Housing Issues of the 1990s

HOUSING ISSUES OF THE 1990s

EDITED BY
Sara Rosenberry
and
Chester Hartman

PRAEGER

New York
Westport, Connecticut
London

Copyright Acknowledgments

Chapter 7, "The Changing Structure of Housing Finance in the United States," is reprinted from the *International Journal of Urban and Regional Research*, by permission of Edward Arnold, Publishers. Parts of Chapter 11 are reprinted from the *Journal of Planning Education and Research* with the permission of the Association of Collegiate Schools of Planning.

Library of Congress Cataloging-in-Publication Data

Housing issues of the 1990s / Sara Rosenberry and Chester Hartman, editors.
p. cm.
Papers presented at a conference held in May 1985 by the College of Architecture and Urban Studies and the Urban Affairs and Planning Program of Virginia Polytechnic Institute and State University and the Institute for Policy Studies.
Includes bibliographies and index.
ISBN 0–275–92362–2 (alk. paper)
1. Housing policy—United States. 2. Housing—United States. I. Rosenberry, Sara. II. Hartman, Chester W. III. Virginia Polytechnic Institute and State University. College of Architecture and Urban Studies. IV. Virginia Polytechnic Institute and State University. Urban Affairs and Planning Program. V. Institute for Policy Studies. VI. Title: Housing issues of the nineteen-nineties.
HD7293.H63 1989
368.5′8′0973—dc19 88–15560

Library of Congress Catalog Card Number: 88–15560
ISBN: 0–275–92362–2

First published in 1989

Praeger Publishers, One Madison Avenue, New York, NY 10010
A division of Greenwood Press, Inc.

Printed in the United States of America

The paper used in this book complies with the Permanent Paper Standard issued by the National Information Standards Organization (Z39.48–1984).

10 9 8 7 6 5 4 3 2 1

CONTENTS

ILLUSTRATIONS

TABLES

FIGURES

EXHIBITS

ACKNOWLEDGMENTS

Special thanks go to Ellen Bowyer and Scot Lawrence, graduate students in the Urban Affairs Program at Virginia Polytechnic Institute and State University, who made significant contributions as editorial assistants, and to Nora Bentley, Denise Farnwalt, and especially Vickie Carroll, members of the staff of the same program, who typed, and in many cases retyped, the manuscripts as revisions were made.

Housing Issues of the 1990s

INTRODUCTION

Sara Rosenberry and
Chester Hartman

Housing policy initiatives developed over four decades by the federal government have produced significant improvements in the quality of the nation's aggregate housing stock. These have been achieved through policies which not only accept but also reinforce and institutionalize a dual or two-tier housing market. On one level, the private sector produces and markets housing units to households able to pay the price of those units. Using tax laws, mortgage insurance, and other approaches, the federal government has subsidized demand for these units while at the same time helping to define the kind of units the market will offer. As a result, we are a nation in which the single-family detached owner-occupied unit is accepted as the norm and in which there have been constant increases in the size and quality of the nation's stock of owner-occupied units. The United States has one of the highest rates of homeownership in the world, and the average American is better housed than are the average citizens of almost any other country of the world.

Average or aggregate figures can be misleading, however. Despite judicial, legislative, and administrative actions designed to reduce legal, social, and economic barriers to the open housing market, a significant share of the American population remains unable to compete in that market and thus unable to own or occupy the housing units it produces. As a result, a second tier of housing and policies to support that housing have been necessary.

Policies in this second tier focus on those groups whose housing needs are not met in the market. In that sense they represent an acknowledgment of the fundamental inadequacy of the market as the mechanism by which the nation's housing needs will be met. Policies within this tier include provision of public housing, direct and deep subsidies for the production of rental units, encouragement of production of nonconventional units (such as modular or group housing), and the support of nonconventional financing institutions and housing sponsors.

It is generally accepted that the record of the federal, state, and local governments in responding to the needs of groups who rely on housing units produced within this second tier is inadequate—whether that record is measured in relative or absolute terms. As a result, households who cannot obtain housing through the private market very often spend a larger share of their incomes to obtain less housing than that enjoyed by households who can compete in the open market. Housing within this second tier is generally regarded as second-class housing.

While federal policy over the past four decades has encouraged a general expansion of the private housing market, it has not been able to prevent short-term fluctuations in its capacity. The housing "crisis" of the early and mid–1980s, which brought to a halt an extended period of expansion, was largely the result of the increased cost of credit, which drove up the price of mortgages. The open housing market suddenly became significantly more exclusive as the share of the population able to compete for the housing it offered became smaller. One result was intense attention, on the part of industry, public analysts, academics, and the press, to the situation in which middle-income potential home buyers found themselves. The alternatives they faced—the same options available to low- and moderate-income households in normal times—were seen as unacceptable. Attention focused on the questions of how to restore the health of the open housing market and ensure its future resiliency, and how to improve the quality of options available to those unable to compete in the market.

On the one hand, the housing crisis of the early and mid–1980s can be seen as another example of the tendency for social problems to become recognized as such only when they affect the average citizen. On the other, it represented an opportunity to focus national attention on the nonconventional, second tier of housing. Policies affecting that housing could be assessed, and options could be developed that were designed to benefit not only those who had recently been excluded from the open market but also those who had never been included.

In May 1985, the College of Architecture and Urban Studies and the Urban Affairs and Planning Program of Virginia Polytechnic Institute and State University, and the Institute for Policy Studies jointly sponsored a conference to consider issues raised by the housing crisis of the 1980s. The organizers chose to structure the conference to explicitly acknowledge the inherently political nature of any debates dealing with the causes of the crisis and the character of appropriate responses. Individuals representing a wide range of experience in the field of housing and diverse political perspectives were asked to present or respond to papers. Our aim was to select respondents who would be able and willing to criticize the papers both on technical and philosophical grounds. The objective was to produce a conference, and ultimately a manuscript, that anticipated the debates we hoped would take place among those responsible for policy analysis and policy development at the federal, state, and local levels.

The papers selected for inclusion as chapters in this volume fall into groups defined by three general issues. Those in the first group are concerned with establishing criteria for evaluating the nation's housing stock and assessing progress toward meeting the nation's housing goals. They allow us to consider the question of the adequacy of the nation's aggregate housing stock and the stock contained in its first and second tiers. The second group of papers focuses on the issue of specialism and also examines the characteristics and problems of groups with special housing needs and the consequences of policies that attempt to target resources and attention to those groups. Papers in the third group examine a range of policies or strategies designed to address the housing needs of households for whom the market currently fails to offer adequate options. They illustrate the diversity of perspectives brought to debates on improving the nation's effort to meet its housing objectives.

Chapters by John Weicher and William Apgar constitute the first group. Weicher addresses the question of how to assess progress in meeting the nation's housing goals and considers the impact of rising expectations regarding housing standards on the criteria we use to assess progress. He argues that when absolute and static standards are employed, there is little doubt that the housing stock available to every group has improved significantly over the past decades, and to the extent that housing inadequacy continues to be a problem, it is mainly a function of inadequate income rather than a failure of the housing market. According to Weicher, the tendency over time to employ new and more demanding criteria of housing adequacy leads us both to underestimate the progress we have made and to divert our attention from the income issue. On the other hand, Apgar argues that the rate of progress in improving the nation's housing stock in fact "stalled in the period since 1974." According to Apgar, if we link this fact to increases in real rents and real costs of homeownership during the same period, we can explain the real deterioration in the housing conditions of many households. He focuses on the situation of low- and moderate-income households and, using data based on the Annual Housing Surveys, reports that when a unit's neighborhood setting is evaluated along with its structural characteristics, there has been very little progress toward improving the quality of housing enjoyed by groups who are at a disadvantage in the open market. According to Apgar, these groups include blacks and families with children. In apparent opposition to Weicher, he argues that "inadequate income alone cannot explain the recent increases in the rent burden, nor the growing concentration of inadequate housing in metropolitan areas."

These chapters, along with responses by Anthony Yezer and George Sternlieb, force the reader to consider the implications of using different measures of housing adequacy. As they make clear, our conclusions regarding the amount of progress we have made toward ensuring that all households have access to adequate housing and our expectations regarding future policy initiatives will depend in large part on the definitions we use.

The second group of chapters focuses on the issue of responding to groups that have special housing needs or special problems gaining access to housing. The papers range from Peter Marcuse's consideration of the implications of defining groups as the objects of special policies, Phillip Clay's and Eugenie Birch's examinations of the problems blacks and women face as they attempt to obtain housing, to Ann Schnare and Sandra Newman's evaluation of the interrelationship and impact of benefits provided through HUD and HHS programs for households with special income problems. These papers, along with comments by Cushing Dolbeare, Mary Nenno, Ellen Bowyer, and Peter Dreier, make clear that it is very difficult to develop policies that target benefits equitably and effectively to groups with documented special needs or claims. In order to be effective, targeting policies must clearly address the factors that create the special need and must avoid stigmatizing recipients. As noted by Marcuse in his careful analysis of the issue of specialism, there is a need to distinguish between those groups whose inherent special circumstances or special housing-related needs make it difficult for them to find satisfactory housing in the open market and those who are simply excluded from the market for reasons having nothing to do with their housing needs. While those in the first group may benefit from targeted or special programs, those in the second have a right to expect policies that eliminate and compensate them for the unwarranted discrimination they currently face.

Women heads of households fall into the first category. As made clear in Birch's paper, the difficulties faced by women trying to compete in the housing market are largely a product of their special circumstances—including resource limits and special service needs. These circumstances make it very difficult for them to compete successfully for the limited number of adequate units available through the open market. The needs of this group are unlikely to be met without policies designed to encourage the production of units designed specifically to match those special circumstances. In contrast, as noted by Clay, the problems faced by blacks as they attempt to compete for housing very often are not the result of any special needs but rather are a reflection of the racial barriers institutionalized in labor and housing markets. Low income, which often is the result of discrimination in the labor market and the housing market, results in reduced access to housing. Without policies that address the effects of discrimination, policies that focus on problems created by inadequate income will have only limited success.

Newman and Schnare show that even when policy objectives—such as providing housing subsidies to poor households—are well understood, it often is difficult to develop programs that use available resources to address those objectives in an equitable, effective, and efficient manner. Focusing on the standards of equity and effectiveness, the authors argue that HUD and HHS programs, both separately and in combination, fail to provide benefits equitably, in that there is enormous variation in the benefits received by households of similar circumstances. They are less critical of the programs' effectiveness, but argue that these programs would benefit from the introduction of more explicit and universal standards, increased coordination between departments and, in the absence of increased funding, improved strategies for targeting available resources to the permanently poor.

Clearly, recognition that there are groups with special housing needs or that are handicapped when competing in the housing market does not automatically lead to the development of policies to adequately address those needs. The papers in this group demonstrate, however, that careful analysis of the characteristics and requirements of special groups and of the specific factors that reduce access to housing is a prerequisite to developing strategies that come close to meeting those groups' needs.

The final group of chapters examines a range of policies that have the potential for alleviating the problems confronted by different groups as they attempt to obtain adequate and affordable housing. The policies or strategies considered in papers by Ann Meyerson, Michael Stegman, Dennis Keating, Emily Achtenberg, Rachel Bratt, Richard Appelbaum, and Michael Stone cover a wide range. They include community-based efforts and federal programs, incentives for the private sector and creation of a new social housing sector, highly targeted programs, and initiatives that, in effect, reinforce the process of trickle-down. These papers, and the comments by Andrew Carron, Anthony Freedman, Douglas Porter, Marilyn Melkonian, Howard Sumka, Peter Salins, and Morton Schussheim, make it abundantly clear that however well-documented the shortcomings of the housing market and the needs of particular groups unable to obtain housing through the market, there will be disagreement regarding the character and scale of the appropriate public response. Even among those who agree that the public sector should assume responsibility for assuring that adequate and affordable housing is available to every household, there will be disagreements regarding the most effective and equitable means for achieving that goal.

Meyerson considers policy initiatives developed during the early 1980s for the purpose of increasing the flow of credit to the housing industry as a whole. She challenges the rationale behind these initiatives: that reducing the cost of housing finance would encourage expansion of the nation's housing stock and thus result in increased housing opportunities for all groups. She argues that deregulation of thrift institutions is likely to weaken the traditional bond between them and the housing industry and encourage them to redirect their investments to "the highest yield investment, housing or not." Most important for low- and moderate-income households is that while large developers who specialize in low-risk, middle- and high-income large developments may be able to compete for financing, relatively high-risk, low- and moderate-income smaller developers are likely to find it more difficult to obtain financing.

Stegman considers the potential for using tax expenditures as leverage to encourage the private sector to produce low- and moderate-income housing and compares the relative leverage provided by tax expenditures to support two different types of multi-family developments—owner-occupied and rental units. He concludes that when comparing low-income developments, benefits available from housing cooperatives are less costly than are benefits from housing built for rental occupancy.

The chapter by Keating focuses on the policy of "linkage," by which localities require developers to provide either direct or indirect support for the production of low-income housing. These "housing exactions" are obtained as a condition of development approval. Keating considers several cities in which linkage programs have been enacted, in order to identify the circumstances under which the strategy is likely to be feasible and successful. He acknowledges that it is not appropriate in all cities but argues that, when appropriate, it provides an effective and efficient means to expand the number of housing units available to inner-city, low-income residents.

Achtenberg examines the troubled history and uncertain future of a number of programs designed to use federal resources and leverage to encourage the private sector to produce housing units for different groups of low-income households. She provides detailed assessments of the inherent weaknesses of the strategies employed up to this point and considers the likely effect of the tax reforms initiated during the Reagan administration on the private sector's willingness to develop low-income housing. Based on an exhaustive analysis, Achtenberg expresses concern regarding the future of the nation's privately-developed subsidized housing stock and predicts that, in the absence of new initiatives to protect that stock, much of it may be lost through conversion to middle- and upper-income units. In conclusion, she suggests strategies that might help conserve that housing stock for its intended beneficiaries.

Community-based, nonprofit housing developments for low- and moderate-income households are the focus of Bratt's paper. She explores the potential for using community-based organizations as sponsors for such developments. Based on a detailed case study of efforts in Massachusetts, she identifies factors, including a committed leadership, supportive public sector environment, and managerial capacity, that increase the likelihood such projects will be successful. She acknowledges that it may be difficult to replicate the Massachusetts experience, but argues that community-based housing programs have the potential for making a significant contribution to the production and preservation of housing units available to groups unable to compete in the open market.

Chapters by the Institute for Policy Studies Working Group on Housing (presented by Appelbaum) and by Stone offer a more holistic solution to the nation's housing affordability problem. The IPS/Appelbaum approach focuses on the national level and the causes of the country's growing incomes-housing costs squeeze, proposing a program that relies on creation of a large non-speculative "social housing" sector, reduction of reliance on the central element in housing costs, credit, by substituting capital grants for new and rehabilitated housing and by permanent debt retirement for large sectors of the existing housing stock.

Stone focuses on what a locality, in this case a "hot" housing market with a booming local and state economy, can do to make housing more affordable to its residents, via a range of subsidies, regulatory devices, and institutional changes.

Attempts to draw specific substantive conclusions based on the papers included in this volume are hampered by the range in subject matter and in the authors' perspectives. In that sense, it seems that we were in fact able to meet one of our objectives, which was to use the volume to produce a sharply defined dialogue among housing experts and advocates on key issues relating to the problems faced by groups unable to compete successfully in the open housing market. While that dialogue did not produce a consensus on specific substantive issues, it does give the reader insights into the complex political and technical character of efforts to address those problems.

There seems to be a strong aversion among policymakers to confronting the inadequacy of policies and programs currently in place to address the needs of those groups effectively excluded from the market. This fact makes it imperative that members of and advocates for those groups who must rely on second-tier, second-class housing continue to draw attention to issues relating to the adequacy of the nation's housing stock, the need for special targeted programs, and the range of programs that might be used to improve the housing options available to those groups. We hope this volume contributes to the dialogue on those issues and increases the likelihood that we can move beyond dialogue to action.

1

HOUSING QUALITY: MEASUREMENT AND PROGRESS

John C. Weicher

This chapter discusses low-quality housing in the United States. It first considers definitional problems; then trends in low-quality housing since World War II; the nature and extent of inadequacy today; and what we know about the causes of inadequacy. It asserts that we have made steady and substantial progress in eliminating inadequate housing, but the progress is not widely recognized because of the definitional problems. Moreover, the improvement has attracted very little interest among researchers; its causes are therefore not well understood.

This paper does not attempt to evaluate housing quality or trends for the average American household, but concentrates instead on the low end of the quality distribution. It addresses only the housing conditions within the occupied housing stock—not vacant units, which to a substantial extent are units either entering or dropping out of the stock. It does not consider institutionalized or homeless individuals, partly because of data limitations, but more fundamentally because in my judgment the serious problems confronting these people are not housing problems (although that conclusion might be reversed by further information, at least about the homeless). Finally, the paper ignores the neighborhood context of housing. It looks at the quality of the housing unit itself, without regard to where it is located.

For the purposes of this paper, housing quality is defined in terms of physical features of the housing unit rather than financial ones. Rent and value are certainly

This chapter was written before the author entered government service. The views expressed are the author's, and not necessarily those of the Office of Management and Budget.

the best broad measures of quality in that they automatically reflect far more dimensions of housing than any physical standard, and assign weights to those dimensions. In most discussions of housing quality, however, rent and value are ignored, or misinterpreted as indicators of quality; thus, high rents are seen as a problem, rather than as a measure of high quality. In a subsequent section, the problem of affordability and briefly described changes in real rents are considered, but the discussion focuses on physical measures because they have been the more commonly accepted measures of housing quality.

For the most part, the paper is descriptive rather than analytical. This reflects the state of knowledge about low-quality housing. Thus, I have used the chapter to discuss what is now known, rather than try to break new ground.

EVOLUTION OF HOUSING QUALITY STANDARDS: THE CENSUS DEFINITION

It is convenient to start by reviewing the development of housing quality standards. Concern with housing quality began in the nineteenth century in reaction to the growth of slums in rapidly growing northeastern cities with substantial immigrant populations. At that time, there was a flurry of activity that included some effort to set standards—and, around the turn of the century, even some data collection—but the basic national concern started during the Depression. The 1936 Democratic platform enunciated a goal of decent, adequate housing at an affordable price for all Americans (Johnson 1978). The term ''decent'' was repeated in the 1949 Housing Act, as part of the national housing goal of a ''decent home and suitable living environment.'' Neither the platform nor the Act defined ''decent'' (or for that matter, ''suitable'' or ''living environment'').

During this period the federal government also began to collect information about housing quality. The first decennial Census of Housing was conducted in 1940; households were asked, among other questions, whether their housing had complete plumbing facilities. Census enumerators also evaluated the overall structural condition. The various combinations of these attributes were reported in the published volumes. During the immediate postwar housing crisis, the Congressional Joint Committee on Housing conducted extensive hearings, and as part of its report offered a tentative definition of standard quality housing: a unit with complete plumbing (in urban areas) and not in need of major structural repairs (U.S. Congress 1949). This definition is as close as the federal government has ever come to establishing a standard, and was commonly used by housing policy analysts until the early 1970s.

Using this definition, housing quality appeared to be dramatically improving, as Table 1.1 shows. In 1940, almost half the housing stock was substandard; in 1970, less than 10 percent was. Closer examination revealed that the main reason was the reduction in the number of units without complete plumbing. Inadequate plumbing had become almost entirely a rural and southern phenomenon, and was not a reliable indicator of housing problems in urban areas.

After the 1960 Census of Housing, the Census Bureau concluded that its

Table 1.1
Measures of Substandard Housing, 1940–1970 (percentage of all occupied units)

	1940	1950	1960	1970
Substandard	48.6	35.4	16.0	8.4
Overall physical condition*	18.1	9.1	4.6	3.7
Lacking complete plumbing	44.6	34.0	14.7	5.5

*"Needing major repairs" in 1940; "Dilapidated" in later years.
Sources: Data are from the following U.S. Bureau of the Census sources: *Sixteenth Census of the United States: 1940, Housing*, vol. 2, part 1; *1950 Census of Housing*, vol. 1, part 1; *1960 Census of Housing*, vol. 2, part 1; *1970 Census of Housing: Components of Inventory Change*, HD(4)-1.

enumerators could not properly identify "dilapidated" housing (the successor category to "in need of major repairs") (U.S. Census Bureau 1967). A post-Census evaluation showed a high incidence of classification error. The Bureau therefore decided to discontinue the question. The decision to conduct the Census by mail in 1970 undoubtedly contributed to this action, but the main motive seems to have been the enumeration problem. City governments and planning departments, which relied on the data, strongly objected to the elimination of the question, and the Bureau partially reversed itself. The question was included in a smaller sample of units surveyed in 1971, rather than the 25 percent sample of 1960. The incidence of dilapidation for these units was then correlated with other characteristics, and the total number of dilapidated units in the country was inferred from the overall incidence of these other characteristics. Because the sample was smaller, the data were only tabulated for large cities and metropolitan areas, not for tracts, small cities, or rural countries. No similar question was asked in 1980.

Thus by the early 1970s a new measure of housing quality was needed. One of the components of the traditional definition was no longer available, and the other was essentially irrelevant. This created problems for housing policymakers, who no longer had a measure of the magnitude of the housing problems they were supposed to address. Ironically, it was just at this time Congress, in the Community Development Block Grant program, mandated the allocation of funds for housing on the basis of objective measures of housing need, only to find that the traditional objective no longer existed. Congress was therefore forced to develop indirect measures, which were widely recognized as less than satisfactory. During these three decades that the Census definition was readily available, it had never been used on the federal level as part of any program, either to allocate funds or to determine eligibility. As a result, both prior to and following the 1970s, data collection and analysis and program design functions were carried on independently of each other.

NEW DEFINITIONS: THE ANNUAL HOUSING SURVEY

Fortunately, and perhaps even foresightedly, just as the decennial Census measure of substandard housing was being phased out, the Annual Housing Survey (AHS) was being created. Beginning in 1973, the AHS has provided new and much more detailed information on housing quality than was available from the Census. (Since 1981, the Annual Housing Survey has been cut back to biennial and renamed the American Housing Survey, to maintain the initials, if not the data.)

Many of the questions in the AHS were also contained in the decennial Census, so that trends can be studied over a long period. Unfortunately, however, the AHS does not contain any evaluation of overall housing quality by the enumerator, even though the survey is conducted by an enumerator at the housing unit, and even though the enumerator is asked to evaluate other aspects of the unit (such as the presence of abandoned buildings in the neighborhood). Instead, the resident is asked to evaluate the overall quality of his or her unit on a simple qualitative scale—excellent, good, fair, or poor. While it is somewhat tempting to treat the household evaluation as a continuation of the enumerator rating, it clearly is inappropriate to do so. On the whole, occupants rate their housing as better than Census enumerators do. For example, in 1970, 8.4 percent of the occupied stock was substandard; in 1974, the first year the question was asked, only 3.3 percent of all households rated their unit as "poor." An additional 15.4 percent rated it as "fair," making a total of 18.7 percent in the two lowest categories. Table 1.2 reports the incidence of units classified as "poor" annually since 1974.

While the AHS does not include the enumerator's overall measure of housing quality, it does provide information on some 30 kinds of housing deficiencies—far more than the decennial Census or any other previous data source. Questions are asked not only about the presence of facilities, but also about how well they work—for example, not only, "Do you have complete plumbing?" but also, "Has it broken down within the last year? If so, how often? For how long?" Similar questions are asked about the heating, electrical, and other major systems. The AHS also includes information on the presence of a number of specific structural problems, such as leaky roofs, damp basements, holes in floors, walls, or ceilings, broken plaster, and peeling paint.

The data on individual structural flaws and system attributes have been used by a number of research analysts in efforts to develop a new working definition of "standard" or "decent" housing. Some of the first research projects tried to identify a single attribute, or a small group of them, that would serve as a direct replacement for the traditional Census definition. No one of the AHS questions has the intuitive appeal of the Census composite measure, so the analysts sought

Table 1.2
Occupant's Subjective Rating of Housing, 1974–1983

Year	Percentage of all Occupied Units Rated "Poor"
1974	3.3
1975	2.6
1976	2.8
1977	2.9
1978	2.5
1979	2.6
1980	2.5
1981	2.3
1982	N.A.
1983	2.2

Source: U.S. Bureau of the Census and U.S. Department of Housing and Urban Development, *Annual Housing Survey: Part B*, Annual.

to identify problems that occurred in the same units to a substantial extent, in the hope that one or two deficiencies could stand as proxies for overall quality. This line of analysis proved to be unsuccessful. Jeanne Goedert and John Goodman (1977), for example, examined more than 20 measures of inadequacy and found little tendency for defects to cluster in the same unit; instead, individual deficiencies were spread across different units.

Failing to find a simple criterion, analysts began to develop more complicated measures. Their definitions have typically used the same framework, although differing, sometimes substantially, in detail. Attributes are usually grouped into categories, such as "plumbing" or "maintenance." A criterion of adequacy is then formulated for each category, and a unit is deemed inadequate if it fails to meet the criterion in any category. (Since most categories have more than one attribute, and most criteria require more than one defect, it is possible for a unit to have one or several defects and still be deemed adequate.) Several federal agencies have developed these definitions and tabulated the number of inadequate units. In recent years, most of this work has been conducted at HUD and to a lesser extent at the Congressional Budget Office (CBO), where definitions of "inadequate" and "seriously inadequate" (HUD) and "needing rehabilitation" (CBO) have gradually evolved; the current definitions depart in several significant ways from earlier versions. For convenience, these definitions are presented here as Exhibits 1.1 and 1.2. In the remainder of the chapter I will generally utilize the HUD definitions, but occasionally will be forced to report findings based on others, especially earlier versions of the HUD or CBO definition.

QUALITY TRENDS: CONTINUING PROGRESS

Using these definitions, what can we say about housing quality? First and most obviously, we have enjoyed gradual but steady improvement in our housing, continuing the trend from 1940 through 1970. Table 1.3 reports the incidence of inadequate housing using both the current HUD and CBO definitions, insofar as data are available. (In 1979 and 1980 all of the questions about quality were not asked in the AHS; Richard Clemmer and John Simonson (1983) have inferred the incidence of inadequacy for those years from the data that were collected.) As can be seen, the CBO definition showed more variability; this probably can be attributed to differences in the phrasing of some questions from year to year. Since individual attributes are more important in the CBO definition—there are fewer categories for which multiple defects are necessary to classify a unit as inadequate—the changes in question have greater effects on the reported incidence of inadequacy.

This continuing improvement is unremarked in most policy discussions, for perhaps two reasons. First is the problem of documenting improvement when the standards are changed. A comparison of Tables 1.2 and 1.3 with Table 1.1 demonstrates that HUD and CBO measures are incommensurate with the traditional Census measure. In 1970 the Census measure indicated that 8.4 percent of the occupied stock was "substandard." In 1973 the HUD definition indicated that 11.8 percent was "physically inadequate," while in the same year 10.0 percent was "in need of rehabilitation" according to the CBO standard. There is no reason to believe that housing quality deteriorated during those three years, and several reasons to believe that it continued to improve. The early 1970s were years of rising real incomes and record levels of both private and subsidized housing production; however, the numbers make it possible to infer that housing quality has not improved in recent years.

The difference from year to year between the HUD "inadequate" criterion and the CBO measure probably occurs primarily because of a problem with HUD's treatment of heating systems. Units are classified as inadequate by HUD if they are heated by an unvented gas, oil, or kerosene space heater, a heating system that is quite common in the South. In a study of individual metropolitan areas (Weicher 1986), I found that this attribute alone increases the incidence of inadequate units quite dramatically, particularly in Texas. For example, Dallas has a 3.9 percent inadequacy rate in 1977 if unvented space heaters are not counted as a defect, but a 15.9 percent rate if they are. While my study did not investigate national patterns, it is possible to estimate the overstatement on the basis of the Census data from standard metropolitan statistical areas (SMSAs). It appears that the HUD inadequate criterion overstates the national incidence

Exhibit 1.1
HUD Definitions of Inadequate Housing

"Seriously Inadequate"

A unit is classified as seriously inadequate if it has any of the following five problems:

Plumbing lacking hot or cold piped water or a flush toilet, or lacking both bathtub and shower, all inside the structure for the exclusive use of the unit.

Heating having three or more breakdowns of the heating equipment last winter, each lasting at least six hours.

Electric having no electricity, or having all of the following three electrical problems: exposed wiring; a room with no working wall outlet; and three blown fuses or tripped circuit breakers in the last 90 days.

Upkeep having any five of the following six maintenance problems: leaky roof; leaky basement; holes in the floors; holes or open cracks in the walls or ceilings; more than one square foot of peeling paint or plaster; or rats or mice in the last 90 days. If the unit has no basement, any four of the remaining five problems would be enough to count the unit as seriously inadequate.

Hallways having all of the following three problems in public areas: no working light fixtures; loose or missing steps; and loose or missing railings.

"Inadequate"

A unit is considered inadequate if it has any of the following six problems:

Plumbing same as "seriously inadequate," or having only one toilet, which broke down three times, at least six hours each time, in the last six months.

Heating same as "seriously inadequate," or having unvented gas, oil, or kerosene heaters as the main source of heat.

Exhibit 1.1 (continued)

Electric	same as "seriously inadequate."
Upkeep	having any three of the six problems listed for "seriously inadequate," regardless of whether the unit has a basement or not.
Hallways	having any two of the three problems listed for "seriously inadequate."
Kitchen	lacking a sink, range, or refrigerator, all inside the unit and for the exclusive use of the unit.

Source: Louise Hadden, et al., *Codebook for the Annual Housing Survey Data Base*, Cambridge, Mass.: Abt Associates, Inc., November 1984, pp. C-1 to C-4.

of inadequacy by about 2.2 percentage points each year. If this is correct, the HUD criterion would show an incidence very similar to the CBO measure. Since the South has been a growing region, relative to the rest of the country, the incidence of inadequacy may have been declining slightly more rapidly than the official measure indicates.

The CBO criterion does not include the type of heating system, but merely how often the system breaks down. This probably is preferable to the HUD criterion.

The problem of incommensurability arises essentially because the various dimensions of quality cannot be measured on a continuum. This can be seen by comparing measures of physical adequacy to measures of crowding, which has sometimes been included in broader measures of housing problems. In 1949, the Congressional Joint Committee on Housing considered a ratio of more than 1.5 persons per room to be overcrowded. By 1967, this ratio had been superseded by a ratio of more than 1.0, with hardly any notice. The incidence of overcrowding measured by this criterion has also continued to decline. In a few years another standard for overcrowding may be established, perhaps 1.00 or more persons per room. Raising the standards tends to obscure the improvement, but in this instance only for the most casual observer, because it is easy to trace either criterion over time and measure progress consistently. There is a much more complicated problem, however, for quality characteristics along dimensions in which gradations are not continuous. If a unit has complete plumbing, it is not obvious what the next step up should be.

The other reason, less important now than a few years ago, is the tendency to confuse housing production with housing improvement. The 1968 Housing

Exhibit 1.2
CBO Definition of Housing "Needing Rehabilitation"

A unit is classified as physically inadequate if it has *at least one* of the following conditions:

1. the absence of complete plumbing facilities.
2. the absence of complete kitchen facilities.

and/or if the unit has *two or more* of the following conditions:

3. three or more breakdowns of six or more hours each time in the heating system during the last winter.
4. three or more times completely without water for six or more hours each time during the prior 90 days, with the problem inside the unit.
5. three or more times completely without flush toilet for six or more hours each time during the prior 90 days, with the problem inside the unit.
6. leaking roof.
7. open cracks or holes in interior walls or ceilings.
8. broken plaster or peeling paint over greater than one square foot of interior walls or ceilings.
9. unconcealed wiring.
10. the absence of any working lights in public hallways for multi-unit structures.
11. loose or no handrails in public hallways in multi-unit structures.
12. loose, broken or missing steps in public hallways in multi-unit structures.

Source: "Measures of Housing Need: Findings from the Annual Housing Survey," Human Resources and Community Development Division, Congressional Budget Office, September 12, 1978, p. 8.

Act established a national housing production target of 26 million units in ten years. That target was much more visible than the basic national housing goal of "a decent home." Year-to-year, even month-to-month, data on starts, completions, occupancy, and more, were and are published. When the production target was not met, it was easy to conclude that the country was not achieving the national housing goal, and to overlook the quality improvement.

A second, more subtle, conclusion about housing quality is that not only are we reducing the incidence of inadequate housing, but that inadequate housing is getting better. We have reached the point at which criteria used in defining units as inadequate are very often individual defects that simply go wrong from time to time in many housing units, rather than fundamental structural problems. Kenneth Wieand (1983) has analyzed the persistence of defects within the same units over time for the mid–1970s. He found that very few problems that occurred in one year continued over three years; there were only four defects that were

Table 1.3
Physically Inadequate Housing in the United States, 1973–1983 (percentage of occupied units)

Year	Inadequate Units (HUD)	Seriously Inadequate Units (HUD)	Units in Need of Rehabilitation (CBO)
1973	11.8	N.A.	10.0
1974	11.0	N.A.	9.3
1975	10.6	4.3	8.1
1976	10.1	N.A.	7.7
1977	10.1	3.9	7.4
1978	10.1	N.A.	8.3
1979	9.8*	N.A.	N.A.
1980	9.6*	N.A.	N.A.
1981	9.3	3.6	N.A.
1982	N.A.	N.A.	N.A.
1983	8.9	3.4	N.A.

*Estimated.

Source: Richard B. Clemmer and John C. Simonson, "Trends in Substandard Housing, 1940–1980," *AREUEA Journal*, Vol. 10 (Winter 1983), pp. 442–464; Iredia Irby, "Attaining the Housing Goal?" and "Housing Problems in 1983," unpublished papers; U.S. Department of Housing and Urban Development, July 1984 and June 1985, respectively.

reported in all three years for more than half the units reporting them in the first year. Three were indeed basic problems—incomplete kitchen, incomplete plumbing, and absence of a sewer connection or septic tank. The fourth was the use of non-vented heat sources, not a defect where such systems are most common. Five others (including two "physical structure" defects) persisted in roughly 20 to 30 percent of all units; 12 (including the other four physical structure defects and heating system breakdowns) persisted in fewer than 15 percent.

The significance of these findings lies in the fact that the physical structure criterion is the most common reason for inadequacy. Several years ago Anthony Yezer (1981) analyzed an earlier version of the HUD definition; he found that almost 30 percent of the inadequate units in 1975 and 1977 were so classified only because they failed the physical structure category. It seems very likely that these were largely different units in the two years. Only about one-third were inadequate because they lacked complete plumbing or kitchen facilities, and thus were likely to be inadequate year after year.

A more sophisticated analysis has been conducted by Sandra Newman, Raymond Struyk, and Donald Manson (1982), with rather different results. They attempted to identify the number of units that were "permanently deficient," defined as having one of a specified set of defects for at least three of the five years from 1974 to 1978. They calculated that 16 percent of all occupied units were permanently deficient, compared to only 10 percent that were inadequate by the HUD definition in 1978. As they noted, however, their criteria were significantly different from the HUD measure. In particular, one of the most frequent of their eight measures is "leaks in basement," which is by far the most common physical structure problem, the hardest to eliminate, and also the least serious. It would be interesting to see the incidence of permanently deficient units if this defect were eliminated (as it is in the CBO definition, and was in earlier versions of the HUD definition).

It is not new to discover that many housing units are only temporarily inadequate. As far back as the 1956 Components of Inventory Change survey, analysts have known that many substandard units are upgraded rather than allowed to continue deteriorating (Muth 1969; Duncan and Hauser 1960). The magnitude of the year-to-year changes must be documented if we are to understand housing quality today.

HOUSING PROGRESS FOR SPECIAL GROUPS

All the data cited in the previous section are aggregate figures for the total population. It is much more difficult to construct similar time series for subgroups within the country, even the largest, that have frequently been of special concern to housing policymakers. For example, data were published for nonwhites in 1940 and 1950, and for blacks since that time; for Hispanics on a national basis only beginning in 1970; and by income classes only since 1950. The most consistent available data for the last five Censuses are shown in Table 1.4 for five special groups: blacks (nonwhites before 1960), Hispanic Americans, rural residents, and two low-income categories—those in the bottom quarter of the income distribution, and those with real incomes of $10,000 or less in 1980 dollars. Because of the definitional problems, the Table includes only units lacking complete plumbing. There are some data on the incidence of dilapidated housing for nonwhites and rural residents, showing a corresponding decline by half for each group from 1940 to 1960. In addition, data on crowding since 1960 are shown: prior to 1960, there are data on nonwhites in 1940 and rural residents in 1940 and 1950, but none for the other groups. While these data are not as detailed as we would like, they nevertheless indicate continued progress for all of these groups, just as for the nation as a whole.

The AHS has provided more data on all of these groups since 1973. Data on individual defects have been published for blacks and Hispanics, and by income classes. The incidence of eight important deficiencies is shown in Table 1.5 for the ethnic groups. There is only one increase for each group: the presence of rats or mice for blacks, and leaky roofs for Hispanics. The other seven deficiencies show improvement. The Table also shows these deficiencies for low-

Table 1.4
Substandard Housing for Special Groups, 1940–1980 (percentage of occupied units)

Lacking Complete Plumbing					
Group	1940	1950	1960	1970	1980
Blacks*	79.6	70.9	41.9	16.3	6.1
Hispanics	N.A.	N.A.	N.A.	6.6	2.4
Rural residents	74.8	61.6	31.5	13.8	4.8
Lowest quartile of income distribution	N.A.	60.1	33.9+	7.9	5.0
Real income below $10,000 in 1980 dollars	N.A.	51.6	30.0++	13.0	5.0
Crowding					
			1960	1970	1980
Blacks*			28.3	19.2	9.1
Hispanics			N.A.	25.7	19.2
Rural Residents			20.6	9.9	4.7
Lowest quartile of income distribution			12.1	7.1	4.3
Real income below $10,000					

*Nonwhites in 1940 and 1950.
+Estimated; correct percentage lies between 31.2 and 35.2.
++Estimated; correct percentage lies between 27.4 and 31.1.
Sources: Data are from the following U.S. Bureau of the Census sources: *Sixteenth Census of the United States: 1940, Housing*, Vol. 2, part 1; *1950 Census of Housing*, vol. 1, part 1; *1960 Census of Housing*, vol. 2, part 1; *1970 Census of Housing: Components of Inventory Change*, HD(4)-1.

income households, defined for ease of comparison as those with incomes below $10,000 in 1983 dollars ($5,000 in 1973 dollars). The incidence of six deficiencies has declined, and the 1983 AHS warns that the data for the two exceptions—interior wall or ceiling cracks and holes in floors—"should be used with caution" because of evidence that they were particularly subject to reporting errors.

The broader measure of inadequacy, using the HUD criterion, shows improvement for several special groups between 1975 and 1983: both ethnic groups, the elderly, female-headed households, and very low-income households (corresponding roughly to those below $10,000 in Table 1.4, a slightly larger group than the low-income households in Table 1.5). These data are shown in Table

Table 1.5
Incidence of Housing Defects in Black, Hispanic, and Low-Income Households, 1973–1983

Defect	Blacks		Hispanics		Low-Income Households*	
	1973	1983	1973	1983	1973	1983
	(percentage)		(percentage)		(percentage)	
Shared or no bathroom	11.0	5.3	5.0	2.6	10.8	5.5
Shared or no kitchen	7.9	2.8	2.5	1.5	6.0	2.2
Presence of rats or mice	26.0	26.6	19.9	19.3	14.3	10.4
Exposed wiring	6.2	4.0	4.7	4.1	5.9	4.1
Lacking working outlets in some rooms	12.6	5.8	6.4	4.3	9.4	5.2
Leaky roof	15.6	12.2	9.9	10.7	11.4	10.5
Interior wall or ceiling cracks	16.0	15.3	13.0	11.5	9.6	10.7
Holes in floors	7.2	6.3	4.4	4.3	3.7	4.4

*Below $5,000 in 1973 and below $10,000 in 1983.
Source: Annual Housing Survey, Part B, 1973 and 1983, and No. 1, 1973.

1.6. Thus, while the limitations of the data for these and other groups are often frustrating, they do not invalidate the general pattern of improvement. Where we have consistent time series data for any major group, inadequacy shows a consistent downward trend.

While progress within subgroups parallels progress for the population as a whole, it is nevertheless true that the housing of each of the subgroups is typically worse than that of the population as a whole. Table 1.7 shows the incidence of inadequacy in 1983 among demographic groups within the total population as well as for all renters and very low-income renters within these groups. The Table indicates that housing inadequacy is concentrated among poor renters. Almost one-fifth of all renters with incomes below 50 percent of the local median (which amounts to about 2.4 million households) live in inadequate housing. There are also disproportionate problems among all four of the demographic groups, but to a very substantial extent their housing problems reflect the fact that they have lower income and more often are renters (which itself reflects their lower incomes) than the general population. Among female-headed households and the elderly, after adjusting for income and tenure, there is a lower incidence of inadequacy than for the nation as a whole. This is not true for black and Hispanic households, however, particularly the former (U.S. President's Commission on Housing 1982).

Even these data do not adequately illustrate the very strong link between

Table 1.6
Incidence of Inadequate Housing for Selected Groups, 1975 and 1983 (percentage of occupied units)

Household Category	1975	1983
Inadequate		
All households	10.6	8.9
Very low-income	20.5	16.3
Blacks	27.6	27.4
Hispanics	20.2	17.6
Female-headed	13.9	11.6
Elderly	14.0	9.7
Seriously Inadequate		
All households	4.3	3.4
Very low-income	9.8	6.9
Blacks	12.5	8.8
Hispanics	5.9	5.4
Female-headed	5.8	4.5
Elderly	6.4	3.9

Source: Iredia Irby, "Attaining the Housing Goal?" and "Housing Problems in 1983," Housing and Demographic Analysis Division, U.S. Department of Housing and Urban Development, July 1984 and June 1985, respectively.

housing quality and income. Table 1.8 reports findings from a study in which the incidence of some individual housing deficiencies is related to household economic and demographic characteristics, using the AHS for 1974. As summarized in the Table, income was significantly negatively related to 23 of the housing deficiencies. With income in the regressions, the only other important attributes, in more than a few instances, were demographic and locational: single-parent households, and those living in the South or in rural areas, showed high incidences of deficiencies more often than would be expected by chance. Race and age were significant in only a very few instances. Yezer (1981) reports essentially similar findings for 1976, using an earlier version of the HUD inadequacy definition. He found that as household income doubled, the incidence of inadequacy was halved, but also that, holding income constant, inadequacy was disproportionately more frequent among blacks and Hispanics, although not among female-headed households or the elderly.

Table 1.7
Incidence of Inadequate Housing for Different Groups in the U.S., 1983 (percentage of occupied units)

	All Households	All Renters	Very Low-Income Renters
U.S. Total	8.9	13.8	18.5
Blacks	22.4	25.1	28.9
Spanish Origin	17.6	20.8	23.3
Female-Headed Households	11.6	13.9	17.2
Elderly	9.7	13.3	15.1

Source: Iredia Irby, ''Attaining the Housing Goal?'' and ''Housing Problems in 1983,'' Housing and Demographic Analysis Division, U.S. Department of Housing and Urban Development, July 1984 and June 1985, respectively.

On the basis of available evidence, it appears that housing inadequacy is primarily a problem of the poor, and to a significantly lesser extent a problem for minorities, as a manifestation of discrimination. (For a contrasting approach to the problems of special groups, see Chapter 3 by Peter Marcuse.)

EXPLAINING THE PROGRESS

What are the reasons for our continuing reduction in inadequate housing? Stated bluntly, we do not know very clearly, nor have we tried very hard to find out. But when the question is stated more broadly—for example, what are the reasons for the continued improvement in housing quality in general?—then there is a wealth of literature, although some questions still remain.

In an economist's analysis, there are three basic explanations for greater housing consumption, either for the population as a whole or for the poor in particular: lower price, higher income, or a change in tastes. Each of the various possible housing policies can be fit into one of these categories.

For example, the concept of ''filtering'' or ''trickle-down''—the notion that stimulating the construction of housing for high-income households leads to a looser housing market and ultimately to better housing for the poor—is fundamentally a statement about the responsiveness of housing consumption to a change in price, and also a statement about a means of changing price. Policies that would stimulate this process are federal efforts to lower mortgage rates directly through explicit subsidies, indirectly through mortgage insurance, and still more indirectly through the establishment and preservation of a specialized housing finance system. These approaches are not usually targeted to the housing

Table 1.8
Incidence of Twenty-Six Deficiencies by Household Type, 1974* (percentage of all occupied units)

Household Type	Higher Incidence Than Normal	Lower Incidence Than Normal
Poor	23	2
Black	3	1
Hispanic	4	12
Other race	4	0
Young (under 35)	11	6
Old (over 65)	1	8
Household with children	13	4
Male head, no wife	14	0
Female head	19	3
Single person	15	4
Living in South	16	2
Living in central city	2	11
Living in rural area	16	2

*The twenty-six deficiencies considered are:

Lacking complete plumbing facilities (tub or shower, toilet, hot and cold piped water).

Crowded (more than 1.0 persons per room).

Lacking complete kitchen facilities (installed sink with piped water, range or cookstove, mechanical refrigerator).

One or more bedrooms lacking privacy (necessary to pass through bedroom to reach another bedroom or bathroom).

Three or more persons sharing a bedroom.

Signs of mice or rats.

Loose, broken, or missing steps on common stairways (for units located in apartment buildings).

Loose, broken, or missing stair railings on common stairways (for units located in apartment buildings).

Light fixtures in public halls not in working order (for units located in apartment buildings).

Exposed electrical wiring (not in walls or metal coverings).

Table 1.8 (continued)

One or more rooms lacking at least one electric wall outlet.

Leaky basement.

Leaky roof.

Holes in the interior floor of the unit.

Open cracks or holes in interior ceilings or walls.

Broken plaster or peeling paint covering at least one square foot of ceiling or wall.

Breakdown in water supply during previous three months.

Lacking piped water.

Breakdown in sewage disposal system during previous three months.

Breakdown in toilet during previous three months (only for units with one toilet).

Electrical fuse blowout during previous three months.

Breakdown in heating system during previous winter.

Additional heat source (*had* to use additional sources of heat during previous winter because regular heating system did not provide enough).

One or more rooms closed during previous winter because they could not be kept warm.

One or more rooms with no heat during previous winter.

Subfamily sharing unit (married couple with or without children, or one parent with one or more single children under 18 years living in household and related to head of household--e.g., young married couple sharing home or husband's or wife's parents).

Source: Annual Housing Survey, tabulations from computer tape files: cited in John C. Weicher, *Housing: Federal Policies and Programs*, Washington, D.C.: American Enterprise Institute, 1980, p. 29.

of the poor. If they affect low-income housing, they do so by changing prices through much or all of the housing market. Some policies are targeted, at least in part, to the poor. These include the tax treatment of housing (with differential incentives for low-income housing production and rehabilitation), zoning and land-use controls, and (for those affected by it) federal, state, and local policies to combat housing market discrimination.

On the other hand, generalized income redistribution programs—such as the welfare programs Aid to Families with Dependent Children or Supplemental Security Income—may improve housing conditions for the poor by enabling them to afford better housing, along with more of other goods and services. (For a detailed treatment of this question, see Chapter 6 by Sandra Newman and Ann Schnare.) Low-income housing programs can also be categorized in the same way by affecting either prices or incomes for a particular group. But these programs incorporate additional constraints that complicate the analysis. Subsidized housing production programs, for example, lower the price of housing for program beneficiaries, but as far as any one household is concerned, only the price of the one specific unit offered to it is affected. Other units still cost the same. Subsidized production programs, however, may lower the price of decent housing for other low-income households by loosening up the housing market. Housing allowances or vouchers are similarly more complicated than generalized income redistribution programs because they typically incorporate a minimum quality constraint.

There have been very few systematic empirical efforts to explain the postwar decline in substandard housing. In part the nature of the data—a handful of observations over time, for a very large number of places each time—has meant that most studies have been restricted to cross-sectional analysis. But it seems fair to say that most analysts have been interested primarily in the implications of their results for housing quality and housing policy in the future; they have wanted to use their cross-sectional results to make inferences about time-series, while recognizing the problems inherent in doing so. A review of that work is useful.

The first study, by the geographers George Hartman and John Hook (1956), was a simple correlation analysis of the incidence of inadequacy across cities with a population of 10,000 or more in the 1950 Census. They found that income and race were significantly correlated with substandard housing; they did not include any measures of housing prices or any housing policies in their analysis.

A few years later Richard Muth (1969) returned to the 1950 Census, performing a multiple regression analysis for cities with populations above 100,000, and also investigating Census tracts on the South Side of Chicago, using both the 1950 and 1960 Census. The former is the more relevant for my purpose. Muth found again that income was negatively correlated with substandard housing, but that race was unrelated. He also found that there was more substandard housing in SMSAs with high construction costs. He did not include subsidized housing. Muth used his cross-section results from 1950 to infer the probable change in quality for the decade of the 1950s; his simulation was reasonably close to the actual change.

Shortly after the 1970 Census, Otto Davis, Charles Eastman, and Chan-I Hua (1974) studied changes in inadequacy from 1960 to 1970 for the 50 largest cities. This study was the most direct investigation of the factors that might be causing the improvement. Unfortunately, it was hampered by the change in data on quality in the 1970 Census. Davis, Eastman, and Hua wrote before the estimates of dilapidated units were published, and thus were able only to analyze changes in the incidence of units lacking complete plumbing. The reduction in such units was positively correlated with rises in income, and unrelated to their proxy for subsidized housing production. They did not have measures of housing price or private construction. They also attempted to analyze the change between the incidence of substandard units in 1960 and the incidence of units without complete plumbing in 1970, without very clear results.

A more recent study looked at inadequacy for the 59 selected SMSAs in the Annual Housing Survey for the mid–1970s (Weicher, Yap, and Jones 1982).

Using the HUD criterion of inadequacy, we found inadequacy to be related to private housing construction, income, race, and some demographic characteristics; for the CBO measure of units needing rehabilitation, private housing construction, income, and race were related. A subsequent, more sophisticated analysis confirms most of these findings and also derives similar results for the traditional Census definition for the 1960s (Weicher and Thibodeau, 1988). In both studies, the bulk of the evidence indicates that subsidized production does not have a significant effect on the quality of housing.

In addition, there have been a handful of other studies testing specific hypotheses about housing quality, more or less rigorously. Over 20 years ago William Grigsby (1963) tried to study filtering by looking at nine metropolitan areas from 1950 to 1960, concluding that housing quality improved more where more new units were built. More recently, Werner Hirsch and C.K. Law (1979), while studying the effect of changes in landlord-tenant law using a larger sample of metropolitan areas from the AHS, found no relationship between subsidized production and substandard housing. Finally, Donald Vitaliano (1983), in a study of cities and towns in New York state, found no relationship between public housing construction and substandard housing.

The studies that comprise this limited literature have seldom attempted to compare alternative hypotheses: some have studied the effect of income but not prices, others the effect of subsidized but not private production and so on. Thus, one needs to be cautious in drawing general conclusions. The safest seems to be that increases in income result in less inadequate housing. There is also recent evidence indicating that private housing production, presumably most of it for high-income households, results in quality improvement for the poor. But clearly there is room for much further research. With the wealth of data, it is odd that there has been so little.

There is a much larger literature on the broader issue of housing quality improvement. The price and income elasticities of demand for housing are certainly relevant to the question of housing quality improvement for the poor, although the relationship between these elasticities and the incidence of inadequacy has rarely been investigated, and probably cannot be formulated very precisely.

In recent years the consensus on the magnitudes of these elasticities has been steadily shifting toward lower numbers. About 15 years ago most economists would have argued that both elasticities were around unity or higher (deLeeuw and Ekanem 1971), probably implying that increases in income, or reductions in housing prices, would result in significant quality improvement for the poor. Now the consensus is probably around 0.5 to 0.7 for both (Quigley 1979), implying much less improvement. Indeed, if the elasticities really are this low, then they probably cannot explain the observed quality improvement. The evidence from the Experimental Housing Allowance Program is the most extreme, and most puzzling. Both price and income elasticities, as estimated in the demand experiment, are well under 0.5 (Friedman and Weinberg 1982). These results would seem to imply that much of the quality improvement is the result of changes in tastes, but the estimated elasticities for various demographic groups—the simplest and most direct categorization of taste differences among households—are very similar to those for the population as a whole. Taken at face value, these results seem to imply that the quality improvement we have witnessed in the last 40 years should not have occurred.

HOUSING AFFORDABILITY

In recent years the cost of housing has emerged as an alternative to physical condition as a measure of housing problems. The most common cost measure is a rent/income ratio, or a housing expense/income ratio for homeowners. A ratio of 25 percent or greater has typically been regarded as evidence of financial burden, and therefore a housing problem, although in the last few years, as housing costs have been rising, 30 percent has been used. These ratios are drawn from the rules of thumb used by mortgage lenders and family financial advisors. (See also Chapter 13 by Michael Stone.)

In contrast to the measures of housing quality, the incidence of "affordability problems"—households with high expense/income ratios—has been steadily increasing. The fraction of renters with ratios above 25 percent has risen from 32 percent in 1960 to 36 percent in 1970, 50 percent in 1980, and 55 percent in 1983. Data for homeowners are only available beginning in 1974; they also show an increase, albeit at a much slower rate and with a much lower incidence of high expense/income ratios.

The rent/income ratio is much simpler and intuitively more appealing than the new measures of housing adequacy, but is itself misleading and even inadequate as a measure of housing problems. A rise in the rent/income ratio is usually interpreted, at least implicitly, as evidence of rising cost—in economic terms, as evidence of a reduction in the supply of housing. But expenditures on housing, and therefore rent/income ratios, are determined simultaneously by demand and supply conditions in housing markets, and will change when either changes. There is no reason to expect rent/income ratios to remain constant over time. They would do so only if the price and income elasticities of demand are both unity, and if tastes do not change. If the elasticities are less than unity, as the current consensus holds, then rent/income ratios would be expected to fall as real incomes rise, and to rise as the relative price of housing rises.

The most important limitation for the rent/income ratio is that it is unadjusted for quality changes. The data from the postwar period clearly show that as incomes rose, households have chosen to buy better housing as well as more of other goods and services. In the case of housing, the observed level of expenditures, and therefore the rent/income ratio, is higher because of the improved quality, chosen by consumers in addition to any change in rents for a given level of quality.

Based on these observations, it would seem that a more appropriate way of measuring affordability is to compare the change in income to the change in the rent on a constant-quality housing unit over time. This approach has the drawback that it is ordinal rather than cardinal. It does not measure how many households have an affordability problem, but rather whether the problem is getting better or worse. Nonetheless, it does provide that more limited information with much less ambiguity than the rent/income ratio.

The best-known constant-quality price index is the rent component of the Consumer Price Index (CPI), which is calculated from the changes in rents on a sample of apartments resurveyed each year. Over the postwar period, and for most subperiods, affordability improved by this measure. Between 1950 and 1970 the median renter income increased by about 125 percent, while the rent index rose by about half as much. Since 1970 the improvement has been smaller and more erratic. The rent index increased faster than income in the early 1970s, but this pattern reversed in the last half of the decade, and from 1980 to 1984 the two rose at almost exactly the same rate. In the last three years, the rent index has again been rising more rapidly. Since 1970, median renter income has increased by about 180 percent, and the rent index by 165 percent.[1]

The rent component of the CPI can also be used to construct measures of housing quality changes. As noted above, real rents and values are probably the best overall measures of housing quality because they take into account far more attributes than any physical measures can. Real rents have risen substantially in the postwar period. From 1950 to 1980 the median real rent for all households doubled; from 1970 to 1980 it rose by over a quarter. Very similar increases occurred for poor renters (defined as those with incomes below $10,000, in 1980 dollars, as in Table 1.4). These increases in rent reflect increases in quality.

Putting these figures together with the data on physical inadequacy, it seems necessary to conclude that the quality of our housing stock—including our low-income housing stock—is getting steadily better, but that recently it has become harder to afford that decent housing. The affordability problem, however, is not growing nearly as rapidly as most discussions of it would suggest.

CONCLUSION

Some years ago I wrote that we would probably be meeting the national housing goal of "a decent home," as originally envisaged, by 1978—the target date established in the 1968 Housing Act—but that we would be unaware of it because of the data problems (Weicher 1977). That proved overoptimistic; Clemmer and Simonson (1983) have estimated that about 6.5 percent of the occupied stock was substandard in 1978, by the traditional Census definition. But we continue to make progress toward it, as best we can tell.

At the same time, we continue to establish new standards of adequacy which make it difficult to meet our goal. George Stigler (1952) has written that "from an Olympian peak, one may say that the economic system has as its purpose forcing people to find new scarcities." Housing is certainly a case in point: as we eliminate substandard housing, we set new goals, and thus, by definition, are never satisfied.

Setting higher standards and expectations is a perfectly reasonable thing to do, but as we raise standards, we should be aware that we are doing so. We should also be aware that the new standards are not only more complicated but more arbitrary. Basic standards such as complete plumbing and structural soundness are reasonable minimum standards that can be justified on health and safety grounds, although structural soundness has apparently been difficult to measure. Newer criteria such as a leaky basement are more specific, and therefore easier to measure, but are much less appealing as measures of obvious housing deficiencies.

Newer and higher standards also provide less of a guide to housing policy. The standards do not clearly identify a subset of the housing stock in need of special attention. The maintenance problems that now account for a large share of inadequate units can be remedied easily in many instances, and in fact the vast majority at any point in time are apparently taken care of within a year or two. More fundamentally, because the new standards lack the universal and intuitive appeal of the old one, housing policy discussions tend to be conducted outside any commonly accepted frame of reference. Indeed, as we set higher standards, it is less clear that they should be used as guidelines for public policy. The inadequate housing identified by the Census is worse than that occupied by the majority of American households, but, unless it lacks complete plumbing or other basic facilities, it is not obviously "bad." The newer standards allow for a description of the distribution of housing quality but are less useful as a precise measure of the adequacy of the nation's housing stock. To the extent that we are interested in redistribution, such standards can be very useful. The traditional standard served that purpose, but it also set an absolute standard that could serve to measure progress toward the national housing goal—progress over time, and progress for different groups in the population. We are still making progress, but it would be easier to evaluate our progress and perhaps even to make policy if we were still using the same yardstick with which we started.

ACKNOWLEDGEMENT

The author thanks Anthony Yezer for helpful comments on an earlier version of this chapter.

NOTE

1. Income by tenure is taken from the decennial Census from 1950 to 1970, from the Annual Housing Survey through 1983, and from the Current Population Reports for 1984. The last two sources report the same incomes for recent years where both are available.

REFERENCES

Clemmer, Richard B., and John C. Simonson. 1983. "Trends in Substandard Housing, 1940–1980." *AREUEA Journal* 10 (Winter): 442–64.

Davis, Otto A., Charles M. Eastman, and Chan-I Hua. 1974. "The Shrinkage in the Stock of Low-Quality Housing in the Central City: An Empirical Study of the U.S. Experience over the Last Ten Years." *Urban Studies* 11 (February): 13–26.

deLeeuw, Frank, and N.F.Ekanem. 1971. "The Demand for Housing: A Review of Cross-Section Evidence." *Review of Economics and Statistics* 53 (February): 1–10.

Duncan, Beverly, and Philip M. Hauser. 1960. *Housing A Metropolis—Chicago*. Glencoe, IL: Free Press.

Friedman, Joseph, and Daniel H. Weinberg. 1982. *The Economics of Housing Vouchers*. New York: Academic Press.

Goedert, Jeanne C., and John L. Goodman, Jr. 1977. *Indicators of the Quality of U.S. Housing*. Washington, DC: The Urban Institute.

Grigsby, William. 1963. *Housing Markets and Public Policy*. Philadelphia: University of Pennsylvania Press.

Hartman, George W., and John C. Hook. 1956. "Substandard Urban Housing in the United States." *Economic Geography* 32 (April): 95–114.

Hirsch, Werner Z., and C.K. Law. 1979. "Habitability Laws and the Shrinkage of Substandard Rental Housing Stock." *Urban Studies* 16 (February): 19–28.

Johnson, Donald Bruce. 1978. *National Party Platforms: Vol. 1 1840–1956*, rev. ed. Urbana, IL: University of Illinois Press.

Muth, Richard F. 1969. *Cities and Housing*. Chicago: University of Chicago Press.

Newman, Sandra J., Raymond J. Struyk, and Donald Manson. 1982. *Poverty, Housing Deprivation, and Housing Assistance*. Washington, DC: The Urban Institute.

President's Committee on Urban Housing (Kaiser Committee). 1967. *Technical Studies*. vol. 1. Washington, DC: U.S. Government Printing Office.

Quigley, John. 1979. "What Have We Learned About Urban Housing Markets?" In *Current Issues in Urban Economics*, edited by Peter Mieszkowski and Mahlon Straszheim. Baltimore: Johns Hopkins University Press.

Stigler, George J. 1952. *The Theory of Price*, rev. ed. New York: Macmillan.

U.S. Bureau of the Census. 1967. *Measuring the Quality of Housing*. Working Paper No. 25.

U.S. Congress, Joint Committee on Housing. 1949. *Housing Study and Investigation: Final Majority Report*, Part 1. March 15.

U.S. President's Commission on Housing. 1982. *Report*. Washington, DC: U.S. Government Printing Office.

Vitaliano, Donald F. 1983. "Public Housing and Slums: Cure or Cause?" *Urban Studies* 20 (May): 173–83.

Weicher, John C. 1986. "Simple Measures of Inadequate Housing: An Empirical Investigation." *Journal of Economic and Social Measurement* 14 (October): 30–45.

———. 1977. " 'A Decent Home:' An Assessment of Progress Toward the National Housing Goal and Policies Adopted to Achieve It." In *A Decent Home and Environment: Housing Urban America*, edited by Donald Phares. Cambridge, MA: Ballinger.

Weicher, John C., and Thomas G. Thibodeau. 1988. "Filtering and Housing Markets: An Empirical Analysis." *Journal of Urban Economics*. 23 (January): 21–40.

Weicher, John C., Lorene Yap, and Mary S. Jones. 1982. *Metropolitan Housing Needs for the 1980s*. Washington, DC: The Urban Institute Press.

Wieand, Kenneth F. 1983. "The Performance of Annual Housing Survey Quality Measures in Explaining Dwelling Rentals in 20 Metropolitan Areas." *AREUEA Journal* 11 (Spring): 45–68.

Yezer, Anthony M. 1981. *The Physical Adequacy and Affordability of Housing in America: Measurements Using the Annual Housing Survey for 1975 and 1977*. Annual Housing Survey Studies no. 7. U.S. Department of Housing and Urban Development, June.

HOUSING QUALITY: COMMENT

Anthony M. J. Yezer

There is surprisingly little literature on the measurement of and change in housing quality. John Weicher has contributed to this literature and, in his chapter, provides an excellent summary of prior results, suggesting that small differences in approach still lead to similar conclusions. These comments first review the major findings in the chapter and then discuss some limitations of his analysis which arise because several important problems concerning the definition and measurement of housing quality are not addressed.

Weicher's chapter makes a number of significant arguments that are well-supported. These are listed below with brief comments.

1. Housing quality, measured by the presence of plumbing in occupied housing units, has increased rapidly. When this measure was replaced in the mid–1970s by measures based on the AHS data, more flawed units appeared. But during the 1970s, these more complex housing quality measures also showed significant quality improvement.
2. These new and presumably better definitions of housing quality have been used to count inadequate units, but are not used as the basis for public programs.
3. Cross-section studies of the probability of living in physically inadequate units find that increasing income raises housing quality. For example, using the 1976 AHS, I found that doubling household income halved the percentage of inadequate housing when household characteristics and location are held constant (Yezer 1981). This study also showed that, holding income and location constant, Hispanic, black, and larger households tended to have a higher probability of residing in inadequate units. Age and sex of the household head did not make a significant difference.

4. Much of the observed decrease in the percentage of physically inadequate housing units is due to rising real income. If anything, Weicher understates this conclusion by suggesting that other, mysterious forces were very important also. If we include in rising real income cash, transfers, taxes, and adjustments for under-reporting, then Peter Gottschalk (in a study for the Brookings Institution) finds that the percentage of persons below the poverty line fell by 50 percent between 1964 and 1980 (Gottshalk 1985). These conclusions are based on detailed analysis of the Current Population Survey and they suggest that economic growth and "Great Society" programs may have worked better than we are generally led to believe.
5. There has been a notable lack of HUD-sponsored research on the questions of measuring housing quality and its change or the causes of changes in the measure of housing quality over time. Indeed, the current measures of housing inadequacy do not have a scientific basis.

Weicher's five arguments are compelling. He fails to acknowledge, however, that the fifth argument calls into question the previous four. Given the lack of research on the definition and measurement of housing quality, reliance on the meager menu of existing studies and measures without questioning their adequacy is questionable. Thus the major shortcoming of the paper is that it fails to address the question of how we should define adequacy. It would have been much more satisfactory if it had looked critically at the implications of focusing on occupied housing units as the basis for measuring changes in the quality of U.S. housing and at the specific manner in which housing units are classified as inadequate under current definitions. The implications of ignoring those two points can be considered separately.

First, defining housing quality in terms of the percentage of occupied units lacking certain characteristics raises the following questions:

1. Housing quality is measured in terms of occupied housing units and not in terms of people. This measure excludes group quarters and reservations, as well as the institutionalized and the unhoused. Given recent debates over the number of homeless in the U.S., some attention should be paid to housing problems of people who do not live in housing units.
2. Housing quality changes are stated as changes in the percentage of units flawed. If the number of all housing units is increasing, then the percentage of inadequate units may fall even as the actual number of inadequate units rises. Both numbers and percentages are important.
3. Quality and availability of vacant units are ignored even though they are the units that are available for occupancy by people on the margin of society. Differences between occupied and vacant units may be particularly important in markets with rent control where vacancies may not be available.
4. Crowding, location within the city, neighborhood characteristics, and affordability are treated as separable from housing quality. Clearly, if the physical quality of housing has improved at the expense of location near places of employment, for example, then the "solution" of the housing problem may aggravate of labor market problems.

Second, there are specific problems with the multi-flaw definitions of housing quality currently being used.

1. Housing units are judged inadequate if they fail to pass a checklist of possible problems, that is, if one, two, or three specific conditions are found. There is very limited ability to trade off desirable features against these flaws. For example, a unit may have several rooms with adequate heating or electrical connections but if any rooms are inadequate, the entire unit is inadequate. In practice, consumers may be willing to trade off some features of units listed as flaws for other features that they desire. But this tradeoff is not reflected in the measure of housing quality.
2. The current quality measures tend to ignore the fact that larger units are more likely to have some flaws simply because they have more rooms. For example, a seven-room unit with one room lacking electrical connections will be judged inadequate while a two-room unit with no rooms lacking electrical connections will be adequate.
3. The housing unit is judged adequate independently of the characteristics of the household occupying the unit. This means that housing flaws must be defined in such a general manner that they apply to any household type. Some households, however, particularly those with children, the aged, and infirm, may find a unit physically inadequate when it would be adequate for a young single household. The converse may be true also.

Given these considerations, Weicher's chapter would have been more complete if it had challenged the traditional literature on housing quality measurement and considered the possibility of defining quality more in terms of housing people rather than occupied units. But even if one sticks to the traditional literature, there are some important questions about the way inadequacy is traditionally defined that should be acknowledged when reporting results based on the standard measures.

REFERENCES

Gottschalk, Peter. 1985. "Overview of Economic and Demographic Factors Affecting Poverty." Report prepared for the Food and Nutrition Service, U.S. Department of Agriculture. March.

Yezer, Anthony M. J. 1981. "The Physical Adequacy and Affordability of Housing in America: Measurements Using the Annual Housing Survey for 1975 and 1977." Annual Housing Survey Study, Series no. 7 (HUD 0002668). June.

2

RECENT TRENDS IN HOUSING QUALITY AND AFFORDABILITY: A REASSESSMENT

William C. Apgar, Jr.

Echoing the conclusions of many policy analysts, the 1982 report of the President's Commission on Housing declared that "basic data point to a continuing improvement in the housing of most Americans." Noting the improvements in broad measures of housing quality—such as the share of units lacking some or all plumbing—the Commission argued that "the quality of America's housing has vastly improved since World War II." Despite the considerable concern about housing affordability in the popular press, the Commission declared that simple measures of affordability—such as the ratio of rent or housing expenditure to income—conceal the actual improvements made in the affordability of both renter and owner housing over the last three decades.

Though the Commission points to the obvious improvement in the housing situation of most Americans over the last 30 years, this paper suggests that improvement in housing conditions has stalled in the period since 1974. While housing lacking inside plumbing continues to disappear from the housing inventory, more sensitive measures of overall housing and neighborhood quality suggest that inadequate housing persists and in some portions of the country, is actually on the increase. Moreover, while rent increases did in fact lag behind the general rate of inflation and real homeownership costs did fall for much of the past three decades, since the mid–1970s real rents have increased slightly and real homeownership costs have turned up sharply. As a result of these trends, the housing situation of many low-income households has taken a serious turn for the worse.

Just as the housing problems of many low-income renters have increased since 1974, so has the spatial distribution of inadequate housing changed. The recent rapid growth of households in nonmetropolitan areas has swept away much of the nation's most severely inadequate housing, while at the same time adding a substantial number of units of good-quality housing to the national inventory. Unfortunately, the reduction in the number of structurally inadequate units in non-metropolitan areas was largely offset by increases in inadequate housing in metropolitan areas.

While the plight of the low-income residents of metropolitan areas can still be viewed as largely a problem of inadequate income, this paper argues that inadequate income alone cannot explain the growth of the housing affordability problem in recent years, nor the growing concentration of inadequate housing in inadequate metropolitan area neighborhoods. Moreover, this paper notes that housing allowance programs, even if made available to all low-income households, might prove to be an insufficient remedy to the growing problems associated with the concentration of inadequate housing in selected metropolitan areas.

The call for a careful balancing of demand- and supply-side programs is hardly new. Neither does this paper offer any specific suggestions concerning the design of programs that can achieve an appropriate balance. Rather, it concludes by observing that such an appropriate program mix will not be developed unless policy analysts have available good empirical data on the causes and extent of current housing affordability and housing quality problems. In attempting to put a good face on the presumed improvements in the nation's housing situation, the report of the President's Commission on Housing not only failed to include the true picture of the housing problems of low-income households, but also helped to foster numerous misconceptions concerning the housing market dynamics of the late 1970s and early 1980s. This paper represents an attempt to provide a sounder empirical basis on which to construct policies to address the nation's housing needs.

STRUCTURAL ADEQUACY AS A MEASURE OF HOUSING QUALITY

In proclaiming the continuing improvement in the housing of most Americans, the President's Commission on Housing offered as its first statistical exhibit a graph depicting the long-term trends in the share of units that are lacking some or all plumbing, that have more than one person per room, that are dilapidated or needing major repairs, or that have more than one and one-half persons per room. As shown in Figure 2.1, each of these measures has declined since 1940. The downturn in the two crowding measures follows the increase in the average number of rooms per unit, coupled with the decline in the average size of households. Interpreting the two measures of housing quality is somewhat more difficult. Over the period, many otherwise adequate dwelling units were modernized with the addition of plumbing facilities. With the advent of building codes in most jurisdictions in the 1950s, it has been virtually impossible to

Figure 2.1
Measures of Housing Adequacy

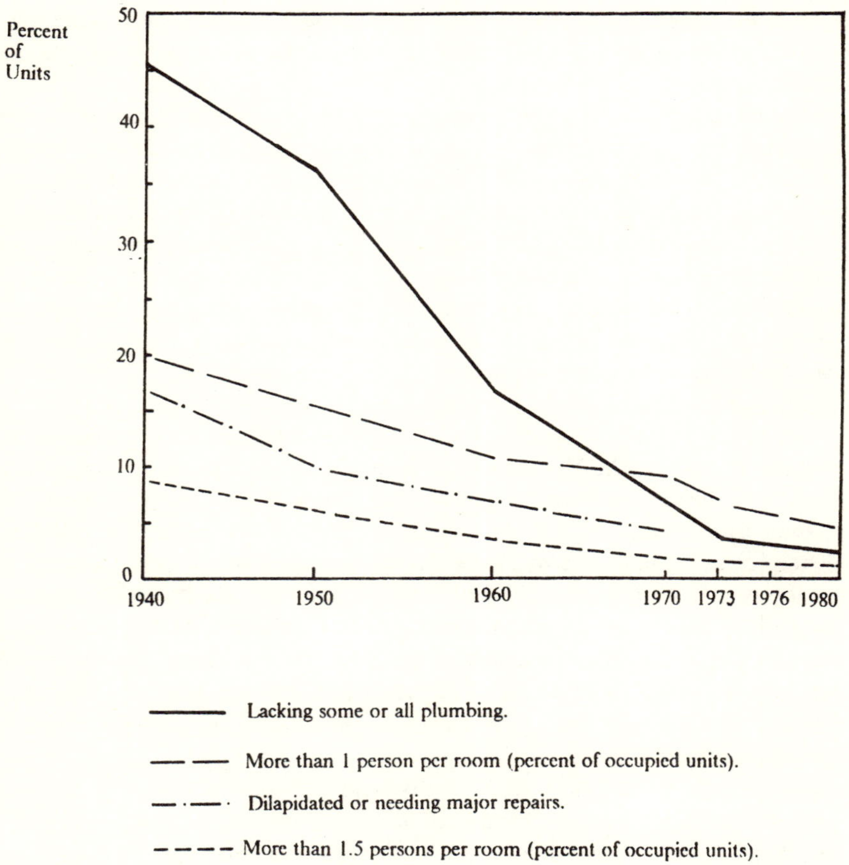

Source: Compiled from data supplied by the U.S. Department of Commerce, Bureau of the Census, and The Report of the President's Commission on Housing, Washington, D.C., 1982.

construct a new unit that lacks minimum plumbing such as a flush toilet, or hot and cold running water.

Recognizing the limited value of the presence of complete plumbing as a measure of housing condition, from 1940 to 1970 the Bureau of the Census produced a broader measure of housing quality—units that are dilapidated or need major repairs. Unfortunately, this measure is not without its difficulties. Post-enumeration surveys suggested, for example, that there was little consistency in how enumerators judged individual dwelling units. The Census prepared estimates of this variable in 1970, but decided to drop the variable from future decennial and mid-decade housing data collection efforts. Despite these problems, the data on dilapidated housing do point to the fact that the sharp decline in units without plumbing did not produce an equally sharp decline in units judged inadequate by the broader measure. By 1970, three million dilapidated units remained in the housing inventory, a number that was widely cited as a rationale for continued federal effort to improve the condition of the nation's housing stock.

The difficulty faced by Census enumerators in determining which units were dilapidated is understandable, given the heterogeneity of the nation's housing inventory. Not only do units differ with respect to the presence of complete plumbing, but they also differ according to the presence or absence of a number of other so-called mechanical subsystems such as electrical service, heating or cooling equipment, and the like. Moreover, units differ according to the extent to which these subsystems work as initially designed, and by other features that relate to the general upkeep or maintenance of the property. Finally, even the best-built and best-maintained unit will have little appeal unless it is located in a neighborhood that meets certain minimum standards.

Beginning in 1973, in an effort to better measure the adequacy of the nation's housing inventory, the Department of Housing and Urban Development combined with the Census Bureau to produce an Annual Housing Survey. In addition to basic data about the household, the AHS collects data on more than 25 housing deficiencies. As indicated in Table 2.1, questions probe not only the presence or absence of a piece of equipment (for example, whether the unit has one or more flush toilets, or central heating), but also whether the item is in good working order. The single decennial census question on the need for major repairs has been expanded in the AHS to include questions on a number of structural defects, such as leaky roofs, presence of cracks or holes in the walls or ceiling, or holes in interior floors.

As was true from 1940 to 1970, units lacking complete plumbing, complete kitchen facilities, or private bathroom facilities continued to decline from 1974 to 1981. Table 2.1 suggests, however, that the number of occupied units deficient in basic maintenance and upkeep was on the rise. In 1981, 4.9 million dwelling units had a leaky roof, an increase of more than 200,000 units or 4.0 percent. As indicated in the Table, some 4.6 million units had cracks or holes in the walls or ceiling, 1.9 million experienced a breakdown in the water supply, and 10.5 million showed signs of rats or mice. It is important to note, however, that since the number of occupied dwelling units increased over the same time period by 17.4 percent, in most instances the proportion of units reporting specific defects declined. New construction added many good quality units to the inventory while demolitions continued to remove the worst quality housing. Yet despite these factors, the absolute number of units with selected deficiencies grew.

While it is easy to measure individual defects, translating a detailed list of defects into a single comprehensive measure of housing condition is more difficult. Three widely used AHS-based indices of housing quality are those de-

Table 2.1
Number of Occupied Dwelling Units With Selected Structural Defects, 1974 and 1981

Defect	1974	1981	Percentage Change 1974 to 1981
Mechanical Sub-Systems			
Shared or Not Complete Kitchen	1,582	1,330	-15.9
Shared or No Bathroom	2,633	2,120	-19.5
Lacking Some or All Plumbing	2,076	1,626	-21.7
No Heating Equipment	329	447	35.9
Maintenance and Upkeep			
Some or All Wiring Exposed	2,375	2,375	0.0
Lacking Working Outlets in Some Rooms	3,078	2,728	-12.8
Breakdown in Water Supply	1,549	1,850	19.4
Breakdown in Sewer/Septic/ Cesspool	833	923	10.8
Inadequate Heat	2,890	2,937	1.6
Cracks or Holes in Walls or Ceilings	4,024	4,647	15.5
Holes in Interior Floors	1,308	1,561	19.4
Roof Leaks	4,737	4,928	4.0
Signs of Rats or Mice	6,676	10,499	57.3

Source: U.S. Department of the Census, *Annual Housing Survey* (Washington, D.C.: U.S. Government Printing Office, 1974 and 1981).

veloped by HUD, the Office of Management and Budget (OMB), and the Congressional Budget Office (CBO). Though these indices are very subjective about which AHS variables to include, analyses of the three alternative measures suggest that conclusions based on these measures do not differ significantly. In their analyses of participation in the Section 8 program, analysts at Abt Associates used each of these three measures of inadequate housing, but concluded that the results were similar (Abt Associates 1981).

Regardless of which measure is selected, it is important to remember that the AHS data on housing condition are based on the respondents' own assessments of their units. As a result, assessments on quality depend in part on the characteristics of the household making the assessment. For example, some studies suggest that a homeowner is less likely than a renter to report defects. Similarly, low-income and elderly households tend to under-report defects, while higher-income households and households headed by a younger person tend to be more critical of their dwelling units. (For a discussion of the design of inadequacy

Table 2.2
Definition of Structural Inadequacy

A unit is inadequate if it has one of the following problems:

PLUMBING	Lacking hot or cold piped water or a flush toilet, or lacking both hand basin and shower, all inside the structure for the exclusive use of the household, or having only one toilet, which broke down three or more times in the last six months.
HEATING	Having three or more breakdowns of the heating equipment last winter, or having unvented gas, oil or kerosene heaters as the main source of heat.
ELECTRICITY	Having all of the following three electric problems: exposed wiring; a room with no working wall outlet; and three or more blown fuses or tripped circuit breakers in the last 90 days.
UPKEEP	Having three or more of the following five problems: leaky roof; holes in the floors; holes or open cracks in walls or ceilings; more than a square foot of peeling paint or plaster; or signs of rats and mice in the last 90 days.
HALLWAYS	Having at least two of the following three problems in public areas: no working light fixtures; loose or missing steps; or loose or missing railings.
KITCHEN	Lacking a sink, range, stove, or refrigerator, all inside the unit for the exclusive use of the unit.

indices, see Abt Associates, *Annual Housing Survey Data Project Codebook*, Cambridge, MA 1983.)

Table 2.2 presents the measure of housing quality used in this paper. The measure rates a unit in each of six areas: plumbing, heating, electricity, upkeep, hallways, and kitchen. The measure is similar to the widely used HUD index, but unlike the HUD measure it combines the categories ''seriously inadequate'' and ''moderately inadequate'' into one category. While admittedly arbitrary, by

Table 2.3
Number of Occupied Dwelling Units By Tenure and Structural Adequacy, 1974 and 1981

Tenure and Structural Adequacy	1974	1981	Percentage Change 1974 to 1981
	(in thousands)		
Owner-Occupied			
Adequate Structure	39,679	48,587	22.5
Inadequate Structure	6,105	5,755	- 5.7
All Structures	45,784	54,342	18.7
Renter-Occupied			
Adequate Structure	19,523	23,118	18.4
Inadequate Structure	5,523	5,715	3.4
All Structures	25,046	28,833	15.1
Total Occupied			
Adequate Structure	59,202	71,705	21.1
Inadequate Structure	11,628	11,470	- 1.4
All Structures	70,830	83,175	17.4

Source: Harvard Joint Center for Housing Studies, special tabulations of Annual Housing Survey data for 1974 and 1981.

combining information from 18 separate AHS questions the variable does represent a comprehensive measure of housing condition that is consistently defined over the period 1974 to 1981.

As Table 2.3 indicates, 11.6 million units (or 16.4 percent) of all occupied dwelling units in 1974 were structurally inadequate. The number of structurally inadequate units fell slightly from 1974 to 1981. Despite the claims by the President's Commission and others that the housing situation of renters has improved steadily, in actuality nearly 200,000 more renters lived in structurally inadequate housing in 1981 than in 1974.

In interpreting the data presented in Table 2.3, it must be recognized that even for renter households, the number of adequate units grew at a greater rate than the number of inadequate units. Over the period, new construction added more than 12 million units of good-quality housing to the nation's inventory. At the same time, demolitions and other losses removed nearly four million units, with as many as one million of these losses coming from the inadequate portion of the inventory. Despite these changes, the number of structurally inadequate units declined by only 158,000. As these statistics suggest, while new construction may have added to the number of good-quality housing units, lack of maintenance and repair led to a deterioration of the existing inventory. Thus, for every thousand inadequate units removed from the inventory from 1974 and 1981, 842 units of existing housing moved from the adequate to the inadequate category as a result of lack of maintenance and upkeep.

NEIGHBORHOOD CONDITIONS AND HOUSING ADEQUACY

Although neighborhood amenities and local public services are important components in a household's determination of the adequacy of a particular dwelling unit, such factors are not included in the HUD, CBO, or OMB analyses of housing condition. Thus, when the President's Commission proclaims the continued improvement in the nation's housing stock, it refers implicitly to improvement in structural adequacy. Yet with the continued high levels of abandonment in selected inner-city neighborhoods, and the growing difficulties that cities and towns have in raising sufficient funds to maintain adequate levels of public services, there is ample reason to believe that the condition of many neighborhoods has actually deteriorated since 1974.

Comparison of AHS data on household attitudes concerning basic neighborhood amenities and public services suggests that the quality of America's neighborhoods has deteriorated significantly since 1974. For in addition to the questions on structural defects, the AHS also asks respondents to rate their neighborhood according to a number of neighborhood and public service variables. As indicated in Table 2.4, from 1974 to 1981 there were sharp increases in households who felt that crime was a problem in their neighborhood, or that police protection was inadequate. As the number of households increased by 17.4 percent from 1974 to 1981, both the number and the incidence of households reporting neighborhood crime, unsatisfactory police protection, the presence of abandoned buildings, or trash, litter, or junk in their neighborhood increased as well. Little change was noted in the other two measures (streets in need of repair; odors), perhaps reflective of the increases in street repair work funded by the Community Development Block Grant program (CDBG), or the substantial improvement in ambient air quality resulting from the more stringent environmental regulations put in place over the period.

Table 2.4 also combines the information on the six neighborhood measures into a single index of the number of neighborhood deficiencies present. In 1981,

Table 2.4
Number of Occupied Dwelling Units By Selected Neighborhood Deficiencies, 1974 and 1981

Condition Present in Neighborhood	1974	1981	Percentage Change
	(in thousands)		
Crime	12,115	18,371	51.6
Unsatisfactory Police Protection	6,357	8,460	33.1
Abandoned Buildings or Structures	4,834	6,396	32.3
Trash, Litter, or Junk	10,308	12,730	23.5
Streets in Need of Repair	13,741	14,399	4.8
Odors	7,240	6,640	- 8.3
No Deficiencies	37,072	43,825	18.2
One Deficiency	20,101	22,715	13.0
Multiple Deficiencies			
Two	8,683	9,939	14.5
Three	3,449	4,367	26.6
Four	1,055	1,713	62.4
Five or More	467	615	31.6
All Units	70,830	83,175	17.4

Source: Harvard Joint Center for Housing Studies, special tabulations of Annual Housing Survey data for 1974 and 1981.

43.8 million households reported no deficiencies, while 22.7 million reported only one deficiency. Over the period, the number of households reporting multiple deficiencies increased substantially, with especially sharp increases in the number of households reporting one or more neighborhood deficiencies.

As was true with the measures of structural inadequacy, answers to questions concerning the presence of certain neighborhood deficiencies could vary from one respondent to another. One household might complain about junk in the street, while another might ignore the condition. This is a common problem in demand studies. Households differ by a number of characteristics, not the least of which is taste and preferences. As these tastes and preferences change, so does an individual's opinion about a commodity. In developing constant-quality indices of any commodity, an effort must be made to include those important elements of the product that influence a consumer's perception of the commodity.

Given the complexity of the many housing and neighborhood attributes that comprise the housing bundle, the housing consumption decision is a particularly difficult one. Some households might check with their local police station concerning the most recent crime reports, but most households will rely on less formal sources of information. A household's perception that crime is on the upswing in a neighborhood could very well contradict police department data that show otherwise. It may be true that there are fewer abandoned houses in the neighborhood or that the neighborhood has less litter, but the perception of neighborhood deterioration could nonetheless cause a household to move, or reduce the willingness of a household to pay for housing in the area. In developing constant-quality measures of the housing inventory, the perception of what constitutes quality is important, even if the perceptions are based on less than perfect information concerning actual conditions.

Whether increased complaints about neighborhood deficiencies represent a change in perceptions or a change in actual conditions, the data in Table 2.5 suggest that much of the increase in perceived neighborhood deficiencies is associated with renter households. Table 2.5 defines an adequate neighborhood as one with zero or one of the six neighborhood deficiencies, while an inadequate neighborhood has two or more deficiencies. The choice of a cutoff point was, of course, arbitrary, and was selected to make the number of housing units judged to be in an inadequate neighborhood in 1974 roughly equal to the number of structurally inadequate dwelling units. As Table 2.5 indicates, the number of units with two or more neighborhood deficiencies increased from 13.7 million in 1974 to 16.6 million in 1981, with nearly two-thirds of the increase the result of increases in renter-occupied units in inadequate neighborhoods. Indeed, for renters over the period, the incidence of neighborhood inadequacy increased from 20.2 percent in 1974 to 23.9 percent in 1981.

Table 2.6, which combines the structural inadequacy and neighborhood inadequacy measures, provides further evidence of the slow pace of housing progress, especially for renter households, during the period 1974 to 1981. As indicated in the Table, the number of households living in structurally inadequate units and/or inadequate neighborhood settings increased by 11.1 percent, from 22 million in 1974 to 24.4 million in 1981. The two measures are correlated, but are by no means substitutes for one another. Of the 22 million households living in an inadequate structure and/or neighborhood in 1974, 3.3 million lived in both an inadequate structure and in an inadequate neighborhood. By 1981, the number of households living in both an inadequate structure and an inadequate neighborhood had grown to 3.7 million.

As indicated in Table 2.6, for renter households, the number of dwelling units that are either structurally inadequate or located in inadequate neighborhood settings has increased faster than the number of all renter units. The number of units with both types of deficiencies has increased even faster, moving from 1.6 million in 1974 to 2.2 million in 1981, an increase of 33.4 percent. These numbers result from the fact that over the time period, an increasing share of structurally inadequate renter units are located in inadequate neighborhoods.

Table 2.5
Number of Occupied Dwelling Units By Tenure and Neighborhood Adequacy, 1974 and 1981

Tenure and Neighborhood Adequacy	1974	1981	Percentage Change
	(in thousands)		
Owner-Occupied			
Adequate Neighborhood	37,182	44,622	20.0
Inadequate Neighborhood	8,602	9,720	13.0
All Neighborhoods	45,784	54,342	18.7
Renter-Occupied			
Adequate Neighborhood	19,992	21,929	9.7
Inadequate Neighborhood	5,054	6,904	36.6
All Neighborhoods	25,046	28,833	15.1
Total Occupied			
Adequate Neighborhood	57,174	66,551	16.4
Inadequate Neighborhood	13,656	16,624	21.8
All Neighborhoods	70,830	83,175	17.4

Source: Harvard Joint Center for Housing Studies, special tabulations of Annual Housing Survey data for 1974 and 1981.

REGIONAL TRENDS IN STRUCTURAL AND NEIGHBORHOOD ADEQUACY

The previous section noted that the small decrease in the number of structurally inadequate units was more than offset by an increase in units in inadequate neighborhood settings. As indicated in Table 2.7, the reduction in the number of structurally inadequate units was the result of substantial decline in the inadequate housing stock in nonmetropolitan areas. In spite of substantial increases in the number of dwelling units, the number of structurally inadequate units in

Table 2.6
Number of Occupied Dwelling Units by Tenure and Neighborhood and Structural Adequacy, 1974 and 1981

Tenure and Neighborhood and Structural Adequacy	1974	1981	Percentage Change 1974 to 1981
	(in thousands)		
Owner-Occupied Units			
Adequate	32,748	40,361	23.2
Inadequate	13,036	13,981	7.2
Total Structures	45,784	54,342	18.7
Renter-Occupied Units			
Adequate	16,089	18,376	14.2
Inadequate	8,957	10,457	16.7
Total Structures	25,046	28,833	15.1
Total Occupied			
Adequate	48,837	58,737	20.2
Inadequate	21,993	24,438	11.1
Total Structures	70,830	83,175	17.4

Source: Harvard Joint Center for Housing Studies, special tabulations of Annual Housing Survey data for 1974 and 1981.

nonmetropolitan areas fell from 5.4 million to 4.5 million. In nonmetropolitan areas, the greatest improvement was in the owner-occupied stock, with the number of inadequate units falling by 19.3 percent from 1974 to 1981. In contrast, the number of structurally inadequate units in metropolitan areas increased by more than 10 percent, with equal percentage increases recorded for both owner and renter units.

Though the number of units in inadequate neighborhood settings increased in both metropolitan and nonmetropolitan areas, the increase was markedly slower for owner units in nonmetropolitan locations. Surprisingly, the number of non-metropolitan renters reporting two or more neighborhood deficiencies rose fastest

Table 2.7
Number of Structurally Inadequate Dwelling Units or Dwelling Units in Inadequate Neighborhoods by Tenure and Metropolitan Status, 1974 and 1981

Tenure and Location	Inadequate Structure			Inadequate Neighborhood		
	1974	1981	% Change	1974	1981	% Change
Metropolitan						
Owner	2810	3097	10.2	5511	6435	16.7
Renter	3471	3838	10.6	4150	5551	33.8
TOTAL	6281	4935	10.4	9661	11986	24.1
Non-metropolitan						
Owner	3295	2658	-19.3	3091	3285	6.3
Renter	2052	1877	- 8.5	904	1353	49.7
TOTAL	5347	4535	-15.2	3995	4638	16.1

Source: Harvard Joint Center for Housing Studies, special tabulations of Annual Housing Survey data for 1974 and 1981.

of all, suggesting that the growth of rental housing in the more densely populated nonmetropolitan areas was bringing with it a measure of the neighborhood problems more traditionally associated with metropolitan areas. Thus, while nonmetropolitan areas recorded substantial reductions in the number of structurally inadequate units, this progress was offset, in part, by growing neighborhood problems.

Despite the fact that the housing inventory was growing faster in nonmetropolitan than in metropolitan areas, problems of housing inadequacy were becoming increasingly concentrated in metropolitan areas. Historically, much of the nation's worst housing inventory has been located in nonmetropolitan areas, particularly the low-income marginal farming areas of the North Central and Southern states. The recent surge of growth in nonmetropolitan areas has helped to sweep away much of the inadequate stock in these areas, while at the same time adding new standard units to the inventory.

As indicated in Table 2.8, the combination of a growing inventory and an absolute decrease in structurally inadequate units has had a pronounced effect on the incidence of structural inadequacy in nonmetropolitan areas. As shown in the Table, by 1981 only 13.6 percent of all owner-occupied units in nonmetropolitan areas were structurally inadequate, down sharply from the 20.5 percent figure of 1974. Similar reductions in the incidence of structural inadequacy were recorded for the nonmetropolitan renter stock. This decline in the incidence of inadequacy of nonmetropolitan housing was widespread, with only

Table 2.8
Structurally Inadequate Dwelling Units as a Percentage of Total Occupied Units by Tenure, Region, and Location Status, 1974 and 1981

Region and Location	Owner		Renter	
	1974	1981	1974	1981
Metropolitan				
Northeast	7.1	8.0%	20.4	19.1
North Central	7.7	7.7	14.8	16.2
South	14.7	13.2	24.1	21.1
West	7.9	5.8	12.3	13.1
TOTAL	9.5	8.9	18.3	17.5
Non-metropolitan				
Northeast	11.3	11.7	22.3	16.1
North Central	15.2	10.3	23.1	17.2
South	29.0	17.2	48.7	38.6
West	13.5	10.2	21.0	20.7
TOTAL	20.5	13.6	33.8	27.0

Source: Harvard Joint Center for Housing Studies, special tabulations of Annual Housing Survey data for 1974 and 1981.

the owner-occupied stock in the nonmetropolitan Northeast failing to exhibit a similar decline.

Although the absolute number of inadequate owner and renter units in metropolitan areas increased from 1974 to 1981, the incidence of inadequacy did fall slightly as a result of the growth of the total inventory. Thus, for all metropolitan areas in 1981, 17.5 percent of all rental units and 8.9 percent of all owner units were inadequate, down slightly from the corresponding figures in 1974. The incidence of structural inadequacy of renter-occupied units showed most improvement in the South, but nonetheless remained high. The renter stock of Northeastern metropolitan areas also improved somewhat, but the metropolitan areas in North Central and Western states ended the period with increased shares of their renter stock in a structurally inadequate condition.

Table 2.9 presents similar information on the share of units located in inadequate neighborhood settings, and again, the differences by region are striking. Metropolitan area renter households have the greatest chance of living in an inadequate neighborhood, but neighborhood inadequacy is an increasing problem for non-metropolitan renters as well. By contrast, the incidence of neighborhood inadequacy has declined sharply for nonmetropolitan area owners. At the be-

Table 2.9
Dwelling Units in Inadequate Neighborhoods as a Percentage of Total Occupied Units by Tenure, Region, and Metropolitan Status, 1974 and 1981

Region and Location	Owner		Renter	
	1974	1981	1974	1981
Metropolitan				
Northeast	16.5	19.9	23.9	30.4
North Central	18.6	17.5	23.5	27.4
South	21.0	21.3	20.6	23.5
West	17.7	14.6	19.0	20.2
TOTAL	18.7	18.5	21.9	25.4
Non-metropolitan				
Northeast	17.6	10.6	19.3	19.6
North Central	15.0	15.4	11.7	15.6
South	22.2	19.3	14.4	21.5
West	21.4	18.4	18.7	24.6
TOTAL	19.2	16.8	14.9	19.5

Source: Harvard Joint Center for Housing Studies, special tabulations of Annual Housing Survey data for 1974 and 1981.

ginning of the period, nonmetropolitan areas had a higher share of their owner-occupied units located in inadequate neighborhoods than was true for metropolitan areas. By 1981 the incidence of neighborhood inadequacy was lower in nonmetropolitan areas. Indeed, with the exception of the Western region, nonmetropolitan owners had the fewest complaints about their neighborhoods.

WHO LIVES IN INADEQUATE HOUSING?

Historically, housing policy has focused on specific groups with severe housing problems. In part this reflects the goal of national policy that each household is entitled to a safe, decent, sanitary dwelling unit located in a suitable living environment. Despite more than three decades of federal, state, and local government effort, however, large shares of households remain poorly housed. As indicated in Table 2.10, inadequate housing is far more common among renters than owners, and such housing tends to be concentrated in the lower end of the income distribution. In 1981 28.0 percent of all renters with incomes of $5,000 or less lived in structurally inadequate units, and 28.2 percent lived in inadequate neighborhoods. A somewhat lower share of low-income owners live in inade-

Table 2.10
Percentage of Households Living in Inadequate Structure or Inadequate Neighborhood by Tenure and Income, 1981

Income Class	Percentage Living in Inadequate Structure		Percentage Living in Inadequate Neighborhood	
(in thousands)	Owner	Renter	Owner	Renter
$ 0 to 5	21.3	28.0	19.5	28.2
5 to 10	15.4	22.5	22.0	22.8
10 to 15	12.9	18.0	18.9	23.9
15 to 20	10.9	15.1	21.7	23.6
20 to 25	10.4	14.8	17.3	25.5
25 to 30	7.9	15.8	16.1	20.7
30 to 40	6.3	14.7	15.5	20.1
40 or more	6.1	9.9	13.9	15.2
TOTAL	10.5	19.7	17.8	23.9

Source: Harvard Joint Center for Housing Studies, special tabulations of Annual Housing Survey data for 1981.

quate structures and/or inadequate neighborhoods, but nevertheless 21.3 percent of all owners with incomes less than $5,000 live in structurally inadequate housing. With but one exception, for renters with incomes of $25,000 to $30,000, the inadequacy decreases steadily as income increases.

Similar findings concerning structural inadequacy have previously been reported by the President's Commission and others. Homeowners have more control over the maintenance and upkeep of their unit than renters. As a result, for households with incomes in excess of $15,000, the incidence of renters living in inadequate housing is anywhere from 50 to 100 percent higher than for owners. Note that these same owners do not share a similar advantage over renters with respect to neighborhood inadequacy. These differences make sense. Neither owners nor renters can directly influence the level of neighborhood amenities. The difference between the structural and neighborhood inadequacy for owners is simple: most owners will, in fact, fix a leaky roof or repair a broken fixture, but fewer owners apparently are willing to move to avoid neighborhood problems. As a result, inadequate neighborhoods are not simply associated with low-income renter households.

Occupants of inadequate housing are more likely to be black and/or families with children. The differences by race are particularly striking. As Table 2.11 shows, in 1981 32.2 percent of all black renter households lived in structurally inadequate housing, compared to 17 percent for white households. Similar gaps between blacks and whites exist for the incidence of neighborhood inadequacy.

Table 2.11
Households Living in Inadequate Structure or Inadequate Neighborhood by Family Type and Race, 1981

Family Type and Race	Percentage Living in Inadequate Structure		Percentage Living in Inadequate Neighborhood	
	Owner	Renter	Owner	Renter
Households with No Children				
Head Age 64 or Younger				
Married Couple	8.9	17.6	16.9	21.6
Other Household	12.7	17.8	18.9	24.2
Head Age 65 or Older				
Married Couple	8.0	16.1	13.3	19.4
Other Household	16.0	18.3	17.5	16.0
Households with Children				
Married Couple	9.5	23.0	18.7	24.7
Other Household	15.8	24.9	25.4	32.7
Race of Household Head				
White	9.6	17.0	16.8	20.9
Black	23.4	32.2	30.2	37.2
TOTAL	10.5	19.7	17.8	23.9

Source: Harvard Joint Center for Housing Studies, special tabulations of Annual Housing Survey data for 1981.

Even among owners, blacks are almost twice as likely as whites to live in inadequate housing and in inadequate neighborhoods. Households with children—especially female-headed households—are more likely than other household types to live in inadequate structures and inadequate neighborhoods.

The President's Commission argues that the high incidence of inadequate housing among renter populations is in part the result of the declining real incomes of renters. There is some merit to this claim. As measured in real 1981 dollars, the share of renter households with incomes less than $5,000 increased from 15.3 percent in 1974 to 20.2 percent in 1981. (For more on this, see discussion of Table 2.14). Over this same period, the share of renter households with real incomes less than $5,000 living in structurally inadequate housing fell from 34.5 percent to 28.0 percent.

Yet improvements in the incidence of structural inadequacy mask the fact that the number of renter households with real incomes less than $5,000 living in structurally inadequate housing actually increased from 1.3 million in 1974 to 1.6 million in 1981. In absolute terms, low-income owners fared little better, with the number of households in structurally inadequate housing increasing from 827,000 in 1974 to 920,000 in 1981. Thus, over the period, the problems of structural inadequacy were becoming increasingly associated with very low-income households.

The continued growth in the absolute number of low-income households living in inadequate dwelling units is somewhat surprising, especially in light of the fairly substantial increases in the number of subsidized housing units available, and the increased efforts to target these units for low-income renters. In 1981 3.1 million households reported in the Annual Housing Survey that they lived in either public housing or other types of subsidized rental housing. This compares with the 2.2 million households reporting that they lived in public or subsidized rental housing in 1974. Over the period, then, the stock of subsidized units increased by nearly 900,000 units, or more than 40 percent.

Many people, of course, are unaware of whether or not they live in a subsidized rental unit, especially if the subsidy consists of below market rate financing or other types of concessions granted the builder/developer or owner of the property. As a result, the AHS figures on subsidized housing correspond only roughly to actual counts of subsidized units prepared by HUD. Nevertheless, AHS data point to a serious problem with the maintenance of a large segment of the nation's subsidized housing stock.

As illustrated in Table 2.12, at least part of the reason that increases in the subsidized inventory failed to have more effect on the number of poorly housed low-income renters is that many of the subsidized units are themselves structurally inadequate or located in inadequate neighborhoods. In 1981 457,000 subsidized renter units were in inadequate structures, up by 62.6 percent over 1974. Similar percentage increases were observed in the number of subsidized units located in inadequate neighborhoods. Since the total number of subsidized units increased by only 40.8 percent, these figures indicate that the share of the subsidized inventory that was structurally inadequate or located in inadequate neighborhoods increased over the period. Thus, by 1981 14.8 percent of all subsidized rental units were structurally inadequate and another 30.0 percent were located in inadequate neighborhoods.

TRENDS IN HOUSING AFFORDABILITY

In summarizing its findings in this area, the President's Commission on Housing concludes that for all households, renters and owners alike, adequate housing has become more affordable over the postwar period. The Commission bases

Table 2.12
Number of Subsidized Rental Housing Units by Structural and Neighborhood Adequacy, 1974 and 1981

	1974	1981	Percentage Change 1974 to 1981
	(in thousands)		
Total Number of Subsidized Units	2,178	3,067	40.8
Adequate Structure	1,897	2,610	37.6
Inadequate Structure	281	457	62.6
Adequate Neighborhood	1,623	2,147	32.3
Inadequate Neighborhood	555	920	65.8

Source: Harvard Joint Center for Housing Studies, special tabulations of Annual Housing Survey data for 1974 and 1981.

this conclusion on analyses of data through 1980, and their findings mirror the reports, available at that time, of numerous prominent housing market analysts. Recently available data suggest, however, that in the 1970s the real cost of housing actually began to rise, reversing the long-term trends presented in the President's Commission report. Since 1979, the real costs of homeownership have increased dramatically, while real rents, properly adjusted for changes in housing quality, have increased steadily since at least 1975.

In discussing homeownership costs, the Commission's report correctly observes that the decision to buy a home represents both investment and consumption considerations. While the actual purchase price of the unit is of course a central component, the cash cost of homeownership entails several ongoing expenses, including mortgage interest payments, fuel and utility costs, maintenance and repairs, real estate taxes, and insurance. In addition to cash outlays, there are other costs associated with owning a home: the loss of cash income on the homeowner's down payment and accumulated equity indirectly increases costs. At the same time, though, the deductibility of interest and property taxes from taxable income and the expectation of capital gain appreciation indirectly reduce costs. Change in either the cash, direct, or indirect costs can thus affect the total costs of homeownership.

In a recent study on housing affordability, James Brown, Karl Case, and Kermit Baker (1983) examined how homeownership costs have changed relative to income since 1965. Figure 2.2 traces the cash cost, the direct cost, and the total cost of owning a home (the latter two measures adjusting out-of-pocket costs for the effects of tax savings and the effects of expected capital gains, including the foregone interest on equity). Thus adjusted, the total cost of owning

Figure 2.2
Homeownership Costs as Percentage of Median Family Income, 1965–1983

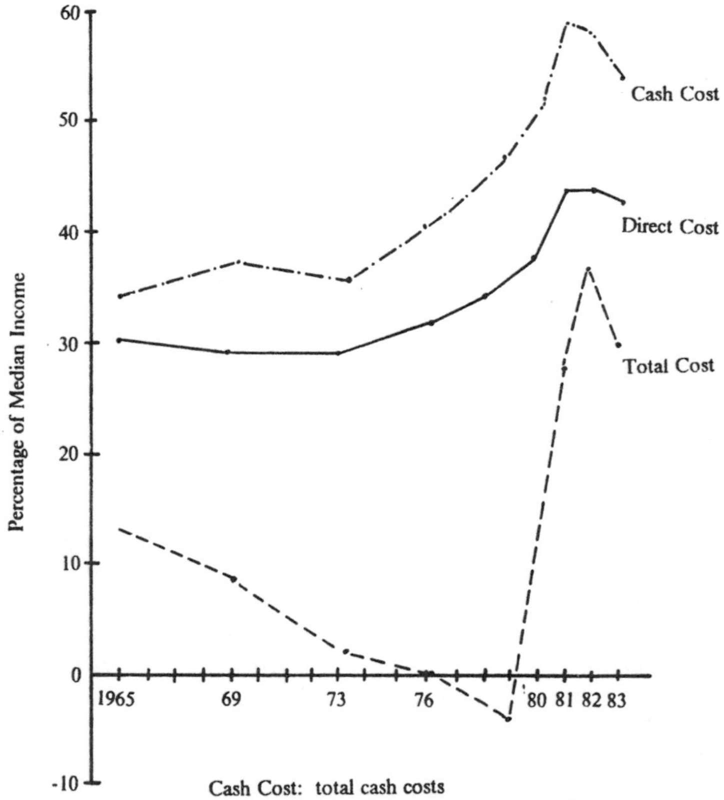

Cash Cost: total cash costs
Direct Cost: total cash cost net of tax saving
Total Cost: total cash cost net of tax saving and expected capital gain, including forgone interest on equity

Source: H. James Brown, Karl Case, and Kermit Baker, "Homeownership and Housing Affordability in the United States, 1963–1983." Joint Center for Urban Studies, paper prepared for National Gypsum Company, September 1983.

a home declined steadily for much of the period and may have even become negative in the period 1977 to 1979. After 1979, however, total homeownership costs rose sharply. By 1982, higher home prices, interest rates and utility costs—together with a reduction in the expected gains from appreciation—combined to raise the total costs of owning a home to nearly 40 percent of median family income.

The recent increases in the real costs of homeownership have been matched by equally significant increases in the real cost of rental housing. As indicated in Table 2.13, from 1974 to 1981 the proportion of renter households paying

Table 2.13
Renter Households Paying 35 Percent or More of Income for Rent, 1974 and 1981

	1974	1981
Households with No Children		
Head Age 64 or Younger		
Married Couples	8.1%	16.7%
Other Households	28.2	34.9
Head Age 65 or Older		
Married Couples	24.6	32.2
Other Households	42.0	36.7
Households with Children		
Married Couples	9.5	21.1
Other Households	41.6	49.6
TOTAL	23.1	32.0

Source: Harvard Joint Center for Housing Studies, special tabulations of Annual Housing Survey data for 1974 and 1981.

more than 35 percent of their income for rent increased from 23.1 to 32.0 percent. In absolute terms, the number of renter households so overburdened increased from 5.8 million in 1974 to 9.1 million in 1981. As should be expected, the nation's poorest households faced particularly severe payment burdens. In 1981 6.4 million renter households with incomes less than $5,000 paid more than 35 percent of their income for rent. Further, as indicated in Table 2.13, the incidence of overpayment increased for a wide range of family types, with particularly sharp increases occurring among married couples with children.

Increases in the rent/income ratio can, of course, be a misleading indicator of changes in the affordability of rental housing. The President's Commission

Table 2.14
Distribution of Renter Households by Real 1981 Incomes: 1974 Actual, 1981 Predicted, and 1981 Actual

Thousands of Dollars	1974 Actual	1981 Predicted	1981 Actual
less than 5	15.3%	17.8%	19.7%
5 to 10	20.7	22.2	23.1
10 to 15	17.1	19.2	21.2
15 to 20	14.3	13.3	13.4
20 to 25	10.6	9.4	8.8
25 to 30	9.0	6.8	5.5
30 to 40	7.2	6.3	5.6
40 or more	5.8	5.0	2.7
TOTAL	100.0	100.0	100.0

Note: 1981 predicted distribution assumes that rate of owner-occupancy for each real income class equals 1974 actual owner-occupancy rates.
Source: Harvard Joint Center for Housing Studies, special tabulations of Annual Housing Survey data for 1974 and 1981.

notes that a ratio can change as a result of changes in the denominator (in this instance, income) as well as changes in the numerator (in this instance, rent). While conceding that nominal rents increased over the period, the Commission argued that the real driving force behind the increased rent/income ratio was the declining real incomes of renters. Over the postwar period, the growth of the real income of renters did in fact lag behind that of owners. Moreover, during this period, many upper-income renters did become owners, reducing the average income of those who remained as renters. Finally, as the Commission observes, lower-income people have always had difficulty paying for rent, as evidenced by the high rent/income ratios for that group in all time periods. Thus, argued the Commission, it was the movement of upper-income renters into homeownership that explained the sharp increases in rent burden that have occurred in recent years.

While these explanations are plausible, the data for the period 1974 to 1981 fail to support the central features of the argument. The rate of homeownership did increase from 1974 to 1981 for households with real incomes in excess of \$15,000 (in constant 1981 dollars). Similarly, for households with real incomes of less than \$15,000, the rate of homeownership fell. Yet this shift in the relationship between the rate of homeownership and real income is not sufficient to explain the decline in real incomes of renter households. By way of illustration, Table 2.14 presents information on the distribution of renter households by income in 1974 and 1981. As in the previous discussion, incomes are measured in constant 1981 dollars. In addition to the actual data for 1974 and 1981, the Table also presents a predicted distribution based on the assumption that the ownership rate for each real income category remained at 1974 levels.

As these calculations reveal, even without changes in the income/tenure relationship, the share of renters in the lower-income categories would have increased over the period. The declining rates of homeownership among lower-income households added to the share of low-income renters, but this alone explains only a portion of the trend. Another way to illustrate the same point is to note that over the period, the median income of renter households declined from $14,100 to $11,400 in constant 1981 dollars. Of this decline only $1200, or approximately 44 percent, is the result of changing patterns of homeownership for households in a given real income category.

In seeking to explain the declines in renter income in terms of shifting patterns of homeownership, the Commission missed an obvious point: during the period 1974 to 1981, inflation substantially eroded the real incomes of households that remained renters. That the income of permanent renters should lag behind inflation is most plausible, especially since the long-term renter population includes many of the nation's most economically disadvantaged citizens. The Commission's argument seems to suggest, though, that the peeling away of upper-income households merely served to reveal a problem among low-income renters that had existed for years. Yet, in fact, the failure of the incomes of large numbers of renter households to keep pace with inflation was exacerbating an already severe housing affordability problem.

Just as changing patterns of homeownership are an insufficient explanation for the declines in real incomes of renters, so are declining real incomes of renter households an insufficient explanation for the increases in households with high rent/income ratios. As noted above, the number of renter households paying more then 35 percent of their income for housing increased from 5.8 million in 1974 to 9.1 million in 1981. The growth of the total number of renter-occupied households accounts for 874,000 of the increase, while the decline in the real incomes of renters accounts for an increase of another 1.5 million. Thus, more than 960,000 renters were added to the list of households paying more than 35 percent of their income for housing as a result of factors other than the growth of total renter households or the declining real incomes of renters.

The President's Commission does note that in addition to declining real incomes, the growth of rent/income ratios could result from the general improvement in the condition of the housing stock. Given the previous evidence on the absolute increase in units with structural and neighborhood deficiencies, this seems hardly plausible. The Commission report presents information on trends in real housing prices, but limits the analysis to the period 1970 to 1979. Following its lead, Table 2.15 presents similar (and in most instances identical) information for the period 1970 to 1980, but unlike the Commission, breaks the data into two periods. As measured by the then official Consumer Price Index

Table 2.15
Selected Measures of Change in Prices, Rents, and Incomes, 1970–1980

	Percentage Change		
	1970 to 1975	1975 to 1980	1970 to 1980
Consumer Prices Index Old Series Total	39	54	113
Consumer Price Index Old Series Residential Rents	25	39	73
Consumer Prices Index New Series Total	36	47	99
Lowry* Residential Rents	34	51	103
Median Income of Owners	40	46	104
Median Income of Renters	25	33	67
Median Gross Rents	44	55	123

For a definition of the Lowry rent index, see Ira S. Lowry, ''Inflation Indexes for Rental Housing,'' RAND Corporation, Santa Monica, California, 1981.

Source: Annual Housing Survey and periodic reports of the Bureau of Labor Statistics on consumer prices. For a discussion of the effect of alternative measures of homeownership affordability on the Consumer Price Index, see U.S. Department of Labor, Bureau of Labor Statistics, *CPI Issues*, #593, February 1980.

(CPI), consumer prices increased by 39 percent in the first half of the decade, and at a somewhat sharper rate in the second half. In both periods, residential rents, as measured by the CPI, lagged behind. These declines in real residential rents as measured by the CPI continued a pattern that had been in effect since the 1950s.

Though the CPI residential rent index is the best-known measure of real rents, it has certain flaws. The CPI rent component is derived from rents on the same dwellings, which are resurveyed from year to year, with adjustments being made only for major changes in the quality of the dwelling units. As a result, minor changes attributable to depreciation are not picked up, nor are cost increases on utilities paid directly by the tenant. Recognizing these difficulties, Ira Lowry prepared a constant-quality rent index that incorporates adjustments for both factors. As shown in Table 2.15, the Lowry rent index increases more rapidly than the CPI residential rent index, suggesting that the deficiencies in the CPI index substantially overstated the extent to which real rents declined during the period.

In addition to the concern about the ability of the CPI to correctly measure residential rents, there has been equal concern about CPI measures of homeownership costs. Prior to 1983 the CPI homeowners cost measure was based primarily on the cash costs of homeownership. Yet, as argued earlier in this paper, and indeed by the Commission itself, for much of the period such cash cost measures substantially overstate the total cost of homeownership, when allowance is made for equity build-up. After several years of experimentation, the Bureau of Labor Statistics in 1983 introduced an improved measure of homeownership costs that essentially calculates the rental-cost equivalent of owner-occupied housing.

While the above discussion is somewhat technical, it goes to the heart of the rental affordability issue. As shown in Table 2.15, the failure to correctly measure homeownership costs not only distorted the measurement of the changes in all consumer prices, but added to the false impression that constant-quality real rents were falling over the period. Thus, for the entire period 1970 to 1980, the adjusted CPI increased by only 99 percent. Since the Lowry residential rent index increased by 103 percent, the data suggest that real rents actually increased. Moreover, the data also suggest that constant-quality rents may have increased faster than all other prices at the beginning of the decade, but this was more than offset by the relatively faster increases in constant-quality real rents at the end of the decade.

The supposed decline in real rents is an important element in many attempts to explain what happened to housing consumption in the 1970s. In a widely cited article, Lowry (1981) argued that declining real rents could have induced households to consume more housing. Thus, at least a part of the increase in rent burden reflects the fact that households are consuming more housing. Yet, as Lowry conceded at the conclusion of that article, he was unable to explain why real rents fell during the period. To Lowry's credit, in his subsequent work he answers his own question: in fact, rents did not lag behind correctly measured inflation by much, if at all. As a result, most of the increases in median rents paid during the period were in fact the result of rent inflation. Faced with declining real incomes, there were few rental housing bargains to aid the increasingly beleaguered low-income renters.

SUMMARY AND CONCLUSION

Low-income households, and particularly low-income renter households, have historically been consigned to live in inadequate housing in marginal urban neighborhoods. While the President's Commission argues that the housing conditions of all Americans—rich and poor alike—have improved in the postwar period, this progress has stalled since 1974. This paper presents evidence that, since 1974, the rapid inflation in housing costs, combined with the inability of renter income to keep pace with inflation and the seeming decline of many basic urban services, have exacerbated the problems of affordability and inadequate housing for many low-income renters. By 1981 1.6 million renters with incomes less than $5000 lived in structurally inadequate housing and another 6.4 million paid more than 35 percent of their income for rent. Both figures were up sharply from the 1974 numbers for households with equal real incomes.

Just as the income distribution of housing problems has changed, so has their spatial distribution. The recent rapid growth of nonmetropolitan areas has swept away many of the most severely inadequate housing units, while at the same time adding substantial numbers to the stock of new adequate housing. Unfortunately, the improvement in the structural adequacy of non-metropolitan housing was largely offset by increases in the number of structurally inadequate metropolitan housing units. In 1974 54 percent of all structurally inadequate housing was located in metropolitan areas. By 1981 this increased to 60 percent. Further compounding the problem was an increasing number of reported deficiencies in metropolitan neighborhoods.

While the plight of the low-income residents of metropolitan areas can still be viewed as largely a problem of inadequate income, this paper notes that inadequate income alone cannot explain the recent increases in rent burden, nor the growing concentration of inadequate housing in inadequate metropolitan neighborhoods. While a universal housing allowance program that provides cash assistance to the more than 6.4 million low-income households now paying excessive amounts for housing undoubtedly would help, a program by itself might prove insufficient. Instead, this paper points to a surprisingly persistent housing quality problem, a problem that may respond only slowly, if at all, to such a universal housing allowance program.

The call for a careful balancing of demand- and supply-oriented programs is hardly new. Yet such a program cannot be developed unless policy analysts are more fully aware of the extent of current housing problems and better understand the housing market dynamics of the recent period that produced them. In attempting to put a good face on the presumed improvements in the housing situation, the report of the President's Commission on Housing not only failed to state the true magnitude of current housing problems, but also helped to foster numerous misconceptions concerning recent housing market dynamics. The nation's housing problems deserve more careful attention.

REFERENCES

Abt Associates. 1981. "Participation and Benefits in the Urban Section 8 Program: New Construction and Existing Housing." Cambridge, MA: Abt Associates.

Brown, H. James, Karl Case, and Kermit Baker. 1983. "Homeownership and Housing Affordability in the United States, 1963–1983." Paper prepared for the National Gypsum Company by the Joint Center for Urban Studies, Cambridge, MA.

Lowry, Ira S. 1981. "Rental Housing in the 1970s: Searching for the Crisis." In Rental Housing, Is There a Crisis?, edited by John C. Weicher, Kevin E. Villani, and Elizabeth A. Roistacher. Washington, DC: The Urban Institute Press.

U.S. President's Commission on Housing. 1982. Report. Washington, DC: U.S. Government Printing Office.

RECENT TRENDS IN HOUSING QUALITY AND AFFORDABILITY: COMMENT

George Sternlieb

The issue of housing quality and the priorities given it are a microcosm of our nation's history and changing levels of priority. It is barely 50 years since FDR, in his second inaugural address, described one-third of all Americans as ill-housed. In 1940, for the first time, the Census Bureau began a systematic attempt to describe the nation's housing. This was relatively easily, if imprecisely, measured in terms of lack of central heat, plumbing counts, and other comparable physical attributes. As described by Professor Apgar in his paper, once we move from these obvious parameters of necessity into issues of quality, affordability, and environmental context, the adequacy of the status quo become much less positive.

The development of the Annual Housing Survey in the early 1970s was a response to the inadequacy of the data available from the 1970 census. The Census Bureau itself noted that a replication of fieldwork conducted during the decennial count produced results very different from those of the initial surveys. Unfortunately, the AHS—which had been anticipated as producing worthwhile results not merely in terms of counts (e.g., do you have central heat?) but performance (e.g., how many times and for how long has it not worked?)—has had a mixed record as a tool for identifying housing problems and encouraging effective policy responses.

This record is due in part to the fact that the AHS became available as a policy tool just as the economic conditions of the country and its political climate began to shift markedly. Trends toward real gains in personal income during the 1950s and 1960s were truncated abruptly in 1973, the base year of the AHS, as Americans began to look closely at a range of expensive and theoretically open-ended commitments. These included housing programs.

There are a number of possible explanations for the waning support during that period for national housing programs. On one hand, it is possible to argue that by the mid–1970s middle-class housing demands generated by post-World War II expansion had been largely met. In addition, the moral fervor—and fear—generated by the urban riots had abated. America had moved into suburbia and had left its troubles and obligations behind. Private housing production, particularly as it was sustained by increasing inflation, was the major consideration of national housing policy. Support for the concept of social housing waned, even among former advocates, while critics focused on the modest results and huge costs of the 235/236 programs and the Section 8 effort.

On the other hand, a case could be made that by 1973 the war against inadequate housing had largely been won. It was possible to argue that future public sector efforts should concentrate on cleaning up pockets of resistance in isolated rural areas and urban slums. Remaining problems were seen as largely site-specific and, as a result, there was sympathy for the argument that responses should be developed by localities themselves. The federal government's most effective role would be to provide lump resources and let the programs be established and administered by states and localities. This approach was consistent with the rhetoric of the Nixon administration as it pushed toward its policy of New Federalism. By the 1980s, the federal government had largely talked itself out of being responsible for solving the nation's housing problems.

It is noteworthy that even with the crash of 1981–82 (which produced the most radical downturn in housing starts since World War II), there was no major housing initiative at the federal level. It seemed that by that point, both parties accepted that assuming responsibility for housing low- and moderate-income families was a losing proposition. Since 1976 only lip service has been given to issues relating to housing by either party.

Professor Apgar's chapter is an effort to dispel the mood of complacency that has largely governed the housing arena. True, alarms have been sounded repeatedly on the plight of the first-time home buyer, especially when the housing market becomes tight. It nevertheless remains true that deep subsidies have largely disappeared as an incentive for encouraging new low- and moderate-income housing starts. The major responsibility in this area has been delegated to states and municipalities. As a result, localities have taken what could be described as desperate measures as they attempt to meet the need. In New Jersey, zoning indulgences are now being sold in the public interest, *à la* Mount Laurel, and inclusionary housing ordinances are being tested, as in Orange County. These ordinances give density bonuses to developers in return for generating a given number of low- and moderate-income housing units. Their equivalents in urban areas are the linkage approaches being used in San Francisco, Boston, and other cities. Linkage programs attempt to load subsidy costs on nonresidential development in order to secure subsidy dollars. (See Chapter 9 by Dennis Keating for a more complete discussion of the concept of linkage.) These efforts are exceptional, and the levels of productivity they secure are relatively trivial. Even the effort to reduce the awesome flow of tax-exempt financing for housing by restricting it to structures that will incorporate 20 percent low- and moderate-income housing (as under Section 103 (b)) has largely been evaded.

America's current preoccupation is with employment opportunities and overseas competition; its interest is much more stimulated by the question of whether it is "de-" or "re-industrializing" than by the question of whether or not it is providing a decently built environment for the poor. As the elderly, who traditionally have made up a significant share of the poor and represented a very sympathetic constituency, have largely been made secure through increments in Social Security, advocacy for the poor has been further undermined. Today, despite increasing evidence to the contrary and efforts to dispel misconceptions, the poor are generally characterized as inherently separate or different from the rest of America. (See Chapter 4 by Eugenie Birch for an example of such evidence.) As such, they generally lack an effective link to institutional interests that might serve as advocates on their behalf.

The efforts of housing analysts to address the needs of low- and moderate-income families have been divided. More traditional analysts call for new housing construction, that is, more units, based on the assumption that until there is adequate supply, those with the least ability to make demands will remain outside the market. Insurgents of both the left and the right, however, argue with equal force that the issue must be seen as one of income constraints. The assumption implicit in this perspective is that the market will respond if adequate demands are made on it.

What does Professor Apgar's paper tell us as we view both the present scene and the future? First, he makes it clear that the house-buying power of practically all Americans has been reduced over the past decade. In the case of those fortunate enough to have boarded the housing train before inflation, this loss has been modified by significant increases in housing prices. Those who were left behind, however, are less able than ever to compete for available housing. These are the individuals still looking for refuge from the elements and the families seeking a housing unit with enough space in which to raise their children in decency; it is the household struggling to locate in a safe and decent environment in which the amenities expected in America in the 1980s are available.

Second, his paper points out that to the extent that the complacency about the need to upgrade the nation's housing stock is premised on assumptions about progress over the past decades, it is subject to question. As Apgar makes clear in his careful analysis of available data, there is a small, though important, increase in the number of units which, at least gauged by self-reporting techniques, require some form of reasonably significant capital input in order to qualify as adequate. If we define adequate as having available a toilet, then we have more adequate housing than ever in history. If we are willing to define adequate more broadly, however, perhaps as including protection from crime, then we must make more modest claims about our progress.

Apgar does not address the fact that there is distinct evidence that there has been a decrease in the rate at which housing at the bottom of the chain is being retired from the market. In short, the 'scrappage rate' seems to have declined. We can speculate that as the buying power of Americans declines, that which at one time would have been scrapped now becomes potentially charming to those with the resources to support recycling. To the extent this process leads to increased competition for units at the bottom rung of the ladder, however, it only intensifies the problems faced by those with the fewest resources.

Is it appropriate to characterize the problem as a crisis? Certainly, a careful analysis of the data available from the AHS and other sources gives little basis for complacency. It does not, however, provide a means to act. Meaningful action is unlikely unless a rationale is found to link the interests of the middle of the market with those of the poor.

3

THE PITFALLS OF SPECIALISM: SPECIAL GROUPS AND THE GENERAL PROBLEM OF HOUSING

Peter Marcuse

> Those ill-served by the private [housing] market [include]: the elderly, the handicapped, low-income single-parent households, [and] the working poor (National Association of Housing and Redevelopment Officials 1984, 28).

This statement suggests that the market does adequately serve the needs of all but those who fall into special groups, thereby implying that it is the presence of those groups that makes necessary action by the public sector to direct and/or regulate the market. It raises the issue of "specialism," the tendency to see social problems as the special problems of particular groups, brought about or made severe by the particular characteristics of those groups. Specialism stands in apparent opposition to the concept of a "general problem of housing," and in particular to the idea that the root of the nation's housing problem is the general provision of housing only for profit: the "commodification of housing."

Specialism is dangerous because (1) it conceals the general (structural) nature of many problems; (2) it tends to blame the victim for his/her problems; (3) it makes political problems appear technical; and (4) it divides those affected from the larger population. Ignoring special problems is also dangerous, however. Such "generalism" conceals the particular, special oppression of particular groups, and makes it appear their problems will disappear when more general problems have been solved.

The correct balance between addressing problems as special and/or general is difficult to achieve. It involves differentiating among problems and among groups. It requires recognizing that certain problems are structural while others are merely the results of inefficiencies, that certain problems are political while others are merely technical, and that certain problems are common to many groups while others are not. Balancing the dangers of specialism and those of generalism also requires being able to differentiate among special groups. Blacks, women, and Hispanics, for instance, constitute a quite different type of "special group" than do the poor, on the one hand, or the disabled, on the other. These differentiations among groups and the types of problems they face are essential to developing effective strategies to meet their needs.

SOME CASES THAT ILLUSTRATE SPECIALISM AT WORK

A press release from New York City's Comptroller reads as follows:

> Goldin Warns Council: Teenage Pregnancy Increase Will Result in Feminization of Poverty. Citing statistics dramatizing the alarming increase in teenage pregnancy . . . this phenomenon is likely to lead to an irreversible escalation of poverty and the creation of a growing category of dependent poor people, namely, women. . . . The startling incidence of teenage pregnancy and motherhood threatens to make our country and City one of rigid classes in which those at the bottom have no hope of escaping poverty and disadvantage (Goldin 1985).

Emanuel Tobier recently wrote a generally excellent study of poverty in New York City. When it was released by the Community Service Society of New York, it made political waves because it pointed out convincingly that poverty in the city was increasing—and that all indications were that it would continue to increase. The report contained the following formulations:

> A second and even more compelling reason why the 1960's did not bring a further reduction in poverty in the city was the changing family circumstances of a significant portion of the city's population. In 1970, 80 percent of the city's poor were in family households. Women headed 42 percent of those households. The number of female headed households in the city rose by 24 percent between 1960 and 1970, while married couple families fell by 6 percent . . . .The city's Hispanic males also fared poorly during the 1970s. . . . The principal reason for this poor performance was the dominance of Puerto Ricans in the city's Hispanic population. . . . Part of the reason for New York's extremely poor showing with respect to the teen labor market is a result of the fact that it includes a disproportionate concentration of hard-to-employ Black and Hispanic, mostly Puerto Rican, youth. (Tobier 1984)[1]

The following assertion comes from a special issue of SIGNS on Women and the City:

> The concentration of women and female-headed families in the city is both cause and consequence of the city's fiscal woes (Freeman 1980, 13).

A proposed New York State bill addressing landlord-tenant relations is summarized as follows:

> A.4418/S.3418 . . . would prevent automatic evictions of those 65 and older by requiring landlords to state whether the respondent in a dispossess petition is age 65 or older; if the elderly tenant does not have an attorney, the court would appoint one, and could stay proceedings for up to 90 days to protect the potential evictee.[2]

As the preceding quotations indicate, the critical problems of poverty in the 1980s are often addressed as problems among special groups—female-headed households, teenage parents, Hispanics and blacks in central cities, and the elderly. Policies that attempt to address these problems increasingly are directed primarily at the victims as opposed to the system itself. Is this focus on the victim as opposed to the system the proper direction for social policy addressed to problems of housing?

DIFFERENT TYPES OF HOUSING PROBLEMS

Not all housing problems are alike. Frictional problems arise from inefficiencies in the housing system or from conflicts among users. They are technical rather than structural in nature. Problems of efficiency can by solved, leaving some better off and none worse off. Problems of commodification and oppression cannot because they are structural rather than technical. The commodification of housing is a structural problem because if housing is provided only in proportion to the profits to be made from its provision, those having too little money to buy adequate housing in the market will be ill-housed regardless of how efficiently the market is organized.[3] Oppression is a problem that afflicts certain groups whether or not they have money, and regardless of how efficiently the housing system otherwise works. Racism and sexism are forms of special oppression that confront special groups, while practices reinforcing power relations among groups defined in terms of their economic situation (among working, middle and upper classes, for instance) may be regarded as general oppression.

This way of categorizing housing problems is more than just a convenient taxonomy of miscellaneous issues; it is directly relevant to the formulation of housing policies. It sees housing problems neither as a collection of miscellaneous and separable special problems nor as problems resulting simply from inadequate incomes. While individuals' incomes may be limited, the United States as a nation clearly could house all of its residents well if it chose to do so. Inadequate housing is not inevitable, but rather the result of specific types of problems in the housing system.

Frictional Problems

Frictional (or technical) problems include problems of efficiency, technical organization, externalities, information, economic pricing, and marketing. They also include problems arising from conflicts among users (as distinguished from conflicts between users and suppliers, where one side's loss is the other side's gain).

The market is an effective distribution device in many ways, but in other ways it is inefficient, even in its own terms. The inefficiencies of the housing market are well known: inadequate control of externalities; lack of information; cyclical variations in pricing, availability, and financing; inefficient and often corrupt public controls; unwillingness to take risks or difficulty in spreading pricing risks; inadequate research and development; and fragmentation of the industry with consequent unavailability of economies of scale.

These are technical problems that make life even harder for many adversely affected by the economic and housing systems, and often particularly for members of certain groups. But they are, by their nature, not insoluble, nor are there major conflicts of interests involved in their solution. They do not involve a zero-sum game. At the same time, precisely because they are technical and thus generally noncontroversial, efforts to develop solutions can sometimes lead to an attack on wider problems. An example is the relationship of architectural solutions to the larger housing problems faced by women. By themselves, architectural solutions do not address the sources of women's oppression or deal with the systemic problems of housing women face. Yet the search for architectural solutions may open the door to a consideration of wider issues and help proponents of a more general approach make that case more clearly.

Conflicts among users of housing, such as competing for a particular location, or having different ideas about the aesthetics of a particular style, or simply wanting to cut their lawns while others want to listen to a ball game, are also frictional. Solutions may be hard to find, and some may end up better off while others end up worse off. But intelligent planning can often leave everyone better off. The crucial characteristic of frictional user conflicts, in analyzing the issue of specialism, is that the user groups affected are not systemically defined; conflicts are distributed almost randomly. They do not stem from the position of one group systemically oppressing another group.

User conflicts, like inefficiencies, are likely to occur in any system of housing. Both are remediable without dealing with the systemic problems of commodification and oppression, and both are likely to remain, in one form or another, even if deeper systemic problems are solved.

Commodification

Commodification is an integral, indeed perhaps the defining, characteristic of the system of providing housing in the United States (Achtenberg and Marcuse 1986). Housing is designed, built, financed, sold, managed, and disposed of for profit. Profit determines how much housing there is, where it is, what it looks like, who owns it, who manages it, how much is paid for it. Profit thus also determines who will live in it. Those unable to pay the price for what they want, or for what by social norms is adequate, will not get it through the market system. That is simply how the system operates: housing is a commodity, and it is supplied in accordance with economically effective demand. (For an alternative approach to the housing system, see Chapter 12 by the Institute for Policy Studies Working Group on Housing.)

Commodification is a general, structural characteristic of the housing system. It affects individuals directly, those with the least incomes most adversely. If it makes sense to talk of those thus adversely affected as a "group," then the group consists of the poor: working people, the unemployed, and those excluded from the labor market. The system of providing housing as a commodity *must* affect the poor adversely; there is no other way it can function.

Oppression

Oppression adds the non-economic element to the quality and cost of housing.[4] Oppression in housing is that function of housing which circumscribes opportunities, dictates roles, inhibits protest, subtly produces conformity and acceptance, undermines resistance, integrates and makes tolerable a system against which an individual might otherwise protest. Inadequate housing is not necessarily oppressive, but the form in which it is provided, the logic by which it is imposed and accepted, can be. Homeownership, as an example, can be oppressive, regardless of the quality of housing that is involved: it can impede mobility, it can force individuals into stereotyped roles, it can set neighbor against neighbor, it can create a fear of loss that inhibits protest, it can stereotype women's roles, it can produce a vicious cycle of behavior in which ever-increasing consumption leads to ever-increasing willingness to work harder and avoid risks that might jeopardize what has already been acquired. Oppression is the political and social aspect of exploitation.

Oppression in housing, then, is that set of housing problems that neither money nor technical changes will solve. The source of the oppression of the poor is economic. That is to say, the poor are defined along economic lines: poverty is a question of money and economic situation. That basis for oppression is here considered "general"; other bases for oppression are called "special."

Special Oppression

Special oppression is a category whose clearest and most prevalent forms are racism and sexism. Racism is an ingrown feature of housing, as it is of most aspects of societal existence in the United States; the vested interests in the patterns it has created and the depth of its social and psychological roots justify considering it structural (see Chapter 5 by Phillip Clay). The patterns of sexism and of gender-based discrimination and stereotyping are also so ingrained and so functional to major portions of the social, economic, and political system, including housing, that the oppression of women is structural as well (see Chapter 4 by Eugenie Birch).

Because of the deep-seated character of these three forms of oppression—economic, racial, and gender-based—the problem of housing for those affected by such oppression cannot be solved without solving the problems that led to such oppression as well.

The connections among the three forms of oppression are many, and are matters of first-hand experience to the poor, unemployed, and underpaid, to women, blacks, and Hispanics. For these groups, the problem of what they must pay for their housing is consistently linked with the problems of oppression and exploitation from which they suffer. Women and members of minority groups are, because of sexism and racism, likely to be at the bottom of the economic ladder, and thus to be victimized by the general problems of commodification and oppression in housing. But racism and sexism are also special issues which must be dealt with in their own terms, not simply as part of the general economic problem.

The fundamental contradiction within the housing system is an economic one: housing suppliers may be racist and sexist, but these attitudes will generally be seen by them as consistent with the pursuit of profit. They redline, they will argue, because loans in black neighborhoods are economically risky. If economic risk is removed, for example by government insurance, redlining will decline; enough builders and developers don't mind building housing for blacks if they can profit from it. The same is true of housing oriented to the special needs of single women or single parents. Nevertheless, redlining exists, and special purpose housing is in short supply. As long as there is special oppression of women, blacks, and others in the larger system, these groups will not be well-housed. Neither income redistribution nor decommodification within the housing market alone can solve the housing problems of minority group members and women.

In any case, income redistribution and decommodification of the nation's housing stock are unlikely to come soon, for the economic system as a whole depends on the differentiation of groups by income, status, wealth, power, and role in the productive process. The skewed distribution of resources and roles is not accidental; it plays a major role in the system as a whole. Faith in income redistribution as a means to solve the housing problem is doomed to result in disappointment.

Manuel Castells refers to economic, racial, and gender-based practices as three "axes" of oppression and exploitation, a formulation that both graphically suggests their importance and picturesquely neglects the relationship among them.[5] Of the three, poverty is general and directly rooted in the economic conflicts of interest on which housing provision rests in the U.S. The other two, racism and sexism, are similarly structural, but result in an additional form of oppression separate from (and in addition to) that created by economic relations.

DIFFERENT PROBLEMS AFFECT SPECIAL GROUPS DIFFERENTLY

Structural problems involve major conflicts between groups; their resolution is difficult, involves significant changes in existing patterns, and ultimately will be decided by power. Nonstructural problems can be solved by adjustments in the existing situation, although they may coincidentally also involve relationships of power. Commodification and oppression are structural problems; frictional problems are not.

As an example: if demographic changes result in smaller households, and apartments have for years been built for large families, singles will have problems finding small units, but one would not talk of oppression of singles. Such a problem is a problem of technical organization: a frictional problem. Singles are not a structurally special group.

Some groups have both structural and frictional problems. Female-headed single-parent households, for instance, have problems finding units they can afford. There is a direct link between household composition and quality of housing, because of structural discrimination (sexism). There is thus a structural component to the special difficulties of such households. There is also a technical (frictional) component: correctly predicting the need for apartments of a given size within a subsidized housing project, or the type of facilities—daycare, recreational, etc.—needed, is also a problem, but a technical rather than a structural one. The technical problems of special groups need to be separated from their more structural problems, because the solutions are quite different: one requires technical competence, the other political power.

One way in which technical problems can be separated from political ones (generally structural and involving economic and social conflicts) is to ask whether greater knowledge of the characteristics and needs of the special group would assist in the solution of the problem. The problems poor single women with children have in finding suitable daycare, for instance, goes beyond ascertaining the nature or extent of the need. It requires finding the resources to meet that need. It is a political problem.

Market research addressed at special groups is an interesting indicator of the difference between technical and structural problems. There is substantial market research addressed to the special needs of many groups: the elderly, teenagers, rural residents, the disabled. The purpose of such research is to develop products for which there will be demand among groups with resources. Research addressed to clarifying the needs and preferences of poor single mothers is virtually nonexistent.

Public policy research addressed to the characteristics of special groups can similarly be a test of the nature of the problem. Except in unusual times, such research will be directed toward ferreting out the nonstructural aspects of their problems, that is, those that can be dealt with within the existing framework, or those that in effect "blame," control, or disarm the victim.[6] Much research on identifying the homeless is a classic case in point. The structural issues of a housing system and a health care system that systematically provide less than the poor need are forgotten. Instead, the focus becomes how the particular individuals at that particular point on the streets, in shelters, or in welfare hotels can be most efficiently (i.e., most cheaply) gotten out of their immediate desperate (and visible) plight. The answer tends to be either segregating them in special quarters where they will be out of sight and/or using social service interventions that will modify their behavior. The knowledge as to their characteristics leads to social control, not social reform.

Thus, particular groups whose characteristics require simply that they be taken into account in an efficient manner in order for their particular problems to be solved can be differentiated from special groups whose characteristics bear a structural relationship to special oppression. The distinctions among types of problems lead us to distinctions among the types of "special groups."

DIFFERENCES AMONG "SPECIAL GROUPS"

All special groups are not alike. The working poor, the permanently unemployed, women, blacks, Native Americans, the disabled, single-parent households, Hispanics, the mentally ill, the elderly, the homeless all share the distinction of being different from the stereotypical housing consumer, but they also differ a great deal from each other. In particular, they differ in the nature and causes of the housing problems they face. We can distinguish among four distinct categories of special groups: the specially oppressed, the atypical, the working poor, and the excluded poor.

The Specially Oppressed

The specially oppressed include women, racial minorities, illegal immigrants, and others whose problems are in part traceable to a special exploitation that holds their incomes below the average for what they do in the regular labor market. Blacks and Hispanics are discriminated against in the level of their wages, divided from their white peers through prejudice, separated from them by residential segregation, denied opportunities for education and advancement. Many women are confined to unpaid labor in the home, discriminated against in rates of pay, divided from their male peers by prejudice, held back in their opportunities and aspirations. For illegal immigrants, or those whose residency status is insecure, their vulnerability is used to pay them substandard wages in sweatshops or for home work. The restricted possibilities available to Native Americans on reservations, and the prejudice they encounter elsewhere, results in substandard compensation for the work they do. Discrimination and segregation are forms of special oppression that permit special exploitation to take place.

Housing patterns both contribute to and are shaped by special exploitation and special oppression. Blacks and Hispanics are confined to ghettos, limited in where they can live, excluded from major areas of most metropolitan regions. They are thus also restricted in their choice of jobs by the limited accessibility their housing provides—many jobs in the suburbs, for instance, realistically are not available for them. They are charged more than whites for comparable housing, and receive less than comparable transportation, education, recreation, and other public services. They are more insecure in their everyday lives, more dependent on fragile linkages to make things work, more subject to disruption in the pursuit of the day's necessities. They are thus also less well situated to climb the ladder of success, to improve their incomes, to resist exploitation. The lack of childcare connected with or near their housing severely restricts the job choices of many women. Others are restricted to jobs they can reach from suburban locations with limited public transport, to unpaid work within the household, or to jobs in locations not of their choosing but chosen by men on whom they are dependent. Their locational choices are restricted by discrimination in the housing market, in the granting of mortgages or the preferences (and prejudices) of landlords. For immigrants worried about their legal status, vulnerability to the whims and overcharges of landlords or sellers is extreme, and the insecurity of their housing reinforces their vulnerability to exploitation at work.

Segregation by income, race, national origin, sex, or household composition confines individuals to living with persons similar to them and excludes them from the benefits of accessibility to a variety of services, goods, amenities, interchanges, cultural offerings, and information available to others. Housing can function as a direct control device, permitting the overseeing and regulation of groups forced to live in regimented and controlled environments, in public housing projects, group homes or accommodations from which they can be evicted if they do not comply with the norms externally established for them.

The Atypical

The atypical range from deliberate nonconformists to those who, through no doing of their own, have special needs requiring particular types of housing. Artists may exemplify the former, the elderly and disabled the latter. The problems confronting atypical groups have two sources: the lack of comfort many feel in the presence of those who are unlike themselves or who reject their values, and market frictions in meeting unusual demand. The pressure for uniformity is visible throughout U.S. housing. Suburbia, of course, is the classic example: the single-family house, built for commuting husband, wife at home, two children, car and dog, is a symbol of the homogeneity to which not only housing, but advertising, cultural institutions, political rhetoric, and other pervasive aspects of our society lead. Nonconformity is disfavored: the greater the difference, the more it is frowned on, rejected, or ignored. Thus, virtually any special need or different circumstance is likely to run up against a system designed to accommodate and produce only a single type of person, of household, of life. Gays, lesbians, single-parent households, night people, home workers, and even trombone-players will find themselves pressured to conform. Housing suppliers will expect the neighbors to object to nonconformists next door, or they may themselves object. Nonconformists will find a housing system structurally uninterested in their needs.

Even where the atypical do not meet social resistance to nonconformity, they may encounter market frictions in having their needs met. Conventional marketing tends to make production for the majority more profitable, and certainly more risk-free, than production for the minority. Thus, housing for anyone whose needs do not conform to those of a large and known market segment presents difficulties for purely market reasons having nothing to do with prejudice or social pressure. It is simply safer to produce for the middle of the market range than for its extremes. In this sense atypical people will face problems in housing regardless of their means until the housing industry is convinced it can meet those needs and still make a profit. The market needs time to adjust—but structurally can do so—to acceptable atypicals, and will ultimately meet their needs as long as the costs of doing so can be passed along to consumers.

Covering the costs of providing improved access to public spaces is a different matter. Because the costs of making a store, lobby, or parking lot handicapped-accessible cannot be charged only to the handicapped who benefit from the additional accessibility, the real estate industry has generally protested building code requirements of the type New York and several other states now have (for example, requiring wheelchair accessibility in certain types of buildings).

Atypical households that are also poor cannot afford the increased cost of housing adapted to their needs. Because of age or disability, their earning capacity is impaired at the same time their housing needs are different from the ordinary. Inevitably and structurally, the private market will not meet their needs; there either has to be some non-market redistribution of costs within the housing sector (a skewing of rents) or a direct public subsidy. Both will encounter private market resistance.

While atypical groups face special problems in housing, they are not specially exploited. Unlike blacks and women, for instance, whose special oppression ultimately contributes to the profits made in the private sector, the special needs of the elderly and the disabled contribute to no one's profits. Their needs simply cannot be met at a profit. The end result is much the same, but the political battles that need to be won to change that result are different. No special vested interests profit from the exploitation of the atypical.

The elderly have in fact been successful in fighting many battles. They are well organized, vocal, active, and often militant. Their numbers are large and their interests are clear. Perhaps most importantly, they are atypical only in some ways. While they have special needs and interests, they are also disproportionately white. While they are also disproportionately female, the strength of sexism as it affects them is lessened by the fact that most are no longer in the labor market, and thus are not currently subjected to special exploitation there, too. As a result, they have been more active than other groups in using political power to gain access to benefits from governmental programs (Marcuse 1987b). They have pioneered in broadening the concept of housing to include residential services and neighborhood, and they have led fights for improvements not only for themselves but for other ill-housed groups.

The disabled are not in as favorable a political situation. Some are among the worst-housed in the nation. They cannot compete for much of private housing, which in any case does not meet their needs, yet they are not numerous or powerful enough to determine the design, construction, and management of alternative housing (Yasmin 1985). There are examples where they have been able to use their limited economic resources and political power to achieve significant victories, but most disabled do not have access to suitable housing.

The Working Poor

The working poor will have difficulty obtaining housing as long as housing is provided as a commodity. Given the gap between the family income necessary to purchase the average-priced new single-family house in the U.S. today and actual median family income of the working poor, and given that more than half of all tenants pay more than 25 percent of their incomes for rent (Hartman 1983), it would take a virtual revolution in the structure of income distribution in the United States to solve the housing problem through a redistribution of income alone. In a very fundamental sense, the housing problems of the poor are thus not special. They are instead structural. Housing is commodified, and the poor are those who cannot afford that commodity.

The Excluded Poor

The excluded poor are not always to be a special group. Some argue that permanent poverty distorts values and modifies behavior to a point at which the permanent poor become different people from the rest of society. Culture of poverty theories tend to support this view.

Over the last several decades change has occurred in the economic structure of the country to produce a qualitatively new phenomenon: an increasing permanent redundancy of a large segment of the population, who are permanently excluded from the labor force, in whose welfare there is thus barely any economic interest in the business community. Basic changes in the productive machinery of the country are responsible for the effective permanent exclusion of many from the workforce and, as a result, from the housing market. Some of the excluded poor are perhaps a special group to the extent that the depth and duration of poverty has produced special and individual forms of adaptation that in turn create problems for them, but for many a change in economic conditions will erase such special characteristics. Applying the label of "the small hard core" (Wood 1957) to this group may be realistic, but it is potentially treacherous, because it implies that their exclusion is explained by their individual characteristics, neglecting the reverse chain of causation.[7]

THE DANGERS OF SPECIALISM AND GENERALISM

Specialism—the definition of a societal problem as the special problem of a particular group, brought about or made serious by the particular characteristics of that group—has four dangers: it can conceal the general (structural) nature of a given problem; it can blame the victims for their problems; it can conceal political problems with a technical cover; and it can divide those affected by common problems.

Concealing the General Nature of Structural Problems

The cataloguing approach to housing problems—listing the particular groups that can be isolated as having problems over and above the average—suggests housing is no longer a problem for the majority. The policy inference is that housing programs should be targeted to special groups, and any assistance given to others is unnecessary. Much of the discussion of homelessness, addressing it in terms of the characteristics of the homeless instead of the supply of housing, leads to similar conclusions.[8]

Blaming the Victim

From viewing a problem as that of a special group to blaming the problem on the special characteristics of that group is an easy step. Specialism focuses attention on the particular characteristics of the victim (household status, age, place of origin, skills, demographic or physical characteristics) and makes it appear that helping the victim change those characteristics, or compensating for their disadvantages, will eliminate the problem.

Concealing the Political Under the Technical

Submerging political under technical issues, obscuring conflicts of interest or denying their existence, contributes to the perpetuation of political (and economic and social) relationships that cause major housing problems. Specialism does this by lumping together all groups with problems, whether or not they suffer from special exploitation or oppression. Some groups are simply atypical; their desires are inefficiently met in the present housing market, and those inefficiencies can be met simply by technical changes. Other groups are specially oppressed, and their problems cannot be solved without more basic change.

Considering them all indiscriminately as "special groups" suggests that technical solutions may suffice for all of them.

Dividing the Ill-Housed

The structurally ill-housed—the poor, members of oppressed groups, and social non-conformists—face similar problems arising out of similar macro-economic and housing supply patterns. By focusing attention on the characteristics of particular groups among the structurally ill-housed, the common threads running through the causes of their problems are obscured, and common action is made more difficult.

This "divide and disarm" effect is not unique to housing; it runs throughout most areas of social policy. As Friedland, Piven, and Alford (1977) have pointed out:

> Political structures tend to encourage the multiplication and fragmentation of groups focused on relatively minor forms of group recognition, patronage, and service delivery. . . . [This] splinters the middle, working and lower classes . . . [and] heightens non-class bases of identification [such as] territorial and ethnic bases.

Generalism

Generalism—ignoring the special problems affecting particular groups in addressing general societal problems—has one main, and important, danger: it can divert attention from the critical problems facing particular groups. It is debatable whether blacks or women, for example, suffer more from the general problem of poverty than from the specific problems of racism or sexism. Sexism and racism certainly aggravate the problem of poverty. A recently completed study of housing in New York City (Marcuse 1986) shows that, even holding rent constant, blacks receive worse housing than whites, at the same time that incomes for blacks—and thus rent-paying ability—are much lower than for whites. Generalism ignores such facts.

This danger of generalism is much more acute for the specially oppressed than for the atypical, because of the dominant desire to conceal the special oppression of any group. To be specific: conceding that some of the disabled need ramps for accessibility does not require that one acknowledge the existence of any structural flaw in the system of providing housing, while conceding that blacks pay more for housing does. With adjustments, the private market system could provide ramps for those handicapped who can afford it; it cannot provide freedom from discrimination even for blacks who have money. Nor is it likely to provide an adequate range of housing opportunities for women even when they can afford it.

CONCLUSION: A UNIFIED APPROACH TO HOUSING PROBLEMS

Many distinctions thus exist among forms of the housing problem and among the groups affected by them. Must conflicts around housing issues therefore be fragmented, or are there grounds for a general response that will address all the problems of special groups? If a general response is possible, would it gain the support of middle-class consumers as well?

Although the middle class is economically differentiated from the poor in housing and is neither structurally ill-housed nor oppressed in the senses used here, its members have housing interests paralleling those of the poor.[9] As users, middle-class residents are interested in holding down the profits from the sale of housing as a commodity. While the market "works" for most members of the middle class as it does not, and cannot, for the poor, the middle class and the poor nevertheless are on the same side of a major dividing line: those whose interests are in the use of housing, as opposed to those whose interests are in its profit potential.[10] Both classes are users of housing and thus share a common interest.

But the interest of the poor is also different from the interest of the middle class in regard to housing. The middle class may be badly served by the commodification of housing, but the housing situation of the poor is often intolerable. Further, while the middle class can sometimes negotiate satisfactory compromises in the market, the poor rarely can. For the poor, a social and political response is a necessity; for those better situated, it may simply be desirable.

As between the poor and the specially oppressed, both long-run and short-run interests are much more congruent. Every specially oppressed group is also ill-served by the commodity character of housing. Over and above this common interest, special groups—the specially oppressed—have an interest in ending the special disadvantages imposed on them in housing. A solid alliance toward that end between special groups and the poor can be grounded in their common opposition to commodification, but opposition to special oppression must be included if the alliance is to last.

Particular groups that are not specially oppressed may also have particular problems in housing (the atypical, the well-off elderly, and so on), but their alliance with the poor is not inevitable. In some cases, such groups can only be served by the decommodification of housing. In other cases, simply improving its handling as a commodity will suffice. In the latter case, alliances among such groups will be transitory and fragile.

Both specialism and generalism are major obstacles to the improvement of housing. The relationship between general and special is complex, but disentangling the relationship is important both to design sound policies and to develop effective strategies for their adoption. The first step is to recognize that both general and special problems must be dealt with if either is to be overcome.

NOTES

1. For criticism of a parallel analysis from an earlier period, see Marcuse 1966.

2. Summary from letter by the Gray Panthers of New York City, 28 May 1985, urging support.

3. The term 'commodification of housing' is awkward, but frequently used, and no better one has been suggested. See Harloe 1981, and Achtenberg and Marcuse 1986.

4. The term 'oppression' is not ideal; 'discipline' might be substituted. For a fuller discussion, see Marcuse 1987c.

5. Castells (1984) in fact has discussed the relationship among them extensively. The "axes" formulation itself, however, is useful to clarify the existence of the three (actually, Castells adds a fourth, culture) rather than to deal with that relationship.

6. Thus, Daniel Patrick Moynihan has apparently moved from blaming the "black family" for society's disorders—an approach calculated both to blame and further control the victim—to blaming the disintegration on "the family" in general—continuing to blame, while generalizing the victim. For a later discussion of the same issue that by contrast treads perilously close to "blaming the victim," but then moves to "structural unemployment" and governmental responsibility, see Norton 1985.

7. For a discussion of the issue in the context of treatment of the homeless (among the poorest of the very poor), see Marcuse 1987a.

8. See the report of the Coalition for the Homeless et al. 1986, which analyzes newspaper coverage of homeless issues and calculated that less than 10 percent of all articles ever refer to housing issues as a part of their discussion of homelessness.

9. There is an extended discussion in the socialist literature on this point, touched off by Engels' analogy of the relationship between housing consumer and housing supplier to the relationship between buyer and seller of any ordinary commodity on the market: a shopkeeper/customer conflict, not a class conflict. The analogy, while having merit, needs to be modified by two considerations: the commodity housing is necessary to sustain life, and the cost of its provision at a socially acceptable level influences the wages employers must pay. The conflict around what is a socially acceptable level of housing thus becomes a conflict in which different classes have different interests.

10. The two interests often coexist, as in a homeowner who also sees his or her home as an investment or as financial security for old age. Nevertheless, the motivations arising from the perspective of use and from the perspective of profit are quite different, even if one household may have both at the same time.

REFERENCES

Achtenberg, Emily and Peter Marcuse. 1986. "Towards the Decommodification of Housing." In *Critical Perspectives on Housing*, edited by Rachel Bratt, Chester Hartman, and Ann Meyerson. Philadelphia: Temple University Press.

Brecher, Charles and Bailey Waldinger. 1984. "A Skills Mismatch in New York's Labor Market." *New York Affairs* 8:3ff.

The Builders Institute. 1985. *Impact* 26 (8), May. White Plains, NY.

Castells, Manuel. 1984. Untitled talk at Urban Conflict and Change Conference, Sussex, England.

Coalition for the Homeless et al. 1986. *Stemming the Tide of Displacement: Housing Policies for Preventing Homelessness*. New York, mimeographed.

Freeman, Jo. 1980. "Women and Urban Policy." *Signs* 5 (3) Supplement: S4-S21.

Friedland, Roger, Frances F. Piven, and Robert R. Alford. 1977. "Political Conflict, Urban Structure, and the Fiscal Crisis," *International Journal of Urban and Regional Research* 1:447–73.

Goldin, Harrison. 1985. *Report of the Comptroller of the City of New York*, vol. 10, no. 6, December 1984–January 1985.

Harloe, Michael. 1981. "The Recommodification of Housing." In *City, Class and Capital*, edited by Michael Harloe and E. Lebas. London: Edward Arnold.

Hartman, Chester. 1983. *America's Housing Crisis: What Is To Be Done*? Boston: Routledge & Kegan Paul.

Marcuse, Peter. 1987a. "Why Are They Homeless?" *The Nation* 244 (13): 426–29.

———. 1987b. "Are the Elderly Especially Ill-Housed?" Paper delivered at the Brookdale Conference, The Housing of the Elderly.

———. 1987c. "The Other Side of Housing: Oppression and Liberation." In *Between State and Market: Housing in the Post-Industrial Era*, edited by Bengt Turner. Göteburg, Sweden: Almqvist & Wiksell.

———. 1986. "The Uses and Limits of Rent Control." Report to the Commissioner of the New York State Department of Housing and Community Renewal, December.

———. 1985a. "Gentrification, Abandonment and Displacement: Their Linkages in New York City." *Washington University Journal of Urban and Contemporary Law* 28: 195–240.

———. 1966. "Scholarship and Burning Issues" (review of Oscar Ornati, *Poverty Amid Affluence). The New Republic*, August 13.

National Association of Housing and Redevelopment Officials. 1984. *Better Places to Live: The Future of the Public Role in Housing and Urban Development*. Washington, DC.

Norton, Eleanor Holmes. 1985. "Restoring the Traditional Black Family." *The New York Times Magazine*, June 2, 1985, pp. 43ff.

Ornati, Oscar. 1966. *Poverty Amid Affluence*. New York: The Twentieth Century Fund.

Tobier, Emanuel. 1984. *The Changing Face of Poverty: Trends in New York City's Population in Poverty: 1960–1990*. New York: Community Service Society.

Wood, Elizabeth. 1957. "The Small Hard Core: The Housing of Problem Families in New York City. A Study and Recommendations." New York: Citizens' Housing and Planning Council of New York.

Yasmin, Adib. 1985. "Housing the Disabled." *City Limits*, October 1983, p. 6ff.

THE PITFALLS OF SPECIALISM: COMMENT

Cushing N. Dolbeare

Both Peter Marcuse and I start from the perspective that decent, affordable housing should be regarded as a basic human right. I fully agree with him that an adequate national housing policy must go beyond addressing some specialized needs (such as special housing for the elderly) to confront the basic inequity of the housing system itself. Finally, I concur that the current effort, which provides massive subsidies, primarily through the tax system, for middle- and upper-income people while failing to provide adequate support for programs that provide decent housing to low-income people, cannot be described as adequate.

Where we part ways is on the question of how best to use our energies to bring about a more just national housing effort. I believe that the most critical challenge is to convince policymakers to support and adopt specific policies that will reduce the inequities in our housing system and address the housing needs of low-income people and other groups with special housing needs. Quite simply, I question the extent to which it is necessary to link reform of national housing policy to comprehensive efforts to reform the larger economy. Is it necessary or even useful to assume that we cannot, or will not, meet our nation's housing needs as long as housing is defined as a speculative commodity? I do not think so. If we frame the question as a choice—between focusing on specific objectives, such as the provision of housing as a right, and moving from there to broader social reform, or beginning with attempts at fundamental social and economic reform as means to bring about specific objectives—I would argue for the former while Marcuse suggests the latter.

This difference should not, I believe, be regarded as a question of a "right" or a "wrong" approach, but rather of with which strategy each of us, personally and professionally, is most comfortable. Rather than regarding them as mutually exclusive, we should try to make them complementary. Thus, instead of rejecting Marcuse's argument, I will argue both for a pragmatic policy-specific approach to reform of the housing system and for efforts to link such an approach to Marcuse's broader social reform strategy.

My preference for focused, policy-specific reform strategies rather than broad, theoretically-based efforts reflects my 35 years of experience. I have learned that when the objective is change, it is necessary to frame arguments for change in a way that makes that change seem realistic and desirable. When one testifies before a Senate committee headed by a conservative, the chance to be taken seriously would be eliminated by stating that housing should no longer be bought or sold for private profit. If, however, one begins by discussing the nature and scope of housing needs of particular constituencies and moves on to propose specific measures to address those needs, one can have at least a marginal influence on policy. And it is possible, once the ground has been laid, to assert that the private sector is unable to meet low-income housing needs and that one must look for new approaches that treat ownership of housing as a public trust and that prevent speculation for personal gain at the expense of vulnerable groups. Clearly, neither conservatives nor others on the housing committees of Congress have yet accepted the notion that allowing housing to be treated as a commodity is at the heart of the nation's housing problems, but some of the more thoughtful members have at least been moved to consider the need for alternatives to the private market for meeting housing needs. These members, who cannot possibly be expected to accept the idea that housing should be removed from the private market, are potential allies in the effort to solve the nation's housing problems. It is critical to remember that in these troubled times for housing, we need all the support we can get to save alternative housing programs and avoid losing ground in the short run.

I do not mean to imply that it is not important to have a clear sense of the larger issues and goals. Marcuse's analysis is helpful, and much of it rings true. But having said that, I am not sure the analysis gets us very far in dealing with housing as a political problem. Indeed, his arguments remind me of experiences at the Housing Association in Philadelphia in the late 1960s. We concluded that much of the work we had been doing on housing analysis and advocacy was irrelevant or even counterproductive because the real problem was racism. With benefit of hindsight, I question our decision to shift our emphasis to the "larger" more fundamental problem of racism. In the end we did not get very far on racism (Frank Rizzo was elected mayor soon thereafter), and we did not have as much impact as we might have had on housing issues.

An alternative approach would have been to build a broad coalition of different racial and income groups interested in housing reforms and to use that coalition to address larger political issues. Based on the lessons learned over the past decades in Philadelphia and elsewhere, I believe that it is not only possible but practical to use a broad housing coalition, such as the National Low Income

Housing Coalition, to bring about specific policy reforms and, ultimately, broad social change. Such a coalition brings together a range of groups with interests in specific policy initiatives, such as elderly housing or rural housing, into a mutually reinforcing effort to deal with the broad housing problems of all groups who cannot obtain decent, affordable housing in the communities where they wish to reside.

I also believe that it is critical to include credible political actors in the coalition. Their participation gives visibility to the effort and facilitates access to the political process. An example is found in the recent priority given by the National League of Cities to the inequity of our housing subsidy system, which gives $3 (including tax-expenditures) to the affluent for each $1 of housing assistance going to low-income households. While for years the National Low Income Housing Coalition has been pointing out this inequity, the ''finding'' clearly had far greater impact when it came from the National League of Cities. Whenever it is possible to include political actors in a coalition and to convince them to take a public stand consistent with the coalition's objectives, the leverage of the coalition is increased.

During 1984, the National Low Income Housing Coalition used this approach to involve dozens of national, state, and local organizations and hundreds of individuals in an exchange of views and review-and-comment process. This culminated in the adoption of an outline designed to be used as a vehicle for organizing and mobilizing constituencies for reform of national housing policy.

The policy outline which emerged from the process rests on three basic principles that are certainly consistent with those underlying Marcuse's arguments. They are that:

- Decent, safe, and sanitary shelter is one of the basic necessities of life. All people share the basic human right to live in dignity, safety, and security. The federal government bears the fundamental responsibility for ensuring that the opportunity to obtain decent, affordable housing with a choice of location is available to all in our society—regardless of race, creed, age, family composition, or income level. All housing programs should be responsive to consumer, tenant, neighborhood, and community needs and preferences, and accessible to all without regard to race, creed, or handicap.
- The federal government has the responsibility and the resources to ensure that adequate housing for low-income people is provided throughout the United States: in inner cities, in suburbs, in small towns, and rural areas. Only the federal government can mount programs that provide uniform standards and protections, while leaving flexibility to states, local governments, and other institutions, including the private sector, to adapt them to the range of housing needs that exist in our country.
- Federal housing expenditures should give highest priority to those with the most critical housing needs: people living in inadequate housing; people displaced or threatened by displacement, from whatever cause; and people whose incomes are too low to bear the high cost of decent shelter.

Building on these three principles, eight specific policies were proposed. The policies were complementary in that they each focused on different elements of the housing problem or different groups' needs. As such, they provided a basis for holding the coalition together and allowing it to build a larger constituency for general housing policy reform. At the same time, they provided the vehicle by which the coalition could appeal to policymakers.

The policy outline developed by the National Low Income Housing Coalition provides the basis for addressing the nation's housing needs. It provides the basis for proposing specific policies and quantifying their costs. And it provides a context for raising housing as a political issue and letting people engage it in whatever way they are most comfortable. A community group can engage it around the issue of community housing supply. Fair housing groups can engage it around the fair housing issue. Specialized groups can engage it around issues relating to their specialized interests. Each group will be encouraged to consider their issue as part of a larger effort. By doing so, the policy outline provides the basis for pursuing the reforms that Marcuse calls for. Most importantly, however, it does what housing policy has thus far failed to do: it articulates the means of making decent, affordable housing a reality for everyone in this country.

4

WOMEN AND SHELTER: NEEDS AND ISSUES

Eugenie Ladner Birch

INTRODUCTION

Nearly one-third of the nation is experiencing a housing problem. The ill-housed population consists of over 23 million households. They are a diverse group—the elderly, families with children, and single people of all races. Most significantly, they tend to be women. In fact, numerically, female-headed households are the largest subgroup of the poorly sheltered.[1]

Included in today's definition of a housing problem are two issues: housing quality and tenure status. The housing quality concept employs three criteria to form an index that sets the minimum standard for decent housing in America: the physical adequacy of a dwelling, the extent of overcrowding, and the level of affordability. Tenure status is a term identifying a householder as an owner or renter. In the United States, 65 percent of all housing units are owned, yet only 48 percent of the nation's female householders are homeowners.[2] Renters are more likely to be afflicted with housing quality problems than are owners. For example, 30 percent of all renters are cost-burdened,[3] and 15 percent live in physically inadequate shelter. By contrast, in the homeowner group only 8 percent are cost-burdened and 6 percent live in physically inadequate housing. Female householders, homeowners as well as renters, have a higher incidence of housing quality problems than does the general population. For example, 17 percent of female homeowners are cost-burdened—almost three times the national rate—and 32 percent live in physically inadequate shelter—five times the national rate.

This evidence adds a new dimension to understanding American housing conditions. It suggests the importance of incorporating gender as a factor in identifying and elaborating housing issues. This paper will explore how and why gender has become an essential analytical variable. It will detail important demographic characteristics of the female householder population and outline the dimensions of its housing problem. In particular, it will outline housing conditions for different groups of women—single parents and the elderly—and will contrast women's situation with that of minority groups. (A related treatment of the problems of special subpopulations may be found in Chapter 3 by Peter Marcuse.)

AMERICAN HOUSEHOLDS: THEIR COMPOSITION AND LOCATION

While the housing problem has long been associated with women's concerns, its definition as a gender issue has traditionally been articulated within the context of conventional family structure. Early housing advocates such as Jacob Riis and Edith Elmer Wood documented that women, particularly mothers, bore the brunt of inadequate shelter. Yet the women they were concerned with were usually part of conventional families. Their successors, too, regarded the traditional household—mother, father, and children—as the norm. Consequently, their solutions were premised on the collective belief that they were treating a family housing problem (Birch 1983).

Until about 1950, they may have been correct. However, at about that time major changes in household composition began to occur. As Table 4.1 indicates, the family household, while still a majority, became a smaller proportion, and the nonfamily, single-person household experienced dramatic growth.

Adding the gender factor to the analysis, Table 4.1 also demonstrates that women increasingly are heads of households. Historically, they have dominated the nonfamily class, and between 1950 and 1980 they increased from 9 percent to 15 percent of all families. By 1980 the 27 percent female-headed households constituted 22 million units.

Growth rates of these households, exhibited in Table 4.2, demonstrate the extent of this demographic transformation. While female households more than doubled in the last generation, the nonfamily household, composed largely of single, elderly women, who are 48.5 percent of the group, experienced the most dramatic expansion.

The majority of female householders, as Table 4.3 demonstrates, live in metropolitan areas. In both categories, family and nonfamily, they are a little more urban than the general population. They also show a slight tendency to be more concentrated in central cities than are other American households. This is especially true of female-headed families. While female householders are urban, they do not live exclusively in central cities. Almost one-half of the metropolitan female householders live in the suburbs. This identification of the concerns of female householders will have to include consideration of a variety of issues

Table 4.1
Distribution of U.S. Households by Type, 1950–1980

	1950	1960	1970	1980
All Households (in thousands)	43,554	52,799	63,799	82,368
All Families	38,838	44,905	51,456	60,309
As a Percentage of All Households	89.2%	85.1%	80.7%	73.2%
Female-Headed Families	3,594	4,422	5,500	9,082
As a Percentage of All Families	9.0%	9.7%	10.7%	15.3%
All Non-family Households	4,716	7,895	11,945	22,059
As a Percentage of All Households	10.8%	14.9%	19.3%	26.8%
Female-Headed Non-family Households	3,048	5,179	7,882	12,780
As a Percentage of All Non-family Households	65.9%	66.7%	65.5%	57.9%
Total Female Households	6,642	9,601	13,382	21,862
As a Percentage of All Households	15.1%	18.2%	20.9%	26.6%

Source: U.S. Bureau of the Census, *Census of Population*, 1950, 1960, 1970, 1980, and U.S. Bureau of the Census, *Statistical Abstract of the United States*, various years.

tied to location, among them the equity question of whether female-headed families are more concentrated in central cities by choice, and what kinds of dwellings and services different groups of women need in their respective locations.

INCOME AND AGE

An analysis of the distribution of income among households is essential to a full appreciation of gender-related housing issues. In comparison to other Americans, female householders are poor. Their median (1980) income ($8,931) is less than half of the national figure ($19,074) and only 35 percent of married

Table 4.2
Growth Rates of Female Households in the United States, 1950–1980

	1950-60	1960-70	1970-80	1950-1980
		(percent increase)		
All households	21.1	23.6	29.8	89.1
Family	15.7	14.5	17.3	55.3
Female-headed	25.6	25.0	65.5	152.2
Non-Family	65.9	52.6	85.7	367.6
Females	67.7	50.0	64.1	319.3
Total Female Households	45.5	38.5	64.7	229.1

Source: U.S. Bureau of the Census, *Statistical Abstract of the United States, 1982–83*.

couples' ($25,106). Furthermore, as Table 4.4 demonstrates, almost three-quarters of female householders have incomes under $15,000, while only one-quarter of married couples fall into this category. At the other end of the scale, only 6 percent of female householders earn enough to purchase a new home having the 1983 $93,000 median price tag. In contrast, almost 40 percent of married couples can undertake such an obligation.

Table 4.5, which correlates female householders, distributed by age categories, with income, reveals that 60 percent of heads of families are in their childbearing years and almost half of the single-person households are over sixty-five. The poorest are the female heads of family, with median incomes ranging from $5,000 to $12,000. (The precarious position of many of these women is underscored by the fact that most are supporting one or more minor children in their homes. In fact, the average size of a female-headed family is more than three people.) The elderly, who constitute almost half of female single-person households, are among the poorest. Their median income of less than $6,000 also places them

Table 4.3
Location of Female Householders in the United States, 1980

	Total U.S. Households (in thousands)	Percentage of U.S. Households Within SMSA's	Distribution of Households Within SMSA's: Percentage Inside Center Cities	Distribution of Households Within SMSA's: Percentage Outside Center Cities	Percentage of U.S. Households Outside SMSA's
All Female Householders	21,723	72.6	52.4	47.6	24.8
All U.S. Householders	83,526	68.2	46.0	54.0	30.8
Female-Headed Families	9,403	72.6	52.8	47.2	27.3
All U.S. Families	61,019	66.6	39.1	60.9	33.4
Female Non-Family Households	12,320	77.1	52.1	47.9	22.9
All U.S. Non-Family Households	23,913	72.7	49.5	50.5	27.8

Source: U.S. Department of Commerce, Bureau of the Census, *Money Income of Households, Families and Persons in the United States, 1981; General Population, U.S. Summary, 1980.*

Table 4.4
Household Income in the United States, 1980: Comparison of Female Householders and Married Couples

	All Householders	Female Householders	Married Couples
	(in percent)		
	(N = 83,527,000)	(N = 21,775,000)	(N = 49,630,000)
Under $5,000	10.5	26.6	2.9
$5,000- 9,999	14.9	27.8	8.7
$10,000-14,999	14.4	17.9	12.3
$15,000-19,999	12.3	11.1	12.5
$20,000-24,999	11.4	7.1	13.2
$25,000-29,999	9.7	3.9	12.3
$30,000-34.999	7.6	2.1	10.3
35,000 +	19.3	4.0	27.7
Median Income	$19,074	$ 8,931	$25,106

Source: U.S. Department of Commerce, Bureau of the Census, *Money Income of Households, Families and Persons in the United States, 1981* (Washington, D.C. 1983).

in precarious situations: half have less than $500 per month to cover all their expenses, including their (probably rising) health care costs.

HOUSING QUALITY

The U.S. Department of Housing and Urban Development biannually (and, until recently, annually) surveys several indicators of the quality of individual dwelling units. It looks at physical inadequacy, including an assessment of systems (plumbing, electrical, heating) and facilities (kitchens and bathrooms); the incidence of overcrowded units (more than one person per room); and the existence of excessive costs.

As Table 4.6 indicates, slightly over one-fourth of all American dwellings are problem-ridden. Perhaps most importantly, female householders, representing over 10 million households, occupy over 40 percent of these units.

Notably and predictably, women are most affected in the cost-burden category. With over one-third of them paying more than they should for their shelter, they

Table 4.5
Age Distribution and Median Income of Female Householders, 1980

Age	Female Head of Family (N = 9,403,000)		Female Single Person (N = 13,051,000)	
	Percent	Median Income	Percent	Median Income
15-24	8.3%	$ 4,879	8.1%	$ 8,334
25-34	25.9%	8,113	14.3%	13,768
35-44	24.2%	12,595	6.2%	13,828
45-54	17.2%	14,680	6.7%	10,264
55-64	11.3%	14,001	16.2%	8,593
65+	13.1%	12,429	48.5%	5,625

Source: U.S. Department of Commerce, Bureau of the Census, *Money Income of Households, Families and Persons in the United States, 1981* (Washington, D.C. 1983).

Table 4.6
Housing Quality in the United States, 1981

	All Households	Female Households	Female Households as % of Problem
Occupied Units	83,203,000	22,603,000	---
Percentage of units With:			
Any Housing Problem	27.8	42.9	41.8
Physical Inadequacy	9.3	10.1	35.6
Crowding	3.0	2.1	18.8
Cost Burden	15.5	29.3	51.3

Source: Special tabulations based on 1981 Annual Housing Survey, U.S. Department of Housing and Urban Development.

constitute half of all those having this hardship, due primarily to their low incomes. (For a more complex view of housing affordability standards, see Chapter 13 by Michael Stone.) Their high representation among those living in physically inadequate dwellings is also related to their poverty. For many, all their earnings can support is a substandard house.

THE MORE SEVERELY IMPACTED WOMEN: THE SINGLE PARENT AND THE SENIOR CITIZEN

Among female householders, two groups stand out as requiring separate analysis: the single parent with children under the age of 18, and the elderly female household head. Although they occupy 15 percent of the nation's housing stock, they live in one-quarter of the units experiencing housing problems, and they are two of society's most economically vulnerable groups.

They have extremely low median incomes ($9,210 for the single parent, $4,757 for the elderly) and little likelihood of increasing their incomes without some outside support, such as daycare provisions allowing mothers to work or pensions or insurance for the senior citizens. As between the two groups, the single parent has the greater difficulties with her housing (Table 4.7). In fact, comparing data from this table with those of Table 4.6, it can be seen that the rate for this group is twice as high as the overall rate for all U.S. households.

Analyzing housing quality among renting single parents and seniors uncovers even more startling conditions. The female householders of this group (Table 4.7) are more than twice as likely as other American households to have a housing problem, three times more likely to be cost-burdened.

Female family householders with minor children are the most problem-ridden group among those living in substandard shelter. While the comparisons drawn in Table 4.8 are somewhat imprecise because female householders are not separated out from the comparison groups, the analysis is useful for its measurement of the severity of impact.

Given the high incidence of female householders living in inadequate housing, policymakers should single them out for special attention. Included in this population should be the very low-income mother with children who rents. This latter group constitutes one-third of female family householders with children, and over 53 percent of them have a housing problem.

TENURE PATTERNS: WOMEN AND OTHER GROUPS[4]

As noted above, female households are less likely to be owners than American households in general. The obverse side of the picture is women's status as renters. In 1981 they constituted 41 percent of all American renters (Table 4.9). Only four years earlier they were 32 percent of all renters (Downs 1983). They have grown to be a larger proportion because other households have increased their share in ownership faster than women.

Compared to other groups usually considered deprived in American society, women are only marginally better off. They own their homes with more frequency than minorities (Table 4.10). This favorable position can be attributed to the higher proportion of women among the elderly, who have higher rates of homeownership. Among the female elderly are frequently widows whose spouses' income purchased their housing.

Table 4.7

Housing Quality of the Female-Headed Family and the Elderly Female and of Severely Impacted Female Heads of Household Who Rent, 1981

	Total	Female-Headed Households With Children < 18	Elderly Female-Headed Hsehlds	Total Severely Impacted Households	Female-Headed Femalies With Children < 18 (renters)	Elderly Headed Households (renters)
Occupied Units	13,169,000	5,856,000	7,313,000	6,304,000	3,639,000	2,665,000
Percentage of Units With:						
Any Housing Problem	45.4	53.9	38.4	63.6	67.7	58.0
Physical inadequacy	12.5	14.7	10.8	15.7	18.4	12.1
Crowding	0.3	6.2	0.2	4.6	7.8	0.1
Cost Burden	29.9	33.1	27.5	43.3	41.5	45.8

Source: Special tabulations based on 1981 Annual Housing Survey, U.S. Department of Housing and Urban Development.

Table 4.8
Female Heads of Family With Minor Children Compared to Other Groups, 1981*

	Females With Children < 18	Blacks	Hispanics	Elderly
Occupied Units	5,856,000	9,025,000	4,346,000	16,906,000
Percentage With a Housing Problem	53.9	51.2	51.4	28.3

*Groups are not mutually exclusive.
Source: Special tabulations based on the 1981 Annual Housing Survey, U.S. Department of Housing and Urban Development.

Table 4.9
Tenure Patterns of U.S. Households Compared to Female Households, 1981

	All	Female Households	Female Households as a Percent of All Households
Total	83,203,000	22,603,000	27.2
Owner	65.4	48.2	19.9
Renter	34.6	51.8	40.6

Source: Special tabulations based on 1981 Annual Housing Survey, U.S. Department of Housing and Urban Development.

The ramifications of the difference in housing tenure patterns are not as immediately obvious as quality issues. But in analyzing the spatial, economic and, finally, intangible qualitative aspects of housing tenure in the United States, it becomes apparent that this low percentage of female homeownership represents a housing problem for women.

LOCATION

There are intra-regional and inter-regional dimensions to the location of owner-occupied and rental housing in the U.S. Within a region, rental units tend to be located within urbanized areas and specifically in central cities. In 1980, 69 percent of rental units were in urbanized areas and 42 percent were in central cities. (This compares with 31 percent of all housing units located in central

Table 4.10
Tenure Patterns of Selected Groups* of U.S. Households, 1981

Household	Total	Percent all Households	Owners	Percent all Households	Renters	Percent all Households
			(in thousands)			
Female	22,603	27.1	10,899	20.0	11,704	40.0
Percentage	(100)		(48.2)		(51.8)	
Black	9,025	10.8	3,901	7.2	5,123	17.0
Percentage	(100)		(43.2)		(56.7)	
Hispanic	4,346	5.2	1,822	3.3	2,524	8.0
Percentage	(100)		(41.9)		(58.1)	
Elderly	16,906	20.3	12,390	27.6	4,516	15.0
Percentage	(100)		(73.2)		(26.7)	

*Groups are not mutually exclusive.

Source: Special tabulations based on 1981 Annual Housing Survey, U.S. Department of Housing and Urban Development.

cities in the same year.) Female renter households (because of their inability to purchase housing units) are therefore also concentrated in urban areas and especially in central cities. This in itself is not of critical importance except for what it says about the degree of choice that female households have in selecting a location, neighborhood quality, and other services and attributes that should be considered in the definition of decent housing. All neighborhoods carry with them certain amenities and disamenities. Choice in a freely functioning housing market permits a household to choose a bundle of services desired. For female households, selection of services is severely circumscribed by where they can afford housing units.

As Tables 4.11 and 4.12 indicate, the South and West had far higher rates of increase in personal income in the 1970–1980 decade than did the Northeast and North Central regions; and in these two high-growth Sunbelt regions housing prices also rose much more rapidly than in the Frostbelt. Consequently, new housing units in the Sunbelt were more likely to be built for homeownership than rental use: in that same decade, the proportion of owner-occupied units in the South rose from 64.7 to 67.0 percent, and in the West from 59.0 to 59.8 percent. Thus, the type of housing being built tended to inhibit the migration of lower-income female households (who could not afford homeownership) to areas of the country where a booming economy could provide enhanced economic opportunity.

The concentration of female-headed households in rental units represents a lack of choice that has ramifications beyond the psychic satisfaction of having options or the opportunity of moving where economic growth is taking place.

Table 4.11
Personal Income (in constant 1972 dollars)

	Percent Increase 1970-80	Percent of U.S. Population	
		1970	1980
U.S.	38.6	100.0	100.0
Northeast	18.0	27.0	23.0
North Central	29.1	28.1	26.2
South	57.6	26.6	30.2
West	56.0	18.3	20.6

Source: U.S. Bureau of the Census, *Money Income of Households, Families and Persons in the United States, 1981* (Washington, DC: U.S. Government Printing Office, 1982).

Table 4.12
Price Index of New One-Family Houses Sold, by Region, 1970–1980

	U.S.	Northeast	North Central	South	West
1970	55.3	61.5	58.2	58.7	48.8
1975	81.7	89.8	82.5	85.1	76.2
1977	100.0	100.0	100.0	100.0	100.0
1980	145.2	138.5	135.4	144.3	154.2

Source: George Sternlieb, James W. Hughes and Connie O. Hughes, *Demographic Trends and Economic Reality* (New Brunswick, N.J.: Center for Urban Policy Research, 1982).

It means that these individuals are more likely to be excluded from areas with higher-quality schools, lower crime rates, and other desirable features.

The fiscal aspects of the tenure question come into play in two ways. First, homeownership allows a build-up of equity for the owner which never occurs for renters. It is the major form of wealth most American families ever accumulate and provides the owner with a significant asset and with financial flexibility. An owner has the ability to borrow against its worth or sell this asset. (For a different view of the social costs and benefits of homeownership, see Chapter 12 by the Institute for Policy Studies Working Group on Housing.)

In addition, mortgage interest and property tax payments are tax deductible, a deduction not available to renters. There are, of course, certain advantages to rental housing. These units will usually take a smaller proportion of monthly income than owned units. Also, less expense is involved when moving. The problem is that female households do not have the option to make tenure decisions as freely as other households.

CONCLUSIONS

One of the first questions asked in this chapter is, who is the poorly sheltered woman? The answer is clear. She is either a young mother not yet 35, with minor children, probably living in rental housing, or an elderly single person living alone in either a rented or owned unit. She is urban, yet she has an equal chance of living either in the central city or the suburbs. Above all, she is poor, in all likelihood having an income less than 80 percent of the nation's median. (In fact, one in two female householders earns less than 50 percent of the median.)

These characteristics, poverty and life-cycle position, define her prominent place among the ill-housed one-third of the nation. Being a female householder means that a woman has a one-in-three chance of being cost-burdened and a one-in-eight chance of living in an inadequate dwelling. If she is a single parent, she has more than a 50 percent chance of having a housing problem. A comparison of these odds with those of blacks and Hispanics, groups generally studied by housing analysts, reveals that female householders, on the whole, are as badly off; but in spite of their numbers, which exceed that of the other groups, they are not often singled out for special attention.

The poverty of female householders creates another phenomenon that is rightly considered a housing problem: low rates of homeownership. Today, a female householder has less than a 50 percent chance of achieving homeowner status; a single female parent has a 40 percent chance.

This portrait of the female householder is complete only with the recognition that she is fast becoming an important subgroup in American society. Only 30 years ago the female householder comprised 15 percent of the total—today she is approaching one-third. Her needs, particularly for low-cost, decent shelter, cannot be ignored.

How these needs should be met is the subject of a lengthy policy debate whose outlines can only be suggested here. One approach, to improve the purchasing power of the female householder, can be developed through a variety of programs ranging from income-targeted solutions such as job training, child care, pensions, and other devices, to shelter-targeted solutions, including Section 8-type arrangements or housing vouchers. Another strategy, to increase the supply of low-cost rental and ownership housing, can be implemented by programs designed to reduce the costs of construction, rehabilitation, and home purchase through any number of devices used in the past, from public housing to interest subsidies. The method is less important than the goal: to reduce the number of poorly sheltered women. What is lacking is the political will.

This discussion has been limited to defining American housing problems according to the availability of data that can measure preselected parameters—

physical qualities, cost, and tenure status. It does not touch upon larger issues, such as the suitability of the actual dwellings and their location. Since affordability is the crux of the problem, however, the data do suggest that dwellings designed for households of the past, which differ radically in composition from almost one-third of today's households, may not be appropriate. It may be that the female householder needs specially designed dwellings that meet more than shelter needs and also address broader issues such as economic opportunity. Inherent in the latter concept is the idea that certain designs, such as intergenerational housing, might be organized to blend the physical features of shelter, the economic advantages of sharing, and the social aspects of service delivery. Thus, new designs and financial programs to implement them should be part of the demands of the poorly sheltered woman.

NOTES

1. Female householders are defined by the U.S. Bureau of the Census as female heads of families and single-person households.

2. Tenure figures are drawn from special tabulations based on the 1981 Annual Housing Survey, Housing and Demographic Analysis Division, U.S. Department of Housing and Urban Development. The author is grateful to Duane McGough and Iredia Irby of HUD, who assembled these data.

3. Cost-burdened is defined by HUD as renters paying 30 percent or more of their income for rent, or owners paying more than 35 percent of their income for mortgage and maintenance (30 percent for maintenance of a mortgage-free unit).

4. The author is grateful to Carol Smolenski for her contributions to this discussion of tenure.

REFERENCES

Birch, Eugenie Ladner. 1983. "Woman-made America, The Case of Early Public Housing Policy." In *The American Planner*, edited by Donald A. Krueckeberg. New York: Methuen.

Downs, Anthony. 1983. *Rental Housing in the 1980's*. Washington, DC: The Brookings Institution.

Milgram, Grace. 1983. "The Rationale for Assisted Housing." In *Housing—A Reader*, by Congressional Research Service. Washington, DC: U.S. Government Printing Office.

WOMEN AND SHELTER: COMMENT

Mary K. Nenno

For more than a decade, housing analysts have recognized the need for national housing policies that respond to the special requirements of single persons (particularly single women), and one-parent households (particularly female-headed households). The Housing Act of 1976 opened up eligibility for the first time to single persons for initial admission into federally-assisted housing. Recognition of this need mushroomed with the release of the 1980 Census data revealing the depth of the changes that had taken place in household structure in the United States. The unprecedented move to homeownership by newly-formed households in the 1970s left revealed in stark contrast a residual rental housing inventory that was physically deficient and heavily concentrated among the lower income groups—many of whom were single women and female-headed households. Eugenie Birch has made a significant contribution by condensing into one concise and readable paper the essence of the situation, carefully documenting the changes that have taken place since 1950. In summary, she notes that the female householder is fast becoming an important subgroup in American society, whether she is an elderly single person living alone or a young mother not yet 35 with minor children. She is poor—with an even chance of having income less than 50 percent of the median. She likely lives in substandard shelter.

Birch's work raises important policy questions, and I would like to comment briefly on two of them:

LOW INCOME

I do not believe we can discuss this issue without reference to public assistance shelter allowances for female-headed households, for example, Aid to Families with Dependent Children (AFDC). My own calculations based on 1981 data showed that only ten states still had separate shelter allowances, with the balance of 40 states folding housing allowances into one flat grant. Over two-thirds of the 50 states provided shelter support that was less than 40 percent of the existing fair market rent in the largest urban place in that state. (For states with flat welfare grants, the estimate is based on families paying 30 percent of their public assistance grant for rent.) In 18 states, the existing fair market rent level for the HUD-assisted Section 8 Leasing Program was greater than the maximum allowable total AFDC grant. It is not surprising that a substantial proportion of AFDC-supported housing is substandard. (For a more detailed discussion of this issue, see Chapter 6 by Sandra Newman and Ann Schnare.) Pioneering work has been undertaken in both Westchester County (New York) and the state of Connecticut (largely through the efforts of Liz Rosenbaum[1]) to address the quality of housing occupied by AFDC households. A proposed national demonstration based on this work was authorized in the 1983 Housing Act, but has not been funded.

THE HOUSING SETTING

Birch notes that dwellings designed for households in the past, which differ radically in composition for almost one-third of today's households, may not be appropriate. What is needed is a recognition of both the shelter and service requirements in a housing setting. This concept of optional housing choices and specially-designed housing has been largely recognized and researched, and is in the process of being implemented in the case of the elderly, but not for single-parent households. We need to stimulate more of the kind of research and demonstration described in a recent article by Jacqueline Leavitt (1984). Beyond the shelter itself (which can take several forms), the article identifies the following as essential: assistance with food preparation, overcoming adult isolation, reducing transportation costs, and securing well-paying jobs. One option described is the design of a congregate structure that can house more than one household, where privacy is preserved, but tasks can be shared. There is a need for intensive research and demonstration on a full range of options. Ironically, more than a decade ago we succeeded in having included, in Section 507 of the 1974 Housing and Community Development Act, a provision that authorized such research and demonstration in federally assisted housing. This section specified that:

> The Secretary [of HUD] may undertake special demonstrations to determine the housing design, the housing structure, and the housing-related facilities, and amenities most effective or appropriate to meet the needs of groups with special housing needs including the elderly, the handicapped, the displaced, single individuals, broken families, and large households . . .

[He] is authorized to undertake demonstrations involving the actual planning, development, and occupancy of housing utilizing the contract and loan authority of any federally assisted housing program. He is also authorized to set aside any development, construction, design, and occupancy requirements, for the purposes of these demonstrations, if in his judgement they inhibit the testing of housing designed to meet the special housing needs.

It is past time that this section be implemented. Based on the work of Birch and others, we now know enough about the character of the problem to know what kind of response is appropriate. Funding of the 1983 Act demonstration on welfare shelter, and the 1974 Act demonstrations on housing for special households would represent an important first step. There is no excuse for further delay.

NOTE

1. Elizabeth B. Rosenbaum, Urban Initiatives, Woodside Green (120-1B), Bridge and Summer Streets, Stamford, CT 06905.

REFERENCE

Leavitt, Jacqueline. 1984. "The Shelter Plus Issue for Single Parents." *Women and Environments* (April).

5

SOCIAL ISSUES AND THE FUTURE OF FAIR HOUSING

Phillip L. Clay

Following four decades of significant federal effort to meet the nation's housing needs and use the federal government's power in order to advance the goal of open housing, we now have, and have had since 1981, an administration that suggests that these are not proper goals for the federal government. Despite strong evidence to the contrary—such as the more than ten million families who still are deprived of decent, affordable housing and the significant difference in opportunities for blacks and whites owing to documented discrimination (Wank et al. 1979)—the administration has argued essentially that we do not have a housing problem and that the federal government should be divested of responsibility in the area of housing.

TRENDS TO MINORITY ACCESS

The data make it quite clear that there are problems in the area of minority access to housing opportunity. In 20 years the minority percentage of the nation's suburban population has increased from less than 4 percent to about 8 percent, yet blacks clearly face more hurdles than do whites as they attempt to make the move to the suburbs. One result is that it is not uncommon for recent black migrants to have a higher socioeconomic status than their white neighbors. Though working-class blacks are represented in suburban populations, particularly those of older suburban cities, recent black migrants to the suburbs are typically middle-class.

We also see a documented pattern in which suburban blacks are not dispersed across the suburbs in a manner that reflects their socioeconomic status, but rather are clustered in less desirable areas (Clay 1979a). Most suburban desegregation is concentrated in about a dozen metropolitan areas, and within these regions, more than half of the migration is concentrated in a few communities, mainly older working-class or middle-class suburbs. In regions with the most extensive black suburbanization (including Washington, DC and Los Angeles) it remains true that only about 25 percent of the blacks in the metropolitan area live in the suburbs while for whites the figure is 70 percent.

Despite the extremely modest progress in black suburbanization, segregation is still the norm within the central city itself. University of Wisconsin sociologist Karl Taeuber's 1983 study of the 28 largest central cities found they had an average segregation index of 85, where a score of 100 reflects total segregation and 0 indicates total integration. Region, size of city, and the proportion of black residents were not found to be related to the variation in index scores among cities. While these figures clearly represent progress since 1970, when the score for these same cities was 91, the change must be seen as inadequate relative to the magnitude of the problem.

Other data suggest that there is a growing concentration of the poor in cities. In a crude way, this is a measure of the degree to which the poor (who in the largest cities are mainly but not exclusively black) are segregated from others, including middle-class blacks. In 1970, for all races, 14 percent of central city households had incomes below the poverty line. By 1980 the proportion had increased to 20 percent. Among blacks, the numbers rose from 26 percent to 37 percent during the same period. During the same time, the incidence of poverty in the suburbs rose only marginally (from 7 percent to 9 percent) for all races and not at all for blacks. While middle-class blacks may be able to escape to suburban communities (though usually to areas with a socioeconomic status lower than that of their household), working-class and poor black families remain less able than working-class and poor white families or middle-class black families to leave inner-city areas of poverty. Increases in poverty during the 1970s are concentrated in the largest cities and particularly in tracts with more than 20 percent poor in 1970.

In order to produce acceptable results, policies designed to address fair housing issues must take into account the context of the viability and economic future of the communities to which blacks will be encouraged to move. Too often, when blacks with low or moderate incomes are found in the suburbs, it is often in those suburbs that are not significantly different from "crisis ghettos" in cities. Typically these are former manufacturing communities and working-class suburbs—places that have lost jobs, have few services, and suffer from a declining tax base and housing stock. They also are often experiencing declining populations. These suburbs remain desegregated only as long as it takes whites to move out and take with them institutional commitments and investment resources. This pattern is characteristic of a significant share of the black suburbanization that does occur, and is not progress as conventionally defined in this country. Instead, the pattern underscores the need for action designed to counter market forces that direct blacks largely to areas being abandoned by whites.

Those policies must also address the problems encountered by blacks when they do attempt to find housing through the open market. These problems are documented in numerous studies. HUD's 1978 testing program demonstrated that blacks have a 72 percent chance of encountering discrimination in searching for rental housing and a 48 percent chance when they attempt to purchase a home. Various local studies and anecdotal data update and reinforce these conclusions (HUD 1984).

Despite the overwhelming evidence of the inadequacy of existing efforts to address the issue of fair housing, there is insufficient federal commitment to an expanded effort. Despite wide agreement that there is a need for new fair housing laws and more effective enforcement of existing laws, there has been no administration action either to significantly expand enforcement under existing laws or to develop new, more effective legal tools.

PERSPECTIVES ON FAIR HOUSING

No groups—conservatives, liberals, or radicals—have proposed adequate strategies to address the shortcomings of existing fair-housing policies. The fact that the three groups communicate with each other across a wide ideological divide and through the thick fog of political posturing has made it even more difficult to forge a strategy that reconciles competing expectations. That process might begin with delineation of areas where the different perspectives complement one another, as well as where they do not.

Liberals are correct in their notion that central government leadership is important to ensuring equity and promoting equal opportunity. Their sense of mission with respect to alleviating the pains suffered by the poor and minorities is welcome. Many of the programs they pioneered over the years have not failed so much as they have been inadequately tested, misapplied, or proved too inflexible for the variety of contexts in which they have been applied. The liberals' estimates of the power and effectiveness of regulations and bureaucracies have sometimes proven too optimistic and have had perverse results or encouraged perverse behavior on the part of various parties, including the private sector, clients, and local government. Too often liberal rhetoric ran ahead of resources and social technology, with unrealistic expectations and unfulfilled promises being the result.

Even as we criticize a generation of liberal policy, however, we are obliged to give it credit for substantial achievements. The number of ill-housed in the country is now very much smaller than the one-third figure cited by FDR, in large part because of the availability of more than 1.2 million public housing units developed under liberal administrations. These units generally are better than those that the private market offers for a similar rent. Many millions more households have benefited from government programs designed to make homeownership possible for moderate-income families.

While blacks and other minorities have not shared equally in these gains, the progress they have made in the area of housing has been in large part the result of liberal housing programs. These programs developed over the past decades simply cannot legitimately be called failures. While liberals' programs have not solved the nation's housing problems, they have provided a vehicle for addressing those problems and contributed to their solution.

Conservatives' successes in recent elections can be traced in part to their ability to reveal flaws in the liberal approach to the provision of housing. Ignoring what might have occurred had no action been taken, conservatives have focused attention on imperfections in the strategies used, on new problems, and on unanticipated consequences, and labeled these as evidence of program failure. Regulatory inflexibility, program inequities, high costs, delays, thwarted private initiative and self-help have been identified by conservatives as evidence in support of the argument that the government should withdraw from direct involvement in the housing market. Conservatives insist that the market, whose failures spurred corrective action by liberal administrations in the first place, is more capable than the public sector of addressing the nation's housing problems.

There is little evidence that the private market will ever live up to conservatives' expectations. Their mainly *laissez-faire* approach to social issues, including desegregation, relies on the notion that rising tides lift all boats. While there is some evidence to support the claim that expansion of the aggregate housing market can have positive effects on the various groups that rely on the market, there also is evidence that the process of trickle-down is blind to the effect of discrimination in determining how those benefits are allocated. Fighting discrimination in the allocation process is a battle separate from, though related to, the effort to expand the aggregate housing stock to a point at which all families can have access to a decent housing unit. Fair housing objectives require that we ask not only how much decent housing is available, but also who has access to what components of that housing stock and why.

Radicals of all stripes have stood as the loyal opposition to mainstream perspectives of housing policy. Their diagnostic skills have been and continue to be superb. They have told us why we have a housing problem, and in drawing out the implications of treating housing as a commodity they suggest strategies to respond to the problem. (See Chapter 12 by the Institute for Policy Studies Working Group on Housing, and Chapter 13 by Michael Stone). The fundamental problem, however, is that radicals tend to prefer to focus on class issues, with the view that once class issues are resolved, say by decommodification, then fair housing will be a more attainable goal. In essence, they prefer to assume the viability of a class-based alliance rather than to address the need to assist one victim in making claims against another. While I part company with some of them on the relative importance of class versus race in explaining the different outcomes for blacks versus whites, and on some proposals that I consider too impractical in the absence of major structural transformations, I nevertheless am positive about some of their specific ideas for local or self-help programs and for cooperative enterprise.

It is important to note that there are areas of commonality among the current agendas of liberals, conservatives, and radicals. All three groups currently are advocating self-help and cooperative strategies for producing housing and are calling for local rather than central initiatives. While their assumptions, reasons, and expectations may differ, these points of commonality may well provide a basis for forging a national housing policy. Perhaps now, more than at any point in recent memory, there is at least an opportunity for a constructive dialogue on the issue of the objectives of such a policy.

THE CHANGING CONTEXT OF FAIR HOUSING

There are a number of issues that must be considered in any dialogue about fair housing. These issues are related to changes in the legal, economic, and demographic context in which fair housing has to be considered. Instead of the city being a low-valued piece of real estate, the battle over turf outside of the downtown is growing, both from the white gentry who want to establish middle-class neighborhoods or convert apartments to condominiums, and from economic interests seeking "back office" space.

On the one hand, the Gautreaux decision—which required that public housing be located so as to reduce segregation—makes siting of subsidized housing more difficult and discourages low- and moderate-income housing production programs (*Hills v. Gautreaux*, 425 U.S. 284 1976). On the other hand, high development costs, combined with fewer tax incentives, have decreased the feasibility of developments targeted to low-income households, while the lack of a national production subsidy program impedes local self-help efforts. Effective programs to produce housing for the poor are likely to require both legal incentives and multiple subsidies.

Attention to fair housing issues is further complicated by two recent demographic developments. First, we have had a substantial increase in the black middle class. Depending on the thresholds used, this group increased from between 12 and 20 percent to between 18 and 33 percent of black families in the 1970s. While this group continues to have higher unemployment rates, less wealth, and more limited access to traditional middle-class amenities than their white middle-class cohorts, its growth and progress over the past decade is nevertheless impressive.

This group's progress and its role in desegregating certain suburbs has been interpreted as visible evidence of substantial progress toward integration of residential areas. This interpretation fails to acknowledge the fact that blacks still are not distributed across metropolitan areas in ways that reflect either their income distribution or the distribution of house prices or rents. Given the growth of the black middle class over the past decade, if residential integration depended primarily on economic progress of blacks, then the rate of segregation would be significantly less than is currently the case. Quite simply, because of discrimination, significant numbers of blacks are unable to locate in areas of their choice despite the fact that they can afford to compete in the private housing market. The effect of documented racial steering in the housing market is the concentration of blacks in particular areas and their exclusion from others.

While there is at least some evidence of progress toward increased integration of certain suburbs, there is also growing evidence of the devastating consequences of concentrating blacks in the older inner cities. This is a fair-housing problem, a community planning problem, and a compelling argument for looking at the process by which committees develop and redevelop land.

THE CHALLENGE OF FAIR HOUSING

Traditionally, fair housing has been directed toward improving access for minorities in suburban locations from which they have been excluded. Such a narrow perspective is now recognized as an inadequate means to enlarge housing opportunities for minorities. Two observations underscore this view. First, this approach to fair housing benefited mainly middle- and upper-income blacks who could afford suburbia and were prepared to take immediate advantage of the opportunities offered by successful fair-housing activities. Few low-income blacks have been able to take advantage of suburban opportunities, with the occasional exceptions leading to low-income enclaves.

Second, the rise in house prices and rents over the past decade means that the price barriers to the poor are even more serious than in the past. While suburbs are selectively more open to multi-family housing, the absence of deep subsidies means that little benefit from the recent flexibility on apartment development (mostly upscale rental and condominium development) accrues to the poor. All of this suggests that new approaches will have to be developed if fair-housing goals are to be met.

A concern with fair housing also requires an assessment of the impact of the increasing incidence of reinvestment. This reinvestment very frequently results in the displacement of long-term residents who very often are older, poor blacks. These blacks, who are prevented from moving to the suburbs because of a combination of racial barriers and cost differentials, are thus also prevented from remaining in the city neighborhoods where a more sensitive and well-managed process of revitalization might yield the racial and income integration that has eluded us in suburbia. The forces have produced inequities that underscore the need to develop and implement fair-housing initiatives that ensure both the right to open access and the right to reside in place.

The Right to Open Access

As pointed out above, traditional fair-housing efforts have served to help mainly middle- and upper-income minority families. While this has been an important service, it is insufficient because these are not the only families who ought to have choices and because the price of housing should not be the principal basis for residential settlement patterns. Moreover, efforts at advocacy for low- and moderate-income housing in the suburbs have not been successful even when there were resources to increase the supply of new subsidized housing. Advocacy for the working poor remains necessary, for all the reasons it ever was needed and, additionally, because increasingly scarce subsidy resources make it even more difficult for lower-income households to compete for housing in the open market.

Opening access requires taking account of the new context described above. The new context calls for extending fair-housing concerns to housing opportunities created in the city. That in turn involves a host of activities, including disposition of publicly controlled or influenced development opportunities, zoning and planning, regulatory protections in rental housing and the management of public and subsidized housing resources. In these areas, the use of Urban Development Action Grants, mortgage revenue bonds, disposition of distressed property, and the targeting of block grant funds become important fair-housing tools.

The Right to Reside

Since the late 1970s, there has been a resurgence of interest and reinvestment in older urban neighborhoods. Revitalization and reinvestment activities have involved both new and long-term residents. While the sum of this effort is less than concurrent disinvestment in residential neighborhoods, the volume is large enough to be a significant local urban phenomenon.

Many long-term urban residents want to remain rather than move. The right to be free from exploitative removal and displacement is what is meant by a "right to reside" (Davidoff 1983). This right does not mean that each person has life tenure on a piece of real estate or that one group can keep out other groups, but that, as redevelopment and reinvestment proceed, low- and moderate-income residents will not be involuntarily displaced by activities which are part of the land's "highest and best" use (Clay 1979b).

Under existing policy it is not uncommon for long-term residents to be forced out of their neighborhoods as a result of the actions of speculators and gentry. Blacks and poor renters have been especially hard hit by this process, since they face the greatest difficulties in relocating to a comparable setting and situation. Managing the reinvestment process in order to minimize losses to vulnerable groups is a key frontier for promoting fair housing in cities. Taking advantage of reinvestment offers a practical opportunity, with potential benefits in both racial and economic justice. Maintaining a commitment to long-term residents is a necessary preamble to a plan for managing reinvestment to ensure fair-housing practices.

One of the least discussed aspects of the right to reside issue is the displacement that results from disinvestment. For every neighborhood that has experienced gentrification in recent years, a larger number experienced disinvestment. Some of this disinvestment results from a deliberate policy to withhold investment funds based on the assumption that investment would be a waste of money. The result of such a decision, which usually is not debated publicly, is that as decline accelerates, the possibility of residents fixing up their neighborhood becomes virtually nil. Perhaps most importantly, decisions that determine the level of investment to be made in an area are made in many cases without resident input and without thoughtful efforts to use public and private resources effectively to prevent decline.

Columbia Point, Boston's version of Pruitt-Igoe, is an example of the destructive outcome of withholding investment. Unlike Pruitt-Igoe, Columbia Point was not demolished. Instead, it was allowed to deteriorate. Like Pruitt-Igoe, however, the result has been the loss of housing units to low-income households. At the end of its slide, it has been proposed that one-quarter of Columbia Point's original units be upgraded for the poor and the rest be converted into a middle- and upper-income community. This result is as much a threat to the right to reside as is gentrification. Blacks are often the victims of this process, and the result is to deprive them of a decent place to live.

Some disinvestment is part of a ruse directed toward creating reinvestment opportunities for higher-income groups. Challenging these tactics or negotiating for a just deal are appropriate ways to address fair-housing issues. What this discussion suggests is that the fair housing and social housing agenda now is far more complex. No longer is it simply that we need to find ways to make the market nondiscriminatory and promote the development of housing affordable by those at the bottom of the income distribution. Now we have to worry about: (1) the interaction (in non-additive ways) of race and class; (2) the development of a more complex mosaic of urban and suburban neighborhoods; (3) reinvestment and conversion in existing stock as a source of new housing opportunities; (4) how to join local public, private, and nonprofit forces in a partnership that can make housing progress happen in the absence of federal production programs; and (5) how to protect and improve housing resources now used by the poor, but under stress and in demand by the middle class and developers. This is a full and more complex agenda, particularly because in any community all of the challenges must be addressed at once. It also is one that pulls at all of the tender parts of our belief systems and challenges many conventions of the housing market.

NEW POLICIES TO PROMOTE SOCIAL GOALS

There are several specific actions that would produce progress toward the goal of fair housing. These actions focus on the dual objectives of open access and right to reside.

Open Access

- enforce existing fair housing laws and enact new ones that provide stronger enforcement tools;
- develop new programs and allocate additional resources to provide more housing opportunities for low- and moderate-income households, especially in areas not already open to them;
- develop new planning strategies to deal with transition issues in older suburbs that are losing population and are likely targets for exploitative racial and class steering;
- develop new approaches for involving minority housing professionals in the real estate industry in non-minority areas;
- develop counseling and outreach efforts to increase the pool of blacks who want to move to nontraditional areas;
- mandate the development of performance-based standards and incentives for development, rather than relying on affirmative marketing and good faith efforts.

The Right to Reside

- develop anti-displacement tools that recognize the need to promote reinvestment in urban neighborhoods on a non-exclusive basis by class and race;
- encourage neighborhood development plans that assess and attempt to balance the competing interests. In the long run "no-displacement" mandates will neither protect nor help the poor, but negotiation based on the principle of protecting their interests may do both;
- direct public funds to community development projects, including joint ventures between the private and community-based sectors that affirmatively promote housing for low- and moderate-income minority incumbents, especially renters and families;
- incorporate fair-housing provisions and goals in all laws and regulations relating to anti-speculation, rent control, property disposition, large-scale development, use conversion, and public subsidy. Use linkage arrangements to pay for the externalities imposed on city residents by downtown development;
- develop opportunities within urban neighborhoods for the elderly who want or need alternatives to the conventional family home but who do not want to leave the familiar setting in the neighborhood;
- preserve existing low- and moderate-income housing resources such as public and assisted housing. Develop more extensive mechanisms, such as cooperative housing, that stabilize housing for the poor and extend secure tenure without requiring ownership.

CONCLUSION

What we have argued here is that as conditions change, we must change the way we think about and approach our social housing goals. While the goals of open access and right to reside represent a considerable challenge, there are points of leverage that provide means to meet the challenge. Before we can use those leverage points, however, we must be willing to reaffirm both our fundamental commitment to justice and equality and our willingness to use the public sector to address social objectives.

Commitment to the goal of fair housing is not fashionable today. The fact that most of the issues raised here are old issues is itself a political liability in an era of new ideas and new approaches. I am a bit like the preacher who responded to a woman complaining that his sermons were redundant. He said, as I say, "I will change my sermon when you change your way of living."

REFERENCES

Blackwell, James. 1985. *The Black Community*. New York: Harper & Row.

Clay, Phillip. 1979a. "The Process of Black Suburbanization." *Urban Affairs Quarterly* (Winter).

———. 1979b. *Neighborhood Renewal*. New York: Lexington, D.C. Heath.

Davidoff, Paul. 1983. "Decent Housing for All: An Agenda." In *America's Housing Crisis: What Is To Be Done?* edited by Chester Hartman. Boston: Routledge & Kegan Paul.

Roof, Wade, and Daphne Spain. 1977. "A Research Note on City–Suburban Differences Among Blacks." *Social Forces* (September).

Taeuber, Karl. 1983. "Racial Residential Segregation, 28 Cities, 1970–1980." Working Paper 83–12. Madison, WI: Center for Demography and Ecology, University of Wisconsin, Madison.

U.S. Department of Housing and Urban Development. 1985. *U.S. President's National Urban Policy Report*. Washington, DC: U.S. Government Printing Office.

———. 1984. *Recent Evidence on Discrimination in Housing*. Washington, DC: U.S. Government Printing Office.

Wank, Ronald et al. 1979. *Measuring Racial Discrimination in American Housing Markets*. Washington, DC: U.S. Department of Housing and Urban Development.

SOCIAL ISSUES AND THE FUTURE OF FAIR HOUSING: COMMENT

Elizabeth Ellen Bowyer

The problems associated with ensuring equitable access to the housing market still exist, despite years of, at times, extensive federal intervention. Social prejudice and ingrained disparities among the incomes and opportunities of different groups have produced persistent neighborhood segregation and a continuing high incidence of substandard housing for racial minorities. Historically, the federal government has played a leading role in initiating fair-housing policies, though the conviction behind those policies has fluctuated from administration to administration.

Phillip Clay's chapter reviews the current state of minority access to the housing market, with specific reference to the need for public sector action to alleviate problems. Clay argues that racial discrimination continues to pose significant difficulties to the minority population in the United States, and correctly observes that the support for fair-housing policies waned under the Reagan administration. His discussion is thus timely and important, reminding us of the need for unslacking attention to the problem of persistent inequity in access to decent housing.

It is unfortunate, then, that Clay's argument against discrimination in housing access has three significant weaknesses. First, his defense for fair housing is made only with reference to blacks. His entire argument for minority access is predicated on black access, and this limitation seriously affects the validity and relevance of his argument. Second, Clay confuses discrimination on the basis of race with discrimination on the basis of income. This confusion deflects attention from the very real problem of racial discrimination at the expense of only a brief discussion of the problem of poverty. Either issue would have been better advanced by individual treatment.

Finally, and most importantly, Clay implies that the negative outcome of some black suburbanization—black concentration in suburban areas abandoned by whites—can be addressed through "action designed to counter market forces" which, he argues, are responsible for "directing" black movement into such areas. Here Clay is confusing economic and social forces. I would argue that, to a great degree, it is racial prejudice acting upon the housing market that directs black movement, not forces inherent in the housing market itself. Therefore, the difficulties blacks face in purchasing housing and the tendency for whites to leave neighborhoods into which blacks are moving are due not to market forces per se, but rather to social prejudice, expressed in the housing market as well as in other institutions. It is certainly not a problem that can be dealt with through increased federal funding alone. Considering the problems blacks face in the housing market as only economic problems obscures the effects of social discrimination, and seriously overestimates the federal government's power (or willingness) to provide relief through market manipulation.

The following critique of Clay's paper will focus on how these three weaknesses of his argument serve to undermine his conclusion that the solution lies primarily in greater federal intervention in the housing market.

MINORITIES VERSUS BLACKS

From the outset of his article, Clay consistently draws on statistics about minorities and then draws conclusions about blacks. In discussing trends to minority access, for example, he notes that "in 20 years, the minority percentage of the nation's suburban population has increased from less than 4 percent to about 8 percent, yet blacks clearly face more hurdles than do whites as they attempt to make the move to the suburbs." If Clay wants to analyze minority access, then he should be using that term consistently. If, on the other hand, he wants to talk about the problems of black access, then he needs to use data that refer specifically to blacks. By using the terms interchangeably, he confuses the extent to which blacks (as opposed to Hispanics) are affected by discrimination, overlooking the possibility that blacks actually suffer greater discrimination in housing access than do other minorities. By using data on minorities as a whole, Clay loses the opportunity to consider differences among minority subgroups, and also weakens his arguments.

Clay fails to distinguish between blacks and minorities throughout his chapter. For example, he argues that the whole issue of fair housing is complicated by recent demographic developments—the growth of the black middle class and the concentration of poor blacks in the central city. Following from this, he then argues that the historical basis for fair housing as improving access for minorities in suburban locations is no longer valid since "this approach to fair housing benefited mainly middle- and upper-income blacks who could afford suburbia and were prepared to take immediate advantage of the opportunities offered . . . '' In discussing the impact of reinvestment, he notes its ''displacement of long-term residents who very often are older, poor blacks''. This particular phrasing indicates that Clay is not simply deliberately deciding to emphasize housing access for blacks as one example of minority access, but that he is justifying doing so on the basis that blacks form a significant percentage of the minority population. In many cities, however, this no longer is the case. An article in the *New York Times* discussing changes in minority populations, provided 1980 Census data (for 26 of the nation's 30 largest cities, representing all regions) which revealed that in Los Angeles, San Diego, Denver, San Jose, San Antonio, and Phoenix, the black population is significantly smaller than the Hispanic population. These data indicate changes in the minority population of big cities which have been caused in part by the slowing of the urban migration by rural blacks (Herbers 1981). The composition of many cities' minority populations has changed dramatically over the past decade. This makes it even less valid to use the terms 'minority' and 'black' interchangeably.

Clay discusses the growing concentration of the poor in the central cities in the same manner. He says that this trend is a ''measure of the degree to which the poor (who in many cities are mainly but not exclusively black) are segregated from others, including middle-class blacks.'' Here, Clay is treating blacks and poverty as synonymous by assuming without documentation that blacks are generally dominant in that subgroup. But even if this assumption were correct, it still does not legitimize using it as any kind of ''measure'': we need to know what percentage of the poor in central cities actually are black before we can draw conclusions about their segregation from middle-class blacks or any other group, or about the type of policies that might most effectively address their needs.

TYPES OF DISCRIMINATION

The second weakness in the argument is Clay's confusing racial discrimination with income discrimination. The fact that housing is an extremely expensive commodity means that access is largely determined by a consumer's income. This is understood by developers and housing officials (among others), who can use zoning ordinances, building standards, or other elements of the residential construction process to limit access to a neighborhood, and thereby reinforce the importance of housing consumption as a status-conferring activity. Clay fails to adequately separate this type of housing discrimination—which can affect all but the highest income groups to one degree or another—from housing discrimination on the basis of race. The implicit justification for linking the two issues is that it is blacks who constitute the majority of the impoverished population. Use of that justification in turn tells us nothing about the extent to which blacks and other minorities suffer discrimination on the basis of income as well as race, or about the extent to which they suffer discrimination based on race alone.

Clay's analysis of access to housing is weakened by confusing different types of discrimination, and his argument against income discrimination is clouded by a disconcerting idealism. After insisting that the right to open access not be limited only to middle- and upper-income minority families, he then suggests that "the price of housing should not be the principal basis for residential settlement patterns." This naive assertion undermines Clay's attempt to focus attention on realistic fair-housing policy. American history records the widespread and continuing use of price differentials in housing to define a household's status. As long as housing plays this role, it is very unlikely that calls for equal access to housing regardless of income will result in significant policy initiatives.

THE FEDERAL ROLE

Clay suggests that the best avenue to improving minority access to housing is through extensive federal subsidies. His observation that "while suburbs are selectively more open to multi-family housing, the absence of deep subsidies means that little benefit from the recent flexibility on apartment development . . . accrues to the poor" reflects his assumption that deep subsidies would enable excluded groups to gain access to the suburbs. Instead of either a basic concern with the racial discrimination that may affect minorities (much more intractable than simple income discrimination) or with simply providing adequate housing at a politically acceptable cost, Clay seems to want to address both of these issues in one expensive swoop.

Clay acknowledges the difficulties of this approach. He points out that "the advocacy for the working poor remains necessary . . . [in part] because increasingly scarce subsidy resources make it even more difficult for lower-income households to compete for housing. . . ." This suggests that the suburban markets be opened to lower-income families by addressing the restrictive elements of the housing construction process through advocacy. While this approach may affect the basic causes underlying rising housing costs more directly than would federal subsidies to individual households, Clay would rely on extensive federal intervention, targeted to assist certain groups, to force integration.

While the federal government certainly has an important role in mediating on questions of equity in the housing market, the degree to which it can or should effectively control the market is more problematic. Federal intervention has occurred on a large scale, with varying intensity, since the 1930s. While there have been improvements in the nation's aggregate housing stock, the process has been extremely expensive and has produced mixed results. We must recognize that in the current political atmosphere it is unlikely that there will be widespread support of increased federal involvement.

NATURE OF THE HOUSING MARKET

Clay acknowledges that the housing market is both an economic and social entity, yet he fails to distinguish between the two aspects in his analysis. He seems unable to discuss one without reference to the other, and tends to assume that social problems can be addressed by manipulation of the market. For example, he says it is market forces that "direct blacks to areas being abandoned by whites," when abandonment very often occurs after black immigration. When blacks move to areas already abandoned by whites, it is often because the property values of these areas are low enough to allow poorer blacks to afford the housing available in the area. By constantly emphasizing the social results of market behavior, Clay overlooks the fact that the housing market not only produces but reflects social relationships. He ignores the fact that people may be willing to pay a significant price to indulge their personal prejudices, and the federal government has limited ability to prevent developers from responding to those preferences. Clay also fails to acknowledge that there may be substantive financial reasons behind many of the problems relating to housing opportunity. He ignores the fact that landlords may proceed with disinvestment or reinvestment because their lower-income tenants cannot pay sufficient rents to generate profits. The problems of housing opportunity are not only fairly intractable—housing is a large, profitable business—but may constitute an integral part of the national economy. Clay does not sufficiently address the economic impact of his proposals, and this diminishes the chances that they will be taken seriously.

THE VALUE OF TARGETING

It can of course be argued that any discussion of fair housing must look both at the situation of blacks (or other special minorities) and at the situation of all minorities as a group. While it may well be true that in most cases the discrimination faced by blacks is more crippling than that faced by other minorities, it is also necessary to consider whether by focusing on the problems of one particular subgroup, and recommending action only relevant to that group, one is not only fragmenting the minority population but the national population as well. This possibility—which potentially lessens chances for more comprehensive, effective action—has been suggested for some time, but has recently received greater attention (Wilson 1985). The argument suggests that the problems that racial minorities and the poor face are due in large part to such macro-level economic and demographic forces. Wilson argues that the recent shift in the American economy from a reliance on manufacturing to one on services, and from the central cities to the suburbs, has severely affected all racial minorities and the poor, by stranding them in largely abandoned areas characterized by high unemployment and low housing opportunity. This analysis suggests that any proffered solutions should not be formulated in terms of one subgroup or another, but rather should look to the amelioration of the national problems that affect all of the poor—for example, unemployment and economic growth.

As Clay himself has observed, traditional approaches to fair housing "benefited mainly middle- and upper-income blacks who could afford suburbia and were prepared to take immediate advantage of the opportunities offered by successful fair-housing activities.'' This observation supports Wilson's claim that ''the urban underclass has not benefited significantly from 'race-specific' anti-discrimination policy programs . . . which have helped so many trained and educated blacks'' (Wilson 1985, 159). In short, any effective, long-term attempt to comprehensively address the problems of poverty in this country must apply itself not only to individual groups but also to the national issues that affect all groups. (See Chapter 3 by Peter Marcuse for a related discussion.) Since race does not stand in a fixed relation to poverty, poverty reform that is specifically based upon race stands a good chance of never reaching the population it is intended to benefit.

CONCLUSION

Any discussion of the issue of fair housing is weakened if problems are couched in terms of only one minority group. While Clay makes this mistake throughout his chapter, this does not negate the validity of his claims that a greater effort is needed in the area of fair housing. A more damaging error is Clay's failure to distinguish between the social and economic aspects of the housing market. Finally, and more pragmatically, Clay does not fully consider the political milieu in which he is making his recommendations. His chapter might have been much more effective had he recognized this constraint and couched his suggestions accordingly.

REFERENCES

Herbers, John. 1981. ''Census Finds Blacks Gaining Majorities in Big Cities.'' *New York Times*, April 16.

Wilson, William Julius. 1985. ''The Urban Underclass.'' In *The New Urban Reality*, edited by Paul E. Peterson. Washington, DC: The Brookings Institution.

6

REASSESSING SHELTER ASSISTANCE: THE INTERRELATIONSHIP BETWEEN WELFARE AND HOUSING PROGRAMS

Sandra J. Newman and
Ann B. Schnare

INTRODUCTION

Recent cutbacks in domestic spending, coupled with the prospects of unprecedented deficits in the foreseeable future, necessitate a hard and objective review of the various ways in which this country meets the economic and social needs of its poor. Any rethinking of the welfare state must consider housing. For most families—and particularly the poor—housing is the single biggest item in the monthly budget. Moreover, housing may represent the highest priority item, since failure to pay each month's rent will ultimately result in eviction. A welfare system that does not enable recipients to obtain decent and affordable shelter is certainly a failure by any standard.

While staggering estimates of the number of homeless across the country suggest just such a policy failure, the housing problems of the poor are in fact even deeper and more tangled (*New York Times* 1984, 1985). Consider the following facts:

- Shelter payments under welfare (for example, Aid to Families with Dependent Children [AFDC]) cover only a fraction of the rent of a modest unit in most jurisdictions.

This chapter describes the initial results of a multi-year study of the relationship between housing and income assistance. More detailed findings for 1983 are presented in *Subsidizing Shelter: The Relationship of Housing and Welfare Assistance*, Urban Institute Press, 1988. Partial funding for the research was provided by a grant from the Aetna Foundation.

- Operating costs of rental units grew faster than inflation during the 1970s, jeopardizing the ability of private landlords to provide low-cost housing for the poor, and increasing the need for public assistance.
- There are stark disparities in the amount of shelter assistance received by the poor; similar people are not treated similarly.
- Two different federal agencies, the Department of Housing and Urban Development (HUD) and the Department of Health and Human Services (HHS), provide shelter subsidies for the poor. But their approaches are uncoordinated and have the potential to overlap.

This evidence raises three serious questions about current approaches to shelter assistance—questions of equity, efficiency, and effectiveness. First, such assistance does not appear to meet the test of fairness. Under current AFDC rules, geography rather than need plays the major role in determining how much shelter assistance an individual or family will receive. A family of four in Mississippi will receive a shelter payment that is only about 8 percent of the estimated cost of standard housing in that area, while the same family in Washington State will receive more than 90 percent of its estimated shelter needs. Moreover, in either state, families enrolled in an assisted housing program will receive a subsidy equal to the full amount of their shelter needs.

Second, the involvement of both HUD and HHS in housing assistance with essentially no coordination between them seems certain to result in inefficiencies. Recent estimates suggest that the welfare system spends approximately $5 billion per year on shelter allowances—about half as much as the $10.6 billion to be spent by HUD in fiscal year 1985 for housing assistance (Nenno 1983). Yet there is little attempt to coordinate program resources or policy goals. As HUD abandons its traditional construction-oriented programs in favor of housing vouchers, the actual and potential overlap between HUD and HHS programs and policy objectives becomes increasingly important.

The third question concerns the effectiveness of current approaches. Estimates of the fraction of welfare recipients who live in substandard housing run as high as 50 percent (Nenno 1983). Thus, a sizable pool of taxpayer dollars appears to be supporting inadequate housing. At the same time, all estimates point to dramatically rising rents in the next few years, further exacerbating the problem of an inadequate supply of affordable units for the poor and the middle class. The growing inability of families to pay for shelter, which may be increasing the ranks of the homeless, combined with extensive housing abandonment across the country, argue convincingly for a rethinking of government's role in housing assistance.

Taken alone, these circumstances are compelling. But they are only anecdotal and fragmentary bits of evidence that "something" is not working. What is needed is an objective review of how the nation attempts to meet the housing needs of the poor, and a determination of the best and worst features of the present system.

This chapter takes a step in that direction, and represents the first product of a larger analysis of the interrelationships between income and housing assistance programs. Its objectives are relatively modest: namely, to document some of the major disparities that exist within and across the major housing and income maintenance programs, and to examine the characteristics and housing conditions of households receiving various combinations of income and housing assistance. The primary emphasis of this paper is on program equity. Issues of effectiveness and efficiency will be addressed in subsequent work.

The chapter has four components. We begin with a brief background statement, highlighting what is currently known (and not known) about the nature of the problem. We then present the results of a recent survey of state welfare offices. The purpose of the survey was two-fold: to collect information on each state's implicit or explicit allocation for shelter assistance, and to compare these shelter allowances to the cost of "decent, but modest" housing as determined by HUD.

The third part of the chapter uses data from the 1981 Annual Housing Survey (AHS) to take a broader look at the overlap between housing assistance and traditional welfare programs. In particular, we examine the number and types of households currently receiving income assistance and direct rental subsidies, the overlap between the two groups, and the housing conditions of each. The first half of the analysis addresses the disparities in the subsidy levels incorporated in Section 8 and AFDC; the second half examines the impact of such disparities on the housing conditions of program recipients. Note that the AHS data do not enable one to identify AFDC recipients per se or to distinguish among various types of subsidized housing. As a result, this component of the study examines all kinds of housing and income assistance, including Section 8, public housing, and other local housing programs, as well as AFDC, SSI, and general relief.

The last part of the chapter draws some general conclusions about the strengths and weaknesses of the current system. While we offer one option for redirecting public policy, at this early stage of our research such findings are quite preliminary and necessarily incomplete. The data presented here would not in themselves support a call for a major overhaul to the current system. As we probe more deeply into the issues at hand, however, we may well find that radical change is the only appropriate policy response.

BACKGROUND

There is growing recognition that the way we currently meet the housing needs of the poor is fragmented at best, and inequitable and inefficient at worst. Yet relatively little systematic information exists about the ways in which traditional housing assistance programs interact with the welfare system or, more fundamentally, about how best to spend scarce public resources while at the same time providing decent housing for the poor.

The geographic inequities under AFDC have long been recognized. Very little that results from disinvestment. For every neighborhood that has experienced gentrification in recent years, a larger number experienced disinvestment. Some of this disinvestment results from a deliberate policy to withhold investment funds based on the assumption that investment would be a waste of money. The result of such a decision, which usually is not debated publicly, is that as decline accelerates, the possibility of residents fixing up their neighborhood becomes virtually nil. Perhaps most importantly, decisions that determine the level of investment to be made in an area are made in many cases without resident input and without thoughtful efforts to use public and private resources effectively to prevent decline.

Columbia Point, Boston's version of Pruitt-Igoe, is an example of the destructive outcome of withholding investment. Unlike Pruitt-Igoe, Columbia Point was not demolished. Instead, it was allowed to deteriorate. Like Pruitt-Igoe, however, the result has been the loss of housing units to low-income households. At the end of its slide, it has been proposed that one-quarter of Columbia Point's original units be upgraded for the poor and the rest be converted into a middle- and upper-income community. This result is as much a threat to the right to reside as is gentrification. Blacks are often the victims of this process, and the result is to deprive them of a decent place to live.

Some disinvestment is part of a ruse directed toward creating reinvestment opportunities for higher-income groups. Challenging these tactics or negotiating for a just deal are appropriate ways to address fair-housing issues. What this discussion suggests is that the fair housing and social housing agenda now is far more complex. No longer is it simply that we need to find ways to make the market nondiscriminatory and promote the development of housing affordable by those at the bottom of the income distribution. Now we have to worry about: (1) the interaction (in non-additive ways) of race and class; (2) the development of a more complex mosaic of urban and suburban neighborhoods; (3) reinvestment and conversion in existing stock as a source of new housing opportunities; (4) how to join local public, private, and nonprofit forces in a partnership that can make housing progress happen in the absence of federal production programs; and (5) how to protect and improve housing resources now used by the poor, but under stress and in demand by the middle class and developers. This is a full and more complex agenda, particularly because in any community all of the challenges must be addressed at once. It also is one that pulls at all of the tender parts of our belief systems and challenges many conventions of the housing market.

NEW POLICIES TO PROMOTE SOCIAL GOALS

There are several specific actions that would produce progress toward the goal of fair housing. These actions focus on the dual objectives of open access and right to reside.

mum quality standards for the housing rented by recipients. HHS's shelter assistance programs do not. But perhaps the more pressing issue relates to the fact that existing AFDC shelter allowances cover such a small proportion of the estimated cost of "decent, but modest housing," suggesting that a sizable fraction of welfare dollars may be flowing into substandard housing. In part, the problem seems to be that some states' specified shelter allowances have little relationship to the cost of standard housing.

Arguments about effectiveness are also beginning to emerge in recent discussions about the growing incidence of homeless families. Alcoholism, combined with the deinstitutionalization of the chronically mentally ill, undoubtedly accounts for much of the homelessness that exists today. Nevertheless, there is evidence that emergency assistance—which is designed to provide temporary shelter to individuals with no other place to go—is increasingly used by families with chronic housing needs. Yet such assistance is extremely expensive and does little to improve the long-term housing situation of the nation's poor.

STATE TREATMENT OF SHELTER ASSISTANCE UNDER AFDC

Our recent survey of state welfare officials was undertaken to develop more precise information on inter-state differences in the shelter standards that are embedded in assistance programs. Two questions are addressed: first, how do states differ in their estimates of shelter need and in their calculations of payment standards for shelter under AFDC? Second, how do these shelter payments compare with the costs of standard quality housing within each state?

Data on states' treatment of shelter assistance under AFDC were collected through a combination of telephone and mail surveys of all states in the continental U.S. plus the District of Columbia, supplemented by analyses of documentation describing each state's approach to shelter assistance under AFDC. HUD's estimates of the rental costs of standard quality units, represented by the Fair Market Rents (FMRs) for existing housing under Section 8, were used to measure the actual cost of adequate housing within each area.

States apply one of three approaches to the treatment of shelter under AFDC. The first, applied by 25 states, involves the establishment of explicit shelter needs and payment standards. This explicit amount, which differs for families of different sizes and in many cases by location within the state, generally takes the form of reimbursement to households for their actual housing costs, up to some maximum.

In another nine states, one can derive an implicit shelter standard from several pieces of information, although there is no single, explicitly stated amount. In some instances, a different overall standard of need (and payment level) is established for individuals who have no housing costs (for example, individuals who live rent-free with another household); here, shelter needs and payment levels can be derived by comparing the grants available to such households with the grants available to families that must pay for housing. In other cases, states were able to give us a rough percentage of the standard of need and payment level that was allocated to shelter.

The remaining states apply a third approach: they have fully consolidated shelter needs standards and payment levels. Only aggregate amounts are provided for overall needs standards and payment levels, and there is no way to derive, either explicitly or implicitly, the portion allocated to shelter. In order to include these states in the national analysis, we set their ratio of shelter need to standard of need (and shelter payment to payment level ratio) at 30 percent, which represents a rough average of these ratios for the 34 states with either explicit or derived shelter assistance components. (This is the same rate adopted in Nenno 1983).

Before turning to a discussion of the differences among the states in their approach to shelter assistance under AFDC, there are several attributes of the states as a whole that are at least equally important. First, of the 49 states for which we have data, only 19 (roughly 40 percent) provide assistance payments to eligible households at 100 percent of the state's own established needs standard (that is, the cost of basic necessities the state deems are required to maintain a minimum standard of living). The rest pay some arbitrary fraction, which falls as low as 31 percent. This characterization also applies to the relationship between the standard set for shelter by the state and the actual shelter payment made to eligible households.

Second, and perhaps more striking, are the large differences in the depth of subsidy to households under AFDC rather than HUD housing assistance, such as Section 8. In 15 locations around the country, the total AFDC payment received by a family of four—which is supposed to cover the cost of all basic necessities including shelter—is smaller than the lowest Fair Market Rent within the state. In another 22 locations, the AFDC payment level is less than one-and-a-half times the lowest FMR.

Beyond these broad patterns, there are at least six additional ways in which states differ in their determinations of how much shelter assistance a household will receive. These include: (1) differences in adjustments for family size; (2) differences in adjustments for location within a state (for example, higher- versus lower-cost areas); (3) differences in the fraction of the needs standard devoted to shelter; (4) differences in the fraction of shelter needs actually funded (that is, the ratio of shelter payment to shelter need); (5) differences in the relationship between shelter payments and the actual costs of standard housing (as measured by the HUD FMRs); and (6) differences in the frequency of updates to shelter payment levels. Some highlights of each of these disparities will be described below. The full detail can be derived from a careful review of Table 6.1. (See the related discussion of ''shelter poverty'' in Chapter 13 by Michael Stone).

Table 6.1
Summary Statistics on Shelter Assistance under AFDC, by State (1984–85 data)

	(1) Standard of Need ($) 4 Persons	(2) Payment Level ($) 4 Persons	(3) Payment Level / Standard of Need 4 Persons	(4) Shelter Need ($) 4 Persons	(5) Shelter Payment ($) 4 Persons
Alabama	480	147	.31	(144)	(44)
Arizona	282	282	1.00	112	112
Arkansas	273	164	.60	40	24
California	660	660	1.00	222	222
Colorado	765	420	.55	207	113
Connecticut					
Region A (High)	636	636	1.00	265	265
Region C (Low)	534	534	1.00	162	162
Delaware	336	336	1.00	101	101
District of					
Columbia	798	399	.50	(239)	(120)
Florida	468	284	.61	135	82
Georgia	432	264	.61	(130)	(79)
Idaho	627	344	.55	142	78
Illinois	752	386	.51	297	155
Iowa	578	419	.73	100	72
Kansas					
Group I (Low)	363	363	1.00	76	76
Group II (High)	422	422	1.00	135	135
Kentucky	246	246	1.00	(74)	(74)
Louisiana					
Region I (Low)	658	217	.33	(197)	(65)

Table 6.1 (continued)

	(1) Standard of Need ($) 4 Persons	(2) Payment Level ($) 4 Persons	(3) Payment Level / Standard of Need 4 Persons	(4) Shelter Need ($) 4 Persons	(5) Shelter Payment ($) 4 Persons
Region II (High)	712	234	.33	(214)	(70)
Maine	640	465	.73	214	1555
Maryland	520	376	.72	191	138
Massachusetts	490	463	.95	125	119
Michigan					
Zone I (Low)	564	516	.92	140	140
Zone II (High)	628	575	.92	195	195
Minnesota	611	611	1.00	(183)	(183)
Mississippi	327	120	.37	60	22
Missouri	365	310	.85	(110)	(93)
Montana	513	425	.83	250	207
Nevada	341	280	.82	(102)	(84)
New Jersey	443	443	1.00	(133)	(133)
New Mexico	313	313	1.00	105	105
New York					
New York City	528	528	1.00	270	270
Erie County	457	457	1.00	199	199
North Carolina	488	244	.50	(146)	(73)
Ohio	757	343	.45	(227)	(103)
Oklahoma					
A (High)	349	349	1.00	(105)	(105)
B (Low)	301	301	1.00	(90)	(90)
Oregon	392	392	1.00	140	140
Pennsylvania	724	429	.59	(217)	(129)
Rhode Island	484	484	1.00	(145)	(145)
South Carolina	229	229	1.00	44	44
South Dakota	371	371	1.00	163	163

Table 6.1 (continued)

	(1) Standard of Need ($) 4 Persons	(2) Payment Level ($) 4 Persons	(3) Payment Level / Standard of Need 4 Persons	(4) Shelter Need ($) 4 Persons	(5) Shelter Payment ($) 4 Persons
Tennessee	300	168	.56	74	51
Texas	593	201	.34	188	64
Utah	809	428	.53	297	157
Virginia					
Group I (Low)	331	298	.90	141	127
Group III (High)	422	379	.90	210	189
Washington	904	561	.62	471	292
West Virginia					
Plan III (High)	332	249	.75	63	47
Plan I (Low)	236	170	.72	0	0
Wisconsin					
Area I (High)	749	637	.85	225	191
Area II (Low)	723	618	.86	217	185
Wyoming	390	390	1.00	80	80
Indiana	375	316	.84	100	84
Nebraska	420	420	1.00	105	105
New Hampshire					
Reg. Housing	442	442	1.00	141	141
Sub. Housing	418	418	1.00	174	174
North Dakota	454	454	1.00	114	114
Vermont	798	523	.66	263	173

Table 6.1 (continued)

	(6) Difference in Shelter Payments 3 vs. 4 per. (%)	(7) Shelter Need Std. of Need 4 Persons	(8) Shelter Pymt. Shelter Need 4 Persons	(9) HUD Fair Market Rents ($) High	Low	(10) Shelter for 4 Persons Low FMR for State
Alabama	(.26)	(.30)	(.31)	356	254	(.17)
Arizona	(.20)	.40	1.00	445	328	.34
Arkansas	.00	.15	.60	331	228	.11
California	.05	.34	1.00	577	335	.66
Colorado	.11	.27	.55	552	307	.37
Connecticut				491	363	
Region A (High)	.12	.42	1.00			.73
Region C (Low)	.07	.30	1.00			.45
Delaware	.17	.30	1.00	421	361	.28
District of						
Columbia	.22	(.30)	(.50)	440	440	.27
Florida	.01	.29	.61	515	283	.29
Georgia	(.17)	(.30)	(.61)	397	261	(.30)
Idaho	.00	.23	.55	361	307	.25
Illinois	-.02	.40	.52	572	247	.63
Iowa	.08	.17	.72	382	287	.25
Kansas				376	232	
Group I (Low)	.00	.21	1.00			.33
Group II (High)	.00	.32	1.00			.58
Kentucky	(.25)	(.30)	(1.00)	386	236	(.31)
Louisiana				375	228	
Region I (Low)	(.24)	(.30)	(.33)			(.29)
Region II (High)	(.23)	(.30)	(.33)			(.31)
Maine	.26	.33	.72	450	339	.46
Maryland	.20	.37	.72	572	418	.33
Massachusetts	.00	.26	.95	533	364	.33

Table 6.1 (continued)

	(6) Difference in Shelter Payments 3 vs. 4 per. (%)	(7) Shelter Need / Std. of Need 4 Persons	(8) Shelter Pymt. / Shelter Need 4 Persons	(9) HUD Fair Market Rents ($) High	Low	(10) Shelter for 4 Persons / Low FMR for State
Michigan				448	298	
Zone I (Low)	.22	.25	1.00			.47
Zone II (High)	.15	.31	1.00			.65
Minnesota	(.17)	(.30)	(1.00)	451	280	(.65)
Mississippi	.10	.18	.37	387	279	.08
Missouri	(.16)	(.30)	(.85)	385	232	(.40)
Montana	(.26)	.49	.83	425	316	.66
Nevada	(.20)	(.30)	(.82)	528	423	(.20)
New Jersey	(.17)	(.30)	(1.00)	548	370	(.36)
New Mexico	.19	.34	1.00	341	280	.38
New York				539	282	
New York City	.11	.51	1.00			.96
Erie County	.03	.44	1.00			.71
North Carolina	(.09)	(.30)	(.50)	377	246	(.30)
Ohio	(.24)	(.30)	(.45)	373	246	(.42)
Oklahoma				424	244	
A (High)	(.24)	(.30)	(1.00)			(.43)
B (Low)	(.29)	(.36)	(1.00)			(.37)
Oregon	.21	.36	1.00	408	302	.46
Pennsylvania	(.24)	(.30)	(.59)	402	237	(.54)
Rhode Island	(.14)	(.30)	(1.00)	420	361	(.40)
South Carolina	.00	.19	1.00	377	279	.16
South Dakota	.00	.44	1.00	364	285	.57
Tennessee	.21	.30	.89	391	253	.20
Texas	.14	.32	.34	434	244	.26
Utah	.08	.37	.53	413	277	.57

Table 6.1 (continued)

	(6) Difference in Shelter Payments 3 vs. 4 per. (%)	(7) Shelter Need / Std. of Need 4 Persons	(8) Shelter Pymt. / Shelter Need 4 Persons	(9) HUD Fair Market Rents ($) High	Low	(10) Shelter for 4 Persons / Low FMR for State
Virginia				415	266	
Group I (Low)	.13	.43	.90			.48
Group III (High)	.09	.50	.90			.71
Washington	.12	.52	.62	461	302	.97
West Virginia				451	387	
Plan III (High)	.09	.19	.75			.12
Plan I (Low)	.00	.00				.00
Wisconsin				451	273	
Area I (High)	.19	(.30)	(.85)			.70
Area II (Low)	.19	(.30)	(.85)			.68
Wyoming	.00	.21	1.00	478	307	.26
Indiana	.04	.27	.84	367	292	.29
Nebraska	.02	.25	1.00	373	273	.38
New Hampshire	.00	.32	1.00			.39
Reg. Housing				496	359	
Sub. Housing	.00	.42	1.00			.48
North Dakota	.00	.25	1.00	491	310	.37
Vermont	.00	.33	.66	478	351	.49

Notes: 1) Figures shown represent 4-person families; 2) numbers in parentheses are estimates for states whose shelter needs and payment levels could not be extracted from state documents; 3) need and payment standard shown is for Chicago; rest of Illinois uses a different need and payment standard; 4) HUD FMR data are for 2-bedroom units; 5) in states with intrastate variations in shelter payments, ''low'' versus ''high'' areas were designated on the basis of AFDC payments and not FMR's; therefore low versus high FMR's do not always correspond to the location that is low versus high for AFDC payments.

Source: Telephone interviews with state AFDC officials, and state documents.

Adjustments for Family Size

As shown in the sixth column of Table 6.1, ten states make no distinction in the shelter payments provided to families of three versus four persons, the modal sizes of AFDC families. In one state, Illinois, the shelter payment actually is reduced for the larger-sized family. In the remaining states, the difference in shelter payments by family size ranges from a low of 1 percent (Florida) to a high of 29 percent (Oklahoma). Since larger families require larger, more expensive dwelling units, they are significantly disadvantaged in states where the payment differential is relatively low.

Differentials by Intra-State Location

Ten of the 49 states for which we have detailed data differentiate their shelter payment levels geographically, recognizing the variation in housing costs by market area. The remaining 39 states apply a single shelter payment level to all locations. Since housing costs are typically higher in urban areas, this would create significant disparities in the effective value of the shelter supplement in urban versus rural areas.

Shelter Need: Standard of Need

There is also a marked variation in the proportion of the needs standard which states allocate to shelter, and this differentiation varies further by family size. For one-person families, the states' estimate of shelter needs ranges from about 20 percent of the total needs standard (Iowa) to about 55 percent of total needs (New York City and Washington State). At the other extreme of family size (not shown here), Arkansas devotes the smallest proportion of its needs standard to shelter for six-person families (about 12 percent), while Washington assigns the highest fraction (about 49 percent). Furthermore, some states more sharply differentiate these ratios for different family sizes; South Dakota, for example, has nearly a 40 percentage point differential between one-person and six-person families, while others differentiate little, if at all.

Fraction of Shelter Need Actually Funded

As shown in the eighth column of Table 6.1, the percentage of shelter need that is actually translated into a shelter payment for AFDC recipients also varies widely across the states. Twenty states (about 41 percent of all states) fund their total shelter need standard, while most of the remaining states fund at least 50 percent of the shelter standard. Six states, however, fund less than half of the standard.

Deviation of Shelter Payment from FMR

A comparison of shelter payments for four-person AFDC families to the lowest FMR in a state should bias the results in the direction of understating the discrepancy between AFDC shelter payments and HUD FMRs. As shown in the final column of Table 6.1, however, even this comparison reveals substantial differences and also demonstrates the shallowness of the AFDC shelter subsidy. Seven states (Alabama, Arkansas, Mississippi, Nevada, South Carolina, Tennessee, West Virginia) have shelter payments that are 20 percent or less of the lowest FMR for any location within their jurisdiction. AFDC shelter payments in another 26 states fall somewhere between 21 and 50 percent of the lowest FMR. Only the state of Washington funds shelter payments that are virtually the same as the lowest FMR in the state.

Updating Data over Time

The striking disparities between shelter payments and FMRs may result in part from the great time lags between updates to components of the AFDC formula. Few states attempt to update their needs standards or payment levels on a regular basis. In a number of states, the last review of standards occurred at least five years ago. In some instances, even when adjustments are made, they do not necessarily bring the standard up to current prices. For example, Georgia last updated its standard of need in 1980, but values were inflated to equal only 90 percent of 1969 estimates. It is also important to realize that even if adjustments are proposed by state AFDC program staff, ultimately the legislature makes the final budgetary decisions regarding funding levels. In the face of budget pressures, recommendations to inflate standards and payments on a regular basis may be futile.

Summary

The current system of shelter assistance under AFDC essentially guarantees that similar individuals living in different locations in the U.S. will not be treated similarly. States differ markedly in their estimates of shelter needs and in their calculations of payment standards for shelter under AFDC. These variations reflect differences in the states' treatment of family size, geographic areas within their borders, the fraction of the need standard devoted to shelter, the fraction of the shelter need that is translated into an actual dollar payment to a family, and how often various elements that comprise the AFDC formula are updated over time. In addition, shelter payments under AFDC in the large majority of locations across the nation fall considerably below the lowest estimates of the costs of standard quality rental housing for those states. The deviations of shelter payments from FMRs also differ a great deal across the states. These findings suggest that geography rather than need plays the major role in determining how much shelter assistance a household will receive.

ANALYSIS OF THE AHS DATA

In this section, we examine the number and types of households receiving various combinations of income and housing assistance. Several key questions are addressed, including:

- What is the magnitude and nature of the overlap between housing assistance and income assistance programs?
- What kinds of households receive various combinations of income and housing aid?
- How do housing conditions vary according to type of subsidy received? In particular, what proportion of welfare families not receiving housing subsidies live in physically inadequate housing?

We present some preliminary answers to these questions based on an analysis of a nationally representative sample of 90,000 households interviewed in the 1981 Annual Housing Survey.

The AHS data identify households with incomes from "welfare payments or other public assistance"; this includes AFDC, SSI, general assistance, and a host of other smaller welfare programs (for example, refugee aid, emergency assistance). Households were also asked if their unit was in "a public housing project" or if they paid "a lower rent because the federal, state, or local government was paying part of the cost." While these identifiers are fairly crude, and while households have difficulty distinguishing between rental assistance and public housing per se, the data should provide relatively good estimates of the number and characteristics of households with income assistance and/or direct housing aid.

Table 6.2 presents estimates of the number of households receiving income or housing assistance in 1981. Three types of households are identified: those receiving income assistance, but not housing assistance; those receiving housing assistance, but not income assistance; and those receiving both types of assistance. The proportion of renters within each group is also identified. While housing assistance is largely restricted to renters, about 30 percent of the welfare population are owner-occupants.

In 1981 about 7.7 million households (or 9 percent of all U.S. households) were receiving some form of housing or income assistance. About 4.6 million households were receiving income assistance alone; almost 1.8 million were receiving housing subsidies but not income assistance; and about 1.2 million were receiving both types of aid. This latter group represents 16 percent of the households served by either housing or income assistance programs. Thus, while there is a significant overlap in the population that participates in housing and

Table 6.2
Breakdown of Households by Type of Assistance, 1981*

	Number of Households (1000s)	Percent Renters +
Total Receiving Income Assistance	5,834	70%
Total Receiving Housing Assistance	3,091	100%
Type of Assistance:		
Income Assistance Only	4,628	62%
Housing Assistance Only	1,885	100%
Both Income and Housing Assistance	1,205	100%
Total Receiving Income and/or Housing Assistance	7,719	

*Estimates obtained from the 1981 Annual Housing Survey.
+ Includes households who neither own nor rent.
Source: Special tabulations based on the Annual Housing Survey, U.S. Department of Housing & Urban Development.

income assistance programs, the majority of participants receive only one form of subsidy.

The first part of the study documented the large differences in the explicit (and implicit) housing subsidies incorporated in welfare and traditional housing assistance programs. As is evident from Table 6.2, however, about 21 percent of the welfare population also received housing subsidies. Among renters with income assistance, the overlap is somewhat higher, with about 30 percent of all such households living in subsidized housing. Viewed alternatively, about 39 percent of all households currently receiving a housing subsidy are also receiving income assistance. If housing assistance were targeted entirely to the welfare population, about half of the total population, or about 75 percent of the households who rent, could be served.

Table 6.3 presents information on the geographic distribution of households by the type of subsidies they receive. The Northeast has the highest concentration of households receiving housing subsidies, while the South has the highest share of households with income assistance. However, the magnitude of the differences is relatively small. In general, the distribution of program participants across the four census regions reflects the distribution of the population at large.

Differences between metropolitan and nonmetropolitan areas are more pronounced. About one-third of all households with income assistance live in the central cities of large SMSAs and about one-third live in nonmetropolitan areas. In contrast, about 46 percent of all households with housing assistance live in

Table 6.3
Distribution of Assisted Households by Location

	Total Receiving Income Assistance	Total Receiving Housing Assistance	----TYPE OF ASSISTANCE---- Income Assistance Only	Housing Assistance Only	Income & Housing Assistance
Northeast	23.2%	29.9%	22.0%	31.1%	27.9%
North Central	24.2	22.1	24.9	22.5	21.6
South	33.3	28.9	34.9	29.9	27.3
West	19.3	19.2	18.3	16.6	23.2
	100.0%	100.0%	100.0%	100.0%	100.0%
Large SMSAs					
Central City	35.8%	45.5%	32.1%	42.8%	49.7%
Suburban Ring	19.0	19.1	19.3	19.8	17.9
Small SMSAs	13.5	14.5	13.4	14.9	13.9
Non-Metropolitan	31.7	20.9	35.2	22.4	18.5
	100.0%	100.0%	100.0%	100.0%	100.0%

Source: Special tabulations based on the Annual Housing Survey. U.S. Department of Housing & Urban Development.

the central cities of large SMSAs, and only 21 percent live in nonmetropolitan areas. This geographic tilt toward urban areas is particularly evident among households receiving both income and housing assistance. About half of all such households live in the central cities of larger SMSAs.

An alternative way to view the geographic distribution by subsidy type (not shown in the Table) is to consider the proportion of households with income assistance who also receive a housing subsidy. This proportion ranges from 12 percent in nonmetropolitan areas to about 29 percent in the central cities of large SMSAs. Part of this difference reflects the fact that the proportion of the welfare population that rents is much higher in central cities (77 percent) than in non-metropolitan areas (42 percent). Among renters with income assistance, the proportion receiving a housing subsidy ranges from 24 percent outside of SMSAs to 34 percent in central cities.

Table 6.4 presents information on the characteristics of households by subsidy type, including household size, age of household head, race/ethnicity, household income, and household composition. Several broad conclusions emerge. First, the welfare and housing assistance populations as a whole appear to be fairly similar. Households receiving housing assistance, however, tend to be smaller, have a higher proportion of elderly heads, and report marginally lower incomes than do households with income assistance. Income disparities may well reflect differences in household size.

Table 6.4
Characteristics of Households by Type of Assistance, 1981

	Total Receiving Income Assistance	Total Receiving Housing Assistance	----TYPE OF ASSISTANCE---- Income Assistance Only	Housing Assistance Only	Income & Housing Assistance
HOUSEHOLD SIZE					
One Person	22.7%	40.2%	19.9%	44.6%	33.3%
2	21.3	21.6	21.7	23.0	19.4
3	18.3	16.1	18.3	14.8	18.2
4	15.5	9.5	16.9	9.2	10.1
5	9.8	5.5	10.1	3.7	8.4
6+	12.5	7.1	13.0	4.8	10.9
AGE OF HEAD					
< 20 years	1.7%	1.1%	1.6%	0.4%	2.1%
20-29 years	21.8	19.6	21.6	17.7	22.6
30-49 years	32.3	29.7	31.9	27.0	33.9
50-61 years	17.3	12.4	17.9	10.8	14.9
62+ years	26.9	37.2	27.0	44.1	26.5
	100.0%	100.0%	100.0%	100.0%	100.0%
RACE/ETHNICITY					
% White[1]	51.2%	49.4%	55.2%	58.0%	36.1%
% Black[1]	33.7	35.3	30.4	28.4	46.2
% Hispanic	11.7	11.3	11.4	9.8	13.1
% Other[1]	3.4	4.2	3.1	3.9	4.7
	100.0%	100.0%	100.0%	100.0%	100.0%
HOUSEHOLD INCOME					
> $5,000	45.8%	44.4%	41.4%	32.9%	62.5%
$5,000- $9,999	29.8	34.6	29.6	37.2	30.7
10,000- 14,999	11.0	12.2	12.5	16.8	5.1
15,000- 19,999	4.8	4.5	5.8	6.7	1.0
20,000+	8.7	4.2	10.7	6.5	0.7
	100.0%	100.0%	100.0%	100.0%	100.0%
Mean Family Income	$8,152	$7,149	$9,141	8,525	$4,997

Table 6.4 (continued)

	Total Receiving Income Assistance	Total Receiving Housing Assistance	----TYPE OF ASSISTANCE---- Income Assistance Only	Housing Assistance Only	Income & Housing Assistance
HOUSEHOLD TYPE					
Single-Person Elderly	12.4%	27.7%	10.7%	33.2%	18.9%
Other Elderly	13.4	6.8	15.7	8.2	4.5
Single-Person Non-Elderly	10.2	12.5	9.1	11.4	14.4
Female-Headed Households w/ Children	32.2%	29.4%	28.5%	18.5%	46.4%
Male-Headed Households w/ Children	16.8	13.0	19.3	16.8	7.1
Other Non-Elderly	15.0	10.7	16.7	12.0	8.7
	100.0%	100.0%	100.0%	100.0%	100.0%

[1]Excludes households who classify themselves as Hispanic.

Source: Special tabulations based on the Annual Housing Survey. U.S. Department of Housing & Urban Development.

When one considers the overlap in assistance programs, however, more significant patterns are revealed. In general, households receiving both income and housing assistance tend to have the lowest incomes, the highest concentration of blacks, and the highest proportion of female-headed households with children. While such households tend to be larger than those with housing assistance alone, they are somewhat smaller than the average "welfare-only" household.

Many of the differences between multiple- and single-subsidy households are quite pronounced. For example, about 62 percent of the households with combined subsidies have incomes that are less than $5000 per year, compared with 41 percent of households with income assistance alone, and 33 percent of house-

Table 6.5
Housing Costs and Affordability by Type of Assistance, 1981

	Total Receiving Income Assistance	Total Receiving Housing Assistance	----TYPE OF ASSISTANCE---- Income Assistance Only	Housing Assistance Only	Income & Housing Assistance
Average Monthly Housing Costs	$210	$155	$232	$169	$133
Average Housing Costs-to-Income Ratio	0.436	0.322	0.457	0.298	0.360
Distribution of Ratios					
< 0.25	35.8%	54.3%	32.1%	57.7%	49.1%
.25-.30	7.3	12.6	6.1	13.2	11.7
.31-.40	12.0	11.0	12.4	11.3	10.7
.41-.50	10.1	6.4	11.0	6.1	6.8
.50+	34.8	15.6	38.4	11.8	21.6
	100.0%	100.0%	100.0%	100.0%	100.0%
Percent Paying More Than 50% of Income for Housing	56.9%	33.0%	61.8%	29.2%	39.1%

Source: Special tabulations based on the Annual Housing Survey. U.S. Department of Housing & Urban Development.

holds with only housing assistance. As a result, average family income by subsidy type ranges from $4997 for households with income and housing assistance to $8525 for households with only a housing subsidy and $9141 for households with income assistance alone. Multiple subsidies are thus clearly targeted to the most needy segment of the population.

Table 6.5 presents information on housing costs and affordability by subsidy type. Note that HUD programs establish the maximum rent/income ratio at roughly 30 percent. Although the actual ratio may vary by household size and housing program, and although utility payments in excess of budgeted amounts may well lead to burdens above the theoretical maximum, the ratio expected under housing programs should be close to 30 percent. In contrast, given the size of the welfare grant in relationship to the cost of housing, housing costs-to-income ratios among welfare households are expected to be fairly high.

These expectations are for the most part supported by the AHS data. The average housing costs of households in assisted housing programs ($155/month) are about 33 percent below the average costs of those receiving income assistance alone ($232). As a result, housing costs-to-income ratios are relatively low among

Table 6.6
Housing Conditions by Type of Assistance, 1981

	Total Receiving Income Assistance	Total Receiving Housing Assistance	----TYPE OF ASSISTANCE---- Income Assistance Only	Housing Assistance Only	Income & Housing Assistance
Percent Substandard	25.3%	8.9%	28.8%	7.1%	11.8%
Fail Major (i.e., Structural Problems)	9.2	1.8	10.9	1.5	2.3
Fail Minor (i.e., Maintenance Problems)	21.7	7.6	24.7	5.8	10.5
Fail Both	5.6	0.5	6.9	0.2	0.9
Average Persons Per Room	0.723	0.640	0.731	0.605	0.695
Distribution by Person Per Room					
> 1.0	88.6%	92.4%	86.1%	94.6%	88.9%
1.1 to 1.5	9.8	6.3	10.0	4.5	9.2
1.6 to 2.0	2.8	1.0	3.2	0.8	1.4
2.0+	0.8	0.3	0.8	0.1	0.5
	100.0%	100.0%	100.0%	100.0%	100.0%

Source: Special tabulations based on the Annual Housing Survey. U.S. Department of Housing & Urban Development.

households that receive a housing subsidy (32 percent). In contrast, households on welfare alone spend an average of 46 percent of their incomes on housing. Sixty-two percent of all such households spend more than 30 percent, and 38 percent spend over half of their income on housing. Thus, affordability is clearly a major problem for this segment of the population.

Even with housing assistance, however, a significant number of households report rents that exceed the "30 percent" affordability standard of federal housing programs. For example, 29 percent of households receiving only a housing subsidy spend more than 30 percent of their incomes on rent, and 12 percent spend more than half. More strikingly, 39 percent of households with both housing and income assistance have housing cost burdens in excess of 30 percent, and 22 percent report ratios of 50 percent or more. Some of these cases may well reflect inaccuracies in the data, as well as differences in affordability standards in state or local housing programs. The relative poverty of this latter group, however, combined with inadequate utility allowances, may well explain these findings.

Table 6.6 presents additional information on the extent of crowding and the physical condition of dwelling units occupied by the various groups. Units have been classified as substandard if they fail to meet housing quality standards similar to those used by HUD to define adequate housing.[3] Similarly, units have been classified as crowded if they have more than one person per room. Although HUD occupancy standards often allow for a higher number of persons per room, this cut-off serves as a rough indicator of the extent of crowding among different household types.

Households in subsidized housing have a relatively low incidence of substandard dwellings, and most of the defects observed reflect building maintenance, as opposed to structural problems. Again, this finding is not surprising, given that most of HUD's programs incorporate fairly stringent construction or maintenance standards that attempt to ensure decent and sanitary housing conditions for program recipients. Although the AHS data do not enable one to distinguish among different program types, the small proportion of households living in units with multiple maintenance deficiencies could well be in the older public housing stock.

The incidence of substandard dwellings is considerably higher among the "welfare-only" population, and major defects are much more prevalent. Nevertheless, the proportion of welfare-only households in substandard units (29 percent) is roughly half the proportion that pay more than 30 percent of their income for housing (62 percent). Thus, the problem of affordability appears to dominate the problem of housing quality regardless of program mix. Much the same conclusion can be drawn with respect to crowding, which appears to be related more to household size than to type of subsidies received. While the incidence of crowding is again highest among the welfare-only population, most of the crowded units have less than 1.5 persons per room.

Table 6.7 presents information on the incidence of multiple housing problems across the different household types. Three types of problems are considered: affordability (the household pays more than 30 percent of its income for housing); crowding (the dwelling has more than one person per room); and physical condition (the dwelling is classified as substandard). As is evident from the Table, a relatively large proportion of assisted households have a housing problem, regardless of the type of assistance received. Affordability, however, is the only problem for at least half of those with a housing need. The incidence of multiple deficiencies is relatively low among those in assisted housing, but fairly high among welfare households. About 76 percent of all welfare-only households have some kind of housing need, and about 22 percent have at least two problems.

Thus far we have treated the welfare-only population as a homogeneous group. As we have seen, however, about 38 percent of all such households own their homes, and thus may face significantly different housing circumstances than those who rent. Table 6.8 presents information on both the income and housing situations of this component of the population, stratified by the household's tenure. The figures in the Table reveal some rather striking differences between the two groups.

Table 6.7
Distribution of Households by Number and Type of Deficiencies, 1981

	Total Receiving Income Assistance	Total Receiving Housing Assistance	----TYPE OF ASSISTANCE---- Income Assistance Only	Housing Assistance Only	Income & Housing Assistance
One Deficiency					
Overcrowded	4.4%	4.7%	4.0%	4.1%	5.8%
Substandard	9.8	4.3	11.3	4.5	4.0
Unaffordable	36.2	27.2	38.0	25.8	29.3
Two Deficiencies	17.8	5.9	20.0	3.6	9.4
Three Deficiencies	2.2	0.5	2.4	0.0	1.4
Total Proportion of Households With a Housing Need	70.4%	42.6%	75.7%	38.0%	49.9%

Source: Special tabulations based on the Annual Housing Survey. U.S. Department of Housing & Urban Development.

Renters in the welfare-only population have significantly lower incomes than their counterparts who own their homes. Forty-eight percent of the renters report incomes of less than $5,000 per year, and only 9 percent report incomes of $15,000 or more. These income figures resemble those reported by households receiving both income and housing subsidies, and are considerably below the incomes of both owners on welfare and households that receive housing assistance alone. Thus, the targeting of multiple subsidies to the lowest income groups is caused by the fact that housing programs are geared to renters. Apparently, there are significant numbers of equally needy renters on welfare who are not now benefiting from housing programs.

Despite their lower incomes, the housing costs of renters are somewhat higher than the housing costs of those who own their homes. As a result, some 76 percent of renters receiving welfare but not housing assistance pay more than 30 percent of their income for rent, and 43 percent pay over half. Thus, the affordability problem within this group is widespread and severe. In contrast, about 47 percent of owners pay more than 30 percent, and 24 percent pay more than half. These ratios are close to those observed among households receiving both income and housing assistance, but considerably above those experienced by nonwelfare households with housing assistance.

Finally, the incidence of crowding and substandard housing is relatively similar between owners and renters. About the same proportion of units have been classified as substandard, and the incidence of major and minor deficiencies is

Table 6.8
Selected Demographic and Housing Characteristics by Tenure: Households With Income Assistance But No Housing Subsidies

	Renters	Owners
Household Income		
< $5,000	48.0%	29.8%
$5,000-$9,999	30.9	27.7
10,000- 14,999	11.6	14.4
15,000- 19,999	4.7	7.8
20,000+	4.8	20.4
	100.0%	100.0%
Monthly Housing Costs		
< $100	6.7%	24.9%
$100-$200	30.6	26.4
201- 300	37.2	23.6
301+	25.6	25.2
	100.0%	100.0%
Mean Costs	244	228
Housing Costs-To-Income Ratio		
< 0.25	18.3%	50.6%
.25-.30	5.9	7.0
.31-.40	13.3	11.8
.41-.50	13.7	7.1
.50+	48.8	23.6
	100.0%	100.0%
Mean Ratio	0.533	0.360
Persons Per Room		
< 1.0	84.8%	87.6%
1.1-1.5	11.0	8.9
1.6-2.0	3.2	3.0
2.0+	1.0	0.5
	100.0%	100.0%

Table 6.8 (continued)

	Renters	Owners
Percent Substandard	30.6%	25.2%
Fail Major (i.e., Structural Problem)	9.8	10.8
Fail Minor (i.e., Maintenance Problem)	24.9	22.3
Fail Both	5.1	7.8
Number of Deficiencies		
None	13.6	38.9
One Problem		
Quality Only	6.6	15.3
Affordability Only	47.2	27.5
Crowding Only	2.7	6.1
Two Problems	26.8	10.7
Three Problems	3.1	1.6
	100.0%	100.0%

Source: Special tabulations based on the Annual Housing Survey. U.S. Department of Housing & Urban Development.

about the same. A somewhat higher fraction of renters have more than one person per room, but the differences are relatively small. Thus, while the incidence of multiple housing problems is considerably higher among households who rent, this is caused by the fact that three out of every four renters have a housing cost burden that exceeds 30 percent. For some 30 percent of all renters on welfare, high housing costs are accompanied by crowding or substandard conditions—a situation that signifies a real and very pressing housing need.

CONCLUSIONS

We began this paper by stating that the current system of housing subsidies in this country raises questions of equity, efficiency, and effectiveness. The analysis presented here primarily deals with the equity and effectiveness issues, and even these are addressed on a highly preliminary basis. As our work proceeds, we will be able to explore the data in more detail, test our hypotheses in a more rigorous manner, and expand the institutional component of the analysis to the other major income maintenance programs beyond AFDC.

There are several broad conclusions supported by the analysis to date. The first relates to the equity issue. Our analysis has revealed an enormous variation in the implicit or explicit housing subsidies received by households both within and between programs. For example, under AFDC, an otherwise similar family of three would receive an implicit housing allowance ranging from $20 in Mississippi to $260 in Washington State. This represents 8 to 97 percent, respectively, of the cost of standard housing in those areas.

In addition, some households receive multiple subsidies while others do not. About 21 percent of the welfare population also receives a housing subsidy which often is as large as the entire AFDC grant. The remaining 79 percent must rely on shelter allowances that are dramatically below those employed by HUD. From the broadest perspective, multiple subsidies are being received by the neediest groups. The average income of the 1.2 million households with both income and housing assistance is less than 40 percent of the average income of the 6.5 million households receiving income or housing assistance alone. Yet the 2.9 million renters who receive income assistance but not housing subsidies have incomes that are just as low as those receiving multiple subsidies. Therefore, the majority of households who appear to be most in need are not receiving HUD assistance.

Less can be said about the effectiveness issue at this stage in the analysis. Some 29 percent of all households with income, but not housing, assistance, or about 1.5 million families, live in substandard dwellings. Eleven percent live in units with major structural defects. Affordability is an even greater problem, particularly among the 2.9 million renters who receive income but not housing assistance. According to our estimates, 76 percent of all such households spend more than 30 percent of their incomes on housing, and 49 percent pay more than half. In contrast, those receiving HUD housing assistance fare considerably better in terms of both quality and affordability, primarily due to the deeper subsidies they receive.

Given the inequities of the existing system, what is the appropriate policy response? Two general kinds of solutions have been proposed. The first would involve increasing the implicit or explicit housing allowances available to needy families, either by creating an entitlement voucher program or by supplementing shelter allowances under AFDC (and, presumably, under the other income assistance programs). All such proposals would involve a significant increase in funding levels—a solution that seems infeasible given current budget constraints. While tax reform potentially could be used to generate additional resources for low-income housing—for example, by reducing the enormous subsidies currently flowing to owner-occupants—such options are not part of the current tax structure.

An alternative set of proposals would involve introducing more explicit housing standards into the administration of income maintenance programs. Such an objective was behind the so-called McKinney Demonstration, which was part of the 1983 Housing Act. Under this demonstration, local welfare offices were to use a mix of approaches ranging from code enforcement to rehabilitation loans to ensure that AFDC families lived in physically adequate units. While the demonstration never was funded, the administrative difficulties associated with expanding the responsibilities of an already overburdened welfare bureaucracy give one reason for concern. Furthermore, while 30 percent of all welfare families not in assisted housing live in substandard units, 70 percent do not. Thus, while such an approach may well make sense on a limited basis, it does not represent a global solution to the problem.

How can the conflict be resolved between the very low probability of bigger budgets for shelter subsidies and the obviously vital role of deep housing subsidies in achieving housing goals? Our results show that HUD assistance is very effective for the three million households who receive it. But among the additional 4.6 million welfare households who do not, there are surely some who are at least equally in need of this type of aid. The question, therefore, is how to provide deeper housing assistance to more of these welfare households. One broad policy option is better targeting: redistributing existing resources among a smaller population identified as most needy. Such a change in policy approach raises several important questions.

First, how do we define "most needy"? One approach which we have examined in other work (Newman and Struyk 1983) is to focus assistance on those who are persistently or permanently poor, rather than the temporarily poor. Since the permanently poor represent a fraction of all those who are poor in a single year, limited resources could be translated into much deeper subsidies per household. For example, of the 7.3 percent of families who were poor in 1974, only half remained poor in at least three of the next five years (Newman and Struyk 1983). Focusing housing assistance on the permanently poor would remove geographic or demographic inequities in the current allocation of HUD funds. It would also reduce administrative costs per assisted household because recipient turnover rates would decline.

A second question concerns the relationship between housing problems and permanent poverty. Do the permanently poor have the greatest housing need? Clearly, the case for concentrating housing assistance on the permanently poor is stronger, the more severe their housing problems are. Here, too, previous research is convincing. Permanently poor households live in physically deficient dwellings at substantially higher rates than the temporarily poor. For example, among renters, 40 percent of the permanently poor live in units failing HUD's basic quality test. This rate is about twice that of the temporarily poor.

Finally, what about the administrative feasibility of identifying the permanently poor and coordinating the work of HUD and HHS to better target these resources? The answer to this question is not known. No assistance programs exist that specifically target this subpopulation. Furthermore, there is no existing mechanism for coordinating the resources and activities of these two independent agencies on such a massive scale. Sadly, these administrative problems may be the greatest stumbling blocks to better addressing the housing needs of the nation's poor.

ACKNOWLEDGMENTS

The authors gratefully acknowledge the capable research assistance of Marc Solomon and Mittie Olion, and computer assistance of Miguel Cordova and Timothy DiLauro.

NOTES

1. These certificates are currently valued at the difference between the rental cost of a standard apartment and 30 percent of the household's income.
2. In this chapter we do not address the efficiency issues.
3. These housing quality standards are as follows:

1. Plumbing: unit either lacks complete plumbing facilities or households must share its use.
2. Kitchen: unit either lacks a complete kitchen or households must share its use.
3. Sewage: one or more of the following three services was unavailable or completely unusable for six or more hours at least three times during the past 90 days: (1) running water, (2) sewage system, (3) toilet.
4. Heat: the heating system was completely unusable for six or more hours at least three times during the past winter.
5. Maintenance: two or more of the following four conditions exist: leaking roof, substantial cracks or holes in walls and ceilings, holes in floors, broken plaster or peeling paint in areas larger than one square foot.
6. Public Halls: the unit is in a building with public hallways and stairs, and two or more of the following three conditions exist: missing light fixtures; stair railings are missing or poorly attached; missing, loose, or broken steps.

In subsequent analyses, we consider items 1 and 2 to be "major" defects and items 3 through 6 to be "minor" defects.

REFERENCES

Nenno, Mary. 1983. "What is the Future for Federal Housing Assistance?" National Association of Housing and Redevelopment Officials. Washington, DC: mimeo.

Newman, Sandra, and Raymond Struyk. 1983. "Housing and Poverty." *The Review of Economics and Statistics* 64:243–53.

New York Times. 1985. "Failure of Plan for Homeless Reflects City Housing Crisis." February 19.

New York Times. 1984. "A Street is Not a Home." Editorial, August 24.

REASSESSING SHELTER ASSISTANCE: COMMENT

Peter Dreier

The debate over "big government" is a constant theme in American politics. While most Americans recognize the need for protection against physical and economic insecurity, they also balk at unwarranted intervention in their private lives. Conversely, while many Americans express a general distrust of government—as well as other large institutions such as the media, business, and unions—they nevertheless resist translating that distrust into support to cut or end specific programs, such as Social Security or programs to protect consumers or the environment.

Conservative politicians have been able to appeal to the voters by using the rhetoric of promising to "get government off our backs," but have found it more difficult than anticipated to cut or end programs that address the interests of specific groups such as consumers, workers, senior citizens, minorities, and environmentalists. At the same time, liberal politicians have a hard time finding ways to translate support for specific programs into general support for positive government action. Individual programs have been caught in the tug-of-war between conservatives and liberals.

Programs specifically directed at the poor—for example, "welfare" policies—are no exception, yet they seem particularly vulnerable to recent conservative initiatives to reduce government commitments. In the early 1960s, during the heyday of the civil rights movement and the start of the War on Poverty, Americans were generally optimistic about the future and supportive of programs designed to end poverty. By the mid-1970s, the public's attitude had shifted measurably. Frustrated by the stubborn persistence of poverty, pinched by economic stagnation, increasingly skeptical of elected officials, perhaps lashing out at the black and anti-war activists whom they blamed for the upheavals of the prior decade, the American public told pollsters (and politicians) that they had changed their minds about the anti-poverty effort.

This reversal stems, at least in part, from two related, but distinct, attitudes. First, Americans increasingly began to blame the poor themselves for their situation. This "blaming the victim" attitude has a long tradition in American life, with its lift-yourself-up-by-your-own-bootstraps individualism, and it is especially appealing when initial efforts to solve the problems of the poor produce disappointing results. There is a tendency to assume that policy failures are due to the intransigence of the objects of policy.

Second, Americans began to lose confidence in the anti-poverty programs themselves. Individual programs became lumped together in general criticisms of the War on Poverty, and Americans became increasingly convinced that the overall effort was wasteful and ineffective.

The escalating rhetoric about inefficient, wasteful "big government" anti-poverty programs could not help but influence people already pinched by inflation and taxes. Resistance developed to expansion of programs, and today there is a growing audience for the argument that the nation—and in fact the poor themselves—would be better off today if the War on Poverty had never been initiated.

These arguments did not emerge out of thin air, of course. Shifts in public opinion reflect, at least in part, changes in the so-called conventional wisdom of opinion leaders such as journalists, intellectuals, and politicians. It is in fact possible to argue that Ronald Reagan's election in 1980 and his subsequent reelection in 1984 is the product of a neoconservative campaign, beginning in the early 1970s, to deliberately affect public opinion.

Books such as Edward Banfield's *The Unheavenly City* and journals such as *The Public Interest* helped spawn this effort, while the work of James Q. Wilson and Nathan Glazer sustained it. By the early 1980s it had produced books such as George Gilder's *Wealth and Poverty* and Charles Murray's *Losing Ground*, which gained a popular audience by attacking government anti-poverty programs. Despite serious and devastating critiques that challenge their basic facts, methodology and conclusions (Danziger and Gottschalk 1985; Greenstein 1985; Levitan 1985; Miller 1985), the books gained a legitimacy with opinion leaders and policymakers. Research that documented the effectiveness of anti-poverty programs (such as John Schwartz' *America's Hidden Success*) received little attention compared to their neoconservative counterparts.

Due in part to the success of the neoconservative campaign, liberals and progressives have found themselves in the position of defending the very existence of public programs rather than being able to focus on questions of how they might be refined or improved. On the whole, it is clear that, in the battle of public opinion and influence on policymakers over the past decade, conservatives have out-organized liberals and progressives. As a result, most government programs for poor and marginal groups have become very vulnerable.

This brief discussion of American attitudes toward anti-poverty programs and the poor provides a context for evaluating the Newman and Schnare chapter on "Reassessing Shelter Assistance." While the authors emphasize the tentativeness of their findings and direct us to more comprehensive analysis presented elsewhere, even their preliminary findings imply challenges to the assumptions of the social policy agenda of the New Right. They do so by providing a basis for defending and at the same time improving existing housing assistance programs. They certainly cannot be interpreted as suggesting that those programs have been a mistake.

Very briefly, Newman and Schnare conclude that:

- For those who receive shelter assistance, either from HUD or HHS, the aid has a positive impact on the poor in meeting their housing needs, although it is not enough.
- The number of poor who receive assistance covers only a fraction of those who need it.
- Even among those who receive assistance, there are dramatic disparities in the amount of assistance provided based on geography and bureaucratic requirements rather than on need.
- The two sources of shelter assistance—HHS and HUD—do not coordinate their programs. As a result, there is considerable waste, inequity and ineffectiveness.

The policy implications of these findings should be reasonably clear.

- The federal government should establish nationwide standards for housing assistance, rather than allow individual states, whose assistance varies widely, to set the levels. There is no good reason why a low-income family from Massachusetts should be treated differently from its counterpart in Mississippi. Flexibility should be allowed for variations in local rent levels, energy costs, and so on, but an adequate minimum must be ensured.
- Housing assistance should be restructured and expanded to meet the well-documented need. As much as possible, federal housing assistance should provide permanent housing rather than "emergency" shelter.
- Responsibility for housing assistance should be placed in one agency in order to reduce, if not avoid, overlap, waste, and turf fights. The poor are disserved by the current welfare bureaucracy, as are the public, the politicians, and the bureaucrats themselves.

There are a number of issues not addressed in the Newman and Schnare chapter. For one thing, shelter assistance programs do nothing to expand the inadequate supply of low- and moderate-priced housing. Poor people with welfare checks, rent subsidies, and housing vouchers thus have to compete in the private housing market with better-off consumers. Many landlords would just as soon avoid contact with both the poor and government red tape, and in a tight market are likely to discriminate against recipients of housing assistance. Demand subsidies must be complemented by programs to expand the supply of adequate affordable housing. The federal government's retreat from housing production under Reagan must be reversed. A new cost-effective supply program, with substantial support to nonprofit developers, should be put in place.

In addition, because the chapter deals with outcomes, and not process, no attention is paid to the bureaucratic settings. HHS and HUD are two massive bureaucracies. Both are known for their administrative waste and programmatic confusion. It is possible to argue that this is not so much an inevitable result of large-scale bureaucracy, but a failure of political commitment to the programs they administer and the constituencies they serve. When the political will is there (as in the early days of Head Start), bureaucrats, politicians, and constituents find ways to cut red tape and improve management. Successful consolidation of the HHS and HUD shelter assistance programs would depend on a commitment toward that end and on strong, competent leadership.

Finally, the paper's focus on assistance levels only scratches the surface of the underlying problem of American housing policy in general and these rental assistance programs in particular: the reliance on the private housing market to meet the housing needs of the poor. Despite neoconservative claims to the contrary, the private rental housing system is exceedingly inefficient. Tax laws encourage speculation, shoddy construction, deferred maintenance, and eventual condo conversion—and drain the federal budget through hidden (that is, tax) subsidies to the rich. Landlords' operating expenses—particularly mortgage debt, but also energy and maintenance costs—require them to constantly raise rents, far beyond what the poor can afford. As a result, government programs designed to close or fill the gap between renters' ability to pay and landlords' costs-plus-profits must constantly expand. Reforming and expanding the current shelter assistance programs—although much needed, as Newman and Schnare document—will not cure this systemic problem. This is no excuse not to begin immediately to undertake the reforms this research suggests as a means to alleviate the intolerable housing conditions faced by many low-income households.

Political realism leads us to acknowledge that neither short-term nor long-term changes are likely so long as the current mood regarding government social programs in general and anti-poverty programs in particular prevails. This mood, in Washington and across the country, can only change if advocates for the poor are well organized and form the necessary coalitions to win elections and lobby effectively. They also need a political program that they can defend with data and promote with slogans.

The Newman and Schnare study represents an important potential contribution to that program. It offers data that constitute a rationale for positive public action in the area of housing policy. It could thus be used—by Congress members and their aides, by housing advocates such as the National Low Income Housing Coalition and tenants groups, by progressive-minded housing officials, as well as by liberal journalists—to challenge the Reagan housing cutbacks, to demonstrate the need for continued and expanded housing assistance, and to call for bureaucratic reform to make these programs more cost-effective.

REFERENCES

Danziger, Sheldon, and Peter Gottschalk. 1985. "The Poverty of Losing Ground." *Challenge* 28 (2), May/June, pp. 32–38.

Greenstein, Robert. 1985. "Losing Faith in 'Losing Ground.' " *New Republic*, March 25, pp. 12–17.

Levitan, Sar A. 1985. "Losing Ground: American Social Policy 1950–1980." *Society*, May/June.

Miller, S.M. 1985. "Faith, Hope, and Charity—The Public Relations of Poverty." *Contemporary Sociology* 14 (6), November, pp. 684–87.

Schwartz, John E. 1983. *America's Hidden Success: A Reassessment of Twenty Years of Public Policy*. New York: W.W. Norton.

7

THE CHANGING STRUCTURE OF HOUSING FINANCE IN THE UNITED STATES

Ann Meyerson

The past few years have seen dramatic changes in the financial structure of the United States. Federal legislation in 1980 (the Depository Institutions-Deregulation and Monetary Control Act), and especially 1982 (the Garn–St Germain Depository Institutions Act), together with regulatory changes on a state and local level, succeeded in substantially deregulating and homogenizing the financial system, producing a restructuring that has not been equalled for a half-century. These developments, like the financial restructuring of the 1930s, are having a tremendous impact on housing in the United States, which is greatly dependent on long-term mortgage financing. Housing finance has lost its formerly insulated status, the mortgage lending process has been altered, and fewer but larger financial institutions are increasingly dominating the financial system.

It was a crisis, in the early 1980s, for the nation's historic providers of mortgage debt—the thrift institutions (savings and loan associations and mutual savings banks)—that in part precipitated financial deregulation. Since the mid-1960s the thrifts had been increasingly unable to attract savings and simply stay in business. As a result of their traditional dependency on short-term deposits with regulated interest rates and their predominant investment in long-term, fixed-rate mortgages, they were particularly vulnerable to steeply rising interest rates, which, beginning in 1966, squeezed their earnings and caused deposit outflows. At the peak of this crisis in 1981, hundreds of savings and loans and mutual savings banks were forced out of business, merging voluntarily with healthier institutions, or being forced to do so by supervisory agencies. The deregulatory response to this crisis, however, was also brought on by the problems of the commercial banking industry, which had been losing deposits to the burgeoning money market mutual funds. Thus, both the thrift institutions and the commercial banks were involved in bringing about change in the financial structure that deeply affects housing finance.

Most of the housing finance analysts who have reviewed the recent changes in the financial structure make the assumption that the system of housing finance prior to the 1980s was untenable—government over-regulation of banks and savings institutions, together with high interest rates, was the key problem—and thus deregulation was necessary to save the financial services industry and benefit the public (Colton 1983; Seiders 1982, 1983; Kaplan 1983; Vartanian 1983a, 1983b; Baer 1983; Tuccillo and Goodman 1983). Almost all take for granted that the public will benefit greatly from this shift to a free market approach and that the housing finance system will become much more efficient.

This chapter departs from that view, finding that the future will not be so rosy for housing, particularly housing consumers, or for the financial structure in general. The earlier system clearly was no longer functioning to properly facilitate the flow of credit to housing. But the new developments resolve that problem primarily in the interest of financial institutions, not in the interest of low-cost and community-responsive housing provision. As such, deregulation represents a significant departure in government housing finance policy. Moreover, although deregulation was supposed to shore up the ailing thrift industry, the forces it set into motion are threatening the industry's very survival. Some financial institutions (mostly non-thrifts) are strengthened by this restructuring, but the entire financial structure itself may become considerably weakened.

THE RESTRUCTURED WORLD OF HOUSING FINANCE

Before examining the structural changes themselves and their impact, it is important to take a brief look at the system governing housing finance prior to the 1980s.

The financial restructuring of the 1930s gave the housing sector a protected status and substantial government support. Housing credit was greatly expanded and mass homeownership was facilitated by federal government programs that shored up the thrifts after the Great Depression and shifted a substantial amount of the risk involved in mortgage lending to the government (and to a lesser extent, the mortgage borrower). The institutions themselves thus were strengthened but requirements and incentives for them to specialize in mortgage lending were also established. Among the programs brought into being were the Federal Home Loan Bank Board (FHLBB) for savings and loans; Federal Deposit Insurance Corporation (FDIC) and Federal Savings and Loan Insurance Corporation (FSLIC) deposit insurance; Federal Housing Administration (FHA) and Veterans Administration (VA) mortgage insurance facilitating a new fixed-rate, long-term, self-amortizing mortgage instrument; a national secondary mortgage market; and tax incentives for thrifts to specialize in mortgage lending.[1]

The thrifts did very well for much of the postwar period. Armed with Regulation Q, which set a ceiling on the amount of interest financial institutions could pay to depositors (with thrifts allowed to pay one-quarter percent more than commercial banks), they could charge borrowers a lucrative two to three points more than the deposit rate ceiling and still offer a reasonable mortgage rate. But all this changed dramatically with the steep and unprecedented rise in interest rates beginning in the mid-1960s. As rate-conscious depositors withdrew their savings in favor of alternative, less regulated investments, and as deposit rates rose faster than returns on mortgage portfolios, thrifts were forced to dip dangerously into surplus funds, sell non-liquid assets at a loss, and/or merge with other institutions to accommodate these deposit losses and low earnings. The mortgage market was deeply affected.

The financial restructuring of the 1980s, like that of the 1930s, was designed to support the financial institutions but, unlike that of the 1930s, has reduced their commitment to housing. It seems there was no longer the same governmental interest there once was in stimulating housing or in using residential construction as a lever to stimulate the economy.

The Garn–St Germain Act of 1982

Although this landmark Act was precipitated by the thrift crisis, it also represented the culmination of many years' efforts at "financial reform" aimed at making the system more "efficient and equitable" (Commission on Money and Credit 1961; President's Commission on Financial Structure and Regulation 1971—the so-called Hunt Commission).[2] Much of the impetus behind the changes in the financial structure, including those affecting housing, came from institutions outside the traditional mortgage lending sector, most particularly the large commercial banks. Indeed, it was not the thrifts but the large commercial banks that primarily benefited from the Act; they too had been experiencing difficulties over the years, although of a lesser magnitude than those of the thrifts.

The Garn–St Germain Act basically provided emergency assistance and expanded investment authority to thrift institutions and further deregulated deposit rates at all depository institutions. Not only were the thrifts subsidized, thereby saving many of them and slowing down an intense period of merger activity, but they were given broad new lending powers similar to those of commercial banks. The emergency capital assistance plan authorized federal regulators temporarily to increase the net worth (assets minus liabilities) of thrifts that had at least 20 percent of their loans in mortgages, through government-backed promissory notes. The government would pay off the notes to a thrift institution's creditors only if the thrift failed. This enabled numerous thrifts to stay afloat without merging during 1983 (Bennett 1983a). On the other hand, the Act eased future merger activity by giving federal regulators wider latitude in selecting merger partners. There now is a procedure and order of priority for certain interstate and interindustry acquisitions, although the legislation stipulated that intrastate mergers between thrifts are preferred over interstate, cross-industry mergers.

The expanded investment authority the Act granted to federally-chartered thrifts consisted of their being permitted to invest up to 10 percent of their assets in corporate, commercial, and agricultural loans, areas dominated by commercial banks. In addition, thrifts were given the opportunity to increase consumer loans from 20 percent to 30 percent of assets and nonresidential mortgage loans from 20 percent to 40 percent of assets. Previous asset limitations on investment in state and local obligations were also removed. And thrifts were given authority to invest up to 10 percent of their assets in tangible personal property and engage in equipment leasing, an activity commercial banks have found very profitable.

Also enhancing the asset side of the thrift problem and thrifts' financial viability in general were the Act's provisions regarding mortgage loan terms and federal chartering. State regulation of "due-upon-sale" clauses, restricting financial institutions from calling in a mortgage whenever a home is sold, were overridden. This meant that lenders could issue a new loan at current market rates.

Savings banks and savings and loans can now more easily switch to federal chartering. Federal chartering, unlike some state chartering, allows mutual savings banks to convert to stock ownership, a form that allows the institutions to raise capital by issuing stock. Since the legislation was passed, many thrifts have successfully gone public and rapidly expanded (Bennett 1983c).

On the liability as opposed to the asset side, the Act directed federal regulators to devise a new federally-insured high interest rate account to be offered by commercial banks and thrifts, equivalent to and competitive with the high-yielding money market mutual funds. These new accounts, first available in December 1982, are free from interest rate ceilings, and, as such, represent a considerable leap in the direction of deposit rate deregulation. Further, unlike the money market mutual funds, they are federally insured. Thus, they have contributed to the winning away of deposits from the money market mutual funds. Commercial banks gained a great deal from this provision, as the chief cause of their deposit losses had been the money market mutual funds. The Act also eliminated the Regulation Q advantage thrifts have enjoyed over commercial banks. As of January 1, 1984, they are no longer able to pay one-quarter percent more on certain deposit accounts.

As a result of this legislation, then, the thrifts received emergency assistance, they were allowed to substantially diversify their portfolios, and the financial structure became largely deregulated and homogenized. The lines between commercial banks and thrifts will become increasingly blurred and the two will be in greater competition with one another. Interest rate ceilings on deposits are, to a large extent, removed, leaving everyone—banks, thrifts, money market mutual funds, and so forth—freer to compete.[3]

Housing Sector Loses Support

Prior to 1982, the special link between the thrifts and the housing sector had already been substantially undermined. In addition to the drying up of mortgage funds during numerous periods of tight money as a result of the viability problems of the industry, thrift institutions had been generally reducing their mortgage loans in favor of more liquid assets,[4] becoming increasingly less important as originators and holders of mortgage loans relative to other lenders,[5] and shifting their traditional mortgage lending role from one of originating and holding long-term mortgages to one of merely originating and then selling them on the secondary mortgage market.[6]

With the Garn–St Germain Act in 1982, many of these shifts became codified and the protected status residential finance had enjoyed since the 1930s was finally ended officially. With the liberalization of thrift asset restrictions, the strong relationship between the thrifts and housing that had been formed and fostered over the years to stimulate housing production—and, in turn, the economy—was largely severed. With the deregulation of deposit rates, especially the termination of the Regulation Q protection, housing will lose a guaranteed cheap pool of money for mortgages. With due-upon-sale clauses and alternative mortgage instruments, housing consumers will lose a certain amount of security in their housing and potentially suffer higher mortgage rates. And in an environment of intense intermediary competition due to deregulation, thrifts will be driven to the highest-yielding investments possible, housing or not.

Housing finance still retains mortgage insurance, deposit insurance, a tax exemption for mortgage specialization by thrifts (but this is less effective, given asset diversification possibilities), and federally-related secondary mortgage market agencies—all established in the 1930s. Nevertheless, a definite shift in housing finance policy and housing policy itself is taking place. The governmental commitment to intervene in credit allocation on behalf of housing is no longer there.

In part, previous governmental support for housing reflected the strong housing lobby in the postwar period, whose interests have usually been tied to those of the thrift industry, and both have historically presented a more or less unified position. But this solidarity broke down with the 1982 Act, as shown by the thrifts' move toward expanded non-housing investment powers. The National Association of Home Builders (NAHB) was, however, in favor of capital assistance for the thrifts even with the expanded investment powers. As a NAHB legislative counsel put it, when interviewed, "We felt that half a thrift was better than no thrift at all." The housing lobby did, for example, push for the 10 percent cap on new asset powers when a higher percentage was requested by the thrift industry. But it seems quite clear that the housing lobby had lost a lot of clout. As Colton observed in 1980:

> Congress has shifted in its outlook concerning housing interests. A few years ago the housing lobby was able to work against financial reform on the grounds that the impact on housing was uncertain. It is no longer clear that they have such power; as one congressional staff person noted, 'People are tired of hearing about more assistance for housing. Housing subsidies have been substantial over the years, and they will continue. But Congress is also interested in finding somebody new who they can assist.' (Colton 1980, 107).

Michael Harloe (1983) adds an important dimension to this shift in government support of housing, particularly housing finance, by pointing to the problem of the housing sector's competition with other economic sectors at particular points in time:

> In several countries concern has been expressed at the effects that a rapidly-growing housing sector has had in diverting possible investment from other 'more productive' sectors of the economy. . . . In Britain and the United States, for example, there has been criticism of the privileged position of the arrangements for housing finance which have often served to make it an attractive alternative to investment in other sectors. . . . Such a conflict only becomes apparent at a time when investment in these other sectors sags and yet investment continues to flow, aided by government support, into housing. . . . So perhaps the continued development of the private market in housing, at the very time when it seemed as if its dominance was generally established, is becoming ever more problematic, and clear divisions may be beginning to emerge between the interests of those active in this sector and those of capitalist enterprise more generally.

Thus, not only is housing no longer seen as an important lever of economic stimulation, but a movement toward reindustrialization is afoot, demanding that capital formation be shifted from housing to other ''sagging'' economic sectors[7] (See also Sternlieb and Hughes 1984).

Whether this departure in government housing finance policy will bring about greater efficiency and benefit the public—particularly housing consumers—is a controversial question. But before examining the implications of the financial restructuring for housing in further detail (for example, questions such as; how much will thrifts diversify? Will the cost of mortgage money go up? Will the supply of mortgage credit be adequate? and so forth), it is important first to look at the implications of the restructuring for the financial industry as a whole. The impact of deregulation on the various sectors of the financial industry has considerable bearing on housing, as well as on the future of the financial system itself. The problems housing will face stem in part from the shifting balance of power within the financial structure, on which housing is so dependent.

Financial Institutions Strengthened

What is particularly striking about the financial restructuring of the 1930s and 1980s is the extent to which, at both times, the government's overriding aim seemed to be to support the interests of the nation's private financial institutions. In the 1930s, the thrifts received mortgage insurance, deposit insurance, a regional banking system, and so forth. In 1982, the failing thrifts were rescued with capital assistance and were granted expanded investment powers. Thrifts and commercial banks were authorized to offer unregulated money market fund accounts. Commercial banks benefited from the regulators' greater flexibility in assisting mergers of troubled institutions. They got Regulation Q rescinded. However, they lost their edge over thrifts in terms of asset powers, although thrifts still are limited to an investment of no more than 10 percent of their assets in the expanded forms.

Lane Kirkland (then secretary-treasurer of the AFL-CIO), in a strong dissent from the Hunt Commission's 1971 report, which, like Garn–St Germain, favored free competition, described the fundamental bias of financial "reform" toward serving the interests of private financial institutions:

> I am persuaded that the basic thrust of these recommendations is designed to promote the interests of private financial institutions without any genuine regard for the most urgent problems and needs of the nation. . . . Unfortunately, the Commission, while giving lip service to the broad public interest, washes its hands of the problems and disclaims any responsibility for seeing to it that a fair share of the financial resources are allocated for social priorities. . . . Besides avoiding the social priority area, it would appear that the net effect of the Commission recommendations would be to channel funds out of the housing market as well as to raise the cost of mortgage money—especially during a tight credit market. . . . These recommendations [wider investment powers] would make the savings and loan associations and mutual savings banks more nearly like commercial banks. It would probably increase their profitability, but it would not generate any additional funds for the mortgage market. In fact, in periods of tight money, the mortgage market would be hard hit (President's Commission on Financial Structure and Regulation 1971, 129–31).

The 1982 restructuring did not simply promote the interests of financial institutions at the expense of social priorities, however. It promoted those interests differentially, thereby affecting (and reflecting) the balance of power among the financial institutions concerned. It also vastly increased concentration in the financial industry as a whole.

Commercial Banks Gain; Financial Industry Becomes Concentrated

Although the restructuring was designed to, and did, temporarily strengthen the thrifts, the large commercial banks have become the major beneficiaries. As a result of their ability to exploit deposit rate deregulation, they have substantially increased their share of the savings market. They are also increasingly able to acquire smaller institutions as a result of new merger procedures, the liberalization of thrift asset powers (paradoxically), as well as the highly competitive deregulatory environment in general.

It is apparent, particularly from the 1982 House hearings, that the stronger push for the legislative changes came from the large commercial banks with their powerful lobby organizations, as they had been increasingly losing deposits to the money market mutual funds on top of more long-standing difficulty in holding on to their corporate deposit and loan business and competing with non-banking "predators"[8] (U.S. Congress 1982, 512; Hendershott and Villani 1977, 126).

The nation's large commercial banks have clear advantages in an environment without deposit rate ceilings. Unlike thrifts, they get most of their deposits from markets where rate ceilings never existed and thus will experience little shifting of passbook balances to the higher-yielding accounts and, hence, no significant added costs. But, more important, large commercial banks invest their funds largely in an international market earning very high rates of return. (For example, at the end of 1981, only 40 percent of Citicorp's $116 billion in assets was invested in the United States [*Savings and Loan News* 1982, 30]). Thus, as all institutions will be able to gain savings on the basis of how much they are willing to pay, limited only by how profitably they can invest their funds, the large commercial banks will come out ahead.

The theory behind deregulation is that free competition will allocate capital most efficiently. Institutions will compete for funds and the market will discipline those institutions that take too much risk. According to this view,

> Depositors will assess the risk of loss associated with the assets of various financial institutions and require large interest premiums from those facing possible losses. If conditions deteriorate, savers may flee, a liquidity crisis could develop and the institution might fold. Of course, to monitor the condition of institutions effectively, savers must have detailed and accurate information concerning the financial institutions bidding for their funds.
>
> [However], in the real world, depositors cannot be expected to measure financial institution risks. For one thing, the saver has very little information concerning financial institution performance. . . . Most depositors in the 1980s depend on federal insurance of accounts to protect them from loss. . . . In the normal course of events, regulator and regulated are in a perpetual tug of war over how aggressive a financial institution's lending practices may be. But the global scope of giant banks' activities makes it impossible for regulators to find out what is really going on. . . . Federal regulators have been unwilling or unable to limit institutions to what would appear to be prudent loans (*Savings and Loan News* 1982, 31).

So there is little impeding the large commercial banks from investing in increasingly risky loans at high returns to pay savings rates higher than other more conservative institutions, especially thrifts, can afford. This obviously has implications for the growth and expansion of large commercial banks at the expense of the thrifts and small commercial banks and tends to lead to greater concentration in the banking industry as a whole. It also has implications for the health and security of the financial system itself as it becomes dominated by institutions that accept an ever-increasing level of risk.

As a result of Garn–St Germain's new procedure and priorities for federal regulators in arranging mergers, large commercial banks can now additionally undertake interstate acquisitions of thrifts, something they have long sought in their drive to capture new markets, diversify, and compete with the substantial branching advantage of federal savings and loans. Moreover, they will now be able to manipulate the regulators in arranging these mergers and, as the Public

Interest Research Group (PIRG) testified at the Congressional hearings, "there is a very serious danger that the agencies will abuse their discretion and in fact take advantage of the current crisis to implement their own version of how the industry should be structured." (U.S. Congress 1982, 535). The agencies, for example, the Federal Home Loan Bank Board, are headed by "deregulation advocates," according to PIRG, who are interested in arranging cross-industry, interstate supervisory mergers.

For example, when Citicorp took over Fidelity Federal Savings and Loan of San Francisco in 1982 and later, Biscayne Federal Savings and Loan and First Federal Savings and Loan of Chicago, making it by far the largest commercial bank holding company and the nation's fourth largest operator of savings and loans, critics felt it had circumvented federal and state laws prohibiting interstate banking. While the FHLBB said that Citicorp's bid on Fidelity was substantially better than the next most favorable one, Jonathan Brown of PIRG disagreed, citing a bid from a California federal savings and loan that would have cost the FHLBB $20 million less than Citicorp's. Overall, he testified,

> Many worry that Citicorp, like a giant vacuum cleaner, will be able to suck massive amounts of money out of California to fund its foreign and other operations. The implications, says [Kenneth] Guenther [Director of Independent Bankers Association of America (IBAA)], could be 'far less funds available for small businesses, small farmers, and small states' and the situation could become even more serious if thrifts gain some commercial lending powers, as a financial reform bill now languishing in Congress [the future Garn–St Germain Act] has proposed. This would allow savings and loans to look more like banks—which would suit Citicorp just fine (U.S. Congress 1982, 545).

The granting of commercial lending powers to thrifts (as well as the deregulation of deposit rates and new merger procedures) thus contributes to the growth and hegemony of the large commercial banks. Rather than create more competition for large commercial banks, the expanded investment powers make thrifts more attractive to take over and thereby engage in interstate banking. Moreover, the thrifts that are taken over undoubtedly will not be run as traditional thrifts. In May 1986, for example, the Federal Reserve Board granted Citicorp's petition to eliminate certain barriers between bank holding companies and their thrift subsidiaries. A broader Fed proposal would permit the sharing of customer information between thrift and bank subsidiaries and certain financial arrangements and transactions; and permit joint marketing and advertising of products and services (Nash 1986).[9]

Through deregulation, then, the large commercial banks gain, but more important, the financial industry as a whole becomes more concentrated. Large commercial banks capture an increased share of the market; commercial banks—but also strong thrifts, non-banks, securities/brokerage houses and non-financial corporations—take over troubled thrifts; institutions merge as curbs against interstate banking are relaxed (Bennett 1985d); and stronger institutions in general acquire weaker ones in the intense competition generated by deregulation (Waite 1981, 30). To be sure, the unprecedented period of rising interest rates beginning in the mid-1960s caused the failure of many thrifts and led to a considerable amount of financial industry concentration. But the new structure established in 1982 brought this development to another, more far-reaching stage. Now it is no longer simply market forces encouraging concentration but explicit government policy as well.

Thus, although much of the industry concentration so far predates the 1982 deregulation, the trend continued into 1985. In 1975 there were 18,791 savings and loans, mutual savings banks and commercial banks, with average assets of $74.0 million, whereas in 1985 there were 18,044 institutions, with average assets of $199.6 million. In 1982 alone, 12 percent of savings and loans were merged. In 1985, 120 banks (commercial and savings banks) closed due to financial difficulty, the largest number by far since 1940; and in the first six months of 1986, 59 banks closed, 12 ahead of the comparable period of 1985.[10]

As the industry becomes more concentrated—particularly with the acquisition of failing thrifts—the nationally- and internationally-oriented institutions that may become dominant, like Citicorp, take the place of the formerly locally-oriented thrifts. Their priorities could very well be overseas investments; or luxury housing, second homes, large-scale real estate development, and land speculation in fast-growing areas; or support a powerful corporation, "such as the Standard Oil Company of California, which recently raised a $14 billion credit in just a few days" (Bennett 1984c). The priority is not likely to be local mortgages or small business loans.

In addition, concentration itself can lead to less local lending and to monopoly pricing on interest rates. For example, the Independent Bankers Association of America provided evidence during the 1982 House hearings that loans to farmers in local communities went down when lending was done by a large bank holding company. Bank concentration also was associated with higher interest rates charged on business loans, consumer loans and mortgages, and lower interest rates paid on time and savings deposits (U.S. Congress 1982, 556–57). Increased earnings pressures from the intensified competition and the initial higher cost of deposits also cause banks to cut costs by reducing their full-service branches. This not only causes inconvenience to the elderly and shopkeepers, but can reduce local mortgage lending, that is, exacerbate redlining. "When the Philadelphia National Bank closed one branch in the West Oaklane section in 1980, mortgage lending in the neighborhood decreased by 62 percent, while the bank's overall mortgage lending increased by 40 percent" (Kerr 1983).

The Role of the State

It seems clear then that the changes enacted in the early 1980s were aimed at more than temporarily bailing out the thrifts and simply creating an efficient and equitable financial structure. The state's role appears as one of facilitating the capital accumulation process (for example, of the big banks), and at the same time making some attempt to legitimize itself in the eyes of the public. Using O'Connor's model:

> Our first premise is that the capitalistic state must try to fulfill two basic and often mutually contradictory functions—accumulation and legitimization. This means that the state must try to maintain or create the conditions in which profitable capital accumulation is possible. However, the state also must try to maintain or create the conditions for social harmony. A capitalist state that openly uses its coercive forces to help one class accumulate capital at the expense of other classes loses its legitimacy and hence undermines the basis of its loyalty and support. . . . The state must involve itself in the accumulation process, but it must either mystify its policies by calling them something that they are not, or it must try to conceal them (e.g., by making them into administrative, not political, issues). (O'Connor 1973, 6).

In financial deregulation and restructuring, the state is clearly intervening to aid the private appropriation of profit, directly in the case of the thrifts—through the capital assistance plan—and less directly in the case of the large commercial banks, which gain a hegemonic position as a result of the legislation's provisions. Deregulation furthermore helps the institutions at the expense of consumers: for example, variable rate mortgages, which shift inflation risk to the borrower, and higher borrowing rates in general to cover the increased cost of funds. Moreover, the costs of this state aid are shifted onto taxpayers, hence "socialized"—for example, capital assistance, costs incurred in regulator-assisted mergers, government insurance of money market fund accounts, tax "losses" declared by failing institutions—although the costs here, by and large, do not take the form of actual budgetary outlays.

The state's "legitimization role," however, is relatively weak in this financial restructuring process. Some attempt has been made to argue that small savers or depositors benefit from deregulation and that, in fact, prior discrimination against them was one of the most important factors behind the deregulation. With deposit rate regulation, small savers in thrift institutions had been precluded from taking advantage of rising interest rates. Now, their savings will earn more competitive yields, and equity will supposedly be returned to the financial system. It turns out, however, that for low-balance depositors, representing as much as four-fifths of the population, the increased interest they get does not offset the higher fees charged by the banks as they pass along the increased costs of consumer deposits and the costs of stepped-up competition. Many banks have imposed monthly or quarterly fees on savings accounts with small balances.[11] The problem of higher fees is becoming so great that the New York state legislature is considering "lifeline banking services," that is, basic banking services for the poor (Bennett 1984a). High-balance depositors, on the other hand, will do quite well.

In this restructuring, then, there seems to be little interest by the state in promoting the appearance of being above class interest. The promotion of financial industry concentration (the capital accumulation of the big banks) and the lack of real equity for the small saver, coupled with the uncertain provisions to channel adequate and low-cost funds into housing (discussed below), starkly reveal the class bias of the restructuring scheme. The state is exhibiting its conservative tendencies typical of the 1980s. It is clear that the political climate is radically different from that of the 1930s, a time of considerable insurgency and leftist political activity.

IMPLICATIONS OF THE RESTRUCTURING FOR HOUSING

The restructuring scheme appears to be an attempt to resolve certain crisis-level contradictions of the finance system in the interest of some private financial institutions. The question remains; what further impact will this have on mortgage lending, the housing sector, and housing consumers? What will the restructured system of housing finance look like?

Thrift Diversification

One of the most important questions concerns the institutional framework of mortgage lending: will the thrifts continue as an important source of mortgage credit or will they diversify?

One would expect them increasingly to channel their savings away from direct, long-term, residential mortgage investment, given expanded investment powers, numerous commercial bank and non-bank thrift takeovers, and intense competitive pressure on returns in a deregulated market, forcing them into higher-yielding and shorter-term non-mortgage uses of funds. The preliminary picture as gleaned from 1983–85 data is surprising, however. In the three years since the 1982 deregulatory changes, the thrifts have sharply increased their mortgage originations in absolute terms and did not reduce their market share of originations until 1985, as commercial banks and mortgage bankers increased theirs (see Table 7.1). This was most likely due to the fact that variable-rate mortgages make mortgage lending more attractive, thrifts still receive preferential tax treatment for investing in mortgages, and the drop in nominal mortgage interest rates during this period produced a large pent-up demand for mortgage loans. But perhaps the comeback in 1983 and 1984 merely represented a short-term reaction to the extremely low 1983 level when interest rates peaked, and the drop in the thrifts' market share in 1985 represented the beginning of their diversifying away from originating mortgage loans. It is too soon to tell.

The thrifts have shifted the type of property on which they originate loans, however—they have become more involved in short-term construction loans and other real estate development and, increasingly, are selling off the mortgage loans they originate on the secondary mortgage market. Multifamily mortgage originations are on the increase for savings institutions, with savings and loans' relative share peaking in 1983 and 1984 (as that of mortgage bankers declined

Table 7.1
Long-Term Mortgage Loan Originations (one-to-four family, multifamily, nonresidential and farm), 1970–1985 ($ million)

Year	Savings + Loans	Mutual Sav. Banks	Comm'l. Banks	Mortgage Bankers	Other*	Total
1970	18,303	4,316	13,568	11,842	11,806	59,835
1971	33,770	7,036	21,982	16,425	14,423	93,636
1972	46,292	9,363	31,173	17,615	17,162	121,605
1973	46,830	10,491	33,568	14,251	22,533	127,673
1974	37,832	7,052	23,775	14,375	23,396	111,429
1975	49,809	7,127	27,062	15,930	20,789	120,717
1976	72,583	9,511	40,648	17,630	21,236	161,608
1977	99,049	11,860	58,596	32,754	26,932	229,191
1978	101,603	12,291	66,863	42,824	33,627	256,208
1979	92,337	11,090	62,101	53,359	38,617	257,504
1980	68,461	6,990	43,429	35,694	40,623	194,197
1981	47,873	5,270	39,151	28,377	37,465	158,136
1982	43,499	5,424	46,528	30,729	27,709	153,889
1983	103,926	14,545	72,263	63,580	35,033	289,348
1984	129,553	18,130	83,353	50,816	32,952	315,204
1985	145,624	21,998	108,897	68,065	42,691	387,275

Relative Shares of Originations:

1970	30.6%	7.2%	22.7%	19.8%	19.7%	100.0%
1971	36.1	7.5	23.5	17.5	15.4	100.0
1972	38.1	7.7	25.6	14.5	14.1	100.0
1973	36.7	8.2	26.3	11.2	17.6	100.0
1974	34.0	6.3	25.8	12.9	21.0	100.0
1975	41.3	5.9	22.4	13.2	17.2	100.0
1976	44.9	5.9	25.2	10.9	13.1	100.0
1977	43.2	5.2	25.6	14.3	11.8	100.0

Table 7.1 (continued)

Year	Savings + Loans	Mutual Sav. Banks	Comm'l. Banks	Mortgage Bankers	Other*	Total
1978	39.5	4.8	26.0	16.6	13.1	100.0
1979	35.9	4.3	24.1	20.7	15.0	100.0
1980	35.3	3.6	21.8	18.4	20.9	100.0
1981	30.3	3.3	24.8	17.9	23.7	100.0
1982	28.3	3.5	30.2	20.0	18.0	100.0
1983	35.9	5.0	25.0	22.0	12.1	100.0
1984	41.1	5.8	26.6	16.1	10.5	100.0
1985	37.6	5.7	28.1	17.6	11.0	100.0

*Includes life insurance companies, public and private pension funds, Real Estate Investment Trusts (REITs), federal credit agencies, mortgage pools, and state and local investment agencies.
Source: HUD, Survey of Mortgage Lending Activity.

and that of commercial banks slightly increased) although, in 1985, as their multifamily originations increased absolutely, their market share fell when mortgage bankers entered that market in an unprecedented way (see Table 7.2). Savings institutions are also catching up to commercial banks' traditional hold on the nonresidential mortgage market, originating more than 30 percent of such mortgages in 1984, up from 20 percent in 1970. Again, in 1985, the thrifts' share dropped slightly as commercial banks and life insurance companies took the lead in participating in the large increase in nonresidential originations spurred by a boom in commercial construction (see Table 7.3). Multi-family and nonresidential loans usually are more profitable than home mortgages (higher return and larger loan size). The shift into nonresidential property also undoubtedly reflects the increased authority to do so from Garn–St Germain.

As for the range of assets in which thrifts invest, again, they did not abandon mortgage lending after 1982 (see Table 7.4). (Net investment in mortgages increased by over 70 percent between 1983 and 1984.) But they seem to be holding the net percentage invested in mortgage loans to that of the early 1980s, about 45 percent, the percentage reached after they had sharply decreased mortgage assets. Additionally, in terms of gross assets, there has been a steady decline in the percentage of assets invested in mortgage loans by savings and loans: from 72.1 percent in 1982 to 60.8 percent in 1985.[12]

Other assets, however, are beginning to gain in importance. The large increase in liabilities in 1982, 1983, and 1984 from the new money market fund accounts

Table 7.2
Multi-family Long-term Mortgage Loan Originations (nonfarm, conventional only), 1970–1985 ($ million)

Year	Savings + Loans	Mutual Sav. Banks	Comm'l. Banks	Mortgage Bankers	Life Ins. Comp.	Federal Credit Agencies	Other*	Total
1970	1,833	1,078	309	787	2,124	217	518	6,866
1971	3,584	1,746	627	963	1,636	141	921	9,618
1972	5,026	1,825	1,211	1,358	1,760	142	857	12,179
1973	3,996	1,895	966	642	2,201	122	1,140	10,962
1974	3,105	1,246	698	502	2,001	201	1,175	8,928
1975	3,525	1,190	755	530	1,134	306	1,061	8,501
1976	5,032	905	1,833	247	754	320	1,226	10,317
1977	6,754	1,327	1,711	997	997	366	1,439	13,591
1978	6,095	937	1,977	731	1,810	461	1,136	13,147
1979	4,783	772	1,896	762	1,552	948	627	11,340
1980	2,992	446	1,207	402	1,426	951	1,192	8,616
1981	2,271	460	1,426	1,330	752	888	964	8,091
1982	3,076	535	1,595	297	438	794	758	7,493
1983	8,401	1,939	3,697	401	1,597	875	392	17,302
1984	13,038	2,042	3,061	311	1,466	1,423	311	21,652
1985	15,389	2,306	4,941	2,387	2,772	1,647	894	30,336

Relative Shares of Originations:

1970	26.7%	15.7%	4.5%	11.5%	30.9%	3.2%	7.5%	100.0%
1971	37.3	18.2	6.5	10.0	17.0	1.5	9.6	100.0
1972	41.3	15.0	9.9	11.2	14.5	1.2	7.0	100.0
1973	36.3	17.3	8.8	5.9	20.1	1.1	10.4	100.0

Table 7.2 (continued)

Year	Savings + Loans	Mutual Sav. Banks	Comm'l. Banks	Mortgage Bankers	Life Ins. Comp.	Federal Credit Agencies	Other*	Total
1974	34.8	14.0	7.8	5.6	22.4	2.3	13.2	100.0
1975	41.5	14.0	8.9	6.2	13.3	3.6	12.5	100.0
1976	48.8	8.8	17.8	2.4	7.3	3.1	11.9	100.0
1977	49.7	9.8	12.6	7.3	7.3	2.7	10.6	100.0
1978	46.4	7.1	15.0	5.6	13.8	3.5	8.6	100.0
1979	42.2	6.8	16.7	6.7	13.7	8.4	5.5	100.0
1980	34.7	5.2	14.0	4.7	16.6	11.0	13.8	100.0
1981	28.1	5.7	17.6	16.4	9.3	11.0	11.9	100.0
1982	41.1	7.1	21.3	4.0	5.8	10.6	10.1	100.0
1983	48.6	11.2	21.4	2.3	9.2	5.1	2.3	100.0
1984	60.2	9.4	14.1	1.4	6.8	6.6	1.4	100.0
1985	50.7	7.6	16.3	7.9	9.1	5.4	2.9	100.0

*Includes public and private pension funds, Real Estate Investment Trusts (REITs), mortgage pools, state and local investment agencies.

Source: HUD, Survey of Mortgage Lending Activity.

went into mortgage loans but also into consumer credit, whose net investment doubled between 1983 and 1984, and miscellaneous assets (which include commercial loans[13] and equity interests in real estate), whose net investment tripled between 1983 and 1984. The thrifts thus seem to be beginning to take advantage of the expanded investment authority granted by Garn–St Germain. In addition, thrifts are shifting resources from long-term mortgage loans toward short-term construction loans, an area formerly dominated by commercial banks, and one which is extremely lucrative but highly risky. Construction loan originations by thrifts have climbed from 18.5 percent of their mortgage originations in 1975 to 22.1 percent in 1985.[14] The thrifts, as well as the rest of the financial industry, also have been pushing highly risky second mortgage loans to tap into homeowners' equity built up over years of rising real estate values. Sometimes these loans are considered second mortgages and other times, personal loans. But the level of second mortgages never has been so high as in 1985–86 (Bennett 1985f).

These high-risk investments were encouraged by the deregulatory environment

Table 7.3
Nonresidential Long-term Mortgage Loan Originations (Nonfarm), 1970–1985 ($ million)

Year	Savings + Loans	Mutual Sav. Banks	Comm'l. Banks	Mortg. Bankers	Life Ins. Co.s	Other*	Total
1970	1,487	1,029	4,269	1,499	2,975	1,232	12,491
1971	3,363	1,611	7,104	1,967	3,744	1,822	19,250
1972	4,129	2,358	10,109	1,534	4,581	1,822	24,532
1973	4,024	2,484	11,484	623	6,338	2,445	27,397
1974	3,588	1,578	9,844	748	6,468	1,754	23,982
1975	4,910	1,325	9,956	1,159	5,832	1,046	24,228
1976	5,402	1,721	11,784	1,277	5,964	923	27,071
1977	5,728	1,705	16,758	5,138	8,634	1,147	39,108
1978	5,301	1,711	17,586	6,528	9,982	1,638	42,746
1979	4,515	1,221	16,472	6,105	10,631	1,427	40,371
1980	4,183	1,013	12,470	4,642	11,059	1,761	35,128
1981	3,470	654	14,516	2,368	9,643	1,834	32,485
1982	5,479	851	17,365	1,774	7,387	1,399	34,265
1983	13,837	1,847	28,563	3,102	13,616	1,483	62,448
1984	20,135	3,393	34,237	2,784	14,696	2,022	77,267
1985	20,482	3,132	49,255	3,011	23,955	2,066	101,901

Relative Shares of Originations:

1970	11.9%	8.2%	34.2%	12.0%	23.8%	9.9%	100.0%
1971	17.5	8.4	36.9	10.2	19.4	7.6	100.0
1972	16.8	9.6	41.2	6.3	18.7	7.4	100.0
1973	14.7	9.1	41.9	2.3	23.1	8.9	100.0

Table 7.3 (continued)

Year	Savings + Loans	Mutual Sav. Banks	Comm'l. Banks	Mortg. Bankers	Life Ins. Co.s	Other*	Total
1974	15.0	6.6	41.0	3.1	27.0	7.3	100.0
1975	20.3	5.5	41.1	4.8	24.1	4.3	100.0
1976	20.0	6.4	43.5	4.7	22.0	3.4	100.0
1977	14.6	4.4	42.9	13.1	22.1	2.9	100.0
1978	12.4	4.0	41.1	15.3	23.4	3.8	100.0
1979	11.2	3.0	40.8	15.1	26.3	3.5	100.0
1980	11.9	2.9	35.5	13.2	31.5	5.0	100.0
1981	10.7	2.0	44.7	7.3	29.7	5.6	100.0
1982	16.0	2.5	50.7	5.2	21.6	4.1	100.0
1983	22.2	3.0	45.7	5.0	21.8	2.4	100.0
1984	26.0	4.4	44.3	3.6	19.0	2.6	100.0
1985	20.1	3.1	48.3	3.0	23.5	2.0	100.0

*Includes public and private pension funds, Real Estate Investment Trusts (REITs), federal credit agencies, mortgage pools, and state and local investment agencies.
Source: HUD, Survey of Mortgage Lending Activity.

in which, initially, interest rates on loans had to be high because newly deregulated interest rates on deposits were high. Moreover, there is some evidence that these investments, particularly in real estate development, may become the final push in the ultimate decline of the thrift industry. In the 1930s, widespread thrift collapse was due to massive home loan default; in the early 1980s, to high interest rates; and now, additionally, to losses on high-risk loans (Bennett 1985c). In the spring of 1985, there were runs on savings and loans in Ohio (triggered by the collapse of Home State Savings and Loan) and Maryland (triggered by the problems of Old Court Savings and Loan) as depositors responded to the reckless investment strategies of some privately-insured institutions. These savings and loans had been aggressively seeking rapid deposit growth, paying very high interest rates, and thus needed high-return investments. Many of these went sour, leaving them with large portfolios of nonearning assets.

The deregulatory and volatile interest rate environment brought a new wave of management to the formerly conservatively managed thrifts: aggressive, risk-taking businessmen who purchase thrifts to finance their own real estate devel-

Table 7.4
Savings Institutions'* Net Investment in Selected Assets and Net Increase in Liabilities, 1975–1984 ($ billion)

Year	Total Mtgs.	Home Mtgs.	Multi-Family Mtgs.	Comm'l Mtgs.	U.S. Gov't Securities	Consumer Credit	Misc. Assets+	Net Increase in Liabilities
				($ billions)				
1975	30.2	22.3	2.6	5.3	9.7	4.8	2.7	56.0
1976	47.6	38.8	3.3	5.6	10.2	6.9	3.3	68.9
1977	61.9	52.0	4.9	4.9	7.0	8.4	2.2	80.3
1978	57.9	49.9	4.4	3.5	5.4	7.8	5.9	76.0
1979	48.2	42.7	2.1	3.4	2.1	6.0	7.0	62.0
1980	29.4	27.7	.1	1.6	21.4	1.7	5.0	68.5
1981	18.2	16.8	-.5	2.0	5.2	2.7	9.4	49.4
1982	-25.7	-31.8	1.3	4.7	48.0	6.4	30.0	77.5
1983	49.6	29.8	4.6	15.1	64.4	15.4	10.7	155.3
1984	84.9	58.4	7.8	18.6	35.8	30.9	32.3	185.7
				Percentage of Net Acquisition of Financial Assets: (percentages)				
1975	52.0	38.4	4.5	9.1	16.7	8.3	4.6	
1976	66.0	53.8	4.6	7.8	14.1	9.6	4.6	
1977	72.9	61.2	5.8	5.8	8.2	9.9	2.6	
1978	61.2	61.4	5.4	4.3	6.6	9.6	7.3	
1979	72.5	64.2	3.2	5.1	3.2	9.0	10.5	
1980	42.5	40.0	0.1	2.3	30.9	2.5	7.2	
1981	41.6	38.4	-1.1	4.6	11.9	6.2	21.5	
1982	-35.2	-43.6	1.8	6.4	65.8	8.9	41.1	
1983	31.8	19.1	3.0	9.7	41.3	9.9	6.9	
1984	45.9	31.6	4.2	10.1	19.4	16.7	17.5	

Table 7.4 (continued)

Year	Total Mtgs.	Home Mtgs.	Multi-Family Mtgs.	Comm'l Mtgs.	U.S. Gov't Securities	Consumer Credit	Misc. Assets+	Net Increase in Liabilities
				Percentage Change				
1975	-	-	-	-	-	-	-	-
1976	+57.6	+74.0	+26.9	+5.2	+43.8	+22.2	+23.0	
1977	+30.0	+34.0	+48.5	-12.5	-31.4	+32.7	-33.3	+16.5
1978	-6.5	-4.0	-10.2	-28.6	-22.9	-7.1	+168.2	-5.4
1979	-16.8	-14.4	-52.3	-2.9	-61.1	-23.1	+18.6	-18.4
1980	-39.0	-35.1	-95.2	-52.9	+919.0	-71.7	-28.6	+10.5
1981	-38.1	-39.4	+4.0	+25.0	-75.7	-58.8	+88.0	-27.9
1982	-241.2	-289.3	+3.6	+135.0	+823.1	+140.7	+219.1	+56.9
1983	+293.0	+193.7	+253.8	221.3	+34.2	+136.9	-64.3	+100.4
1984	+71.2	+96.0	+69.6	+ 23.8	-44.4	+100.6	+201.9	+19.6

*Includes savings and loans, mutual savings banks and credit unions. Figures count mortgage-backed securities as nonmortgage assets; thus mortgage investment is understated.

+Miscellaneous assets include commercial loans, service corporations and subsidiaries, real estate investments (e.g., land held for development), goodwill and other intangible assets.

Source: Board of Governors of the Federal Reserve System, Flow of Funds Accounts, Seasonally Adjusted and Unadjusted, Z1.

opment activities (Klott 1985; Bennett 1984d). The rise and fall of the Financial Corporation of America, owner of the nation's largest thrift, American Savings and Loan in California, provides another example of this trend of rapidly expanding thrifts getting into trouble from problem loans and unwise interest rate speculation (Bleakley 1984; Hayes 1982, 1984a, 1984b).

Hence, the trend of thrift failure and commercial bank takeover continues. Both the Chase Manhattan Bank and the Chemical Bank of New York, for example, have taken over troubled thrifts in Ohio and Chase and Citicorp have expressed interest in Maryland's thrifts (Bennett 1985c). And William M. Isaac, chairman of the Federal Deposit Insurance Corporation, was reported as predicting that the stronger thrifts will survive as commercial banks, and that the others will be absorbed by commercial banks, given these recent losses (Bennett 1985c). Thus, despite the Garn–St Germain bail out, the thrift industry may be unable to survive in the long run; indeed, the very measures taken to shore up the industry (such as diversification) appear to be promoting its decline. But even if the thrifts survive, their asset diversification and shifting priorities and management styles indicate that the traditional, specialized, locally-oriented home mortgage lender is a thing of the past.

New Sources of Mortgage Credit

The mortgage market is being restructured to include greater reliance on the secondary mortgage market. It is becoming common practice, as the secondary markets expand, for lenders to originate and then sell, but continue to service, mortgages rather than to hold them. Indeed, the percentage of loans originated by the five key lender groups that are then sold has increased dramatically since 1977, from just over one out of four loans to over one out of two in 1985; and savings and loans now have the largest ratio of sales to originations, next to mortgage bankers—nearly 75 percent for all property types (see Table 7.5). Further, since 1975 the percentage of home mortgage debt held by mortgage pools, which deal with mortgage-backed securities,[15] has increased dramatically—from just over 5 percent to over 20 percent (see Table 7.6).[16] In addition to the thrifts' increased mortgage banking role, mortgage bankers themselves have been steadily increasing their share of mortgage originations since 1970—from originating under 2 percent of 1-4 family conventional loans to over 15 percent in 1984.[17]

The loss of the specialized housing finance institutions and the reliance on the secondary mortgage market may very well lead to an inflexibility in mortgage lending and an abandonment of those properties that do not conform to a standard, secure type. Examples of such nonconforming properties include older, inner-city, multi-family properties with balloon mortgages in need of refinancing, limited-equity cooperative housing, and so forth. Mortgages, especially those pooled for the pass-through securities market, will increasingly become uniform, standardized, interchangeable investment instruments, an alternative to government bonds or triple A-rated corporate bonds, and thus further removed from individual buildings or homes, which are considered too risky to invest in per se. Older, inner-city properties, traditionally served by the thrifts, thus may not find replacement institutions, given the exigencies of the secondary mortgage market. In essence, the secondary mortgage market (and its agencies) increasingly will be the ones calling the shots in the overall mortgage market. The repercussions of this, as well as of the thrifts' shifting role, can be serious. As Jonathan Brown of PIRG stated:

> There is still a broad public benefit in maintaining a system of savings institutions that are mortgage specialists. Depository institutions that specialize in mortgage lending are needed to assure the broadest possible availability of mortgage credit and accountability to local community housing needs. Savings institutions that specialize in mortgage lending are in a position to adopt more flexible mortgage lending criteria than capital market investors. They also have a clearly defined mandate to serve local community housing needs, which commercial banks do not do (U.S. Congress 1982, 543).

Table 7.5
Long-term Loan Sales by Primary Lenders (all property types: one-to-four family, multi-family, nonresidential, nonfarm), 1970–1985 ($ million)

Year	Savings + Loans	Mutual Sav. Banks	Comm'l. Banks	Mortg Bankers	Life Ins. Co.	Total Sales (5 groups)	Total Origina- (5 groups)
1970	996	283	1,917	12,505	115	15,816	52,318
1971	2,013	270	2,247	15,767	64	20,361	83,325
1972	3,579	341	2,726	17,784	19	24,449	109,024
1973	3,416	266	2,719	17,678	17	24,096	111,728
1974	3,527	376	2,430	16,145	33	22,511	94,785
1975	5,234	269	3,385	16,324	28	25,240	105,154
1976	8,641	548	4,972	19,144	0	33,134	144,905
1977	14,124	284	6,836	33,457	84	54,786	208,876
1978	15,775	352	7,603	42,602	52	66,384	232,909
1979	18,667	577	7,688	51,401	243	78,576	230,867
1980	16,140	782	7,477	36,986	195	61,581	165,777
1981	12,832	484	5,458	30,492	404	49,670	130,006
1982	54,446	2,218	8,298	30,893	345	96,200	132,167
1983	54,194	3,197	14,396	70,282	1,034	143,103	270,455
1984	64,097	3,374	13,610	56,571	2,565	140,217	300,227
1985	108,197	6,001	19,173	76,723	4,248	214,342	373,568

Loan Sales as a Percentage of Originations by Lender Groups

1970	5.5	6.6	15.5	105.6	2.1	30.2
1971	6.0	3.8	11.0	96.1	1.1	24.4
1972	7.8	3.7	9.3	101.3	0.3	22.4
1973	7.3	2.5	8.7	124.4	0.2	21.6
1974	9.3	5.3	9.1	112.4	0.4	23.7
1975	10.5	3.8	13.4	102.5	0.4	24.0

Table 7.5 (continued)

Year	Savings + Loans	Mutual Sav. Banks	Comm'l. Banks	Mortg Bankers	Life Ins. Co.	Total Sales (5 groups)	Total Origina- (5 groups)
1976	11.9	5.8	12.5	108.6	0.1	22.9	
1977	14.3	2.4	12.4	102.1	0.8	26.2	
1978	15.5	2.9	11.9	99.5	0.4	28.5	
1979	20.2	5.2	12.8	96.3	1.7	34.0	
1980	23.6	11.2	18.5	103.6	1.4	37.1	
1981	26.9	9.2	14.5	107.5	3.7	38.2	
1982	125.4	41.0	18.8	100.5	4.1	72.8	
1983	52.2	22.0	19.9	110.5	6.5	52.9	
1984	49.5	18.6	16.7	111.3	15.1	46.7	
1985	74.3	27.3	17.6	112.7	14.7	57.4	

Source: HUD, Survey of Mortgage Lending Activity.

The Adequacy of the Supply of Mortgage Credit

It is not altogether clear whether the volume of mortgage lending, as a result of the deregulation and restructuring, will be adequate to meet future needs and demands. The President's Commission on Housing believes it will "as long as funds could flow freely through financial markets to meet the underlying demands for capital in the economy" (President's Commission on Housing 1982, 120). Similarly, Colton (1983) predicts that the level of investment in mortgages will be adequate, as do Vartanian (1983b) and Tuccillo and Goodman (1983). Seiders (1983) takes the unusual view that mortgage pass-through securities are unlikely to expand greatly in the future, but he believes mortgage credit gaps necessitating such expansion are also unlikely to develop. In addition, the booming secondary mortgage market will allow local thrifts and banks to extend mortgage credit even when their cost of deposits exceeds mortgage interest rates, because they can immediately sell the mortgages.

Others are much more skeptical about the ability of the restructured system to meet mortgage credit needs. For example, Grebler (1983, 169) sees expansion of mortgage credit through the securities market occurring in intense competition with huge credit needs created by the federal budget deficit and nonfinancial corporations (the latter, as they increasingly engage in leveraged buy-outs, takeovers, mergers, and so forth). And, on the demand side, so much of the mortgage demand of the 1970s and 1980s has been and will be to refinance existing

Table 7.6
Percentage of Home Mortgage Debt Outstanding by Type of Lender, 1975–1984

Year	Savings Institu-tions*	Comm'l. Banks	Federal + Related Agencies	Mortg Pools +	Hsehlds	Pension Funds + +	Other**
	(percentages)						
1975	55.3	15.7	8.3	5.2	8.9	.7	5.9
1976	55.9	15.6	7.3	6.7	8.8	.6	5.1
1977	55.8	16.2	6.7	8.2	8.3	.5	4.2
1978	54.2	17.0	7.1	8.6	8.6	.5	3.9
1979	51.6	17.0	7.5	10.0	9.2	.5	4.2
1980	49.4	16.4	7.7	10.9	10.4	.5	4.5
1981	47.2	16.1	8.0	11.8	11.6	.5	4.9
1982	41.7	15.7	8.7	15.7	12.7	.5	4.9
1983	40.5	15.0	8.8	19.7	10.7	.5	4.8
1984	40.8	14.7	8.8	21.0	9.3	.4	5.0

*Savings institutions include savings and loans, mutual savings banks and credit unions.

+Mortgages in pools backing pass-through securities issued and/or guaranteed by the Government National Mortgage Association, Federal Home Loan Mortgage Corporation, or Federal National Mortgage Association.

+ +Includes private and public.

**Includes state and local governments, real estate investment trusts, finance companies and life insurance companies.

Source: Board of Governors of the Federal Reserve System, Flow of Funds Accounts, Assets and Liabilities Outstanding.

residential debt.The demand for new housing units—for example, from the estimated 16 million new households to be formed in the 1980s, 25 percent more than were formed in the previous decade (Van Bogan 1982, 113; Treadway 1982, 102–104)—can only create a greater need for lending activity than in the recent past (Lindsay 1980).

There is also the question of uneven distribution of mortgage funds. As the number of mortgage-specialized thrifts declines, as industry mergers shift lending priorities away from local areas, and as the secondary mortgage market calls the shots, we can expect certain areas, certain types of real estate and certain borrowers to be underserved.

The Cost of Mortgage Credit

Some analysts believe deregulation will create greater competition among financial institutions for consumer business, which will in itself benefit mortgage borrowers (Kaplan 1983; Vartanian 1983b). More convincing, however, is the prediction that the cost of mortgage credit will remain high, although rates may become more uniform throughout the country. Even if the supply of mortgage money vastly increases, this would not lower mortgage rates, as they are not determined by the supply and demand for mortgage credit but by the supply and demand for credit in the capital markets in general.[18] Thus, while mortgage rates do fluctuate up and down with the business cycle, the overall trend has been toward maintenance of the high cost of mortgage credit. For example, as Table 7.7 shows, real mortgage rates began to rise dramatically in 1980 (when interest rate deregulation was stepped up) and have remained high despite a sharp decline in nominal mortgage rates from the early 1980s, and especially between 1984 and 1985. In addition, mortgage rates have been higher than other market rates, although in recent years the spread has narrowed. Mortgage rates also tend to respond less quickly than deposit rates; for example, between 1984 and 1985 mortgage rates declined 6.7 percent, yet banks' cost of funds (deposit rates) declined 8.3 percent (see Table 7.8). When deposit rates fluctuate it means greater competition for deposits among banks and thrifts and less predictable spreads. This puts an upward pressure on loan rates and pushes institutions into higher-risk lending. Financial industry concentration from deregulation, as indicated above, also tends to lead to monopoly pricing on loan rates. Thus, what commercial banks and thrifts have indeed lost with deposit rate deregulation is a guaranteed cheap pool of funds to draw upon for low-cost mortgages. Hence, not surprisingly, thrifts' earnings spread (mortgage portfolio yields minus cost of funds) since deregulation is being restored and net income returns are coming back (see Table 7.8).

CONCLUSIONS

The altered institutional framework of housing finance, the competition and concentration within the financial industry and consequent domination by the large commercial banks, the questionable adequacy of the supply of mortgage credit, the higher cost of mortgage credit, and the changed mortgage lending process all will lead to adverse effects on housing and housing consumers. Buying a home or financing a rental property will most likely be more expensive, less secure, increasingly influenced by locational factors, and more subject to the constraints of the secondary mortgage market.

Moreover, the urbanization process in the U.S. should be affected as well. Neighborhood change processes (for example, abandonment and gentrification) underway in older inner cities will be exacerbated. Financial institutions have traditionally played a crucial mediating role in the urbanization process, mobilizing the surplus which investment in urban infrastructure (housing, transport facilities, community facilities) represents for national economic growth. They have channeled mortgage investment away from one area and into another; specifically, in the postwar period, away from inner cities and toward the suburban periphery. This was part of the policy of stimulating effective demand

Table 7.7
Mortgage Rates and Bond Yields, 1975–1985

Year	Effective Mortgage Interest Rate on Single Family Conventional Homes, All Loans, All Lenders*		U.S. Government Long-Term Bond Yields			Corporate Aaa Seasoned Bond Yields			
	Nominal	Real	Nominal	Real	Spread**	Nominal	Real	Spread***	GNP Deflator****
1975	9.13	-.67	6.98	-2.82	-3.49	8.83	-0.97	-1.64	9.8
1976	9.07	2.97	6.78	0.68	2.29	8.43	2.33	0.64	6.1
1977	9.02	2.32	7.06	0.36	1.96	8.02	1.32	1.00	6.7
1978	9.59	2.29	7.89	0.59	1.70	8.73	1.43	0.86	7.3
1979	10.85	1.95	8.74	-0.16	2.11	9.63	0.73	1.22	8.9
1980	12.84	3.84	10.81	1.81	2.03	11.94	2.94	0.90	9.0
1981	14.91	5.21	12.87	3.17	2.04	14.17	4.47	0.75	9.7
1982	15.31	8.91	12.23	5.83	3.08	13.79	7.39	1.52	6.4
1983	12.73	8.93	10.84	7.04	1.89	12.04	8.24	0.69	3.8
1984	12.48	8.38	11.99	7.89	0.49	12.71	8.61	-0.23	4.1
1985	11.64	8.34	10.75	7.45	0.89	11.37	8.07	0.25	3.3

*Weighted annual average on new homes, existing homes and combined construction purchase; savings and loans, commercial banks, mutual savings banks and mortgage companies; includes fees, commissions and charges.
**Spread = mortgage rate - U.S. government bond yield.
***Spread = mortgage rate - corporate bond yield.
****U.S. Bureau of Economic Analysis series based on 1982 = 100. Source: Statistical Abstract Office, June 1986.

Source: FHLBB; U.S. Bureau of the Census, *Statistical Abstract 1986*, Table Nos. 783 and 856, updated by Statistical Abstract Office, June 1986.

Table 7.8
Mortgage Portfolio Yields, Cost of Funds, and Net After-tax Income of FSLIC-Insured Institutions, 1975–1985

Year	Mortgage Portfolio Yields*	Cost of Funds+	Spread (Mtge. Yield-Cost of Funds)	Net After-Tax Income to Average Assets
1975	7.76	6.32	1.44	.47
1976	8.00	6.38	1.62	.63
1977	8.26	6.44	1.82	.77
1978	8.50	6.67	1.83	.82
1979	8.86	7.47	1.39	.67
1980	9.34	8.94	0.40	.13
1981	9.91	10.92	-1.01	-.73
1982	10.68	11.38	-0.70	-.65
1983	11.17	9.83	1.34	.27
1984	11.65	10.03	1.62	.20
1985	11.52	9.20	2.32	.39

*Interest and discounts earned on mortgages as a percent of mortgage balances.
+Weighted for all types of deposits; includes cost of borrowed money.
Source: FHLBB; U.S. Bureau of the Census, *Statistical Abstract 1986*, Table No. 837, updated by FHLBB.

begun in the 1930s to deal with the effects of under-consumption crises (Harvey 1975). The increasingly competitive drive for funds to flow where the rate of return is highest means that mortgage disinvestment in existing inner-city housing for in-place residents will only continue at a more rapid pace (Meyerson 1986).

Whether funds will be channeled into suburban development as in the past is a different matter. It seems that, as compared with the postwar period, we are now in an era in which housing production, as discussed above, particularly suburban housing production, is not being used to resolve under-consumption crises. According to many analysts, the U.S. is moving away from a pattern of major metropolitan centers ringed by appended suburban communities to the growth of non-metropolitan small and medium-sized cities and heretofore rural areas beyond the suburban ring. The shift to a more national mortgage market, for example, allowing greater geographic flexibility in the flow of funds, is consistent with these urbanization trends. The changes taking place in the financial structure thus have even greater significance than indicated previously. The magnitude of the effects of displacement and population shifts from these changes as certain areas lose the ability to borrow money, for example, can only be speculated upon at this point.

But most notably, deregulation and financial restructuring will exacerbate the housing affordability problem. Just as housing need is expanding, the housing finance system is moving in a higher-priced direction, perhaps preventing this need from being translated into effective demand. And "the basic reality," as George Sternlieb states, "is that the housing buying power of Americans has gone down. . . . The average worker's pay check minus the buying power lost to inflation has fallen 9.7 percent since its peak in 1973, meaning that most potential home buyers have less to spend" (Wald 1983).

In the 1960s the tremendous growth of residential mortgage debt with the low down payment, long-term mortgage instrument contributed to higher interest rates, which aggravated affordability problems. The huge national debt increased competition for capital and hence, interest rates. Rising interest rates led to reduced rates of principal repayment, which added to the need for new funds to finance additional mortgages, increasing competition for funds even further and adding more to interest rates in a self-reinforcing cycle.

In the 1980s deregulation of the financial system (for example, deregulation of deposit rates, variable-rate mortgages, the expanded secondary mortgage market, and so forth) has contributed to higher real mortgage interest rates over the long run, further aggravating affordability problems.[19] Ironically, both the original post-1930s mortgage instrument and the 1980s deregulation were supposed to ease the conflict between housing costs and incomes—that is, the affordability problem—but by increasing interest rates, failed to do so.

As a result, what we will increasingly see is the use of variable-rate mortgage instruments as well as other adjustments to cope with the affordability problem. But by shifting the interest rate risk onto borrowers, variable-rate mortgages represent a severe erosion of the middle-class standard of living. Middle-class families have traditionally looked to the long-term, fixed-rate mortgage for the financial security they sought, seeing it as a shield against inflation relative to other conventional investments. Additionally, the many middle- and low-income families who get priced out of the market altogether will have to scale down their housing expectations by doubling-up, moving in with parents, or remaining as tenants. And everyone's "shelter poverty"—the inability to afford other basic necessities such as food and clothing after paying shelter costs—will increase (Stone 1980).[20] In fact, the tremendous surge in second mortgage lending after deregulation was due as much to the need to maintain spending despite declining purchasing power as to financial institutions' need to find new investment outlets. It is likely these "solutions" to the affordability problem will work in only limited ways and hence may result in some degree of political unrest.

Further, deregulation and restructuring will cause the financial system to become shakier. First, housing affordability problems aggravate people's ability to make their mortgage payments, which can lead to widespread mortgage default, especially with second mortgage lending (Stone 1980).[21] And with deregulation—given the blurring of lines between thrifts, banks, and nonbanks and the merging of residential finance with the general financial structure—not simply savings institutions but the whole financial structure becomes vulnerable to this default.

Second, the fierce competition generated by deregulation gives rise to risky, high-yield investment strategies, as discussed above. Andrew Brimmer, a former governor of the Federal Reserve Board, has said, "The financial system is far more unstable than it was a decade ago" (Bennett 1985b). The risk factor is further exacerbated by the extension of government insurance. If banks are assured that monies raised through their money market fund accounts are guaranteed by the federal government, they have even less incentive to be prudent when investing. If the investments go bad, the government promises to pay back depositors. Unfortunately, however, FDIC and FSLIC resources are finite and could not possibly accommodate widespread failures. Thus, government insurance provides the opportunity for more and more lucrative investment outlets and, at the same time, strains the system.

Moreover, as the financial system becomes more concentrated and banks expand into other fields, many kinds of institutions—thrifts, commercial banks, insurance companies, mortgage companies, corporations, securities/brokerage houses—will be undertaking a wide (and overlapping) variety of activities. Thus, the difficulties that inevitably arise, especially given higher-risk investment strategies, will be increasingly impossible to contain and treat. As Securities and Exchange Commissioner Bevis Longstreth said, "The difficulties of a single financial institution threaten to trigger a chain reaction" (Heineman 1983).[22]

The contribution of the 1980s deregulation and financial restructuring to both the housing availability and affordability problem on the one hand, and the vulnerability of the entire financial structure on the other, looms large indeed. Like earlier mechanisms to shore up the financial system, deregulation seems thus far to have failed. Specific institutions are strengthened, monopoly capital is further consolidated, but the entire system is placed at greater risk. Thus, monopoly capitalism again reveals its penchant for private, short-term gain at the expense of the wider good.

ACKNOWLEDGMENTS

The author wishes to thank Rachel Bratt, Jill Hamberg, Chester Hartman, and Michael Stone for their helpful comments on an earlier draft of this chapter.

NOTES

1. Unlike other financial institutions, thrifts receive tax benefits that encourage them to invest heavily in mortgages. Section 593 of the Internal Revenue Code allows thrifts a special 40 percent bad debt reserve deduction if a minimum percentage (82 percent for savings and loans and 72 percent for mutual savings banks) of their assets is invested in mortgages or other qualifying assets. This provision can present a considerable barrier to asset diversification at thrifts. Nonqualifying investments would have to provide con-

siderably higher net tax yields than those available in qualifying assets to offset the additional taxes from diversifying.

2. Garn–St Germain represented the culmination to date of the deregulation process. It was preceded by earlier regulatory changes such as: (1) introduction of money market and other deposit certificates in 1978; (2) introduction of alternative variable-rate mortgage instruments, offered widely by state initiation by 1976 (Colton 1980, 105) and authorized for federally chartered savings and loan associations in 1979; and (3) expansion of the mortgage-backed securities market by federally-related secondary mortgage market agencies; and also by the 1980 Depository Institutions Deregulation and Monetary Control Act.

This Act phased out over six years the interest ceilings on passbook accounts (a period later shortened by Garn–St Germain); authorized interest on checking accounts (NOW accounts); permanently overrode state-imposed usury ceilings on mortgage rates (unless states acted within three years to reenact them); required, over an eight-year phase-in period, all depository institutions to post reserves at the Federal Reserve Bank; allowed federal savings and loan associations to expand their consumer loan and credit card operations, make second mortgages and originate residential mortgage loans without geographic restrictions; and permitted federal mutual savings banks to invest 5 percent of their assets in commercial, corporate, and business loans made within their state or a 75-mile radius of their home office. As a result of the Act, a Depository Institutions Deregulation Committee was set up to oversee and plan for the eventual deregulation of deposit rates.

3. In addition, since passage of this federal legislation, some states have been enacting banking laws more permissive than the federal law. In June 1984, New York State enacted an omnibus banking law which moves deregulation to new heights. And given New York's prominence as a financial center, its move undoubtedly will be widely copied. The New York State law, for example, allows savings banks to use an unlimited percentage of their assets for commercial loans and to invest in stocks and bonds without restriction. All state-chartered banks, including commercial banks, will be allowed to invest in real estate development and ownership and engage directly in leasing activities, without the need of separate subsidiaries; and restrictions will be removed on where banks can invest their assets (no longer confining them to a 75-mile radius of their headquarters). What is particularly noteworthy in terms of thrift support of local mortgage markets is that the current 20 percent limit will be removed on the portion of savings bank assets that can be invested in conventional mortgages outside of New York State. With this more permissive state legislation, then, New York is better able to stem the conversion of state-chartered banks to federal charter, which had been occurring as a result of the Garn–St Germain Act.

4. For example, net investment in home mortgages relative to other assets fell from almost 64 percent of net assets in 1979 to –44 percent in 1982 while net investment in U.S. government securities grew from 3 percent in 1979 to 66 percent in 1982 (see Table 7.4).

5. The percentage of outstanding home mortgage debt held by savings institutions peaked in 1976 at 56 percent and fell to 42 percent by 1982 as mortgage pools and households increased their shares. And savings institutions' share of home mortgage originations fell from approximately 60 percent in 1976 to 40 percent in 1982 (see Table 7.6 and U.S. Department of Housing and Urban Development 1970 through 1985).

6. Loan sales as a percentage of originations increased from 13 percent in 1976 to

146 percent in 1982 for savings and loans (U.S. Department of Housing and Urban Development 1970 through 1985).

7. Many see this as a positive effect of deregulation of the housing finance system. See, for example, P.H. Hendershott and S. C. Hu (1981) "Inflation and Extraordinary Returns on Owner-Occupied Housing: Some Implications for Capital Allocation and Productivity Growth." *Journal of Macroeconomics* (referred to in Grebler 1983).

8. An American Bankers Association report, dated September 9, 1981, on "Activities in the Financial Institution Marketplace 1981" lists "non-banks offering near bank or partial bank services: (1) American Express and Provident to offer cash management service with Hutton, Shearson and Bache; Provident is advisor to certain Shearson money market funds; (2) E.F. Hutton acquired International Paper Credit Corporation to do commercial financing and correspondent banking; (3) Gulf + Western owns Associates First Capital Corporation, which owns Fidelity National Bank of Concord, which spun off commercial loan portfolio; (4) Sears (savings and loan holding company) to establish money market mutual fund; (5) three major savings and loans—Citizens of California, West Side of New York, and Washington of Florida—merged; the resulting savings and loan, Citizens Saving and Loan, owned by holding company, United Financial Corporation, owned by National Steel Corporation" (U.S. Congress 1982, 487. See also Bennett 1983b.)

9. This move reflected the FHLBB's desire to encourage thrift acquisition, in general, by bank holding companies to save the FSLIC insurance fund, which has been saddled with propping up numerous insolvent thrifts. Similarly, during 1986, bank regulators were encouraging out-of-state acquisition of commercial banks, as well as thrifts, by bank holding companies in the wake of bank failures in the oil and gas regions due to the crisis in energy loans. Merging is seen as the antidote to the industry's problems.

On the other hand, previously, in June 1985, the large commercial banks, like Citicorp, suffered a setback in their aggressive interstate banking drive. The U.S. Supreme Court ruled on June 10, that regional banking pacts—state laws allowing banks within regions to merge while keeping out others from non-neighboring states—were constitutional. Regional banks quickly took advantage of this to expand through interstate merger. Hence the battle among the different sectors of the financial industry continues in Congress (Bennett 1985e).

10. Data gathered from FDIC annual reports and FHLBB communications office.

11. For example, the Manufacturers Hanover Trust Company recently raised consumer fees dramatically. Now, unless a customer keeps a substantial balance in accounts at the bank, the customer must pay a monthly fee of $8 for a checking account, plus 50 cents a check. The California-based First Nationwide Savings, which has offices in New York and Florida, recently imposed an $8 annual fee on its Individual Retirement Accounts, to be waived only if substantial balances are kept (Bennett 1984c; Bennett 1984b).

12. Data from U.S. Bureau of the Census, 1986, Table No. 837, updated by FHLBB.

13. The Dime Savings Bank, for example, has aggressively begun pursuing small and medium-sized businesses as loan customers and is doing quite well (*New York Times* 1983). Other thrifts are forming syndicates of like institutions to offer long-term loan packages to industrial borrowers (Noble 1983). The Golddome Bank for Savings in New York is now using its explosion in deposits from the new money market accounts to lease computer equipment and finance company buy-outs by management and employees (Williams 1983).

14. The mortgage origination data included in the following pages come from the U.S.

Department of Housing and Urban Development Survey of Mortgage Lending Activity 1970 through 1985.

15. A relatively recent development in governmental support of housing finance concerns the issuance and guarantee of pass-through mortgage-backed securities by the Government National Mortgage Association (Ginnie Mae), the Federal Home Loan Mortgage Corporation (Freddie Mac), and, more recently, by the Federal National Mortgage Association (Fannie Mae). These pass-through securities are designed to aggregate individual mortgages and convert them into investments that can be marketed on the private capital market to attract more funds into the intermediation market.

Usually a mortgage banking company issues a liquid, fully transferable investment instrument called a mortgage-backed security, which is backed by a homogeneous pool of conventional or FHA/VA mortgages. Ginnie Mae (dealing mainly with FHA/VA mortgages) guarantees the interest and principal on the security, which passes through from the homeowner to the investor. (Freddie Mac's securities are backed by conventional mortgages.) These mortgage-backed securities have become an important piece of the post-thrift crisis restructuring.

16. It has recently come to light, however, that the packaging of these pooled mortgages has often involved massive fraud, with many thrift institutions, key purchasers of these securities, becoming buyers of essentially nonexistent mortgages (Bennett 1985a). Here the losses have not stemmed from thrift investment in poor quality loans but rather from the activities of fraudulent mortgage poolers. Still, one cannot help but conclude that the thrifts' victimization here is related to their keen profit orientation in a deregulated environment.

17. It is interesting to note that there is little evidence so far to support the prediction that commercial banks, pension funds, and state and local government agencies will become more involved in the mortgage market as the thrifts diversify. Commercial banks may become more involved, however, as (1) they have been interested in decreasing reliance on their corporate loan and overseas loan markets and in expanding consumer credit; (2) they see mortgage loans as a way to cultivate relationships with their best account customers to tap into savings and checking accounts, certificates of deposit, trusts, bank cards, and personal loans; and (3) recent regulatory and legislative changes make mortgage lending more attractive (Lacy 1982, 118).

18. Hendershott and Villani (1980), however, state rather contradictorily that an expansion of the mortgage supply, especially through federal credit agencies, has caused the mortgage rate to decline relative to other market rates, although the impact of this growth was offset in the late 1970s by an explosion in demand for mortgage credit.

19. See Sweezy and Magdoff (1984) for an excellent discussion of the role of the expansion of the nation's financial sector during the 1960s and of deregulation in the early 1980s in creating out-of-control interest rates.

20. Interestingly, in response to the affordability problem, the Mortgage Guarantee Insurance Corporation, in 1980, lifted its permissible level for basic housing debt to 33 percent of income instead of the general 25 percent rule of thumb because median family income had risen only about half as quickly as housing costs. Around the same time, Freddie Mac also decided to rely less on the 25 percent of income criterion. These moves demonstrated the "recognition that people have to devote more of their income to shelter" (Brooks 1980).

21. The mortgage delinquency rate has grown steadily, from 4.97 percent in 1980 to 5.66 percent in 1984 for 1–4 family home loans. (U.S. Bureau of the Census 1986, Table No. 843.)

22. By mid-1986, contradictory trends began to emerge. The large commercial banks began lobbying strongly for product deregulation (permission to enter other businesses, such as insurance), now that they had price deregulation and some degree of geographic deregulation. At the same time, a re-regulation movement is forming, aimed at containing risk; different standards for capital requirements and insurance, based on differential assessments of risk, are being proposed.

REFERENCES

Baer, Herbert. 1983. "Thrift Dominance and Specialization in Housing Finance: The Role of Taxation." *Housing Finance Review* 2:4

Bennett, Robert A. 1985a. "Nationwide Pattern Being Found in Huge Losses on Bad Mortgages." *New York Times*, February 25.

———. 1985b. "World Markets Reacting to Ills of U.S. Banks." *New York Times*, March 20.

———. 1985c. "Dire Thrift Outlook." *New York Times*, May 16.

———. 1985d. "Interstate Banking's Difficult Birth." *New York Times,* June 2, sec. 3.

———. 1985e. "Court Ruling Called Blow to Big Banks." *New York Times*, June 11, D1.

———. 1985f. "Putting the Homestead Deeper Into Hock." *New York Times*, November 24.

———. 1984a. "State Panel Report Due on Banks." *New York Times*, February 13.

———. 1984b. "A Banking Puzzle: Mixing Freedom and Protection." *New York Times*, February 19, sec. 3.

———. 1984c. "Economic Scene: Deregulation's Effect at Banks." *New York Times*, March 16, D2.

———. 1984d "Another Crisis Engulfs The Thrifts." *New York Times*, July 22, sec. 3.

———. 1983a. "U.S. Provides $175 Million to Aid 15 Savings Banks, Mostly in City." *New York Times*, January 4.

———. 1983b. "Inside Citicorp: The Changing World of Banking." *New York Times*, May 29.

———. 1983c. "A Daring New World for Thrifts in the Making." *New York Times*, July 14.

Bleakley, Fred R. 1984. "A Fast-Paced Chairman Comes to Abrupt Halt." *New York Times*, August 29.

Brooks, Andree. 1980. "Making it Easier to Get a Mortgage." *New York Times*, October 12.

Colton, Kent W. 1980. "Financial Reform: A Review of the Past and Prospects for the Future." *AREUEA Journal* 8:1.

———. 1983. "The Report of the President's Commission on Housing: The Nation's System of Housing Finance." *AREUEA Journal* 11:2.

Commission on Money and Credit. 1961. *Money and Credit: Their Influence on Jobs, Prices and Growth*. Englewood Cliffs, NJ: Prentice-Hall.

Grebler, Leo. 1983. "The Commission's Recommendations on Housing Finance." *AREUEA Journal* 11:2.

Harloe, Michael. 1983. "The Recommodification of Housing." In *City, Class and Capital*, edited by Michael Harloe and Elizabeth Lebas. London: Edward Arnold.

Harvey, David. 1975. "The Political Economy of Urbanization in Advanced Capitalist Societies: The Case of the United States." In *The Social Economy of Cities: Urban Affairs Annual Review*, 9, edited by Gary Gappert. Beverly Hills, CA: Sage Publications.

Hayes, Thomas C. 1984a. "Pressure Building for a Thrift Unit Guarantee." *New York Times*, August 8.

———. 1984b. "Financial Corporation Facing Hurdles." *New York Times*, October 29.

———. 1982. "F.C.A.'s Gamble on Mortgages." *New York Times*, September 28.

Heineman, Erich H. 1983. "American Express: Symbol of Change." *New York Times*, July 13.

Hendershott, Patrick H., and Keven E. Villani. 1977. *Regulation and Reform of the Housing Finance System*. Washington, DC: American Enterprise Institute.

———. 1980. "Residential Mortgage Markets and the Cost of Mortgage Funds." *AREUEA Journal* 8:1.

Kaplan, Marshall A. 1983. "Deregulation and New Powers in the Savings and Loan Industry: What This Portends." *Housing Finance Review* 2:2.

Kerr, Peter. 1983. "A Bank's Closing Can Jolt an Area." *New York Times*, July 15, D9.

Kilborn, Peter T. 1984. "Playing the Odds on Mortgages." *New York Times*, January 24, D1.

Klott, Gary. 1985. "Old Court: Fast Growth, But High Risk-Taking." *New York Times*, May 20.

Lacy, William H. 1982. "Innovation Is a Key to Banks' Meeting Home Financing Needs." *ABA Journal* (May): p. 19.

Lindsay, Robert. 1980. "Housing Finance in the 1980s." *AREUEA Journal* 8:1.

Meyerson, Ann. 1986. "Housing Abandonment: The Role of Institutional Mortgage Lenders." In *Critical Perspectives on Housing*, edited by Rachel G. Bratt, Chester Hartman, and Ann Meyerson. Philadelphia: Temple University Press.

Nash, Nathaniel C. 1986. "Fed Proposes Lifting Some Banking Barriers." *New York Times*, May 20.

New York Times. 1983. "Dime Savings Pushes Loans." May 23.

Noble, Kenneth B. 1983. "Thrift Limits: Cautious Rivals." *New York Times*, April 23.

O'Connor, James. 1973. *The Fiscal Crisis of the State*. New York: St. Martin's Press.

President's Commission on Financial Structure and Regulation. 1971. *The Report of the President's Commission on Financial Structure and Regulation*. Washington, DC: U.S. Government Printing Office.

President's Commission on Housing. 1982. *The Report of the President's Commission on Housing*. Washington, DC: U.S. Government Printing Office.

Savings and Loan News. 1982. "Deregulation Brings the Threat of a Riskier Financial System: Who Can Monitor, Let Alone Control, Worldwide Citicorp and Its Ilk?" November.

Seiders, David F. 1983. "Mortgage Pass-Through Securities: Progress and Prospects." *AREUEA Journal* 11:2.

———. 1982. "The President's Commission on Housing: Perspectives on Mortgage Finance." *Housing Finance Review* 1:4.

Sternlieb, George and James W. Hughes. 1984. "Structuring the Future." *Society* 21:3 (March/April).

Stone, Michael E. 1980. "The Housing Problem in the United States: Origins and Prospects." *Socialist Review* 10:4 (July/August).

Sweezy, Paul M. and Harry Magdoff. 1984. "The Federal Deficit: The Real Issues." *Monthly Review* 35:11.

Treadway, P. 1982. "Outlook for Housing and Mortgages: They'll Come Back." *ABA Journal* (May).

Tuccillo, John A. with John L. Goodman, Jr. 1983. *Housing Finance: A Changing System in the Reagan Era*. Washington, DC: The Urban Institute Press.

U.S. Bureau of the Census. 1986. Statistical Abstract of the United States. Washington, DC: U.S. Government Printing Office.

U.S. Congress, House, Committee on Banking, Finance and Urban Affairs. 1982. *Depository Institutions Amendments of 1982. Hearings Before the Subcommittee on Financial Institutions, Supervision, Regulation and Insurance*. (September 21 and 22). Washington, DC: U.S. Government Printing Office.

U.S. Department of Housing and Urban Development. 1970 through 1985. *Survey of Mortgage Lending Activity*. Washington, D.C.: U.S. Department of Housing and Urban Development.

Van Bogan, R. 1982. "The Case for More Mortgage Lending by Community Banks." *ABA Journal* (May).

Vartanian, Thomas P. 1983a. "Regulation and Deregulation of the Savings and Loan Industry." *Housing Finance Review* 2:2.

———. 1983b. "The Garn–St Germain Depository Institutions Act of 1982: The Impact on Thrifts." *Housing Finance Review* 2:2.

Waite, D.C., III. 1981. "Deregulation in the Banking Industry." *Bankers Magazine* (January-February).

Williams, Winston. 1983. "The Explosion in Bank Deposits." *New York Times*, May 1, sec. 3.

THE CHANGING STRUCTURE OF HOUSING FINANCE: COMMENT

Andrew S. Carron

Government involvement in the housing finance system started with the programs of the Great Depression more than 50 years ago. The effects of financial regulation and deregulation on the cost and availability of mortgages began to be studied in earnest within the last 20 years. Since 1978 the topic has frequently dominated analyses of financial markets. Yet despite the widespread interest by policymakers and the importance of housing to the economy and society, few studies have gone beyond merely superficial analyses. Ann Meyerson's chapter represents a commendable effort to explore some of the ramifications of recent financial deregulation for housing finance.

The chapter identifies two potential motivations for change: (1) the growing inability of households to maintain mortgage debt service; and (2) the problems of the traditional thrift industry in an environment of high and volatile interest rates. It is the second of these forces that has created the need for change. While mortgage delinquencies have increased in recent years, they are still relatively low and, moreover, can partly be attributed to speculative excesses and poor underwriting rather than a widespread affordability problem. The difficulties of the thrift industry, however, are seen to involve substantial restructuring of the financial system.

A major theme of the chapter is that the specialized system of housing finance created in the 1930s has now been dismantled, and that this will increase the cost and reduce the availability of funds for housing. The reforms of the 1930s established federally chartered savings and loan associations and required them to invest almost exclusively in residential mortgages. The creation of the Federal Housing Agency (now Federal Housing Administration) to insure long-term, fixed-rate, self-amortizing mortgages further defined the housing finance structure. In 1966 Federal Reserve Board Regulation Q interest rate ceilings were extended to thrift institutions and became binding, thereby providing institutions with a source of below-market rate financing. These three elements—thrift investment limitations, fixed-rate mortgages, and deposit rate ceilings—are the focus of Meyerson's analysis.

The problems of the thrift industry in the late 1970s and 1980s have been widely reviewed (Carron 1982; President's Commission on Housing 1982a, 1982b). The reliance on short-term deposits to fund long-term assets proved not to be viable. Initially the problem was disintermediation—the inability to attract funds at below-market rates to support new and existing mortgage assets. With the decontrol of rate ceilings beginning in 1978, institutions were once again able to gather deposits, and the difficulty shifted from quantity to price. The completion of the process involved asset deregulation to reduce the maturity gap between assets and liabilities (Carron 1983b). The principal changes needed to accomplish this were the removal of restrictions on adjustable rate mortgages and the relaxation of prohibitions on shorter-duration nonmortgage investments. As a result, thrifts may now invest in consumer and commercial loans, certain kinds of corporate bonds, and a wide range of real estate-related loans and securities. Their use of these powers to date, however, has been limited (Katz 1985).

These changes have been described, in Meyerson's chapter and elsewhere, as leading to higher borrowing costs and more risk for borrowers. The problem with this line of reasoning, however, is that the housing finance system had already been opened to market forces by the time of deposit rate and asset deregulation. By then there were virtually no subsidies delivered to borrowers through financial intermediaries.

Rate ceilings and asset restrictions on thrifts did not result in lower mortgage interest rates because thrift institutions were not the marginal providers of funds (Carron 1983a). Thrifts never provided more than about 60 percent of the new residential mortgage originations. Mortgage bankers were responsible for most of the balance. This conduit had no access to below-market funds and has no statutory requirement to invest in mortgages. In fact, the benefits of low-cost deposits were captured by the financial intermediaries themselves in the form of higher profits, salaries, and other expenses (Carron 1982).

It should also be noted that even if low-cost deposits did flow through to borrowers, the income distribution effects would have been adverse. Households with mortgage loans from thrifts have higher net worth than those who borrow from other sources, and borrowers in general tend to have higher incomes than those who do not borrow—that is, depositors. Since higher-income individuals also had market-rate alternatives to deposits, the effect of rate ceilings would have been to distribute income from (or among) lower-income groups.

It was not deregulation in the 1980s that opened the mortgage market to the capital markets, but rather the development of the secondary mortgage markets.

Meyerson correctly notes the importance of the secondary markets in the restructuring process. Beginning with Fannie Mae's mortgage purchases, and continuing more recently with the Ginnie Mae and Freddie Mac pass-through programs, linkages were established that allowed mortgage borrowers to draw from the same pool of savings as government and corporate borrowers. Of course, this implies that mortgage borrowers must pay market rates, which means that some potential borrowers may not be able to afford the debt service. But the alternative to rationing by price is quantity rationing through disintermediation. Social welfare can be adversely affected by quantity restrictions just as much as through the price system, but quantity restrictions are inefficient as well.

The housing finance system should not be used in an attempt to deliver subsidies to lower- and middle-income households. It is both inefficient and ineffective to do so. In fact, the major influences on the cost and availability of housing finance have been, and continue to be, fiscal and monetary policy. The tax system—through the non-imputation of homeowner rents and the deductibility of mortgage interest—has done far more to promote homeownership in the last 20 years than has financial regulation. Restrictive monetary policy can do more to limit mortgage lending than any regulatory policy could overcome.

Consider also Meyerson's characterization of the intent of regulatory reform. For example, the thrift capital assistance program cannot be said to aid profits, because thrifts receiving capital assistance may not pay dividends and must redeem the assistance certificates with interest before any profits can be distributed. Also, the intent of adjustable-rate mortgages was not to force more risk on borrowers, but in fact to offer the option of lower payments (and greater affordability) now with the possibility of higher payments later. In practice, these loans have annual and lifetime interest rate caps that have worked to the advantage of the borrower. Finally, the operation of the Ginnie Mae pass-through program does not involve "the state (or taxpayers) underwriting risk." Investors pay a fee of six basis points to Ginnie Mae for the guarantee, which comes on top of the insurance or guarantee fees charged on the underlying FHA or VA mortgage loans. These fees have been more than adequate to cover Ginnie Mae's losses.

To summarize: Meyerson presents a comprehensive and generally accurate summary of the legal and regulatory changes affecting housing finance. But even with deregulation, thrifts continue to be the major mortgage lending institutions, and they are growing at a more rapid rate than ever before. Mortgage funds are now widely available at rates that (in relative terms) are as low as they have ever been. The characterization of deregulation as villain is unwarranted.

REFERENCES

Carron, A.S. 1983a. "The Political Economy of Financial Regulation." In *The Political Economy of Deregulation: Interest Groups in the Regulatory Process*, edited by R.G. Noll and B.M. Owen. Washington, DC: American Enterprise Institute.

———. 1983b. *The Rescue of the Thrift Industry*. Washington, DC: Brookings Institution.

———.1982. *The Plight of the Thrift Institutions*. Washington, DC: Brookings Institution.

Katz, J.W. 1985. "How Thrifts Use Garn–St Germain." *Outlook of the Federal Home Loan Bank System* 1:14–16.

President's Commission on Housing. 1982a. *Financing the Housing Needs of the 1980s: A Preliminary Report on Housing Finance*. Washington, DC: President's Commission on Housing.

———.1982b. *The Report of the President's Commission on Housing*. Washington, DC: U.S. Government Printing Office.

8

RENTALS, CONDOS, AND CO-OPS: WHICH GIVES MORE BANG FOR THE GOVERNMENT BUCKS?

Michael A. Stegman

The government has many ways of encouraging businesses and individuals to invest in various economic sectors and different types of enterprises. One is by direct subsidies provided through the appropriations process; another is by indirect subsidies delivered through the federal income tax system. These latter subsidies are commonly called "tax expenditures," which the Congressional Budget Office (CBO) defines as "provisions of the tax code that provide incentives for particular kinds of activities or that give special or selective tax relief to certain groups of taxpayers" (Congressional Budget Office 1983, xi). In fiscal 1983, the CBO and the Joint Committee on Taxation (JCT) of the Congress found that 105 provisions of the tax code met this definition (1983, xi). Taken together, these tax expenditures resulted in a revenue loss to the federal government of more than $296 billion in fiscal 1983 and are projected to increase by 37 percent in fiscal 1988 to almost $405 billion (Congressional Budget Office 1983, table A–1).

Nearly all businesses, individuals, and sectors of society benefit from tax expenditures. Military disability pensions are exempt from federal income taxes, as is income earned abroad by United States citizens. Exploration and development costs for oil, gas, and other fuels are subject to preferential tax treatment, as are certain kinds of reforestation expenditures in our nation's timberlands. Interest income earned on state and local government pollution control bonds is free from federal income taxes, and so is veterans' income received under the GI Bill.

Although it does not account for a very large proportion of all tax expenditures, the housing sector benefits substantially from this form of government largess.

Table 8.1
Congressional Budget Office Estimates of Selected Tax Expenditures for Housing, 1983 and 1988 (estimated)

	Fiscal Year 1983 (Actual)	Fiscal Year 1988 (Estimated)
	(in billions of dollars)	
Deduction of mortgage interest on owner-occupied homes	25.07	37.95
Deduction of property taxes on owner-occupied homes	8.77	14.98
Exclusion of capital gains on home sales for persons aged 55 or older	1.26	2.35
Deferral of capital gains on home sales	3.77	7.03
Exclusion of interest on state and local government bonds on:		
Owner-occupied housing	1.51	1.11
Rental housing	.87	2.88
Deduction of construction period interest and taxes	.78	1.70
Accelerated depreciation in excess of straight line for rental housing	.70	1.00
Five-year amortization of rehabilitation costs for low-income housing	.05	.06
	$42.78	$69.06

Source: *Tax Expenditures: Current Issues and Five-Year Budget Projections for Fiscal Years 1984–1988*, Congressional Budget Office, October, 1983; Appendix A, Table A-1.

In fiscal 1983 nine separate provisions of the tax code affecting housing produced tax expenditures of $43 billion, which accounted for almost 15 percent of total tax expenditures (Table 8.1). This total (which is projected to increase by more than 60 percent to $69 billion in fiscal 1988) is dominated by two major tax subsidies to homeowners. Deduction of mortgage interest on owner-occupied homes saved American taxpayers more than $25 billion in personal income taxes in fiscal 1983, and deduction of property taxes saved them an additional $9 billion. In fiscal 1988 these two tax expenditures are projected to grow to nearly $38 billion and $15 billion, respectively.

Not all homeowners benefit from these subsidies because low-income taxpayers, even if they own their homes, generally do not itemize their deductions. For that reason, and because of the progressive nature of the personal income tax system, homeowner benefits accrue largely to upper-income families. According to one analysis, 75 percent of these homeownership benefits in 1981 went to homeowners in the top 15 percent of the income distribution (National Low Income Housing Coalition 1984). Not all tax expenditures for housing accrue solely to the affluent, however. Exclusion of interest earned on state and local government bonds for rental housing, while benefiting upper-income investors, also makes possible mortgage loans below market interest rates to build low-income housing. Similarly, tax provisions governing depreciation of rental housing in general, and of low-income housing in particular, increase the relative attractiveness of these investments to equity investors and assist renters and the poor. Together these tax expenditures totaled more than $1.5 billion in fiscal 1983.

THE ISSUE

An interesting and little-explored public policy issue involving tax expenditures for housing involves the recent rise in multifamily unit ownership in the United States. For a variety of reasons—including high interest and inflation rates, expectations of continuing inflation and lagging rents—the number of cooperative and condominium units nationwide increased substantially during the latter half of the 1970s. On the development side, 717,000 units (or 42 percent of all new multifamily housing starts between 1977 and 1981) were in condominiums or cooperatives. During the same period nearly half a million existing rental units were converted to co-ops and condominiums. In 1980 and 1981 combined, conversions exceeded the number of new, conventionally financed rental housing starts by 7,200 units (Kerry 1982). While the deepening national recession and volatile credit environment of the early 1980s caused a substantial decline in all housing starts and an abrupt end to the condo conversion craze, the fall-off in both market sectors is likely to be temporary.

A tax expenditure issue is embedded in the trend toward higher rates of multifamily ownership. It has to do with whether government subsidies associated with housing cooperatives and condominiums are more or less than those that would occur if the same multifamily buildings had been built and operated or remained in use as rental housing. Subsidiary issues are how tax expenditures associated with condos and cooperatives vary with the incomes of their occupants and whether it is more cost-effective for the government to support low-income co-ops and condominiums or investor-owned rental housing for lower- and moderate-income families.

The initial impetus for a formal analysis of this issue arose out of a situation that is not uncommon in the nation's capital. During a 1981 congressional hearing on reform of the federal income tax laws, a member of Congress questioned whether Treasury would be better off with respect to tax expenditures if all co-ops were operated as rental units. Such pointed questions typically strike terror into the hearts of lobbyists everywhere, including, in this case, officials of the National Association of Housing Cooperatives (NAHC), who decided to engage a real estate analyst, Dennis Eisen, to investigate the above proposition.

I first came across Eisen's analysis in a Congressional hearing on tax reform and decided that his assignment from NAHC would form the basis of an interesting teaching case for my class in real estate investment and low-income housing. I wrote the case during the summer of 1984 and used it in class for the first time later that fall. While student solutions to the problem varied, their work shared two common results. First, they found that the tax benefits associated with middle- (and high-) income homeowners exceeded all others, including those associated with the development of new low-income rental housing. Second, the least expensive tax subsidies were associated with dwelling units owned by low- and moderate-income families.

This chapter provides an opportunity to pursue Eisen's analysis unconstrained by the needs of a particular client. While I have been working in the housing research and policy areas for many years, and am quite familiar with the distinction between tax benefits associated with owner versus renter housing investments, I suppose that subconsciously, I have always associated the former with single family and the latter with multifamily structures. Not until I focused on Eisen's paper and my students' subsequent analyses did I become consciously aware of the fact that tax subsidies associated with the development and occupancy of two otherwise identical multifamily buildings will vary significantly depending upon their respective ownership forms and occupancy mix. To clarify this issue, this chapter will attempt to identify the magnitudes of the relationships between the tax subsidies associated with multifamily renter- and owner-occupied housing, and determine how these "hidden" costs vary with the income characteristics of their occupants. The assumptions that governed it and the results of my preliminary analysis are summarized in the remainder of this chapter.

BASIC ASSUMPTIONS

To begin, we need to define an unambiguous measure of tax subsidies to apply to both co-op/condo and rental projects. The measure I use in this paper is the discounted present value of tax savings associated with the two housing types over 7- and 15-year holding periods, using a 10 percent discount rate. Analysis over two holding periods is necessary to determine whether tax expenditures, as my measure of government cost, distinguishes my definition from that used by the Congressional Budget Office and the Joint Committee on Taxation in their official reports. According to CBO, not all classes of tax deductions constitute tax expenditures.

Certain features of an income tax are considered integral parts of the bias structure of the tax and therefore are not viewed as tax expenditures, which are defined as exceptions to these basic rules. The integral features include the general rate schedules, and exemption levels, the general rules defining who is subject to tax and what accounting periods should be used, and deductions for the cost of earning income (Congressional Budget Office 1983, xi).

Under CBO's definition, tax savings accruing from straight line depreciation are not considered a tax expenditure but those due to the more accelerated write-offs allowed under the ACRS system introduced into the tax code in 1981 are.[1] Nor are savings due to operating losses considered tax expenditures by CBO even though their deductibility from income reduces the taxpayers' liability. The rationale for this is that the investor's outlays which cause operating losses to occur are classified as costs of earning income that are generally deductible under the tax code.

In interpreting the results of my analysis, it is important to understand that while my definition of tax savings to owner-occupants due to the deductibility of home mortgage and property tax payments is the same as the CBO's, my definition of tax savings to rental housing investors is broader than theirs. This means that from the CBO's perspective, I overstate the indirect federal cost of supporting new rental housing investments and understate the differences between the tax expenditures associated with new rental versus owner-occupied housing investments.

THE BASE CASE

Eisen realized that his analysis for NAHC had to be applied to a standardized project so that differences in development cost would not bias his results. Using data from the Washington, DC metropolitan area, he constructed a development cost schedule for a "typical" newly constructed multifamily unit. That new unit, which I also use for my analysis, cost $62,000 (in 1981 dollars), of which $35,000 was for hard construction costs and $10,000 was for land. The remaining $17,000 was for interest ($6,500) and taxes ($500) during construction period and other "soft costs" ($10,000).

Because a substantial proportion of multifamily housing starts is financed by state and local tax-exempt lending programs, Eisen (and I) analyzed two different financing arrangements. When targeted to a middle-income market, a unit would be financed with a conventional 30-year, fixed-rate loan at a 14 percent interest rate for 75 percent of value. When oriented to the lower-income market, the same unit would be financed with a 30-year, 10.5 percent (tax-exempt bond financed) mortgage loan for 90 percent of value.

Eisen and I assumed the following maintenance and operating costs for the first year: property taxes = $1240, insurance = $310, maintenance/operations = $930, utilities = $310, total = $2790. These costs were assumed to increase

Exhibit 8.1
Operating Assumptions for Prototype Units

Initial Rents:	Gross rents are initially set such that the sum of operating costs and debt service equals 90 percent of gross potential rent. For market rate units, rents are assumed to increase by 5 percent a year. For low market rent units, rents are assumed to increase dollar for dollar with operating costs.
Operating Costs:	All operating costs are assumed to increase by 10 percent a year.
Future Value:	Future sales price is the capitalized value of net operating income at the end of the year in which the sale takes place. The applicable cap rate is 10.66 percent, which remains constant over the 15 year analysis period. Since net operating income remains virtually unchanged in the case of the lower income unit, future value remains equal to initial development cost over the holding period.
Selling Expenses:	Expenses associated with sale are assumed to be 6 percent of selling price.

by 10 percent per year. To be conservative, Eisen assumed that first-year gross rental income would be just sufficient to cover the sum of operating costs and required debt service payments, allowing for a 10 percent vacancy and bad debt rate (that is, total costs divided by a factor of 0.90) and to increase by 5 percent per year for the market rate unit (Exhibit 8.1).[2] Eisen assumed that rents for the lower-income unit would be permitted to increase on a dollar-for-dollar basis with operating costs.[3]

Eisen's relevant assumptions dealing with future value and disposition of the units are summarized in the same Exhibit. The market rate new construction project is assumed to have a future value equal to the capitalized value of net operating income, using a 10.66 percent capitalization rate. Eisen "backed into" that rate with the assumption that the relationship between first-year net operating income and initial unit cost would remain virtually constant over time, from which it follows that future value would not stray far from initial development costs. Selling costs were assumed to equal 6 percent of the projected sale price for the rental units. Eisen charged the same selling costs against the co-op since the transfer of shares of stock in the cooperative corporation may involve the payment of a sales commission or brokerage fee.

Table 8.2
Taxable Incomes and Applicable Marginal Tax Rates for Housing/Occupancy Types*

Housing/Occupancy Type	Assumed Adjusted Gross Incomes	Marginal Tax Rate
All investor-owners of rental housing	$60,000-$85,600	42%
Owner of market-rate new construction co-ops/condos	$24,600-$29,900	25%
Owners of low-income new co-ops/condos	$ 5,500-$ 7,600	12%

*Assumes married couple filing joint returns and tax rates in effect for calendar year 1984.

The size of the tax subsidy associated with a given provision of the Internal Revenue Code is partly a function of the taxable income of the affected individual and the individual's prospective marginal tax rates. My assumptions regarding the taxable incomes for rental investor-owners and occupants of market rate and lower-income co-ops and condos are presented in Table 8.2. The reported incomes are net of all exemptions and itemized deductions except for the housing-related benefits to which the respective taxpayers are entitled. My working assumption is that the typical investor-owner in new rental housing is in the 42 percent tax bracket, that owners of new market-rate co-ops and condos are in the 25 percent bracket, and that low- to moderate-income homeowners are in the 12 percent bracket.

As indicated earlier, I treat the calculation of tax subsidies similarly for rental and owner-occupied housing. In the latter case, I define the subsidy as the sum of annual mortgage interest and property tax payments multiplied by the appropriate marginal tax rate discounted back to the present. Thus, for example, for a 25 percent tax bracket homeowner, a deduction of $2,000 in mortgage interest and property taxes will reduce taxes by $500. This tax expenditure, when discounted back to the present and added to those for the other years, will sum to the total tax expenditures associated with owning a co-op or condo. In the case of rental housing, I define tax expenditures associated with rental production and operations as the sum of each year's taxable income multiplied by the investor's marginal tax rate discounted back to the present.

A SUMMARY OF THE ANALYSIS

Before summarizing the results of the analysis and the policy issues the analysis raises, it should be noted that the rents and carrying charges associated with the prototype unit are quite high despite the modest assumption that rents will rise

Table 8.3
Summary of Discounted Tax Expenditures Associated with Prototype Units*

	Holding Period			
	Nominal Dollars		Discounted Dollars +	
	7 years	15 years	7 years	15 years
Middle Income				
Owner-occupied	$14,239	$33,529	$ 9,839	$16,349
Renter-occupied	8,728	8,415	10,156	6,022
Low/Mod. Income				
Owner-occupied	6,426	15,218	4,439	7,404
Renter-occupied	13,149	15,757	9,531	10,434

All middle-income costs are based on 30-year, 14% mortgage for $46,500. Low income costs are based on 30-year, 10.5% mortgage for $55,800.
*See Table 8.4 for details.
+Using a 10% discount rate.

by 5 percent a year. Clearly, when we speak of housing for low- and moderate-income families, the tax subsidies would have to be supplemented by deep rental or occupancy subsidies to make them affordable. Since roughly equivalent occupancy subsidies would be required whether the unit is owned or rented by a lower-income family, we are able to ignore this issue in order to determine how the level of tax subsidies associated with housing varies with its occupancy and ownership status.

It should also be understood that the tax subsidies associated with the four tenure-income alternatives are quite sensitive to the underlying assumptions regarding development, operating and financing costs, and to the assumptions regarding the marginal tax brackets of homeowners and rental housing investors. It is therefore important to treat my conclusions as preliminary, pending more refined analysis.

With the above caveat, the results of the analysis can be summarized. The highest tax subsidy is associated with the middle-income owner-occupied dwelling. The nominal value (undiscounted) of the tax savings associated with this housing type over a 15-year period is $33,529, while the discounted value of the subsidy is slightly less than half as much, $16,349 (Tables 8.3 and 8.4). The second most costly housing alternative is the newly constructed low-income rental unit, which has a nominal 15-year cost to the government of $15,757, and a discounted cost of $10,434. The tax subsidy associated with low/moderate owner-occupied housing is third with a nominal 15-year cost of $15,218 and a discounted cost of $7,404. The least costly alternative is market-rate rental housing for middle-income families, which has a nominal 15-year tax subsidy cost of just $8,415 and a discounted cost of $6,022.

Table 8.4
Tax Expenditures for Homeowners

		Market Rate Loan*	Below Market Rate Loan +
		(Nominal Dollars)	
Total mortgage interest over 15- year analysis period		94,720	87,423
Total property taxes over 15 years		39,398	39,398
Total deductions		134,118	126,821
Applicable tax rates:			
middle income	25%		
low/mod. income	12%		
Tax Savings Middle Income:			
over 15 years	33,529		
over 7 years	14,239		
Tax Savings Low/Mod. Income:			
over 15 years	15,218		
over 7 years	6,425		

*Market rate loan is for $46,500 at 14% for 30 years.
+Below market rate loan is for $55,800 at 10.5% for 30 years.

Several interesting relationships are embedded in these findings. First, although in nominal terms there is little difference in the indirect federal cost of supporting new rental and owner housing for low- and moderate-income families, in present value terms it is more cost-effective to support a lower-income owner-occupant than it is to subsidize a producer to build the same multifamily unit for rental occupancy. Every newly built low-income multifamily unit that was built for owner (rather than rental) occupancy would save the federal government $3,000 (in today's dollars) per unit in tax subsidies over a 15-year period. The differences in real costs between the two housing tenure types is closer to $5,000 when viewed over a six-year operating period.[4] This means that the federal government could provide every newly built owner-occupied multifamily unit with a one-time capital grant of $5,000 to capitalize an operating or replacement reserve fund for the low-income occupant, and still pay no more than it would cost in tax subsidy dollars if the same housing unit were to be built and occupied as rental housing.

The analysis also shows that over the longer term, the tax subsidies associated with market rate rental housing decline, as positive cash flows increase and depreciation shelters become exhausted. Over a 15-year holding period, the discounted tax subsidy to a rental housing investor ($6,022) is less than 40 percent as high as it would be if that same multifamily unit had been developed as a condominium or co-op and purchased by a middle-income family. If, however, we look at the respective tax losses associated with owner- and renter-occupied housing over a shorter, seven-year holding period (which may be more realistic), the tax subsidies to the two are nearly the same. This is because the tax savings to rental investors are front-loaded and the fact that before-tax cash flows are modest in the early years of the investment period.

To summarize, it may be fair to conclude that Dennis Eisen's client had good reason to worry about that off-hand query overheard in the halls of Congress on whether housing cooperatives cost the federal government more in foregone taxes than do otherwise identical multifamily rental developments. While the National Association of Housing Cooperatives did not ask for my advice, I would suggest the next time the question is raised that NAHC respond in terms of the income groups the housing is intended to serve. From a tax subsidy standpoint, low-income housing cooperatives are less costly than housing built for rental occupancy even though this may not be true with respect to middle- or high-income co-ops. When the inescapable realization sets in that we must continue to expand the supply of housing for low- and moderate-income families, perhaps we will return to the issue of cost-effective housing assistance choice.

NOTES

1. Contrary to the CBO and the JCT, the Treasury Department does not define accelerated depreciation under ACRS as a tax expenditure.
2. Eisen assumed that rents would grow by 6.5 percent a year.
3. For the low-income units gross rent in year $t + 1$ equals gross rent in year t plus the increase in operating expenses applicable to year $t + 1$, divided by .90.
4. The discounted value of the differences between new rental and owner-occupied housing for low-income families declines more steeply over time because the rental investor exhausts most of his depreciation benefits after seven years, while mortgage and property tax deductions for the owner decline more slowly with time.

REFERENCES

Kerry, John P. 1982. "Multifamily Housing in the 80s: Market Trends and Countercyclical Stimulus Options." Paper presented at a symposium on Countercyclical Stimulus for Multifamily Housing, General Accounting Office, June 29.

National Low Income Housing Coalition. 1984. "Memo to Members." January, 4.

U.S. Congressional Budget Office. 1983. *Tax Expenditures: Current Issues and Five-Year Budget Projections for Fiscal Years 1984–1988*. October. Washington, DC: U.S. Government Printing Office.

RENTALS, CONDOS, AND CO-OPS: COMMENT

Anthony S. Freedman

Michael Stegman's chapter raises issues that are relevant to practitioners interested in the theoretical implications of policy choices. I hope that my comments, which come from a practitioner's perspective, will be of as much interest to policy analysts who consider issues from a theoretical perspective.

Too often it is the case that, as a result of the pressure to produce theoretically and methodologically tight research, more relevant, interesting, and difficult questions do not get addressed. By choosing to assess the impact of tax expenditures on housing produced as a result of investments rather than focusing on the more conventional and straightforward question of the impact of tax expenditures on housing consumption by households, Stegman obviously has chosen the more difficult—and, to me more interesting—option. For example, it is a relatively straightforward matter to estimate the amount of revenue lost by the federal government as a result of individual homeowners claiming the home mortgage interest deduction. The analysis that has produced such estimates is relatively simple and quite valid. Analysis of tax expenditures resulting from government programs aimed at large-scale housing investors, on the other hand, is not only far more technically complicated, but also raises some thorny theoretical issues.

Stegman's analysis also illustrates the need to make a number of definitional and methodological decisions, each of which requires assumptions about the nature of the phenomenon being studied while at the same time directing the analysis toward certain conclusions. As is the case in most such analysis, Stegman's conclusions are largely dependent on the definitions, assumptions, and even cost estimates he has chosen to use. Acceptance of the results of his study depend in large part on whether the definitions and assumptions built into the analysis are accepted.

While we must be able to accept them as valid, we must keep in mind that very often the definitions and assumptions used in policy analysis are the result of necessary compromise between that which is theoretically preferable and that which is methodologically possible. Having recognized this, I applaud Stegman's decision to go at least as far as treating all depreciation as a "tax cost," even though it doesn't qualify for the pejorative term "tax-expenditure." At the same time I want to argue that he should broaden the definition even further. While his definition of the costs to the government of various programs to encourage investment in housing presents formidable measurement problems, one can argue, on theoretical grounds, that it does not go far enough—that the analysis should include a consideration of opportunity costs, including estimates of the value of alternative uses of capital.

Stegman's work also illustrates that, as often is the case in complicated policy analysis, the effects of definitions and estimates introduced at an early stage are magnified with each additional step in the analysis. Thus, the more complicated the analysis, the more critical it is to begin with defensible definitions, assumptions, and cost estimates. When one finds it necessary to begin with and build on crude estimates, it often is difficult to have much confidence in the results. Sometimes it boils down to a matter of judgment as to whether it is defensible to proceed at all with the estimates that are available.

Having said that, I want to express serious reservations with some of the assumptions upon which his analysis depends. First of all, while understanding the methodological reasons for doing so, I am not persuaded that in today's housing market it is defensible to distinguish between low-income and middle-income types of housing on a project-by-project basis. While we may be able to label a Section 8 project or a public housing project as "low-income," and we may be able to identify specific condominium projects as "middle-income," in today's market most projects are not exclusively one or the other. For example, we simply are not building pure low-income rentals anymore, anywhere. To the extent that any units are being produced for lower-income households, they usually fall within the 20 percent of units set aside for low- and moderate-income in otherwise moderate- and upper-income projects in order to meet the requirements for tax-exempt financing. (This analysis described conditions prior to enactment of the Tax Reform Act of 1986, with its new Low Income Housing Tax Credit. The effect of the 1986 Act has been to discourage mixed-income rental housing and to promote the development of 100 percent low-income projects, where such projects are otherwise feasible.)

While this means that is is difficult to distinguish between low- and middle-income housing at the project level, it also indicates that middle- and upper-income households benefit from tax-exempt financing along with lower-income households, a finding not acknowledged by Stegman. I would be willing to argue that at least half of the new housing units produced in 1985 were middle-income housing built with the assistance of tax-exempt financing. The real question is how much of the 20 percent of units that are required to be held for low- and moderate-income persons actually get to low-income people. In reality, with tax-exempt financing, the same program and the same type of government subsidy serve very different classes of people. You simply cannot make the clean distinction between middle-income and lower-income interests and programs, as is assumed in the first part of Stegman's analysis.

A second reservation I have focuses on Stegman's assumption about what constitutes low income. His definition of low income is really a definition of very, very low income. If, as Stegman does, we define low income as households with incomes of no more than 25–30 percent of the national median, we will exclude many households that would qualify under a more liberal definition, including many residents of public housing. Partly as a result of heavy subsidies, either from the housing system or through traditional welfare programs, most public housing households would not qualify as low income under Stegman's definition. I do not think he would mean to exclude them and would suggest that he look carefully at the implications of the definition he employs.

The third and perhaps most serious reservation about Stegman's analysis concerns the parallel between low-income ownership and low-income rental which he assumes exists and upon which he bases his comparisons of programs aimed at renters and owners. I do not believe that such a parallel exists, and I question the justification for the comparisons produced. In order for such a comparison to be valid, it is necessary to assume that deep subsidy programs are or might be available to carry the bulk of the housing costs in both sectors. Aside from the fact that there are no such deep subsidy programs in existence today, it is not clear what kind of deep subsidy program(s) might exist to produce comparable results for renters and homeowners. The lack of comparability between the situation of renters and owners in fact is a problem inherent in any analysis of the housing market. As was discovered when HUD considered the possibility of providing low-income homeowners with subsidies comparable to those available to low-income renters, it is necessary to take into account the ability of the owner, even the low-income owner, to capitalize that subsidy and produce a profit through sale of the house. Because that is a possibility which does not exist for recipients of rental subsidies, the two types of subsidies are inherently unequal.

Except through the Section 235 program (through Section 221(d) (2) for people as old as I am) and more recently through mortgage revenue bonds, the government has never provided homeownership subsidies targeted to low-income households—and the target groups for these programs are substantially above the low-income definition used by Stegman. I think that it would be very difficult to design a large-scale program to provide such subsidies without also producing significant inequities between the rental and ownership sectors. Without any direct experience with low-income homeownership programs, it is difficult to predict costs, yet it simply is not valid to assess subsidy programs without considering the relative costs and benefits of different forms of subsidies. I do not mean to imply that the analysis is not worth doing, but I do want to argue that until and unless the analysis adequately takes into account the relative costs and benefits of different programs, it will produce misleading conclusions.

Finally, I would argue that Stegman's analysis is excessively mechanistic and simplistic in its calculation of the relative costs and benefits of subsidies provided to different groups. The analysis in essence assumes that the value derived from each tax benefit is equal to its cost and that the costs are equal to the amount of taxes lost. Thus, if the government gives a tax benefit to someone in the 42 percent bracket, it costs \$42 per \$100, while a benefit to someone in the 12 percent bracket costs only \$12 per \$100. I think this analysis ignores the fact that benefits given to upper-income groups—that is, to investors rather than occupants—produce something more than just the ability to buy into housing. With investors you are also buying investment knowledge, management skills, and the ability to carry losses. The value of these factors in producing units of housing is significant and evidenced by the fact that the experienced investor will respond to relatively modest tax incentives.

Developers involved in Section 8 used to express amusement about HUD working so hard to provide investors with a 6 percent or a 10 percent return on capital on invested cash. They knew that investors did not need 6 or 10 percent return on cash. A tax shelter provided them with all the return they needed; in essence they got a return on their investments even if they got no cash yield on the money they put in. For investors, cash paid on cash was an extra.

What HUD and Stegman fail to take into account is that when assessing the impact of producer incentives, it is necessary to look at the larger picture and recognize the lack of parallels to consumer incentives. Put simply, a \$5,000 capital grant to investors produces multiple benefits in that it gives developers access to the capital markets, which is critical to producing housing units. This simply is not the case with a capital grant of equal magnitude to a low-income consumer. Due in part to the package of benefits available through the investor, a \$5,000 capital grant to a family with an income of \$7,500 is less likely to produce new housing, or is likely to produce less housing, than a \$5,000 grant to an investor. This does not mean that I would argue against investing in incentives for homeownership for lower-income households. It does mean that if the overall goal is to expand the supply of low-income housing units, then when comparing strategies to reach that goal we should work with realistic and complete information about the efficacy of each of the alternatives.

While my reservations are significant, I nevertheless think that Stegman's analysis is very useful. It allows us to assess arguments made in favor of directing resources to the rental market, and appears to support the conclusion that incentives to rental production are a cheaper and more efficient means to produce low-income housing than are incentives directed to ownership housing. During the waning days of the Carter administration there was considerable concern about the volume of aging subsidized and unsubsidized rental housing that needed refinancing. It was clear that the future of this much-needed housing stock was threatened by the low income levels of its tenants; without substantial subsidies these units were very likely to be lost to the low-income market through conversion and demolition. Several of us argued that if the objective was to ensure the availability of those units to low-income households, it would be much cheaper in the long run to subsidize rehabilitation and refinancing so that they would continue to be part of the rental market than it would be to allow them to convert into ownership housing available only to highly subsidized low-income families. Stegman's analysis supports that argument. (See also Chapter 10 by Emily Achtenberg.)

This leads us to the issue of the implications of this analysis for housing policy. First, it appears that we need to confront the likely long-term and indirect costs of recent tax reforms. These reforms effectively remove all direct incentives for the production of rental housing—except for the very limited Low Income Housing Tax Credit, a credit which alone will have no effect on rental production. The Tax Credit has, however, provided an incentive for some state and local governments to add their own funds to make projects feasible. This increased financial participation by state and local governments is easily the most promising development in low-income housing in the past two years. The only tax shelter that remains under the tax reforms is that for homeownership (and for the ownership of second houses as well), as the investment incentives to rental production developed over the years as complements to the homeownership subsidies have been eliminated. If one of the objectives of national housing policy is to stimulate the production of housing accessible to low-income families, it appears that the new tax reforms move in exactly the wrong direction. If low-income households are to have access to the housing that is likely to be produced under the new incentives, they will have to depend on deep, and very expensive, consumer subsidies. Under the new tax structure it will be increasingly expensive to provide housing for low-income families.

Stegman's analysis also encourages us to rethink the way we look at affirmative spending programs. In the past we have generally limited our attention to programs that involve direct expenditures in order to target benefits to a specific group (whether an income group, a local jurisdiction, or an institution). Stegman's analysis reminds us of the utility of tax expenditures in targeting benefits. His assessment of the effects of the Tax Act of 1981 makes it clear that it is possible, through the creation of tax shelters and the availability of tax-exempt financing, to stimulate the production of low-income housing. I would estimate that the number of rental units started between 1983 and 1985 as a result of the provisions of the Act is greater than the total number of Section 8 units that were constructed during the four years of the Carter administration. The tax engine has enormous redistributive power, if used effectively. Unfortunately, it is a tool that we tend to underutilize.

Finally, Stegman's analysis forces us to confront the long-debated question of the appropriate balance between production and consumption subsidies. As is often the case with government analysts, I tend to come out squarely on both sides of the issue by arguing that you need to provide income subsidies for lower-income people while at the same time taking direct action to expand the supply of housing. The Reagan administration has expressed a clear preference for income subsidies, deliberately phasing out programs designed explicitly to encourage the production of low-income housing. At the same time, by supporting the 1981 Tax Act, the President also helped put in place a demonstration of the relative advantages of production subsidies. As frequently happened, administration's actions provided support for the position it opposed in principle.

Currently there is a clear need for income subsidies for households who otherwise cannot bid effectively for housing in the open market. At the same time, income subsidies will be extremely expensive and relatively ineffective unless there is an adequate supply of moderately-priced housing. I think the most important conclusion to be drawn from Stegman's paper is that tax subsidies, if designed carefully and used effectively, can make a significant contribution toward the goal of ensuring that such a supply exists.

9

LINKAGE: TYING DOWNTOWN DEVELOPMENT TO COMMUNITY HOUSING NEEDS

W. Dennis Keating

Linkage—or a linked downtown-neighborhood development policy—has been widely debated and often adopted in several American cities that have experienced both strong downtown growth and serious housing problems. As used here, linkage is defined as the mandatory municipal regulation of unsubsidized large commercial development in order to obtain housing "exactions" as a condition of development approval. Linkage housing exactions can take several forms. Commercial developers can build or rehabilitate housing themselves, co-venture with housing developers, or pay "in-lieu" fees (either to finance specific housing programs or projects, or to support a municipal housing trust fund).

To date, housing linkage policies have been adopted in San Francisco (1981), Santa Monica (1981), Boston (1983), Jersey City (1985), and Berkeley (1986). They are under consideration in Chicago and Hartford, and have been rejected in Cambridge, New York, and Seattle.

Linkage must be distinguished from two similar approaches. First, many localities have attached conditions to subsidies for large commercial development projects. For example, San Francisco required major hotel developers subsidized through the federal Urban Development Action Grant (UDAG) program to contribute to the rehabilitation of low-rent single room occupancy hotels in order to prevent displacement caused by gentrification (Hartman 1984, 251–56). In Minneapolis and Oakland it has been proposed that developers subsidized through tax increment financing provide housing assistance, but such proposals have not yet been adopted.

Second, many cities have provided developers with density bonuses (additional floor space exceeding zoning ceilings) in return for amenities provided by developers. These agreements are negotiated on a case-by-case basis. Several cities—Denver, Hartford, Miami, Washington, D.C., New York, and Seattle—have used this "incentive zoning" technique to obtain housing subsidies from private developers (Keating 1986).

THE EMERGENCE OF LINKAGE

In addition to the prerequisites of strong Central Business District (CBD) growth, several other factors have influenced the emergence of linkage as a municipal housing policy. First, linkage proponents see it as at least a partial solution to displacement resulting from the gentrification attributable to downtown development. Linkage exactions can be used to preserve the supply and availability of below-market housing.

Second, linkage is viewed as one way in which municipalities can fund housing in the face of tight budgets. Local budgetary problems have been caused by several factors. One such factor is the limits imposed on municipal taxing powers. For example, cities in California and Massachusetts—two of three states where local linkage programs have emerged—are limited by voter-approved constitutional restrictions on property taxes, a major municipal revenue source. This means that revenue from property taxes on new downtown highrise commercial development is far less than its potential. In addition, since 1981, the Reagan administration significantly reduced federal subsidies for low- and moderate-income housing (Hartman 1986; Hays 1985), and state housing subsidy programs have not been an adequate substitute. Given continued cutbacks in other federal urban programs (for example, general revenue sharing) and the constraints imposed by the Gramm-Rudman budget-balancing legislation, most cities are hard-pressed to maintain their current level of services. Few cities can afford to provide housing without increasing taxes, yet most cities cannot afford to raise taxes—especially if they are earmarked solely for subsidized housing—because of voter opposition to tax increases and "public" housing.

Third, the adoption of linkage programs can be at least partially credited to the emergence of successful progressive coalitions that have gained power in several cities (Clavel 1985). The need for affordable housing, and the expansion of local planning and regulatory powers of municipal government to achieve this goal, have been key features of the electoral platforms of these coalitions, most of which have enjoyed the support of tenant and community housing groups. Conversely, where this progressive political clout is absent, cities (such as New York and Seattle, where the first two factors apply) have not adopted linkage policies proposed by progressive groups.

RATIONALE FOR LINKAGE

The housing linkage concept is premised upon assumptions linking the impact of large commercial development projects to tight housing markets. Linkage proponents have argued that office, hotel, and retail development in the CBD creates housing demand through an influx of new employees who want to live in the central city. In ''tight'' (low vacancy), expensive urban housing markets, this leads to gentrification-caused displacement because these new residents—especially the so-called ''yuppies''—can outbid lower-income residents in neighborhoods that are on the verge of, or actually undergoing, gentrification (Smith and Williams 1986). The conversion of cheaper rental housing (for example, single resident occupancy (SRO) hotels and subsidized housing) into luxury units (especially condominiums), and the demolition of cheaper housing for the construction of more expensive housing to meet new demands, aggravate the existing housing shortage. Given the existence of a significant amount of substandard housing, and the inability of the poor to pay market prices, the result is ''reverse filtering'' (that is, lower-income households being displaced into more expensive and often substandard housing).

In many cities, this phenomenon triggered an anti-displacement movement that demanded both protection against dislocation and the preservation of lower-priced housing (Hartman, Keating and LeGates 1982). In San Francisco, another reaction was a long, and ultimately successful campaign for downtown growth controls to prevent the negative impact of unregulated growth (Hartman 1984; *Planning* 1986).

If the linkage proponents' assumptions are accepted, then housing exactions from commercial developers may be seen as a mitigation measure designed to offset the negative impact of CBD development on the lower-cost housing supply. Legally, zoning exaction fees have been upheld only when a nexus (or connection) between the regulated development and the problem to be mitigated has been demonstrated to exist.

Many developers have denied that either individual downtown commercial development projects or cumulative CBD growth have stimulated excess demand for housing in the central city. They claim that the majority of the CBD workforce is comprised of suburban residents who do not follow jobs to the city. Developers can point to studies that conclude that gentrification does not represent a suburban influx (Gale 1985–86) or that relatively little displacement is caused by gentrification (Schill and Nathan 1983), or that if gentrification does cause displacement, this is the price that must be paid for achieving urban revitalization (Lang 1982). In response to the anti-highrise movement in San Francisco, growth proponents pointed to studies showing that the net benefits of CBD growth in the form of jobs and taxes outweigh the costs of additional public infrastructure and services (Hartman 1984, 263–66). Opponents have commissioned studies that come to the opposite conclusion: that the social and fiscal costs of CBD growth exceed its benefits (Hartman 1984, 263–66; Redmond and Goldsmith 1986). This disagreement is important because the rationale for housing linkage exactions is much weaker if CBD growth produces net benefits, including additional taxes that could be used to subsidize whatever housing is needed. This is a very unlikely scenario, however, given housing costs and the burden housing places on already strained municipal budgets.

The key question then becomes whether CBD development does in fact create a housing demand sufficient to require and justify housing exactions. San Francisco, Santa Monica, and Boston all have done studies to document this pattern in order to justify their linkage policies.

San Francisco's original linkage program was based upon a 1979 downtown planning study (Sedway 1985). It assumed that (1) CBD office use generates one employee per 250 square feet; (2) 40 percent of all office employees in San Francisco reside in the city; and (3) 1.8 working adults occupy each residential unit. These assumptions were later translated into a housing exaction formula requiring office developers to contribute $5 per square foot for housing. In 1984 San Francisco commissioned another study to support a revised housing linkage formula (Recht, Hausrath and Associates 1984). Using similar assumptions, the consultants concluded that a fee twice that later enacted by the city was needed to provide the necessary housing.

Santa Monica commissioned a similar study on the fiscal and housing impacts of new office development, which found that the overwhelming majority (82 percent) of office workers were nonresidents. High housing costs were most often cited as "very important" in these workers' residency location decisions (Hamilton, Rabinovitz, and Stanton 1982). These findings led to the conclusion that a linkage policy could be adopted utilizing a wide range of possible exaction fees, and be directed not toward preventing displacement of city residents by incoming office workers, but rather toward allowing the latter to live in the city through provision of less expensive housing. It should be noted that Santa Monica has had one of the strongest and most effective municipal policies to preserve affordable housing through rent, eviction, demolition, and condominium conversion controls.

Boston has conducted similar studies. A 1973 study indicated that 69 percent of office workers resided outside Boston and only 8 percent of these commuters thought it was likely that they would move into Boston in the near future (Boston Redevelopment Authority 1974). A decade later, however, much of Boston's housing had become much more attractive and expensive. Boston projected that 35 percent of new office jobs in the 1982–92 decade would be held by new Boston residents, generating an annual need for 726 units of low- and moderate-income housing (Boston Redevelopment Authority 1983). This study provided the necessary justification for Boston's housing linkage program.

Where housing is scarce, desirable, and very expensive—as it is in these three cities—and gentrification is either a real or perceived threat, it is relatively easy to justify a housing linkage policy when public financing for subsidized housing is inadequate, and new market-rate housing is beyond the reach of most of the employees of the new businesses generated by CBD growth. It can be argued that these employees will outbid the occupants of less expensive existing housing, causing reverse filtering and displacement, thus justifying the use of linkage to subsidize more affordable housing.

In contrast, it is more difficult to make as persuasive an argument in cities like Chicago and Hartford, which have less expensive housing and higher vacancy rates, and where gentrification is not as serious a threat. Tying new CBD jobs to employment of low-income and minority residents of these cities was seen by many linkage proponents as a more important priority than producing housing exactions. They advocated developer support for construction jobs and employment training for residents, and for investment in neighborhood-based small businesses. Boston and Santa Monica have encouraged resident employment, as well as affordable housing, through their linkage policies.

THE LEGALITY OF LINKAGE

To date the only legal challenge to the existence of the necessary nexus was a developer's suit against San Francisco's transit impact exaction policy. In that case, the city's successful defense was based upon expert support for a $5 per square foot fee on office development in order to mitigate its negative impact on transit (Keating 1986).

The only serious legal challenge to the housing linkage programs came in Boston, where a developer claimed that the city's development impact fee for housing was an illegal tax requiring state authorization (Kennedy 1986). The city argued that it was not a tax but rather a fee already authorized by the state. In 1986 the city won on procedural rather than substantive grounds. Despite these successes, the possibility remains that municipal housing linkage programs may be vulnerable to legal attack on both statutory and constitutional grounds, especially in the absence of state enabling legislation or upon an inadequate showing of the required nexus (Diamond 1983; Bosselman and Stroud 1985).

PROFILES OF HOUSING LINKAGE PROGRAMS

There are numerous accounts of the origin and implementation of linkage programs in San Francisco, Boston, and Santa Monica (Fulton 1985; Gruen 1985; Hartman 1984; Keating 1986; Muzzio and Bailey 1986; Silvern 1985). Rather than repeating the description of events included in those accounts, materials in the descriptions will be used to compare the different form of local linkage policies in the three cities.

Typically, only large-scale projects (for example, in excess of 50,000 square feet) are regulated. Smaller projects are exempt, both to avoid discouraging their development and because, individually, they have a lesser impact on the housing market. Usually, residential and industrial projects also are exempt in order to encourage the development of housing and jobs that are more accessible to lower-income city residents. The Boston Linkage Action Coalition has unsuccessfully attempted to apply the linkage exactions requirements to luxury housing developments. Santa Monica has applied its linkage guidelines to two residential projects. San Francisco has limited its program to projects within the CBD, while Boston's program is citywide.

Boston and Santa Monica limit the use of linkage exactions to the production of low- and moderate-income housing. On the other hand, San Francisco's system gives developers credit if they produce market-rate or below-market-rate units, though more credit is given for the latter (Gruen 1985). Approximately 40 percent of the units produced under San Francisco's Office Housing Production Program (OHPP) have been market-rate units. Community housing groups tried to encourage the city to go a step further and target all of the resources produced through linkage to below-market units. They were partially successful in 1985 when OHPP became a city ordinance.

In San Francisco, Boston, and Santa Monica, developers are given the option of producing the required housing themselves or contributing in-lieu fees to support city housing programs. The 1985 San Francisco legislation requires that all of the housing subsidized by these fees (now amounting to $5.34 per square foot for all commercial development) be used exclusively to benefit low- and moderate-income occupants. In contrast, developers can continue to receive credit for market-rate housing in projects they themselves develop. As of April 1986, 84 percent of the OHPP units have resulted from developers' contributions to city housing programs rather than from their own housing developments. As a result, most of the OHPP-assisted housing has benefited low- and moderate-income persons.

Between 1981 and spring 1986 San Francisco's OHPP had resulted in a total of 4,975 units: 2,720 completed, 1,986 under construction, and 269 "committed." OHPP had been applied to more than 30 CBD office projects totalling 9.7 million square feet and had produced almost $28 million in developer housing contributions. Based on the findings of the 1984 study, San Francisco's community housing groups unsuccessfully lobbied the city in 1985 to double the housing linkage fee to $10 per square foot.

Between 1981 and 1984 Santa Monica's linkage program was implemented on a project-by-project negotiated basis through the state's development agreement statute. Five such agreements resulted in developer subsidization of a total of 181 units (Silvern 1985). After 1984 Santa Monica adopted a new land-use element that contained a housing linkage exaction formula. Office projects exceeding 15,000 square feet must pay a fee of $2.25 per square foot for the first 15,000 square feet and $5 per square foot beyond that threshold.

The majority of a Boston mayoral advisory group recommended imposition of a housing linkage fee of $5 per square foot, to be paid annually in equal installments over 12 years (Advisory Group on Linkage between Downtown Development and Neighborhood Housing 1983). Once this is adjusted for inflation, it will produce only about half that much in constant dollars. Community housing advocates dissented, advocating an up-front lump-sum payment of $5 per square foot. In December 1983 Boston adopted the majority recommendation. In the following two and one-half years, the city received commitments of approximately $40 million payable into a Neighborhood Housing Trust (NHT) beginning in 1987 with the expected completion of the initially-approved projects. Like their San Francisco counterparts, the Boston Linkage Action Coalition has unsuccessfully advocated a higher lump sum of $10 per square foot. The number of housing units Boston's linkage program will actually produce will only be known as the NHT funds are invested in subsidized housing.

THE IMPACT OF LINKAGE HOUSING

The best example for analysis of the impact of a housing linkage program is that of San Francisco's—it is the oldest comprehensive program with the most units produced, underway, and committed. Santa Monica's efforts began later and were less comprehensive. Boston's program was not scheduled to be implemented until the end of the decade.

It is most appropriate to assess the impact of San Francisco's OHPP by comparing its achievements to the city's housing needs. Several estimates of the city's housing needs are available. In November 1980, prior to the initiation of OHPP, San Francisco voters overwhelmingly approved an advisory referendum calling for the production of 20,000 new housing units by 1985. A more reliable estimate may be found in a 1983 study of regional housing needs by the Association of Bay Area Governments (ABAG). According to that study, the city itself would need 14,833 new housing units during the 1980–90 decade. Sixty-eight percent, or 10,087 units, would be needed specifically for low- to moderate-income households (San Francisco Department of City Planning 1984). In order to meet this need, the city would have to produce 1,483 new units annually, of which 1,009 would have to be for low- and moderate-income households.

The first five years of OHPP (1981–86) produced a total of 4,706 new units (either completed or under construction), of which 2,866 (61 percent) were low- and moderate-income units. According to ABAG's projections, OHPP produced about two-thirds of the needed new units, and 57 percent of the needed below-market housing. On its face, this is an impressive achievement, especially when seen as a complement to the units produced by the private market and through subsidized housing programs. Given the high cost of new housing, the continuing elimination of below-market units, escalating housing demand, and the cutback in federal housing subsidy programs, however, OHPP's production appears inadequate. It certainly does not represent a panacea. Moreover, community housing activists have charged that OHPP has been credited with the production of many more below-market units than it actually built (Hartman 1984, 288–9). The lesson of San Francisco's housing linkage program is that linkage exactions alone, even if targeted solely for below-market housing, cannot meet the need for new affordable housing in the face of rising demand, gentrification, a continuing loss of existing low-income housing, and federal and state subsidy cutbacks. On the other hand, housing linkage funds can be leveraged with other available subsidies through a housing trust fund to provide an important source for financing affordable housing (Brooks 1985).

THE IMPACT OF LINKAGE ON DEVELOPMENT

Linkage opponents argue that imposing the additional costs represented by exactions, including housing, will kill the golden goose of development. Exactions may cause developers to build their projects in the suburbs, nearby cities, or other metropolitan areas that do not impose such requirements on commercial developers.

A survey of San Francisco commercial developers covered by OHPP disproves this argument (Keating 1985). Of the one-third who responded, most did not rank OHPP as among the most important factors affecting their decision to build in San Francisco's CBD. Most expected to pass on the costs of OHPP to tenants. It has been estimated the OHPP adds only approximately 3 percent to development costs (Diamond 1983). While developers indicated that OHPP would adversely affect the profitability of their projects, the data were inconclusive since none of the developers had yet completed and rented out their buildings.

This limited study suggests that modest housing linkage programs are not likely to have a negative impact on commercial development where the CBD market is strong. One further way to assist in a housing linkage program's success is to recognize developers' expressed preference for a set linkage fee formula contained in an ordinance rather than being subject to ad hoc negotiations.

THE POLITICS OF LINKAGE

Why have housing linkage programs been adopted in only a few cities when there are so many cities with both downtown growth and serious housing problems? The answer is that progressive and neighborhood-based political movements—which are the type of group most likely to advocate linkage policies—are influential in only a few cities, including Boston, San Francisco, and Santa Monica (Clavel 1985; Fainstein et al. 1983; Ferman 1985; Hartman 1984; Kann 1986; Mollenkopf 1983; Muzzio and Bailey 1986). Where progressive electoral coalitions have gained power and influence and share in the control of city government, linkage becomes a feasible response to housing problems related to downtown growth.

In contrast, where these coalitions have not yet gained political ascendancy, housing linkage policies have not gained acceptance in the face of opposition by developers and their political allies. In New York City housing activists proposed the creation of a housing trust fund, to be partially financed by a fee on commercial development (Shiffman 1985; Tegeler 1984). This proposal was opposed by Mayor Koch, and subsequently rejected by a special mayoral study commission in 1984 (Keating 1986). While New York continues to obtain housing assistance from commercial developers through its incentive zoning policies, it has no linkage policy per se.

Similarly, in Seattle another strong mayor rejected a linkage proposal when the city adopted a new land-use and transportation plan in 1984. Downtown business and developer interests opposed linkage and threatened to sue the city if it adopted such a policy without state enabling legislation (Keating 1986). Like New York, Seattle opted instead for an incentive zoning policy under which developers can make housing contributions and, in return, obtain density bonuses.

In Chicago an advisory committee recommended a linkage program in 1985, with developers strongly dissenting (Keating 1986). Until the reformist mayor Harold Washington gained bare majority control of the Chicago City Council in 1986, there was no possibility that his administration could enact a linkage ordinance. Even though pressured by neighborhood groups that formed part of his constituency, Washington resisted pushing the City Council to adopt this controversial proposal, although he encouraged voluntary (as opposed to mandatory) contributions by developers (Bennett 1986).

In other cities as well, the fate of linkage exactions for housing remains dependent on the political fortunes of local progressive electoral coalitions.

ISSUES, DILEMMAS AND THE FUTURE OF MUNICIPAL HOUSING LINKAGE POLICIES

Housing linkage policies present many unresolved issues. It is not clear how much commercial developers can be forced to pay for housing. While modest fees seem acceptable, if fees for other services (for example, daycare, job training, open space, transit) are added and if housing exactions are increased, many developers may balk.

The example of San Francisco indicates that linkage-subsidized housing cannot meet all of a city's housing needs. Even increased fees that are leveraged are not likely to be translated into adequate amounts of affordable housing. Given the current administration's unwillingness to provide federal housing subsidies, linkage funds may well serve as a substitute for lost federal aid. Community housing groups that have relied on federal funding may find themselves competing with one another for the resources generated through linkage policies.

Determining the most equitable use of linkage funds is another important challenge. Which deserving group of beneficiaries should obtain the housing and who should distribute the funds? Linkage opponents argue that linkage benefits are inherently inequitable regardless of who receives them (Ellickson 1985), yet to date there has been relatively little controversy about the allocation of benefits. A related issue is the need for constant monitoring to ensure that, in the long run, linkage-assisted units continue to remain available to intended beneficiaries (Keating 1986). Linkage proponents have argued that equity requires that all linkage subsidies should permanently benefit only low- and moderate-income persons and not be allowed to be transferred to those who can afford market-rate housing.

The legal fate of linkage remains uncertain. Despite Boston's 1986 victory, other developers may challenge the claimed nexus justifying housing exactions, or claim that linkage exactions require state enabling legislation or else violate constitutional guarantees.

A serious dilemma facing linkage proponents concerns the costs of urban growth upon which successful linkage depends. This dilemma is best illustrated in San Francisco. In 1985 the city adopted a controversial downtown plan that imposes ceilings on allowable CBD growth for several years (Hartman 1984, 273–79). In 1986 a much stronger growth control initiative was passed, culminating a 15-year anti-highrise campaign. If growth is effectively reduced to eliminate the negative impacts of overdevelopment, then pressure on the housing market will be reduced. At the same time there will be a reduction in the housing linkage resource produced as a result of the addition of new office floor space. This is a price that limited-growth proponents may accept, but one that raises difficulties for community housing groups that benefit from housing trust funds subsidized by linkage exaction fees.

The future of linkage is uncertain. By 1986 CBD vacancy rates nationwide had risen as a result of overbuilding, and 1986 tax reform legislation reduced the tax shelter incentive for much commercial development. In view of the limited influence of progressive local electoral coalitions and the opposition of downtown and development interests to regulation, linkage does not seem destined to become a widespread phenomenon. In the face of continued federal cutbacks in urban aid, however, those cities experiencing CBD growth may at least consider inclusionary or incentive zoning policies in an effort to encourage developers to contribute to local housing programs, even if mandatory exactions prove to be infeasible.

In conclusion, downtown-neighborhood housing linkage policies can be seen as a progressive local response to a conservative national regime, and—in those cities fortunate enough to have an enduring downtown development boom that can be harnessed to promote affordable housing and minimize displacement—a creative response to the urban housing crisis. Linkage can be seen either as the reverse of trickle-down urban economic development policies or as an attempt to ensure that lower-income city residents benefit from CBD commercial growth. Linkage can also be characterized as a policy to ensure that private corporate expansion contributes to a more equitable revitalization of the central city.

REFERENCES

Advisory Group on Linkage between Downtown Development and Neighborhood Housing. 1983. *Report to the Mayor*. Boston.

Bennett, Larry. 1986. "When Progressives Collide: Chicago's Save Our Neighborhood/

Save Our City Coalition and the Washington Administration.'' Paper presented at the annual meeting of the Association of the Collegiate Schools of Planning. Milwaukee.

Bosselman, Fred, and Nancy Stroud. 1985. ''Mandatory Tithes: The Legality of Land Development Linkage.'' *Nova Law Journal* 9.

Boston Redevelopment Authority. 1983. *Boston's Prospective Development and the Linkage to Housing Needs*. Boston.

———. 1974. *Boston's New High-Rise Office Buildings: A Study of Employees and their Housing Preferences*. Boston.

Brooks, Mary. 1985. ''Housing Trust Funds: Lessons from Inclusionary Zoning.'' In *Inclusionary Zoning Moves Downtown*, edited by Dwight Merriam, David Brower, and Philip Tegeler. Chicago: Planners Press.

Clavel, Pierre. 1985. *The Progressive City: Planning and Participation, 1969–1984*. New Brunswick, NJ: Rutgers University Press.

Diamond, Susan. 1983. ''The San Francisco Office/Housing Program: Social Policy Underwritten by Private Enterprise.'' *Harvard Environmental Law Review* 7.

Ellickson, Robert. 1985. ''Inclusionary Housing Programs: Yet Another Misguided Urban Policy?'' In *Inclusionary Zoning Moves Downtown*, edited by Dwight Merriam, David Brower, and Philip Tegeler. Chicago: Planners Press.

Fainstein, Susan, et al. 1983 *Restructuring the City: The Political Economy of Urban Development*. New York: Longman.

Ferman, Barbara. 1985. *Governing the Ungovernable City: Political Skill, Leadership and the Modern Mayor*. Philadelphia: Temple University Press.

Fulton, William. 1985. ''On the Beach with the Progressives.'' *Planning* 51:1 (January).

Gale, Dennis. 1985–86. ''Demographic Research on Gentrification and Displacement.'' *Journal of Planning Literature* 1:1

Gruen, Nina. 1985. ''A Case History of the San Francisco Office/Housing Linkage Program.'' In *Downtown Linkages*, edited by Douglas Porter. Washington, DC: Urban Land Institute.

Hamilton, Rabinovitz, and Stanton. 1982. *Office Development in Santa Monica: The Municipal Fiscal and Housing Impact*. Santa Monica: City of Santa Monica.

Hartman, Chester. 1986. ''Housing Policies Under the Reagan Administration.'' In *Critical Perspectives on Housing*, edited by Rachel Bratt, Chester Hartman, and Ann Meyerson. Philadelphia: Temple University Press.

———.1984. *The Transformation of San Francisco*. Totowa, NJ: Rowman and Allanheld.

Hartman, Chester, Dennis Keating, and Richard LeGates. 1982. *Displacement: How to Fight It*. Berkeley: National Housing Law Project.

Hays, Allen. 1985. *The Federal Government and Urban Housing: Ideology and Change in Public Policy*. Albany: State University of New York Press.

Kann, Mark. 1986. *Middle Class Radicalism in Santa Monica*. Philadelphia: Temple University Press.

Keating, Dennis. 1986. ''Linking Downtown Development to Broader Community Goals: An Analysis of Linkage Policy in Three Cities.'' *Journal of the American Planning Association* 52:1 (Spring).

———.1985. ''Downtown Linkage Policies: A Case Study of Developers' Opinions on San Francisco's Program.'' In *Downtown Linkages*, edited by Douglas Porter. Washington, D.C.: Urban Land Institute.

Kennedy, John. 1986. ''SJC Reverses Ruling Against Linkage Laws.'' *The Boston Globe*, August 22.

Lang, Michael. 1982. *Gentrification and Urban Decline: Strategies for America's Older Cities*. Cambridge MA: Ballinger.

Mollenkopf, John. 1983. *The Contested City*. Princeton: Princeton University Press.

Muzzio, Douglas and Robert Bailey. 1986. ''Economic Development, Housing, Zoning: A Tale of Two Cities.'' *Journal of Urban Affairs* 8:1 (Winter).

Planning. 1986. ''California Voters Speak Up On Growth.'' 52:12 (December).

Recht, Hausrath and Associates. 1984. *The Economic Basis for an Office-Housing Production Program*. San Francisco: San Francisco Department of City Planning.

Redmond, Tim and David Goldsmith. 1986. ''The End of the High-Rise Jobs Myth.'' *Planning* 52:4 (April).

San Francisco Department of City Planning. 1984. *Residence Element of the Comprehensive Plan of San Francisco*. San Francisco: San Francisco Department of City Planning.

Schill, Michael and Richard Nathan. 1983. *Revitalizing America's Cities: Neighborhood Reinvestment and Displacement*. Albany: State University of New York Press.

Sedway, Paul. 1985. ''The San Francisco Downtown Plan: Office Boom Brings Housing Boon.'' In *Inclusionary Zoning Moves Downtown*, edited by Dwight Merriam, David Brower, and Philip Tegeler. Chicago: Planners Press.

Shiffman, Ron. 1985. ''A Housing Trust Fund for New York City: One Proposal.'' In *Inclusionary Zoning Moves Downtown*, edited by Dwight Merriam, David Brower, and Philip Tegeler. Chicago: Planners Press.

Silvern, Paul. 1985. ''Negotiating the Public Interest: California's Development Agreement Statute.'' *Land Use Law* 37:1 (October).

Smith, Neil and Peter Williams. 1986. *Gentrification of the City*. Winchester, MA: Allen and Unwin.

Tegeler, Philip. 1984. ''Developer Payments and Downtown Housing Trusts.'' *Clearinghouse Review* 18:6 (November).

LINKAGE: COMMENT

Douglas R. Porter

Dennis Keating's paper provides an excellent overview of current downtown/housing linkage programs and the issues they raise. He rightly observes that in a few cities with strong downtown markets and active citizen coalitions, linkage programs can make significant contributions to meeting mounting needs for affordable housing. Keating concludes, however, that such programs do not offer a panacea for local housing problems, and may raise economic and legal obstacles that many cities will find difficult to overcome. He cautions, for example, that linkage exactions alone cannot hope to meet all needs for low-cost housing, that benefits flow to housing only when downtowns continue to grow, and that the legal fate of linkage remains uncertain. He concludes that, all in all, linkage does not seem destined to become a widespread phenomenon.

The origins of the linkage concept are strongly rooted in the post–1960s spread of exactions and fees placed on development by many urban and suburban jurisdictions. Communities all over the nation, struggling to finance expansion of infrastructure systems and increasingly reluctant to underwrite new development, have turned to requirements for private sharing of costs for erstwhile public facilities. The notion that unwanted effects of development should be mitigated by donations of land, cash, or construction of public facilities has now been carried over to downtown areas. Where once almost every city in the United States was bent on attracting developers to its downtown, the recent vitality of many downtown economies has opened opportunities for public exactions. Experience in San Francisco and Boston testifies to the (grudging) willingness of developers to contribute to public programs in return for approval to build in a strong market. (In both cities, in fact, developers usually have to promise a good deal more than housing payments to win approval.)

Yet the use of the housing linkage concept raises serious questions with regard to legal and equity issues that have troubled such programs from the start. At the most elemental level, linkage programs tap a small group of downtown developers to secure funds for a community-wide housing problem. ''Opportunistic'' is the term John J. Costonis, a noted law professor, applies to this notion, commenting further that the developer is selected ''as the 'houser of last resort' because he's the guy they can most easily hit in the regulatory process'' (Merriam, Brower, and Tegeler 1985). Bosselman and Stroud (1985) also raise questions about the legal foundation of linkage programs. Other lawyers support linkage exactions, however, citing the ''rational nexus'' between office development and housing needs that is offered as the reason for enacting linkage programs (Share and Diamond 1983).

Whether or not one believes in the rational nexus of downtown offices with low-income housing, it is fair to say that the connection between the two is somewhat more remote and difficult to track than is the case with many other types of exactions. The Recht, Hausrath and Associates' study for San Francisco referred to by Keating, for example, offers less than wholehearted support for the existence of a direct cause and effect relationship between office development and the housing market. According to Recht and Hausrath, additional economic activities in an expanding downtown will not necessarily be located in new buildings, nor will new office workers necessarily hold newly created jobs in new office space. Their findings emphasize the cumulative effect of downtown growth on the housing market, rather than the incremental effects of new construction (Recht, Hausrath and Associates 1984).

Furthermore, linkage payments that result in higher prices for downtown space provide windfall gains to existing property owners, who stand to gain both from increased property values and from any suppression of new construction due to linkage costs (Gruen 1985).

Linkage fees represent an unusual form of revenue generation for local governments. Unlike many other fees and taxes, linkage fees affect a very small group of taxpayers. The number of developers who have paid into the Boston program during its four years of existence, for example, is but a few dozen. A similar condition is found in San Francisco, with the added factor that the new voter-enacted limits on office construction will allow only two or three large buildings to be developed each year. Compare this to most excise taxes, such as those on cigarettes, liquor, and even hotel rooms, which are paid by thousands and perhaps millions of consumers in any given community. Or consider typical fees for real estate transfers, business licenses, and automobiles, which, again, affect a great many people and firms.

It can be argued, of course, that linkage fees ultimately may be passed on to tenants and from them to consumers in the form of higher prices of products and services, thus spreading the incidence of the tax. This presumes that developers have not had to absorb the added costs in the form of lower profits or that landowners have not been forced to accept a lower price for their land, reflecting the increased cost of developing new buildings—both scenarios have been advanced by many economists. It is safe to state, however, that public officials, when they adopt linkage fees, believe they are taxing developers of new buildings, but that the ultimate payers of linkage fees are determined by a host of market forces that are difficult to predict.

Linkage fees, therefore, are highly selective in application, excluding great quantities of activities—even other real estate activities in the downtown area—that also affect the housing market. Furthermore, revenues from linkage fees rest on a notoriously unstable base: the cycles of real estate activity that produce office buildings in some quantity. Given present office vacancy rates across the nation, and the chilling effects of the new tax reform act, the construction of new office buildings is likely to dwindle rapidly in the next few years in most cities. This suggests that linkage programs do not offer very dependable sources of revenue for housing assistance programs.

Alternatively, the emerging concept of housing trust funds based on a variety of revenue sources offers a more secure and broadly based financial base for assisting production of affordable housing. Several states and cities have adopted such funds, including those that have established linkage programs. California's housing trust fund, for example, is financed by revenues from taxes on offshore oil. Connecticut, as part of a 1986 package of new housing programs, set up a rental housing assistance trust fund that will accept donations from business firms that, in turn, will receive tax credits on state corporate taxes. At the local level, Montgomery County, Maryland provides rent supplements from a trust fund that receives revenues from a transfer tax on condominium and cooperative housing sales.

Another example is provided by Jersey City, which, like several other New Jersey jurisdictions responding to the housing mandates of the Mount Laurel court decisions, has established an "experimental housing policy" that calls for developers of projects anywhere in the city either to construct housing units or to make payments into a housing trust fund that will sponsor affordable housing projects. The city's policy statement labels this a linkage policy intended to generate affordable housing from developers of market-rate housing and commercial projects (City of Jersey City 1986).

These are but a few of the possible revenue sources that might be tapped to provide capital for housing trust funds. The point is that such funds can draw from a broad base of tax- and fee-payers rather than the slim few on which linkage programs depend. Thus, they represent more durable and equitable sources of funds to assist in the production of low- and moderate-income housing.

It is perhaps useful to return to Keating's conclusion that linkage programs present a creative but inherently limited response to the urban housing crisis.

Given the limits of the linkage concept, housing advocates should cast a wider net for housing assistance funds, a possibility that could be enhanced by establishing housing trust funds.

REFERENCES

Bosselman, F., and N. Stroud. 1985. "Mandatory Tithes: The Legality of Land Development Linkage." *Nova Law Journal* 9:381–412.

City of Jersey City, New Jersey. 1986. *Experimental Housing Policy for Jersey City—Summary*. Jersey City: City of Jersey City.

Gruen, C. 1985. "The Economics of Requiring Office-Space Development to Contribute to the Production and/or Rehabilitation of Housing." In *Downtown Linkages*, edited by D. Porter. Washington, DC: Urban Land Institute.

Merriam, D., D. Brower, and P. Tegeler. 1985. *Inclusionary Zoning Moves Downtown*. Chicago: Planners Press.

Recht, Hausrath, and Associates. 1984. *The Economic Basis for an Office-Housing Production Program*. San Francisco: San Francisco Department of City Planning.

Share, L. and S. Diamond. 1983. "San Francisco's Office/Housing Production Program." *Land Use Law and Planning Digest* 35(10):4–10.

10

SUBSIDIZED HOUSING AT RISK: THE SOCIAL COSTS OF PRIVATE OWNERSHIP

Emily Paradise Achtenberg

In almost 50 years of federal housing assistance, this country has produced barely four million units of assisted housing for low- and moderate-income families—a dismal track record compared with available resources and need. Of some ten million renter households with incomes less than 50 percent of median, only 2.5 million live in subsidized housing (U.S. House of Representatives 1983a, 19). Yet all too often, these units represent the only decent housing available to and affordable by lower-income people.

Since the early 1960s, the federal government has increasingly relied on and encouraged the private sector to provide and maintain housing for lower-income families through a variety of direct and indirect mortgage insurance, rental assistance, and tax shelter subsidies. Today, a significant proportion of the units constructed or rehabilitated under these arrangements is at risk of being lost as viable, affordable housing. Of the 688,000 units developed over the last 25 years through the Section 221d3 Below-Market Interest Rate (BMIR), Section 236, and Rent Supplement programs, fully one-quarter have defaulted on their mortgages and are in various stages of assignment, foreclosure, and/or resale by HUD (see Table 10.1). Moreover, by 1991 at least 69,000 Section 221d3 BMIR and Section 236 units owned by profit-motivated sponsors will have reached the point in their regulatory lives at which their mortgages can be prepaid without restriction, eliminating all future use and occupancy limitations (U.S. General Accounting Office 1986, 25). By 1996 there will be at least 282,000 subsidized units in projects that are ripe for mortgage prepayment.

These trends and the overall experience of the Section 221d3 BMIR, Section 236, and Rent Supplement housing inventory merit careful scrutiny for several

Table 10.1
Status of HUD-insured Subsidized Multifamily Inventory

	Projects	Units	Amount (in billions)
	Currently Insured by HUD*		
Sec. 236	3,425	383,462	$6.6
Sec. 231d3 BMIR	939	113,122	1.7
Rent Supp.	226	15,559	.2
Total	4,592	512,142	$8.5
Percent	72.9	74.4	74.6
	Held by HUD+		
Sec. 236	448	49,506	$.8
Sec. 221d3 BMIR	244	36,440	.5
Rent Supp.	40	2,285	-
Total	732	88,231	$1.3
Percent	11.6	12.8	11.4
	Owned by HUD+ +		
All	45	6,405	N.A.
Percent	.7	.9	

Table 10.1 (continued)

	Projects	Units	Amount (in billions)
	Sold by HUD+ +		
All	831	65,445	N.A.
Percent	13.1	9.5	
	Unknown		
All	97	16,014	N.A.
Percent	1.7	2.3	
	Total Ever Insured by HUD**		
Sec. 236	4,240	464,483	$8.1
Sec. 221d3 BMIR	1,590	191,120	2.9
Rent Supp.	467	32,635	.4
Total	6,297	688,238	$11.4
Percent	100.0	100.0	100.0

*HUD Housing Information and Statistics Division (as of 3/11/86). FOIA Request.

+HUD Housing Information and Statistics Division (as of 6/30/86). FOIA Request.

+ +HUD Office of Multifamily Housing Management and Property Disposition (as of 9/30/85). FOIA Request.

**HUD Housing Information and Statistics Division (as of 4/4/85). FOIA Request.

reasons. First, although this housing constitutes a relatively small portion of the total federally subsidized stock, it plays a vital role by providing shelter primarily for the "working poor," especially for families with children. While tenants in Section 236 units tend to be somewhat better off financially than those in Section 8 assisted or public housing projects, their median income is still well below the poverty level, and less than half the median for all U.S. households. In 1979 (the last year for which data are available), the median income of families certified for occupancy in Section 236 housing was $6,885, compared to $4,252 for public housing; the poverty level for a family of four in 1979 was $7,412 (U.S. House of Representatives 1983a, 20). Moreover, in contrast to Section 8, which has primarily served elderly and small households, 90 percent of the Section 236 units are family-oriented (U.S. Comptroller General 1980b, 78).

Moreover, in many of the nation's larger cities, Section 221d3 BMIR, Section 236, and Rent Supplement projects have become a key resource for the stabilization of inner-city neighborhoods and for the maintenance of racial and economic diversity in rapidly gentrifying markets. In an era of escalating costs and lapsed federal commitment for the construction of new low- and moderate-income housing, conservation of these existing subsidized resources has become a compelling public issue for progressive housing advocates, policymakers, and practitioners at the local and national levels. Finally, the troubled history of these programs calls into question the utility of traditional private sector solutions to social housing problems, and suggests the need—as well as the potential—for alternative ownership and financing strategies.

PROGRAM ORIGINS AND HISTORY

From the beginning, the housing produced under the Section 221d3 BMIR, Section 236, and Rent Supplement programs has been characterized by a fundamental duality of purpose: to meet the housing needs of those the private market is unable to serve, and to accommodate the requirements of the private, profit-motivated housing industry. Central to the original concept and design of the programs, this dichotomy soon became a source of internal tension which the federal government was forced to manage.

The Section 221d3 BMIR program was launched in 1961 by the Kennedy administration, against a background of depression in the homebuilding industry and the growing problem of unmet inner-city housing needs. Its primary purpose was to stimulate housing production, by enabling private profit-motivated entities—for the first time in the history of American housing—to develop subsidized housing for lower-income families. Hitherto the exclusive domain of local housing authorities—with a limited exception introduced in 1959 for nonprofit sponsors of elderly housing—subsidized housing as a public enterprise was increasingly under attack and without a viable constituency for an expanded role.

The new program was aimed primarily at moderate-income families with incomes too high for public housing but too low to secure decent, affordable shelter on the private market. To create incentives for private production, the government provided what in effect was a 40-year direct loan at a reduced interest rate for up to 90 percent of project development costs (100 percent for nonprofit sponsors), insured by the Federal Housing Administration (FHA). Initially, Section 221d3 BMIR loans were issued at the Treasury borrowing rate, but in 1965 the interest rate was fixed at 3 percent, representing the first true government subsidy (the difference between the Treasury borrowing rate and 3 percent interest paid by the project) for privately owned rental housing.

Also in 1965, the Rent Supplement program brought the real estate industry for the first time into the development of housing for low-income families, by providing federal subsidies to pay a portion of the rent in private housing built with FHA mortgage insurance. This program, which represented a direct attempt to shift responsibility for provision of low-rent housing from the public to the private sector, passed the Senate by just one vote—with aggressive support from the real estate industry, which ardently proclaimed the virtues of a private sector solution:

> [G]iven the same advantages available to public housing, we can and will produce more and better housing for low-income families. . . . We can and will do it quicker than can be done by publicly financed and owned housing. . . . We can and will do it at less cost to the federal and local government . . . without the serious disadvantages now recognized by even the most ardent public housers (U.S. Senate 1965, 391).

In 1968, with the discovery of urban poverty as a result of the ghetto rebellions and civil rights protests, a major new subsidized housing initiative launched by the Johnson administration firmly established the role of the private sector. Using the blueprint provided by the President's Committee on Urban Housing (headed by industrialist Edgar Kaiser), the 1968 Housing Act called for production of 26 million housing units over a ten-year period, including six million subsidized units, with "fullest practicable utilization of the resources and capabilities of private enterprise." The Kaiser Committee noted:

> The nation has been slow to realize that private industry in many cases is an efficient vehicle for achieving social goals. . . . One of the basic lessons of the history of Federal housing programs seems to be that the programs which work best—such as the FHA mortgage insurance programs—are those that channel the forces of existing economic institutions into productive areas. This approach has proved to be better than . . . starting afresh outside the prevailing market system (President's Committee on Urban Housing 1968, 54).

The Section 236 program, a cornerstone of the 1968 Housing Act's ambitious effort, was similar in concept and purpose to Section 221d3 BMIR, but featured an improved program design and a somewhat deeper subsidy. Under this new approach, the reduced interest rate was achieved through direct monthly payments to private lenders, making up the difference between debt service at the FHA market rate and at 1 percent interest. This change was designed to assist private developers in serving a somewhat lower-income constituency, but also to encourage the participation of private lenders and to reduce the substantial up-front budgetary outlays associated with direct government loans in the deficit-prone "guns and butter" era of the late 1960s.

While the level of subsidy provided to tenants under these programs was relatively modest and indirect (especially in comparison with public housing), the benefits offered to private developers and lenders were significant. With a minimal equity investment—often effectively reduced to 1 to 2 percent of project costs through standard FHA underwriting techniques—developers were guaranteed a market as well as an opportunity for limited annual cash dividends with seemingly little risk. Lenders were fully protected, since problem mortgages could be assigned to FHA for 99 percent of the outstanding balance plus accrued interest. In exchange, project owners and lenders needed only to submit to FHA regulation of construction and project operations for a minimum of 20 years (40 years for nonprofit and rent supplement projects). Use and occupancy of the project was restricted to low- and moderate-income families for the duration of this regulatory period, after which time the mortgage could be prepaid and all government restrictions eliminated.

Despite these features, in their early years the programs achieved only modest production rates, with about 175,000 insured units by the end of 1969 (U.S. Department of HUD 1979a, Table 6). Many of these early projects were developed by nonprofit sponsors, primarily church-related organizations responding to the desperate housing needs of their inner-city minority constituencies.

In the late 1960s a series of modifications to the tax code were introduced to further stimulate the production of low- and moderate-income rental housing by private, profit-motivated developers. In 1969 accelerated depreciation—a key incentive for all forms of real estate investment since the 1950s—was limited to newly constructed rental housing. Through this device, substantial tax losses could be generated in the early years of project ownership in the form of depreciation deductions that could be used to shelter other income from taxation and to defer and ultimately reduce owners' tax liability.

The 1969 Tax Reform Act also included more favorable rules governing the "recapture" of income sheltered from taxation in subsidized housing, plus a special provision allowing rehabilitation costs for low- and moderate-income housing to be fully depreciated in five years. Earlier changes in the housing laws encouraged individual investors to purchase limited partnership interests in government-assisted rental housing projects, which entitled them to a proportionate share of the total stream of tax losses while limiting their personal liability to the amount of their cash contributions. Because such a large portion of the depreciable cost of these projects was financed with borrowed funds, these highly leveraged tax shelters soon proved extremely attractive to investors, who in turn contributed substantial capital up-front to project developers in the form of syndication proceeds (U.S. Congress 1977).

This preferential tax treatment, in combination with favorable financing terms and interest subsidies provided by the Section 236 program, significantly enhanced the profitability of subsidized housing and set the stage for the production boom of the early 1970s. From fiscal years 1970 through 1974, close to 500,000 subsidized Section 221d3 BMIR, Section 236, and Rent Supplement units were built or substantially rehabilitated, primarily by profit-motivated sponsors (U.S. Department of HUD 1979a, Table 6.)

Early Project Failures

By the end of 1975 the subsidized housing inventory was experiencing failures of major proportions. Of some 640,000 units produced, 90,000, or 14 percent, were in projects with defaulted mortgages already assigned to FHA/HUD.

These failed units were about evenly divided between Section 221d3 BMIR and Section 236, although proportionately the assignment rate for BMIRs was significantly higher than for 236s (24 percent versus 10 percent). More than half of these units had been assigned within the previous two years alone. While approximately three-fourths of this troubled inventory remained ''HUD-held'' (assigned), the remaining 25 percent (22,000 units) had been acquired by HUD through the foreclosure process. Some 8,000 of these units had already been resold to private owners (U.S. Department of HUD 1979a, Tables 20 and 35).

Although these early failures are commonly attributed to unanticipated circumstances beyond the programs' control—specifically, to the inability of tenant incomes and rents to keep pace with rapidly escalating operating costs in a period of rampant inflation—they also reveal a more fundamental set of problems. To begin with, the basic design and incentive structure of the programs emphasized front-end profits and risk-avoidance for private developers and lenders at the expense of long-term project viability. Through the limited partnership vehicle, developers could collect their syndication proceeds and then shift ownership risk to passive investors who were totally removed from project operations. The original mortgagees earned their one-time placement fees and passed their fully insured loans on to permanent lenders, avoiding exposure for faulty feasibility decisions. FHA, under pressure to comply with the 1968 Housing Act's production goals and resistant to its new social welfare role, routinely approved loans with little scrutiny. As a result, many projects were infeasible from the start—including a significant proportion of nonprofit sponsored projects whose owners were well-intentioned but inexperienced.

As costs began to skyrocket and more and more projects developed financial difficulties, this same incentive structure made problems difficult to resolve. Limited partners, who might be concerned with the potential tax consequences of foreclosure, were either unaware of their impending financial liability or content to let the general partners delay foreclosure until depreciation benefits expired. As interest rates rose, permanent lenders had little incentive to avoid or cure mortgage defaults, preferring instead to assign their problem loans to

FHA for 99 cents on the dollar. For most nonprofit sponsors, given the choice of reducing project services or raising rents to levels constituents could not afford, mortgage default seemed the only logical solution.

Faced with this rapidly deteriorating situation, the government's primary response was to avoid any further obligation that might be required to preserve the social purpose of the housing. FHA, still viewing itself as an insurer of untroubled suburban loans, effectively ignored the new tenant- and project-oriented responsibilities imposed on it by the subsidized housing programs. While lenders' assignment claims were promptly paid, the government refused to provide an operating subsidy for the projects, as it had been forced to do in 1969 for public housing. In 1974, when an increasingly besieged Congress was forced to authorize a limited additional subsidy to cover increased tax and utility costs in troubled Section 236 projects, HUD refused to implement the program (U.S. Department of HUD 1978, 22). As one critical report noted: "Behind the Department's [HUD's] failure to act was the long-held belief that the government was not responsible for this housing after it was built except to pay an insurance claim, and, if necessary, dispose of the property" (U.S. Senate 1980, 70).

Indeed, once HUD foreclosed on and acquired title to a formerly subsidized project, its only objective was to dispose of the property as quickly as possible at the highest return to the mortgage insurance funds that guaranteed the subsidized loans, and to divest itself of continuing involvement at the least possible cost. Low-bid custodial management contracts were frequently awarded to unscrupulous firms that provided minimal services. Not surprisingly, during this period HUD gained a reputation as the "nation's largest slumlord" (U.S. Senate 1980, 71).

Moreover, while the average disposition was netting the government only 45 cents on its insurance dollar, the adverse impact of these sales on tenant affordability was substantial. According to one study, almost three-quarters of the projects sold between fiscal years 1967–76 experienced sizeable rent increases, despite the effective capital cost writedown resulting from low resale prices (U.S. Department of HUD 1975, 2).

During this period, community opposition to HUD's policies was led by Preachers United to Save Humanity (PUSH), a Chicago-based coalition of nonprofit church sponsors, local realtors, and mortgage bankers. This group demanded a program of mortgage relief for troubled projects, as well as opportunities for increased private sector involvement (Preachers United to Save Housing, Inc. 1975). While a two-year moratorium on foreclosures was granted, few concrete steps were taken until 1976, when HUD was forced to seek a Congressional appropriation to replenish its depleted mortgage insurance funds. With the recognition that the public would ultimately foot the bill for mounting insurance claims and foreclosure costs in excess of project premiums, pressure for remedial action intensified.

Accordingly, HUD implemented several new initiatives. First it began routinely to grant "mortgage relief," especially to nonprofit owners of troubled projects, through such mechanisms as debt service deferrals which allowed interest and often principal payments to be postponed repeatedly. Second, it authorized the sale of nonprofit projects to profit-motivated purchasers, in order to infuse new capital by taking advantage of preferential treatment afforded to low- and moderate-rental housing by the Tax Reform Act of 1976. These efforts, which had been recommended by PUSH, provided limited and temporary help to some projects but ultimately led to more serious problems.

Finally, HUD agreed to divert a portion of available rental subsidies under the new Section 8 housing assistance program for use in troubled subsidized multifamily projects, under a special Loan Management Set-Aside allocation. This effort was designed primarily to avoid future claims on the mortgage insurance funds, while enabling HUD to meet its Section 8 commitment targets in the face of a faltering production program (*Housing Affairs Letter* 1975). Studies suggest that most Section 8 assistance in these early years was allocated to relatively healthy projects owned by profit-motivated sponsors with no history of default or mortgage relief (U.S. Department of HUD 1977, 2). Not surprisingly, these limited efforts proved insufficient to stem the rising tide of mortgage defaults, assignments, and foreclosures.

The Carter Years: A Quasi-Social Response

By the time the Carter administration took office in 1977, a groundswell of community opposition to HUD's foreclosure and disposition policies had developed, spearheaded by activist tenant groups in Boston. At this time, two-thirds of the assisted multifamily inventory in Boston was seriously troubled, and the local HUD office warned that as many as 7,000 families would face substantial rent increases or displacement if prevailing trends continued (Boston HUD Area Office 1977). A series of Congressional hearings chaired by Senator Edward Brooke of Massachusetts focused attention on the issue and provided a public forum for community demands to keep the housing affordable and viable. The new administration declared a moratorium on HUD multifamily sales and set up a task force to study the issue.

The final report of the Multifamily Property Utilization Task Force, issued in 1978, sought to establish a new view of the HUD-assisted multifamily inventory as "not only an investment in housing units for low- and moderate-income people, but also in neighborhoods and in the well-being of some of the Nation's major cities" (U.S. Department of HUD 1978, 2). Seen in these terms, the government's continued failure to assume responsibility for this housing could be extremely costly, the Task Force warned:

> If present trends continue unchecked, HUD's inventory of assigned and acquired projects could rise to more than 3000 projects by 1983—the equivalent of two years of assisted housing production. HUD could easily find itself owning 1,286 of these projects—an estimated 150,000 units. Losses to the insurance fund[s] alone would be over $3 billion.

The total loss would actually be far greater when the impact on surrounding neighborhoods and the loss of affordable units . . . are considered (U.S. Department of HUD 1978, 2).

Conversely, the Task Force argued, a strategy of restoring and preserving existing HUD-held and HUD-owned projects as affordable housing and of preventing future assignments and acquisitions would be fiscally and socially prudent.

Consistent with this new philosophy, a series of legislative and programmatic initiatives was developed with the participation of tenant and low-income housing advocates, focusing primarily on the management and disposition of HUD-acquired properties. Most significant were the Housing and Community Development Amendments of 1978, which required HUD to manage and dispose of foreclosed projects in a manner that would preserve their low- and moderate-income character, revitalize neighborhoods, maintain decent, safe, and sanitary conditions, and minimize tenant displacement—while protecting the financial interest of the government in the ''least costly manner.'' Although these objectives were somewhat contradictory, Congressional intent, at least, was that ''the principal goal of the [property disposition] program shall be to maintain the existing stock of multifamily projects as decent housing available to and affordable by low- and moderate-income families'' (U.S. Senate 1978).

Pursuant to this legislative mandate, HUD developed a new ''repair and sell'' policy for acquired multifamily projects, authorizing direct expenditures from the mortgage insurance funds for publicly sponsored rehabilitation and improvements. Project and neighborhood residents were required to be employed in repair programs to the maximum feasible extent (Simons 1978). In addition, tenant rental charges in HUD-owned projects were reduced to 25 percent of income, with the balance of operating expenses subsidized through the insurance funds. The combined effect of these indirect rehabilitation and operating subsidies was to place foreclosed, formerly subsidized projects on a comparable footing with public housing, at least temporarily.

Further, while the major purpose of this effort was still to prepare the properties for resale to private owners, the government agreed to sell formerly subsidized projects (and unsubsidized projects currently serving lower-income families) with a project-based rental subsidy at least sufficient to assist all income-eligible tenants and to meet community needs for lower-income housing (U.S. Department of HUD 1979b). Toward this end, HUD authorized a new Property Disposition Set-Aside of Section 8 housing assistance payments and mandated its use for the sale of HUD-owned projects—creating, in effect, the first entitlement subsidy for lower-income tenants (U.S. Department of HUD 1979c). In addition, HUD agreed to finance property sales with direct purchase money mortgages and/or continued mortgage insurance, extending the government's long-term risk-exposure typically for another 40 years. Finally, a new system for selecting purchasers on the basis of technical merit and ability—rather than high bid—was developed (U.S. Department of HUD 1979d), along with measures encouraging negotiated sales to tenant cooperatives and other qualified sponsors at below-market prices.

As a result of these new initiatives, of some 15,000 formerly subsidized units sold during 1980–81, all but 1,000 were sold with project-based rental subsidies for at least 15 years (see Table 10.2). Locally, in cities such as Boston, HUD's repair-and-sell program significantly upgraded the condition of the properties and their surrounding neighborhoods, improved their marketability, and provided jobs for a number of residents (Citizens Housing and Planning Association 1979). Also in Boston, a variety of innovative approaches to involving residents in property management, disposition, and ownership were tested on a demonstration basis, resulting in the eventual conversion of five projects to limited-equity cooperatives. Several other projects were sold to community-based housing organizations representing a new generation of nonprofit sponsors with substantial development experience and capacity (Citizens Housing and Planning Association 1982).

With respect to the remainder of the inventory that still was privately owned, the government took several steps. First, the Section 8 Loan Management program was expanded to address more troubled projects: between fiscal years 1976–79, some 180,000 privately owned units were assisted (U.S. General Accounting Office 1984, 2). Protracted class action litigation on the Section 236 tax and utility subsidy issue was settled with $30 million worth of rent rebates to tenants (Goodwin 1980). In addition, a new Flexible Subsidy program provided direct government grants and/or deferred zero-interest loans for project improvements. While these efforts helped bolster the private ownership and financing arrangements that had led to project problems in the first place—and emphasized improved project feasibility rather than tenant affordability—they also included some concessions toward the view of assisted housing as a social resource. For example, in exchange for receipt of Flexible Subsidy funds, profit-motivated owners were required to contribute additional capital to their projects, to upgrade management, and to preserve the low-income use restrictions for the full mortgage term.

For the most part, however, where the social goals conflicted directly with the requirements of the private owners, the government's message remained mixed at best. For example, an investigation by the General Accounting Office (GAO) in early 1980 revealed that over 70 percent of all multifamily projects (subsidized and unsubsidized) with HUD-held mortgages continued to be in default, often for an extended period. More than one-third of these delinquent loans appeared to be languishing in a perpetual "limbo" state, with no action by the government either to work them out or to foreclose (U.S. Comptroller General 1980a, 2). Moreover, the average time required to accomplish a foreclosure requested by HUD was two and one-half years.

Further, GAO noted that most project owners who failed to make their mortgage payments could continue to deduct their interest obligations for tax purposes and frequently did not report these unpaid accruals if and when their projects

Table 10.2
HUD-subsidized Multifamily Property Disposition Activity, 1970–1985

				Formerly-Subsidized Projects*					
				Method of Sale					
		Acquired	Sold	Project Subsidy	Tenant Subsidy	No Subsidy	Total Without Project Subsidy	Percent Without Project Subsidy	Ending Inventory
Cum.	12/31/75	262	100	--	--	100	100	100%	162
CYE	12/31/76	83	43	--	--	43	43	100%	202
	12/31/77	102	73	N.A.					231
	12/31/78	57	47	N.A.					241
	12/31/79	39	31	N.A.					249
Subtotal	1970-79	543	294						
FYE	9/30/80+	44	118	101	--	17	17	14%	187
	9/30/81	79	91	78	--	13	13	14%	175
	9/30/82	65	107	82	7	18	25	23%	133
	9/30/83	22	124	90	22	12	34	27%	31
	9/30/84	83	51	46	3	2	5	10%	63
	9/30/85	28	46	42	3	1	4	10%	45
Subtotal	1980-85	321	537	439	35	63	98	18%	
				Formerly-Subsidized Units*					
Cum.	12/31/75	21,561	7,947	--	--	7,947	7,947	100%	13,614

				Formerly-Subsidized Projects*					
				Method of Sale					
		Acquired	Sold	Project Subsidy	Tenant Subsidy	No Subsidy	Total Without Project Subsidy	Percent Without Project Subsidy	Ending Inventory
CYE	12/31/76	6,607	4,087	–	–	4,087	4,087	100%	16,134
	12/31/77	8,305	5,764	N.A.					18,675
	12/31/78	4,481	2,303	N.A.					20,853
	12/31/79	2,857	2,693	N.A.					21,017
Subtotal	1970-79	43,811	22,794						
FYE	9/30/80+	3,359	8,494	7,941	–	553	553	7%	19,000
	9/30/81	6,002	6,892	6,410	–	482	482	7%	18,110
	9/30/82	4,758	10,302	7,590	409	2,303	2,712	26%	12,566
	9/30/83	1,311	10,224	7,470	902	1,852	2,754	27%	3,653
	9/30/84	6,743	3,441	2,913	207	321	528	15%	6,955
	9/30/85	2,748	3,298	2,821	102	375	477	14%	6,405
Subtotal	1980-85	24,921	42,651	35,145	1,620	5,886	7,506	18%	

*Section 221d3 BMIR + Section 236; includes Rent Supplement from 1980 on.
+Overlaps with Calendar Year 1979.
Note: CYE = Calendar Year Ending
FYE = Fiscal Year Ending
Source: 1970–1979: HUD Statistical Yearbook, ''Disposition of FHA-Acquired Multifamily Housing Properties and Mortgages.''
1980–1985: Compiled from HUD Office of Multifamily Housing Management and Property Disposition Division data.

were finally foreclosed. In effect, HUD's lack of decisiveness with respect to mortgage foreclosures enhanced the profitability of going into default in the first place. In this way, both the tax and housing policies of the federal government further enriched private owners at the expense of the projects and the public sector, which would eventually foot the bill for increased property disposition repair expenditures and tax revenue losses.

In late 1979 Congressional probes of a few scandal-ridden projects that HUD appeared to be dilatory in foreclosing became a convenient pretext for ventilation of an emerging conservative critique of the entire "troubled projects program" (U.S. Senate 1979 and 1980). Charging that these problems were "symptomatic of a deeply-rooted neglect and mismanagement that pervades the inventory of HUD-held multifamily properties" (*Housing and Development Reporter* 1979), Senator William Proxmire went on to sharply criticize HUD's unauthorized use of the mortgage insurance funds as a "back door" entitlement subsidy for low- and moderate-income tenants which avoided the scrutiny of the budget process. The GAO warned that the repair-and-sell policy was responsible for $19 million in annual losses to the mortgage insurance funds, and that the cost of selling just the inventory of 24,000 formerly subsidized units on hand with 15-year subsidies would run to $1 billion (U.S. Comptroller General 1979, i). Thus, the stage was set for a political counter-attack and a new period of retrenchment.

THE 1980s: DEREGULATION, PRIVATIZATION, AND DEBT COLLECTION

In the 1980s the problems of the privately owned subsidized housing inventory have acquired new and increasingly complex dimensions. While the failed projects of the 1970s have continued to meander their way through HUD's foreclosure/disposition process, those projects that survived the rampant inflation of that decade are now confronted with a new set of circumstances which have greatly exacerbated the tension between their private and social purposes.

First, as the subsidized housing stock ages, many projects have substantial capital repair needs, including major systems in need of replacement. According to one industry estimate, 80 percent of the subsidized projects that will be at least 15 years old by 1987 had repair needs averaging almost $3,000 per unit in 1983. Capital improvement costs for the projects surveyed (roughly one-half of the total inventory) were projected at $606 million, against an estimated $75 million in available reserves (U.S. House of Representatives, Committee on Government Operations 1984, 14).

At the same time, many projects owned by profit-motivated sponsors have reached or are approaching the burn-out point in their tax lives, when available interest and depreciation deductions no longer shelter project income from taxation. Since this unsheltered income in a subsidized project typically is not cash flow but mortgage amortization, investors now confront the problem of having to recognize "phantom" taxable income without actually receiving the cash to cover their tax payments. Coincidentally, many of these same projects are close to the point in their regulatory lives at which their mortgages can be prepaid without HUD approval, terminating the original use and occupancy restrictions. Finally, a growing number of subsidized projects are located in areas in which real estate values are rapidly appreciating, creating the potential for conversion to market-rate housing or commercial use.

In general, the response of profit-motivated owners to these changing circumstances has operated to further undermine the viability and affordability of the housing. For example, faced with the problem of phantom income, many owners opt to generate cash for their newly acquired tax liability by deferring maintenance. This causes project conditions to deteriorate just at the time when additional capital expenditures are most urgently needed. Additionally, rather than reinvest in a burnt-out tax shelter that is nearing the end of its regulatory period, most economically rational owners at this stage would prefer to cash in on the residual value of their equities by selling their projects for the highest possible price, posing a threat to tenant affordability. Even in declining areas where the opportunity for capital gains is limited, mortgage default followed by an appropriately timed foreclosure (to minimize recapture penalties) often is a more profitable course of action than the continued holding of a project that has become a substantial tax burden.

Since the early 1980s the evolution of government policy in relation to the privately owned subsidized inventory can be seen as a series of complex efforts to manage the growing contradictions between the public and private purposes of the housing, in a way that has increasingly enriched private interests at the expense of low- and moderate-income tenants. During this period, federal housing policy in general has been characterized by the philosophy that "the genius of the market economy, freed of the distortions forced by government housing policies and regulations . . . can provide for housing far better than Federal programs" (U.S. President's Commission on Housing 1982, xvii). Consistent with this belief, the Reagan administration terminated all new assistance for subsidized housing, rescinded and slashed commitments to ongoing programs, and minimized its ongoing risk and regulatory role, reversing some 50 years of significant federal involvement in the housing field.

At the same time, with the passage of the Economic Recovery Act (ERTA) in 1981, the government increasingly relied on tax code incentives to accomplish its housing objectives through the private sector. This Act, which significantly enhanced the tax benefits of all types of real estate investment, fueled an estimated 200 percent increase in housing-related investor tax deductions between fiscal years 1980 and 1987, while net new budget authority for low-income housing decreased drastically (Low Income Housing Information Service 1986b).

For the subsidized housing industry, ERTA was particularly important. For one thing, the new Accelerated Cost Recovery System (ACRS), which enabled owners to write off project costs considerably faster than they could under previous accelerated depreciation methods, was especially favorable for subsidized projects. Under the ACRS rules, subsidized projects could be depreciated over 15 years under the 200 percent declining balance method, as compared with 18 years (subsequently 19) at 175 percent for other types of property. Moreover, since the generous ACRS incentives applied to all properties purchased as well as produced after 1981, existing housing for the first time was placed on a par with new construction—with existing subsidized projects providing the most lucrative tax shelter opportunities.

Following the passage of ERTA, the government set about the task of creating a new policy framework for the assisted housing stock, which would explicitly encourage tax shelter-motivated investment, substitute private capital for direct public subsidies, and reduce federal regulatory involvement, financial exposure and risk. Accomplished largely without the benefit of Congressional rule-making and its attendant public scrutiny, this effort has involved promulgation of a series of administrative directives governing the disposition, foreclosure, debt collection, and ownership transfer of subsidized projects. While their full impact has been blunted by community opposition, these policies—together with new physical, market, and regulatory circumstances confronting the subsidized inventory—have markedly increased the risk that assisted units will be lost as viable, affordable housing resources in the years to come, as described more fully below.

Property Disposition

With regard to property disposition, the thrust of federal policy since 1981 has been to get the government out of the property management and ownership business as quickly as possible by expediting sales to tax-motivated purchasers and minimizing the government's interim and long-term project obligations. On its own terms, this policy has been quite successful, with federal holdings reduced to the lowest point in over ten years (see Table 10.2). But the social costs—actual and potential—have been substantial.

To begin with, in 1981 HUD abandoned its repair-and-sell program and returned to a policy of "as is" sales (Winn 1981). While the need for rehabilitation of acquired projects was generally acknowledged, this responsibility was shifted from the public sector to private purchasers who could finance repairs out of tax shelter syndication proceeds.

By restricting its own repair obligations during the interim holding period to routine maintenance and emergencies, the government sought to reduce not only its direct rehabilitation expenses but also the ongoing cost of keeping properties in its inventory at Congressionally mandated income-based rent levels while repairs were made. In contrast to the prior period when the average time between property acquisition and disposition was 38 months, properties were now required to be sold within six months. Moreover, to minimize HUD's future responsibility and risk, properties were no longer to be offered for sale with purchase-money mortgage or insurance commitments.

While this policy maximized the availability of rapid (five-year) rehabilitation tax write-offs to purchasers of HUD-sold properties, the results for project residents proved less than satisfactory. For example, at the Granite Properties, a 2000-unit scattered-site project in Boston, HUD's failure to provide decent, safe, and sanitary conditions during an extended holding period led to increased vacancies, tenant hardship, and protracted litigation (U.S. House of Representatives 1983b, 68). While HUD was ultimately forced to spend more than $8 million on emergency repairs, the continued deterioration of the properties increased the estimated cost of rehabilitation required to be performed by future purchasers to $25,000–$30,000 per unit. At the Stonekey II project in Indianapolis, deterioration caused in part by HUD's failure to repair led to an official determination that rehabilitation was infeasible. As a result, the property was sold by HUD without subsidies attached to the units or purchaser repair requirements (U.S. House of Representatives 1983b, 23).

Finally, in several projects purchaser repairs remained incomplete several years after sales closing. In the wake of mounting protests and lawsuits from tenant groups and housing advocates (Johnson and National Housing Law Project 1985, 333), HUD was forced in October 1985 to amend its policy to allow greater flexibility for field office repairs (Hale 1985). This revised approach also responded to the uncertain investment climate created by then-pending tax reform legislation (see below).

At the same time, HUD in 1982 returned to a policy of auctioning acquired projects to the highest bidder, relying on aggressive marketing techniques such as national advertising, contracting with seasoned real estate brokers, and bulk sales packaging to maximize returns to the mortgage insurance funds (Winn 1982; Abrams 1982a). The ownership capacity and motivation of many of the buyers selected through these techniques, especially in terms of the program's social goals, have been dubious at best. For example, in the notorious "New York Seven" case, HUD attempted to negotiate the bulk sale of seven properties, totalling over 1100 units in three states, to a partnership involving several prominent Republican Party figures. This sweetheart deal, which would have utilized an unprecedented 2.5 percent interest loan from the mortgage insurance funds to finance rehabilitation and conversion of a portion of the package to condominiums, was halted after adverse publicity (Kurtz 1982). A 100-unit Boston project was sold to a company involving the city's largest commercial and residential landlord, who had achieved notoriety for previous HUD defaults and foreclosures as well as civil rights violations and arson-related charges (Wong 1984).

In a number of instances, HUD's revised sales policies have also effectively prevented tenants from purchasing their projects. For example, after agreeing to sell the Huron Towers project in Ann Arbor to a tenant cooperative, HUD increased the price to reflect the project's competitive market value to tax-motivated investors. This pricing policy was fatal to the co-op conversion effort, and the property subsequently was auctioned to the highest bidder. According to Congressional testimony, services were drastically reduced after the sale (U.S. House of Representatives 1983a, 266).

Finally, HUD increasingly has sought to avoid its statutory mandate to preserve the lower-income character of formerly subsidized and other projects serving as a lower-income housing resource. For example, in 1982 HUD proposed to repeal the existing use requirements and other mandatory aspects of the property disposition statute, in order to handle the properties on a more "business-like basis." According to HUD: "Present law mandates a bias toward the continued use of the property for low- and moderate-income housing, without a realistic regard for the economic consequences to the government" (Johnson and National Housing Law Project 1985, 380).

While this proposal was rejected by Congress, HUD has repeatedly sought to amend its property disposition regulations to achieve comparable management and sales "flexibility." In the fall of 1984, HUD proposed new regulations to give it broad discretion relative to such critical matters as rental charges, maintenance obligations, and occupancy requirements during its interim holding period, as well as repairs, use restrictions, and subsidies after sale. Subsidies would be attached to the units only as necessary to ensure project feasibility—not tenant affordability (U.S. Department of HUD 1984b).

Although final implementation of these regulatory changes has been delayed by strong opposition from tenant organizations and low-income housing advocates, HUD has routinely waived its own regulations over the past few years to accomplish the same result. Between fiscal years 1982 and 1985, some 6,500 formerly subsidized units out of 27,000 sold did not receive project-based subsidies (attached to the units). Of these, approximately three-quarters were sold without any subsidy whatsoever, while in the balance voucher-type certificates were provided to the tenants (see Table 10.2).

Available evidence suggests that this "flexible" subsidy approach is not adequately protecting the low- and moderate-income residents of HUD-sold properties or the viability and affordability of the housing. For example, in several projects recently sold with voucher-type subsidies, conditions have continued to deteriorate—not surprisingly, since HUD did not require repairs by the purchaser, and since the buyers would be hard-pressed to secure rehabilitation financing without subsidies attached to the units (see U.S. House of Representatives 1983b, 23; Johnson and National Housing Law Project 1985, 396).

In other projects, conversion to condominiums is proposed to occur in several years (Johnson and National Housing Law Project 1985, 393). Either way, existing low- and moderate-income tenants are likely to be displaced and will find it difficult to locate alternative housing, especially if they are members of traditionally hard-to-house constituencies. On a national basis, more than half of all certificate-holders—and three-quarters of minority households and large families—are unable to utilize their certificates within the required 60 days (U.S. House of Representatives 1983a, 24). And either way, these formerly subsidized units are likely to be permanently lost as viable, affordable housing resources, compounding existing rental shortages.

Foreclosure

In a related effort, HUD in 1982 initiated a new policy designed to facilitate the direct sale of multifamily rental properties to private, tax-motivated purchasers at the point of foreclosure, without the intervening stage of HUD acquisition. This was accomplished primarily through a change in the government's bidding practices at foreclosure sale. Instead of the traditional bid method based on the statutory maximum (outstanding mortgage indebtedness plus associated foreclosure costs), HUD elected to bid the "as is" appraised value of the property wherever it was determined to be lower, and to advertise the amount of its offer in advance. By avoiding the crucial steps of HUD ownership and disposition, the government also could bypass its statutory obligation to preserve the lower-income use and viability of the housing.

This policy was temporarily halted and somewhat modified in response to strong community opposition, but not before its initial results were revealed at a stormy Congressional hearing. At eight projects (one formerly subsidized and seven unsubsidized projects partially serving a lower-income population) where HUD had entered its bid based on the appraised fair-market value, the government was outbid every time. None of the purchasers was required to make repairs, restrict future use to lower-income families, or attach subsidies to the units, although an analysis of two of the properties showed that 40 percent of the tenants were eligible for subsidies (U.S. House of Representatives 1983a, 336). According to one Congressional critic: "Clearly, the agency's main incentive, in formulating this new bidding procedure, is simply to . . . lose the property and avoid its responsibility to preserve the existing stock" (U.S. House of Representatives 1983d, 17).

Another curious chapter in the recent evolution of HUD's foreclosure policies involves the ambiguous effort to expedite foreclosure proceedings against recalcitrant owners through the Multifamily Mortgage Foreclosure Act. Enacted in 1981 at the request of the administration, this statute established an alternative uniform non-judicial foreclosure process at the federal level to address the problem of delays in many states that were seriously jeopardizing the condition of HUD-held properties. In response to tenant concerns, Congressman Barney Frank of Massachusetts added a mandatory requirement that formerly subsidized tenancies be protected in accordance with the terms of any prior regulatory agreement, wherever a purchaser other than HUD acquired title at a foreclosure sale conducted pursuant to this method.

Initially, HUD's response to this effort was to seek to repeal the mandatory section providing for continued low- and moderate-income use (U.S. House of Representatives 1983d, 11). Subsequently, implementing regulations were delayed for two and one-half years and then promulgated in a form that maximized agency discretion (U.S. Department of HUD 1984a). As a result, tenants in projects located in gentrifying Philadelphia and Boston neighborhoods were forced to organize to block unrestricted foreclosure sales that likely would have resulted in their displacement (U.S. House of Representatives 1983a, 214 and 1983b, 4). In the case of West Concord Apartments in Boston, HUD's failure to provide tenant protection that would have facilitated its acquisition of the property also threatened to undermine a planned conversion to tenant- or non-profit-ownership.

HUD's refusal to adequately implement the Multifamily Mortgage Foreclosure Act has been a source of irritation to Congressman Frank, who has persistently sought to determine the reason for this seeming instance of bureaucratic perversity:

> We have here a veto by non-regulation. This bill . . . gave the Secretary a tool which he said he needed. It gave it to him in exactly the legal form which he requested. It simply said that if he used it, however, he would . . . have to protect [the existing tenants]. . . . The only explanation that appears to me is that he refused to use it because it comes to him in a form which requires that subsidized tenancies be protected (U.S. House of Representatives 1983c, 2).

Perhaps more to the point, however, is the explanation offered by HUD General Counsel John Knapp in the course of Congressional oversight hearings:

> A further impact of the imposition of use or other restrictions on the property as a condition of the foreclosure sale . . . is the impact on the value of the mortgagor's interest. . . . [A] mortgagor whose property is foreclosed is entitled to receive the value of his equity, if any. To the extent that imposition of restrictions at the sale . . . might reduce the value of the property and, therefore, the original mortgagor's equity, there might be a cause for complaint by that original mortgagor (U.S. House of Representatives 1983c, 18).

At least in the view of this public servant, the government is obligated to protect private interests at the expense of social purposes, even where an owner has defaulted on all of his contractual obligations.

Quite apart from their social costs, HUD's post-ERTA foreclosure and disposition policies have been of questionable financial benefit to the government and to federal taxpayers generally. Recent property dispositions have returned to the mortgage insurance funds only about 30 cents per dollar expended—approximately offsetting the government's holding costs during the interim holding period (Pierce 1984). Private acquisitions at foreclosure sales avoid holding costs, but the proceeds of these sales have averaged only slightly more than HUD's bids. In one case, HUD's advertised offer was outbid (rather predictably) by just $1 (U.S. House of Representatives 1983a, 336).

At the same time, any short-term savings to the mortgage insurance funds resulting from HUD's diminished repair and holding period obligations must be weighed against the significant revenue losses to the Treasury where sales to tax-motivated purchasers are involved. While the specific tax expenditure consequences of post-ERTA foreclosure and disposition policies have not been analyzed, several earlier studies have documented the general inefficiency of tax shelter subsidies as a mechanism for generating housing equity capital. For example, the Congressional Budget Office estimated in 1977 that less than 50 percent of the government's tax losses from a typical subsidized housing venture are actually available to the developer (and thus potentially to the project), with most of the remainder going to investors in the form of excess depreciation and interest deductions (U.S. Congress 1977, xiv).

In effect, because the Treasury must pay more to induce investors to risk their money than it would cost the government to invest directly in the project, the financial benefits of this back-door approach to subsidizing the renovation of foreclosed HUD properties are extremely questionable. Moreover, to the extent that unrestricted and/or unsubsidized sales of foreclosed and HUD-owned property to tax-motivated investors ultimately reduce the potential for housing viability and affordability, the long-term public costs of today's failure to protect these units must also be considered.

Debt Collection

Government policy since the early 1980s has been directed at substituting private investment for federal mortage and subsidy dollars in order to reduce the government's obligation to existing subsidized projects.

One aspect of this effort has involved the sale of current HUD-held mortgage loans to private bidders at public auction. Under this initiative, which began in 1982, some 500 mortgages (including purchase-money mortgages used to finance HUD property dispositions in an earlier phase of the program, and subsidized as well as unsubsidized loans assigned to HUD) have been sold to HUD-approved buyers. While this program has been disappointing from a debt collection point of view, it has been extremely beneficial to some project owners, who have succeeded in purchasing their own mortgages at a substantial discount, positioning themselves for a future prepayment windfall. Although public opposition has forced HUD to maintain prior rental use restrictions on the mortgages that have been sold—and has stopped one mortgage sale altogether (*Housing Affairs Letter* 1983)—this technique has reduced the potential for preserving long-term project affordability.

Simultaneously, HUD launched a major initiative to bring assigned loans current and eliminate outstanding mortgage delinquencies so that more HUD-held mortgages could be sold. A sweeping policy memorandum issued in June 1982 directed project owners to agree to an acceptable mortgage workout arrangement within 60 days or face immediate foreclosure. Mortgage relief was conditioned upon the infusion of sufficient owner capital to meet the project's financial and physical needs. In this way, HUD hoped to "encourage the private sector to invest in HUD-held properties, since government dollars are no longer available to solve a project's problems'' (Abrams 1982b, 1).

This policy was followed in 1984 by an even more stringent directive, requiring owners to contribute substantial cash up front toward their mortgage delinquencies and to cure all remaining financial and physical problems within a two-year period (Barksdale 1984). To ensure that payments required under the workout agreement would be made, HUD threatened to withhold any Section 8 rental assistance payments committed to the project for application toward the mortgage debt. To discourage owners from allowing their mortgages to be assigned in the first place, HUD promised to employ a variety of financial and administrative sanctions, including raising the interest rates on HUD-held mortgage notes.

At the same time, available public subsidies for troubled HUD projects were dramatically reduced. Between fiscal years 1980 and 1984 approximately 11,500 Section 8 Loan Management subsidy units were allocated, compared with 180,000 units between fiscal years 1976 and 1979. In fiscal year 1984, HUD received applications for Loan Management subsidies covering 20,000 units, but funded only 5,000 (U.S. General Accounting Office 1984, 2 and 5). Since 1983, these subsidies have been targeted exclusively for projects with insurance still in force, in order to avoid future claims on the mortgage insurance funds. Flexible Subsidy allocations have generally followed a similar pattern.

These policies have profoundly affected the low- and moderate-income residents of existing HUD-held projects, as well as the affordability and viability of the HUD-held subsidized inventory, as described in the next section. But in order to fully comprehend the consequences of HUD's debt collection effort, its impact on project owners must first be understood.

To begin with, the new ''get tough'' tactics caught many owners off-guard, including those nonprofit sponsors whose projects had functioned for years under a variety of formal and informal mortgage relief arrangements—the favored way of assisting troubled projects during the 1970s (see above). Typically, debt service and reserve obligations repeatedly had been deferred through multiple and often poorly documented agreements, making it difficult to determine prior payment arrangements and current liabilities. Many nonprofit owners learned about HUD's new debt collection policy for the first time in the form of a notice ordering them to bring their mortgages current within 60 days. Effectively precluded from negotiating new workout arrangements by HUD's restrictive and limited use of subsidy funds, these sponsors were confronted with the unhappy choice of selling and losing control of their projects to profit-motivated partnerships, or facing foreclosure (National Housing Law Project 1984, 1).

For the many profit-motivated owners whose mortgages were seriously delinquent, HUD's new debt collection directives similarly left few alternatives other than a transfer of project ownership. But for most of these owners, the new policies represented a welcome (and often profitable) opportunity to bail out of or reorganize their unwanted subsidized tax shelter investments at or near the ''burn-out'' stage—surely an attractive means of foreclosure avoidance. In this way, HUD's post-ERTA debt collection directives have both forced and facilitated a major process of ownership restructuring within the subsidized inventory, which, in combination with the debt policies themselves, has served to precipitate a new series of problems.

Transfers of Physical Assets

Since the early 1980s Transfers of Physical Assets (TPAs) have been widely touted by the government and the real estate industry as the ultimate cost-effective private sector solution to the problems of troubled HUD projects. Under this procedure, project ownership is transferred to a new entity, subject to the existing mortgage and Regulatory Agreement, generating new capital in the form of syndication or resyndication proceeds. According to HUD policies, TPA approval is conditional on the infusion of sufficient owner cash contributions to meet the project's physical and financial needs (U.S. Department of HUD 1984c).

In the words of one Congressional advocate:

> Since this program was put into place, HUD foreclosures have declined . . . at a very substantial saving to the federal government. . . . The tax benefits received by investors have enhanced the federal goal of preserving and maintaining the existing stock of low- and moderate-income housing at a time when federal deficits are forcing the federal government to reduce drastically the expenditures for such housing. . . . This is the way our nation's housing stock is being maintained (U.S. Congress 1984, S 4523).

Moreover, according to the Coalition for Low and Moderate Income Housing, a lobbying group for subsidized housing developers and syndicators, without this transfer mechanism,

> Six to seven million tenants of existing low-income housing units across the country will experience deteriorating conditions with no hope of any relief. . . . In addition, the number of low-income housing projects that will default on their mortgages will greatly increase. . . . At present, the only effective method for providing capital is the transfer of the projects to a new group of owner-investors (Coalition for Low and Moderate Income Housing 1984, 1).

Indeed, in the absence of government subsidies, TPAs have rapidly become the only program available to aging subsidized projects, whether or not they are in immediate financial difficulty. While HUD has no firm count of the number of TPAs that have occurred, it estimates that 3,000–4,000 projects (subsidized and unsubsidized) have changed ownership for tax purposes in the post-ERTA era—a tenfold increase over previous levels (U.S. General Accounting Office 1985, 4). During 1984 alone, HUD gave preliminary approval to an estimated 1,125 TPAs, as owners rushed to escape certain adverse tax changes imposed by the Deficit Reduction Act of 1984 (Johnson and National Housing Law Project

1985, 124). Based on the preliminary findings of a HUD field study, as much as 30 percent of the older insured or HUD-held inventory has now undergone at least one ownership transfer.[1] According to industry sources, approximately half of these recent TPAs involve subsidized housing (Coalition for Low and Moderate Income Housing 1984, Exhibit B).

The TPA "program" actually began during the late 1970s, when HUD first encouraged the conversion of nonprofit projects to profit-motivated ownership in order to generate additional capital. In a critical audit of this early phase of TPA history, the HUD Inspector General concluded as follows:

> HUD has not achieved the results intended by the transfer of physical assets from nonprofit to profit-motivated owners. Pertinent regulations indicate that the transfers are intended to result in significant benefits to the project, the neighborhood and the tenants, as well as protect the interests of the Government. Our review disclosed that the transfer of assets process has been ineffective in improving the condition of the projects. . . . The Field Offices did not adequately monitor or control the actions required for the profit-motivated purchaser to assure compliance with transfer agreements or perform adequate physical inspections to identify the physical needs of the projects prior to the transfers. . . . [E]quity contributions required by the transfer agreement were not sufficient to meet the physical and financial needs of the projects (U.S. Department of HUD 1982, 1–2).

A case in point is Grant Manor Apartments, a 180-unit HUD-held Section 236 project located in Boston which was transferred from nonprofit to profit-motivated ownership in 1980. While the new investment partnership agreed to allocate $355,000 in capital contributions for project repairs, disbursements were not regulated by HUD and the funds were diverted for non-project business purposes. A subsequent HUD inspection report revealed that more than $700,000 worth of repairs was needed to restore the project to decent, safe, and sanitary condition. A variety of other irregularities, including the owner's failure to execute the HUD-approved Workout Agreement, were uncovered by tenants in the process of contesting a proposed $120 per month rent increase. This failed TPA is one of many now in foreclosure (Achtenberg 1982).

Widespread tenant protest against these and similar abuses led to a 1978 moratorium on nonprofit to profit-motivated ownership transfers and, a few years later, to new HUD regulations tightening the requirements for these TPAs (U.S. Department of HUD 1980). By this time, however, syndicators and investors already had turned to a newer and more profitable TPA frontier: resyndication.

With passage of ERTA, the TPA process could be extended to profit-motivated projects for several reasons. First, as noted previously, the more favorable depreciation rules available to post–1981 buyers substantially increased the value of existing property to new tax-motivated purchasers, especially in the face of dwindling new construction opportunities. For new buyers, ERTA's accelerated depreciation methods applied to the "stepped-up" basis of the property created an attractive tax shelter, generating equity proceeds substantially in excess of pre-ERTA new construction syndications (Smith 1982, 1). With the availability of this extra cash, sellers could now dispose of their burnt-out subsidized housing tax shelters at a profit at least sufficient to cover their original equity investment and to pay their "exit" taxes coming due. Thus, ERTA provided the "grease" that made resyndications profitable and possible.

At the same time, HUD provided the "gravy" by allowing the use of secondary seller financing in conjunction with property transfers. Long used in conventional real estate transactions, this creative device enabled profit-motivated sellers to retain the residual value of their investment in the form of a purchase money note, typically due and payable (with accrued interest) when the project's restricted-use period expired. Indeed, by converting the built-up value of their equities into quantified, interest-bearing indebtedness, and often continuing as a general partner in the buying partnership, many sellers could actually improve their financial position after resyndication.

For the buyer, secondary seller financing offered the benefit of significantly increased and extended deductions, especially through the device of continuing annual interest accruals, which eliminated the problem of tax burn-out for the life of the note. This in turn significantly enhanced the value of resyndication proceeds that could be generated by the transfer: typically 20–35 percent of the equity raised through resyndication has been attributable to interest accruals alone (Pierce 1984). With additional cash potentially available to meet the actual or anticipated needs of the project, as well as the requirements of profit-motivated buyers, sellers, and syndicators, TPAs seemed to offer something for everyone. In the words of one industry spokesman:

> Resyndication makes sense to the federal government, which is losing 68 percent of its original claim payment (through foreclosure and disposition). Resyndication also makes general sense to the private sector: it allows existing owners to receive enough money to cover their built-up contingent federal income tax liability; through the use of secondary financing, it permits sellers to receive compensation for built-up capital value, and for new buyers, it represents an attractive tax shelter investment. . . . ERTA may prove to be the savior of the Section 236 and 221d3 programs (U.S. House of Representatives 1983a, 432).

But has resyndication actually enhanced the affordability and viability of subsidized housing? The evidence suggests cause for considerable concern.

First of all, it appears that only a small fraction of the transfer proceeds generated from these transactions has been allocated for repairs or other uses that directly benefit the property and existing low- and moderate-income residents. Congressional critics have cited instances where 40–58 percent of the resyndication proceeds has been allocated to pay "various consulting and marketing fees and organizational expenses of the partnership, and to provide a profit to the general partners" (U.S. Congress 1984, S 4524). According to HUD estimates, well over half of the cash raised in a typical resyndication transaction is diverted to accommodate the requirements of the seller, with 20 percent at best devoted to project-related purposes (Pierce 1984).

While hard data are lacking, HUD has estimated that 50 percent of the subsidized TPAs contribute approximately $1,000 per unit for repairs (Coalition for Low and Moderate Income Housing 1984, Exhibit B), as compared with a current average capital repair need of almost $3,000 per unit in the older inventory (see above). This is confirmed by the Massachusetts Housing Finance Agency's recent resyndication experience, in which nine subsidized properties with 1,857 units transferred during 1984 netted an average of $1,041 per unit for repairs and replacement reserves (Massachusetts Housing Finance Agency 1985, 1).

One possible explanation for this relatively limited level of capital investment is that many of the subsidized projects transferred in the post-ERTA era have not required substantial repairs. HUD estimates that only 15 percent of the TPA applications received during 1984 involved troubled projects with HUD-held mortgages (Johnson and National Housing Law Project 1985, 124), and that only 20 percent of the subsidized TPAs approved were probable candidates for assignment (Pierce 1984). Of course, for profit-motivated buyers, sellers, and syndicators, a relatively healthy project is an infinitely more attractive resyndication proposition than a troubled one, since the transfer proceeds available to the private parties in the transaction can be maximized. Indeed, there are indications that during the resyndication frenzy of 1984 quite a number of transfers took place that were premature from the perspective of project needs, although timely from a tax standpoint.

At the same time, where troubled projects have been resyndicated, repairs frequently take a back seat to the requirements of profit-motivated buyers, sellers, and syndicators, and to HUD's debt collection priorities. A case in point is Princeton Village, a 150-unit Section 221d3 project located in Lowell, Massachusetts, where a profit-motivated partnership facing foreclosure sought to transfer ownership to a new buyer. Of the $1.4 million in gross resyndication proceeds anticipated to be generated by the sale, some $425,000 was proposed to be paid to the seller, $200,000 to the buyer, and another $200,000 to cover syndication and related sales expenses. An additional $500,000 was targeted for repayment of HUD mortgage delinquencies and related debts. Only $100,000, or approximately 7 percent of the gross proceeds (less than $700 per unit), was proposed to be allocated for project repairs, originally estimated by the purchaser at $500,000 (Achtenberg 1985a).

While the benefits to the project resulting from resyndication often are quite limited, there may also be significant costs to existing low- and moderate-income tenants. In the case of Princeton Village, the property was proposed to be transferred with a $1.4 million note to the seller, accruing interest at 10 percent, compounded annually, and due and payable in nine years (when it would be worth $3 million). The restricted regulatory term of this extremely attractive and well-located project would be completed in just four years, allowing the new buyer to prepay the HUD mortgage and convert the project to condominiums or market-rate rental housing. While the potential for conversion did not originate with the TPA, the existence of a substantial accrual note would have created a financial imperative to refinance the HUD mortgage at an early date, making the loss of low- and moderate-income housing a virtual certainty.

In this instance, vigorous tenant opposition, combined with tax law changes reducing the financial benefits of secondary seller financing (see below), resulted in a restructuring of the TPA to eliminate the contested second note as well as the defaulting seller's up-front cash payments. In exchange for a generous nine-year interest delinquency repayment schedule, the purchaser agreed to fund additional repairs and extend lower-income use restrictions for another four years. In general, however, developers and syndicators involved in the transfer of subsidized projects have opposed any significant extension of low- and moderate-income use restrictions. At recent Congressional hearings on a proposed rehabilitation loan program for subsidized projects, industry representatives uniformly testified in favor of the financing assistance but against extended use restrictions that might suppress future resale value. According to one spokesperson:

> We do not agree than an owner should be required to maintain the low- and moderate-income character of the property to any extent beyond his present obligations. If the owner borrows in good faith, repays the loan on time, sticks by all the rules, and is required to prepay the loan in case of sale or refinancing, we believe that is enough (U.S. House of Representatives 1984, 41).

In the most recent chapter of TPA history, the Deficit Reduction Tax Act of 1984 has significantly reduced the financial incentives available to profit-motivated sellers and investors who rely on secondary financing arrangements. Among other things, sellers now are required to recognize the deferred interest on their notes as current taxable income, which significantly increases their tax liability. The availability of depreciation and interest deductions to purchasers in the early years of ownership is also greatly diminished. These—as well as other uncertainties associated with tax reform changes (see below)—have significantly slowed the pace of resyndications (U.S. General Accounting Office 1985, 9).

Since nonprofit sellers can still hold secondary accrual notes without adverse effect, however, they have once again become the favored target of the syndication industry. Indeed, since 1984 some national syndicators who specialize in the transfer of subsidized projects have been preying on nonprofit housing sponsors—especially those with troubled projects who are grappling with HUD's debt collection directives. Many of these deals have been actively brokered by HUD at the local and national level.

While these recent nonprofit conversions have been structured in a variety of ways, all too often unsophisticated and vulnerable nonprofits have agreed to terms that provide limited benefits to themselves and their projects. Some nonprofit sellers or their affiliates have continued as principals in the purchasing partnerships; however, their control over project operations usually is much diminished. Additionally, while the substantial creditor claims built up through accrual notes held by nonprofit sellers may offer the potential to buy back the project, this promise often is illusory, since the note typically is not due until after expiration of the original 40-year mortgage term (and the nonprofit may not have a formal repurchase option). These extended "Pac-man" notes—so-called for their tendency to "devour" the project's residual equity—are regarded by many in the industry as high-risk and audit-prone. Yet they do generate a substantial and continuing stream of deductions for purchasing investors, which in turn results in more up-front cash potentially available to the project.

At the same time, as with TPAs involving resyndications, a relatively small share of the transfer proceeds generated by these conversions seems to find its way back into the project, especially where there are substantial mortgage delinquencies. A case in point is Roxse Homes in Boston, a severely troubled 364-unit subsidized project that was on the verge of foreclosure when the nonprofit sponsor agreed to turn over its deed to a new profit-motivated partnership. Of some $6 million in gross syndication proceeds anticipated to be raised by this transaction, which involves a 30-year accrual note to the seller, $3.5 million, or close to 60 percent, will be remitted to HUD for mortgage interest delinquencies and related arrearages. Only a fraction of the project's substantial repair needs will be met through this arrangement (Achtenberg 1985b).

Moreover, with the resumption of full mortgage debt service mandated by the TPA, within 18 months project rent increases of almost 80 percent will be required. As a result, 40 percent of the existing low- and moderate-income families currently residing in the development will be forced to pay at least 40 percent of their incomes for rent, and 23 percent will pay at least 50 percent. In this instance, which, unfortunately, is not atypical, a nonprofit to profit-motivated ownership transfer facilitated by HUD's aggressive debt collection policies has created the potential for direct displacement of several hundred low- and moderate-income families.

Finally, the financial benefits to the government and federal taxpayers of HUD's debt collection and TPA programs are at best dubious. In the short run, to the extent that these policies have succeeded in reducing mortgage assignments, some savings may accrue to the mortgage insurance funds. Indeed, HUD has recently experienced a significant reduction in assignment claims, although this may also be attributable to the drop in interest rates, which makes lenders less likely to assign in the first place (Pierce 1984). At the same time, to the extent that workouts negotiated for HUD-held loans result in substantial up-front delinquency payments, the federal housing debt may be somewhat reduced.

However, to the extent that these short-term savings have been achieved through property transfers with substantial take-back financing, revenue losses to the Treasury over time will likely outweigh any immediate financial benefits to the mortgage insurance funds. And for those transferred properties that were not even candidates for assignment, it is unclear that any savings at all have been accomplished. Even the Secretary of HUD has acknowledged, in a candid moment, that "in these cases, I cannot say that the benefits of resyndication outweigh . . . the tax revenue losses that result'' (Pierce 1984). To the extent that aggressive debt collection and property transfer policies result in the premature, permanent loss of viable, affordable units from the subsidized inventory, the long-term cost to the government could be substantial indeed.

Mortgage Prepayment

With the profitability of future resyndications clouded by tax reform, profit-motivated owners of aging but rapidly appreciating subsidized projects increasingly are recognizing the value of holding their assets until the 20-year regulatory period expires, prepaying their mortgages, and then cashing out through conversion to condominiums or other profitable forms of re-use. Thus, the potential loss of subsidized units through mortgage prepayment has begun to emerge as a critical problem in its own right.

Current estimates of the number of projects and units becoming ripe for mortgage prepayment vary widely. In addition to the recent GAO projections, HUD estimates that by 1991 some 106,000 Section 221d3 BMIR and Section 236 units are located in projects that will be eligible for prepayment, increasing to 306,000 units by 1996 (U.S. House of Representatives 1986, 67). The National Association of Home Builders projects that 480,000 units will be at risk by 1996, although their estimate appears to include units in nonprofit projects that are precluded from prepayment without HUD approval for the full 40-year mortgage term (National Association of Home Builders 1986, 71).

To compound this problem, a significant number of the older, use-restricted projects receive additional assistance in the form of Section 8 Loan Management subsidies, which have permitted them to serve very low-income families. Most of these subsidy contracts are funded for 15 years, but at five-year intervals allow project owners to ''opt out''; in any case, contract commitments entered into in the mid-to-late 1970s will expire in the early 1990s, at just about the point when the project mortgages can be prepaid. On a national basis, HUD has estimated that some 100,000 of the Section 221d3 BMIR and Section 236 units located in projects which will be eligible for mortgage prepayment in 1996 also are assisted by Section 8, although the relationship between the use restriction expiration dates and subsidy contracts is not known (U.S. House of Representatives 1986, 67).

In areas with a high proportion of older but attractive projects located in gentrifying neighborhoods, the magnitude of the problem is readily apparent. For example, in Massachusetts some 7,500 units out of the total 28,000-unit Section 221d3 BMIR and Section 236 inventory will be ripe for mortgage prepayment by 1991 (U.S. House of Representatives 1986, 132). Sixteen out of the 37 projects in this category are Section 8 assisted. Most of these properties are located in communities that recently have experienced significant economic growth and housing market pressures. A typical unit in a well-situated project built 20 years ago for $15,000 might now have an outstanding mortgage debt of $8,000 and a current market value of $60,000—offering the potential for substantial equity gains.

In characteristic form, the federal government has responded to this potentially explosive situation by attempting to minimize the scope of the problem and adopting a hands-off posture. According to HUD, over the past five years only 12 projects containing a total of 676 units have elected to terminate their use restrictions through mortgage prepayment (U.S. House of Representatives 1986, 68). At recent Congressional hearings on the subject, a ranking HUD official offered the following perspective:

> Our expectation is that a great majority of owners will keep their projects as low- and moderate-income properties under terms of the original mortgage. . . . [W]e believe that due to local neighborhood conditions and the market for such units a majority of the units would remain available for low- and moderate-income use. Only a few projects in very good areas and in healthy condition would convert to high-income use (U.S. House of Representatives 1986, 67).

Accordingly, HUD has proposed to address the problem by requiring mortgagees to give 30 days' advance notice prior to accepting a prepayment offer in order to allow "sufficient time" for negotiations with project owners (U.S. House of Representatives 1986, 69). Pursuant to recent statutory requirements, HUD will offer Section 8 and Flexible Subsidy assistance on a priority basis to owners who might otherwise terminate their regulatory restrictions, and will provide housing vouchers to tenants displaced by expiring or prematurely terminated Section 8 contracts. Yet growing evidence suggests that these minimal efforts will be far from adequate to prevent mortgage prepayment, especially in gentrifying neighborhoods.

A case in point is the Webb Forest Apartments, a 240-unit Section 221d3 BMIR project located in Dallas (U.S. House of Representatives 1986, 116). Built in 1964 in a depressed, lower-income neighborhood, the project has skyrocketed in value in recent years due to government-assisted highway and commercial/retail construction in the surrounding area. In 1985 the project (now zoned for commercial use) was sold to a developer, who prepaid the mortgage and sought to construct a new office/hotel complex on the site. Fortunately, in this instance the tenants succeeded in negotiating a settlement that provides for retention of a portion of the existing units for two years, temporary rent subsidies to ease the burden of displacement, and a commitment by the developer to provide alternative housing on a nonprofit basis.

That Webb Forest represents just the tip of the iceberg is suggested by a recent field survey of subsidized project owners conducted by the National Association of Home Builders. Six out of ten owners contacted who could prepay their mortgages within the next five years indicated that they would possibly or definitely do so (National Association of Home Builders 1986, 73).

At least one major national securities firm has begun to view the prepayment of subsidized mortgages as a profitable investment opportunity and is actively promoting the termination of use restrictions in subsidized projects. In a recent $200 million mortgage fund investment prospectus, the E.F. Hutton Company specifically targets HUD-assisted projects "with a higher than average probability of early prepayment," and promises aggressive activity by the fund managers to cause "the conversion [of properties underlying the mortgages held] to a use which would not involve federal housing programs" (E.F. Hutton 1985, 31 and 34). By buying the subsidized mortgages at a substantial discount and then facilitating their early prepayment, investors in the fund stand to realize substantial gains. With these forces at work, in combination with HUD's refusal to jeopardize owners' financial interests in order to protect the social purpose of the housing, the loss of a significant portion of the assisted inventory through mortgage prepayment and conversion in the coming years seems increasingly probable.

A PROGRESSIVE RESPONSE

Recent Local Initiatives

In a variety of situations,[2] tenant and community-based groups working in conjunction with progressive local government officials have successfully intervened in the foreclosure, disposition, ownership transfer, or mortgage prepayment of assisted housing projects, to develop alternative solutions that enhance the potential for long-term viability and affordability. Challenging the premise that housing for low- and moderate-income families is best provided and maintained by the private sector, these local initiatives have demonstrated in concrete ways how project ownership and financing might be restructured to be more compatible with the basic social purpose of the housing.

While the specifics of these efforts have varied from case to case, their common goal has been to preserve and expand opportunities for successful ownership by resident, community-based and other nonprofit sponsors whose sole purpose is to maintain and operate the housing for lower-income use on a permanent basis. (See also Chapter 11 by Rachel Bratt.) Also, they have sought to enhance project viability and affordability through capital cost writedowns, direct public debt and equity financing, and other mechanisms that reduce dependence on traditional private credit and tax shelter subsidies.

For example, organized tenants in several Boston projects have blocked the unrestricted foreclosure sale of their developments that could have resulted in their eventual displacement. Aided by city and state technical assistance funding, the tenants subsequently negotiated with project owners to deed their properties voluntarily to HUD, in order to avoid the risks of the foreclosure process. With the city and state continuing to back their efforts throughout HUD's property disposition process, these groups effectively parlayed their conveyance of title into a designated-purchaser status.

Three formerly subsidized projects delivered to HUD through this strategy have now been converted to limited-equity cooperatives, with deed restrictions to ensure their continued use as affordable, nonspeculative housing. At Methunion Manor, a 150-unit project located on a prime downtown Boston site, the cooperative has restricted the transfer value of departing members' shares to the initial cash downpayment (for example, $900 for a two-bedroom unit), indexed to the cost of living. The cooperative is required to maintain the project as affordable housing for at least 30 years. In the event of dissolution or resale, a right of first refusal has been granted to a local charitable corporation to purchase the property for the aggregate transfer value of member shares and to maintain it subject to the applicable deed restrictions.

Two other projects are in the process of being sold to the Boston Housing Authority for permanent use as nonspeculative, lower-income housing, with provision for substantial tenant involvement in property management. In a parallel effort, eight community-based nonprofit sponsors are purchasing and rehabilitating approximately 1,000 units of the Granite Properties, a failed subsidized project acquired by HUD through foreclosure (see above). This bulk nonprofit sale is being negotiated through the Boston Housing Partnership, a consortium of public, private, and community-based groups that has successfully brokered property transfers and aggregated financing and subsidy resources for nonprofit sponsors.

Taken together, these efforts have created an effective local right of first refusal for tenant, public, and community-based housing organizations seeking to purchase HUD-owned property for conversion to social ownership. Additionally, tenant and community based groups are seeking to utilize local land use and regulatory agreements to lever similar purchase arrangements for projects on urban renewal sites that are nearing the end of their restricted lower-income use periods.

The financial restructuring of these and other subsidized projects to meet social objectives has been accomplished in a variety of ways. For properties foreclosed and resold by HUD, substantial capital cost writedowns have been achieved through HUD acquisition (wiping out the existing mortgage debt and delinquencies), partial HUD funding of repairs, and negligible resale prices. At Methunion Manor, HUD wrote off more than $8 million worth of indebtedness, completed more than $1 million worth of repairs, and sold the project to the cooperative for $12,000 ($80 per unit)—an extraordinary accomplishment in view of the project's desirable location. With capital costs reduced to the $5,200 per unit required for additional repairs (financed through a mortgage loan from the National Cooperative Bank), monthly mortgage debt has been reduced to $55 per unit. The city also agreed to a substantial reduction in property taxes, allowing the cooperative to maintain an operating budget with ample reserves and funds for member services. Because of these savings, monthly carrying charges have been kept at affordable levels and the cost of rental subsidies for very low-income tenants has been correspondingly reduced.

At the Granite Properties, substantial public debt and equity financing is being utilized to facilitate the conversion of the housing to viable community-based nonprofit ownership. Rehabilitation financing has been provided by the local housing finance agency at below-market rates for a term well in excess of the 15-year rental subsidy contract, supplemented by loans and grants from city, state, and charitable sources. A similar public financing strategy involving the targeting of state and local capital funds is being developed to facilitate the conversion of projects with expiring use-restrictions to social ownership.

A related example illustrating the use of local public financing to preserve existing social ownership is the Grandville Cooperative in Indianapolis, a 156-unit subsidized project that defaulted on its mortgage when the residents could not afford required debt service and operating expenses (Johnson and National Housing Law Project 1985, 273).[3] In 1982 HUD rejected the cooperative's request to recast the outstanding mortgage debt plus delinquencies over an extended term and demanded that the mortgage be brought current immediately. Reluctant to enter into a TPA and risk loss of control over the property, the cooperative sought and received a $100,000 loan from the city on favorable terms to pay off its arrearages. Additional grant funds totalling $150,000 were obtained from public and nonprofit sources for weatherization and other improvements to further enhance project viability.

In other instances, tenant and community-based groups are working with local government officials to restructure private debt and equity financing arrangements in order to maximize their social benefit. For example, a portion of the capital funding required for the Boston Housing Partnership Granite Properties package has been raised through a pooled sale of the nonprofit equity interests, arranged through a local nonprofit syndication firm. By eliminating or substantially reducing the role of for-profit developers and syndicators, the partnership has generated substantially greater cash contributions for these deteriorated projects than could be provided through a standard tax shelter syndication. While the individual nonprofit packages have been aggregated for investment and financing purposes, ownership at the project level is structured to maximize control for each local sponsor over property management and operations. Also, local nonprofits will have an opportunity to repurchase their projects from investors for continued lower-income housing use, to the extent consistent with the fiduciary responsibilities inherent in such limited-partnership arrangements.

Implications for a National Strategy

At the national level, future prospects and policies for the existing subsidized housing stock will be significantly affected by landmark tax overhaul legislation recently enacted by the Congress. In general, the Tax Reform Act of 1986 dramatically curtails the tax incentives for real estate investment—including rental housing—which reached new and abusive heights in the post-ERTA era. In addition to extending depreciation schedules for new investments, the law significantly reduces the value of existing housing tax shelters to current investors by lowering marginal tax rates and severely restricting owners' ability to offset taxable income with "passive losses" such as depreciation deductions.

At the same time, thanks to aggressive lobbying efforts by low-income housing advocates and the subsidized housing industry, the law continues favorable tax treatment for subsidized housing in several ways. First, under special low-income housing "transition rules," investors in most subsidized projects recently re-syndicated or under development are exempt from the "passive loss" restrictions for several years. This exception was adopted after predictions of massive defaults by subsidized housing investors if their tax benefits were reduced (*Housing Affairs Letter* 1986g).

Additionally, the law creates a new tax credit for investors who participate in low-income housing projects through 1990. This substantial incentive, which allows owners to deduct 4 percent of project acquisition costs as well as 9 percent of project development costs annually for ten years, contains many features that improve on the social utility of prior tax shelter arrangements (Low Income Housing Information Service 1986a). For example, unlike depreciation-based incentives, the tax credit is targeted to projects with a minimum (20 or 40 percent) set-aside of very low-income units and is provided only for those units that continue to meet qualifying income and rent tests. Rather than being available on an entitlement basis, the tax credit will be allocated through state agencies to owners and projects that meet locally determined criteria, with a mandatory 10 percent set-aside to nonprofit sponsors. Finally, since the credit offsets tax liability (rather than taxable income), it is worth the same amount to all taxpayers regardless of income.

Not surprisingly, while the tax credit incentive has been described as "the most generous ever" for low-income housing (*Housing Affairs Letter* 1986f), the risk-averse private sector is approaching this untested device with considerable caution. With passive loss restrictions freezing most traditional tax shelter clients out of the market and low-income set-aside requirements posing potential feasibility constraints, prospective developers of tax credit properties anticipate substantial syndication and underwriting problems, at least initially (*Housing Affairs Letter* 1986d and 1986e).

At the same time, nonprofit sponsors are actively working to improve the viability of the credit by devising marketing strategies to attract potential new investors (such as corporations, which are exempt from the passive loss restrictions) and by accessing state and local subsidies to improve project feasibility (*Housing Affairs Letter* 1986c). When and if these new mechanisms prove sufficiently attractive to overcome the uncertainties of the new tax environment, there are growing indications that the real estate industry will be prepared to jump on the tax credit bandwagon (*Housing Affairs Letter* 1986b).

In any case, existing subsidized projects are likely to be the prime initial candidates for tax credit assistance, for several reasons. Most of these projects already meet the program's income-targeting test, have lower capital requirements than new construction, and can take advantage of below-market rate financing, rental assistance, or other subsidies already in place. Moreover, few new construction projects will be ready to qualify for the initial annual credit allocations assigned to each state, allocations which cannot be carried over into future years. Indeed, HUD is actively working with state agencies to steer the credits towards insured or assisted projects "in danger of default" or with expiring use-restrictions (*Housing Affairs Letter* 1986a).

But despite its advantages relative to prior law, the new tax credit approach is unlikely to preserve the long-term viability and affordability of the existing subsidized housing stock. There are several reasons for this: based on past experience, to the extent that the credit encourages the continued acquisition of distressed projects by profit-motivated owners through foreclosure sales, disposition auctions, or resyndication, the capital investment required to meet project needs will not be made—especially if current HUD policies that maximize financial returns to the private sector and the government continue. And while the credit may extend the lower-income use of a portion of the units in some subsidized projects that are ripe for mortgage prepayment, the long-term affordability of these units once again will be jeopardized when the tax credit expires in ten years. Moreover, in strong market areas, the tax credit will likely be insufficient to prevent profit-motivated owners from converting all or a portion of their projects to market-rate housing or condominiums, especially in the absence of regulatory policies to discourage alternative use.

Additionally, while the tax credit may prove more efficient than the prior system of depreciation-based incentives as a vehicle for housing finance, the cumulative tax expenditure required to support this mechanism over ten years is likely to be substantial. And to the extent that the credit is purchased primarily by corporations and individuals who can continue to offset their tax liability with passive losses, the cost effectiveness of this financing strategy will be considerably diminished.

Finally, as many have acknowledged, additional public subsidies will be required to make most tax credit properties (as well as other housing) affordable to low-income families. While some states and localities that currently are riding a wave of fiscal prosperity may be able to fill a portion of this gap on a temporary basis, clearly the bulk of this subsidy will have to be provided from the federal government through increased social spending—supported by a progressive tax system, as well as a reordering of budget priorities.

In the present era of budgetary restraint, the advocacy efforts of low-income and nonprofit organizations on behalf of continued tax incentives for subsidized housing are certainly understandable. Yet, as the experience of past alliances between nonprofit sponsors and the profit-oriented real estate and syndication industries (such as the PUSH Task Force) should demonstrate, the solutions resulting from such efforts are unlikely to serve the social needs of the housing or its residents on a long-term basis. At the same time, continued support for special-interest tax loopholes such as the low-income housing tax credit weaken the movement for broad-based tax reform begun in 1986, with its potential long-term benefits for the housing system as a whole.

With heightened public awareness of the risks currently facing the subsidized housing inventory and the problems posed by traditional private sector subsidy solutions, the opportunity may now exist to develop a longer-range alternative, consistent with progressive tax reform, that would preserve the viability and affordability of this housing stock on a permanent basis. Building on the experience of recent local initiatives, the cornerstone of this approach would involve a program of direct and indirect public capital subsidies for qualified owners of existing subsidized projects, linked to regulatory measures that preserve and foster social ownership (for a more detailed discussion of the concept of social ownership, see Achtenberg and Marcuse 1983).

For projects with insurance and regulatory controls still in force, the capital subsidy would take the form of a direct grant for needed capital repairs, similar to the Flexible Subsidy program (but with no repayment requirement). For HUD-held projects, an additional subsidy would be available in the form of a permanent writedown of mortgage debt (and forgiveness of delinquencies), to the extent necessary to ensure long-term project viability and affordability. In exchange for these benefits, owners would agree to maintain the projects for permanent low- and moderate-income use. They would also grant an option or right of first refusal to the residents or to a qualified nonprofit entity to purchase the project upon resale at a restricted price, for permanent use as nonspeculative lower-income housing. Capital grants could also be provided to finance a limited owner equity take-out consistent with the housing's continued social purpose.

While acceptance of these subsidies by qualified owners would be voluntary, without the alternative of equity financing through the tax system some might choose this option. Others might elect to transfer their projects directly to qualified nonprofit sponsors (through a Transfer of Physical Assets procedure), who would then have the benefit of the capital subsidy program. To the extent that it is more cost effective to the government to facilitate such transfers, rather than institute foreclosure proceedings, incentives could be provided, such as partial or complete forgiveness of capital gains taxes owed by the seller.

Where owners of deteriorated or delinquent projects refuse to accept (or fail to qualify for) the rehabilitation grants and/or mortgage writedowns, HUD would enforce strict debt collection and repair policies, forcing foreclosure wherever possible. By bidding the statutory maximum at foreclosure sales and requiring any private purchaser to comply with similar long-term use, repair, and resale restrictions, in virtually all cases HUD would acquire the property. With an effective writedown of debt accomplished through foreclosure, HUD then would offer the properties at a negligible price to qualified purchasers, with comparable direct grants for rehabilitation, and use and resale restrictions. In these situations where HUD has direct control of the property, sales could be negotiated directly on a priority basis with qualified resident and nonprofit purchasers, wherever possible.

Finally, in order to encourage use of the program by owners of projects with potentially expiring use-restrictions, the government would create a series of new regulatory controls—for example, with regard to rent, eviction, and habitability standards—to be imposed on "post-prepayment projects." While not precluding owners' contractual rights to prepay their mortgages, these requirements would effectively limit the residual equity gain available from prepayment to a reasonable level more consistent with the program's social objectives (and with owners' original expectations). This approach would increase the relative attractiveness of the publicly assisted preservation and social ownership conversion option. In adopting such measures, the government would recognize that federal action to avoid further exacerbating local housing emergency conditions constitutes a legitimate use of authority for a public purpose, even if private privileges are thereby diminished (as long as the restrictions are not confiscatory).

The cost of such a program would not be insurmountable, even in the present era of budgetary restraint. For example, to write off the outstanding debt on HUD-held mortgages (not including interest delinquencies) would cost approximately $1.3 billion (see Table 10.1). Rehabilitation grants for 600,000 insured and HUD-held units, at $3,000 per unit, would cost another $1.8 billion. Capital grants for the HUD-owned inventory of 6,500 units, averaging $10,000 per unit, would add $65 million, while equity grants to convert to social ownership an estimated 100,000 units with use-restrictions expiring by 1991, at $5,000 per unit, would cost $500 million. The total program cost of $3.7 billion, annualized over five years, would be about $740 million—as compared with the current estimated annual tax expenditure of $525 million which is attributable to HUD-insured subsidized housing.[4]

Through these mechanisms, an increasing portion of the existing subsidized inventory would eventually be converted to social ownership, operated solely and permanently for the benefit of low- and moderate-income residents with no potential for speculative resale or market-rate conversion. With full repairs and written-down mortgage debt, the housing would be viable as well as affordable. Rents could be substantially reduced, since only operating expenses would have to be paid (and property taxes based on restricted use value would also be lower). For very low-income tenants unable to afford even the cost of basic housing operations, rental subsidies would still be needed—and should be provided—but their cost would be substantially less.

In this way, the existing subsidized housing inventory could be conserved and made viable on a permanent basis for low- and moderate-income people, while providing a model of cost-effective social ownership and financing, consistent with progressive tax reform, that has broader applicability for the housing system as whole.

NOTES

1. Telephone interview with Jennifer Stucker, HUD Office of Policy Development and Research, March 21, 1986.

2. Except where otherwise noted, information in this section is based on the author's experience as development consultant to the tenants or other direct involvement with the projects.

3. Information updated via telephone conversation with Roderick Bohanan, Legal Services Organization of Indiana, April 5, 1985.

4. HUD has estimated that approximately 25 percent of total tax expenditures for rental housing (including accelerated depreciation, Section 167k rehabilitation write-offs, and exclusion of interest on state and local rental housing bonds) is attributable to subsidized insured rental housing (U.S. Senate 1985, 1578). The total amount of these tax expenditures is estimated at $2.105 billion for fiscal year 1987 (Low Income Housing Information Service 1986b).

REFERENCES

Abrams, Philip. 1982a. "Marketing HUD-Owned Projects and Projects Covered by HUD-Held Mortgages." U.S. Department of Housing and Urban Development, May 7.

———. 1982b. "Policy for Projects With HUD-Held Mortgages." U.S. Department of Housing and Urban Development, Washington, DC, June 18.

Achtenberg, Emily. 1985a. Letter to Lori Raleigh, Boston HUD Office, Boston, MA, March 22. Unpublished.

Achtenberg, Emily. 1985b. Memorandum to Roxse Homes, Inc. Board of Directors, Boston, MA, April 9. Unpublished.

Achtenberg, Emily, and Peter Marcuse. 1983. "Towards the decommodification of housing: A political analysis and a progressive program." In *America's Housing Crisis: What Is To Be Done?*, edited by Chester Hartman. Boston, MA: Routledge and Kegan Paul.

Achtenberg, Emily. 1982. "Grant Manor: Preliminary Status Report." Memorandum to the Massachusetts Community Economic Development Assistance Corporation, Boston, MA, December 26. Unpublished.

Barksdale, Maurice L. 1984. "Revised Policy for Projects with HUD-Held Mortgages." U.S. Department of Housing and Urban Development, Washington, DC, October 18.

Boston HUD Area Office, 1977. *Assisted Multifamily Projects, City of Boston: A Strategy Paper*. Boston, MA, February.

Citizens Housing and Planning Association. 1982. *Resident Participation in the Management and Disposition of HUD-Owned Multifamily Housing: Final Report on the Boston Area Office Demonstration Program*. Boston, MA, April.

———. 1979. "Response to Senate Appropriations Committee Report on HUD-Held Multifamily Housing." Boston, MA, December 4.

Coalition for Low and Moderate Income Housing. 1984. "Senate Finance Committee Error Seriously Injures Existing Low Income Housing Stock." Washington, DC, April 5.

Goodwin, Michael. 1980. "Tenants of U.S.-Backed Projects Sent $30 Million in Disputed Rent." *New York Times*, November 2.

Hale, Janet. 1985. "Repairs to Multifamily Mortgage-in-Possession and HUD-Owned Properties." U.S. Department of Housing and Urban Development, October 31.

Housing Affairs Letter. 1986a. "Stress Preservation of Existing Stock, Allocators of Housing Tax Credit Urged." November 21:2.

———. 1986b. "Low Income Credit Can Work With Subsidies." November 21:3.

———. 1986c. "LISC Seeking Corporate Investors." November 21:4.

———. 1986d. "Making Low Income Tax Credit Work For You." October 17:3.

———. 1986e. "How Low Income Tax Credit Might Work." September 26:1.

———. 1986f. "Reforms Won't Harm Low Income Housing." September 12:3.

———. 1986g. "Potential for Low Income Defaults Weighed." September 12:5.

———. 1983. "Section 202 Mortgage Sales Cancelled." May 27:4.

———. 1975. "OMB Deflating Balloon Payment Plan." November 28:5.

Housing and Development Reporter. 1979. "Landrieu, Simon Defend HUD Against Mismanagement Charges." December 10:581.

Hutton, E.F., and Company, Inc. 1985. "America First: Federally Guaranteed Mortgage Fund 2," Prospectus, April 1.

Johnson, Sara and the National Housing Law Project. 1985. *Preserving HUD-Assisted Housing for Use by Low-Income Tenants: An Advocate's Guide*. Chicago: National Clearinghouse for Legal Services.

Kurtz, Howie. 1982. "HUD to Sell Seven Projects to Two Prominent in GOP." *Washington Post*, May 11.

Low Income Housing Information Service. 1986a. "Tax Bill Spells Victory for Low Income Concerns." Low Income Housing Round-Up, 105, September.

———. 1986b. "The 1987 Housing Budget and Low Income Housing Needs." Special Memorandum 24, February.

Massachusetts Housing Finance Agency. 1985. "1984 Resyndications." Memorandum, January 2.

National Association of Home Builders. 1986. *Low- and Moderate-Income Housing: Progress, Problems, and Prospects*. Washington, DC.

National Housing Law Project. 1984. "Changing HUD Tactics in Regard to Troubled Projects." *Bulletin* 14(2), March/April.

Pierce, Samuel R., Jr. 1984. Letter to Hon. Donald W. Riegle, Jr., Subcommittee on Housing and Urban Affairs, Committee on Banking, Housing, and Urban Affairs, May 22.

Preachers United to Save Housing, Inc. 1975. "HUD/PUSH Task Force Position Paper," May 5.

President's Committee on Urban Housing. 1968. *A Decent Home*. Washington, DC: U.S. Government Printing Office.

Simons, Lawrence. 1978. *Repair and Management of Acquired Properties*. U.S. Department of Housing and Urban Development, Washington, DC, April 5.

Smith, David. 1982. "Resyndication: The Newest Tax Shelter." *Investor Quarterly* 4 (1st Quarter).

U.S. Comptroller General, General Accounting Office. 1980a. *Analysis of Multifamily Assigned Mortgages*. Washington, DC: U.S. Government Printing Office, January 18.

———. 1980b. *Evaluation of Alternatives for Financing Low and Moderate Income Rental Housing*. Washington, DC: U.S. Government Printing Office, September 30.

———. 1979. *HUD Should Improve Its Management of Acquired, Formerly-Subsidized Multifamily Projects*. Washington, DC: U.S. Government Printing Office, December 19.

U.S. Congress, Congressional Budget Office. 1977. *Real Estate Tax Shelters and Direct Subsidy Alternatives*. Washington, DC: U.S. Government Printing Office.

U.S. Congress, Senate. 1984. *Congressional Record*. Washington, DC: U.S. Government Printing Office, April 12.

U.S. Department of Housing and Urban Development. 1984a. *Nonjudicial Foreclosure of Multifamily Mortgages*. 24 CFR part 27, February 17.

———.1984b. *Management and Disposition of HUD-Owned Multifamily Housing Projects*. Proposed amendment to Interim Rule. 24 CFR part 290, September 13.

———.1984c. *Transfers of Physical Assets: Revised Administrative Procedures for Reviewing TPA Proposals*. Notice 84-37, November 14.

———. 1982. *National Report on the Transfer of Physical Assets in the Sale of Multifamily Projects*. Office of Inspector General. Washington, DC. August 24.

———.1980. *Transfer from Nonprofit to Profit-Motivated Ownership for Multifamily Housing Projects with HUD-Insured or HUD-Held Mortgages*. 24 CFR part 265, August 13.

———.1979a. *HUD Statistical Yearbook*. Washington, DC: U.S. Government Printing Office.

———.1979b. *Management and Disposition of HUD-Owned Multifamily Housing Projects*. 24 CFR part 290, October 30.

———.1979c. *Section 8 Housing Assistance Programs for the Disposition of HUD-Owned Projects*. 24 CFR part 886 subpart C, December 6.

———.1979d. *Processing Instructions for the Sale of HUD-Owned Multifamily Projects with Section 8*. Notice 79-122.

———.1978. *Final Report of the Multifamily Property Utilization Task Force*. Washington, DC.

———.1977. *Section 8 Housing Assistance Payments Program: The Loan Management Set-Aside*. Washington, DC.

———.1975. *Multifamily Property Disposition: A Staff Study*. Washington, DC.

U.S. General Accounting Office. 1986. *Rental Housing: Potential Reduction in the Privately-Owned and Federally-Assisted Inventory*. Washington, DC: U.S. Government Printing Office, June 16.

———.1985. *Impact of Federal Tax Provisions on Resyndication of Federally-Assisted Rental Housing*. Washington, DC: U.S. Government Printing Office, July 10.

———.1984. *Improving the Process for Allocating Loan Management Set-Aside Funds to Multifamily Housing Projects*, Washington, DC: U.S. Government Printing Office, November 16.

U.S. House of Representatives, Committee on Government Operations. 1984. *Preservation of Subsidized Housing and Capital Improvement Loans*. Hearings, 98th Cong., 2nd sess. March 29. Washington, DC: U.S. Government Printing Office.

———.1983a. *HUD Multifamily Property Disposition Programs*. Hearings, 98th Cong., 1st sess. May 24–25. Washington, DC: U.S. Government Printing Office.

———.1983b. *HUD Multifamily Repair and Foreclosure Policies*. Hearings, 98th Cong., 1st sess. July 26. Washington, DC: U.S. Government Printing Office.

———.1983c. *HUD's Failure to Implement the Multifamily Mortgage Foreclosure Act*. Hearings, 98th Cong., 1st sess. October 5. Washington, DC: U.S. Government Printing Office.

———.1983d. *HUD Is Not Adequately Preserving Subsidized Multifamily Housing*.

Hearings, 98th Cong., 1st sess. Washington, DC: U.S. Government Printing Office.

U.S. House of Representatives, Subcommittee on Housing and Community Development. 1986. *Loss of Subsidized Multifamily Housing Units*. Hearings, 99th Cong., 2nd sess. June 18. Washington, DC: U.S. Government Printing Office.

U.S. President's Commission on Housing. 1982. *Report of the President's Commission on Housing*. Washington, DC: U.S. Government Printing Office.

U.S. Senate. 1985. *Hearings, Department of Housing and Urban Development and Certain Independent Agencies FY1985*. 98th Cong., 2nd sess., part 2. Washington, DC: U.S. Government Printing Office.

———. 1980. *Management of HUD's Multifamily Properties: The Clifton Terrace Case*. Hearings, 96th Cong., 1st sess., November 13 and December 5, 1979; January 23, 1980. Washington, DC: U.S. Government Printing Office.

———. 1978. Report no. 871, 95th Cong., 2nd sess. 23. Reprinted in 1978 U.S. Code Cong. and Ad. News 4796.

U.S. Senate, Committee on Appropriations. 1979. *Management and Disposition of the Department of Housing and Urban Development's Inventory of Multifamily Properties*. Report no. 79-10, November.

U.S. Senate, Committee on Banking and Currency. 1965. Hearings, March 29–April 9. Washington, DC: U.S. Government Printing Office.

Winn, Philip D. 1982. "Elimination of Purchase Proposal Selection Procedure for the Sale of Multifamily Projects." U.S. Department of Housing and Urban Development, January 21.

———. 1981. "Policy for Repairs on HUD-Owned Multifamily Projects." U.S. Department of Housing and Urban Development, November 3.

Wong, Jan. 1984. "Harold Brown: Boston's Biggest Landlord Has His Share of Trouble With Tenants and the Courts." *Boston Globe*, September 25.

SUBSIDIZED HOUSING AT RISK: COMMENT

Marilyn Melkonian

Emily Achtenberg reviews 25 years of federal housing policy involving private sector participation in the development and ownership of housing affordable to lower-income Americans. She concludes that the record is dismal for at least two reasons. First, the policy was contradictory because the owners' and tenants' interests were incompatible, and the system tilted against tenants. In addition, she observes that the policy did not create nearly enough housing relative to need and resources. These simultaneous observations are somewhat reminiscent of the old joke told by Woody Allen about the two elderly ladies at dinner in a Catskill resort. Both were complaining about the food, and one of them added, "And such small portions."

Achtenberg's analysis addresses shortcomings of the federal effort over the past four decades to meet the nation's housing needs. She points out that these efforts have fallen short of the expectations of those who believe in delivering on the promise, made in the Housing Act of 1949, to provide "a decent home and suitable living environment for every American family." In the past eight years, however, the promise itself has been removed from the nation's political consciousness, and Achtenberg's criticism focuses on the policies of the Reagan administration. Since 1980 direct federal spending on housing has dwindled to less than 1 percent of the federal budget, a 60 percent reduction and the largest single domestic spending cut. The Reagan administration's rationale for reduced federal support for housing programs rested on the premise that government involvement, in and of itself, is the cause of the nation's housing problems. It is assumed that the market, left free of government meddling, can provide for housing far better than federal programs.

As Achtenberg well describes, the Reagan administration mindlessly pursued a policy of cut and run: dumping property, mortgages, and tenants, and refusing to follow statutory and congressional mandates and requirements. It avoided building relationships with states and localities, which, in the spirit of the ''New Federalism,'' could have supported local efforts to address housing needs. It made no effort to learn from 50 years of federal involvement in a range of housing programs. It developed policies without any understanding of the multiple interests involved and the impact of its policies on tenants, neighborhoods, or housing providers. As evidenced by its ostrich-like approach to the prepayment issues raised by Achtenberg, it showed no concern for the value of housing to the general welfare and Treasury. As a tide of homelessness rises, to the shame of most Americans, the attitude of the Reagan administration was epitomized by its former Attorney General, who saw homelessness as the manifestation of freedom of choice. Against such sophistry, even angels fight in vain.

Ironically, however, while the actions of the Reagan administration precipitated a housing crisis, they also provided an opportunity. Since we currently have no real federal housing policy, we are now forced to reexamine the ways and means to fulfill the promise of decent homes and suitable living environments. This will require developing goals and programs appropriate to our time and place. Achtenberg's arguments are particularly relevant to this endeavor because they provide not only an insightful critique of past housing policies, but also a sharp point of view on strategies for meeting the nation's housing needs. She concludes by calling for policies that would shift ownership of the existing federally assisted stock to nonprofits and tenant cooperatives. Whether or not one agrees with her specific recommendations, her suggestions stimulate the process of developing new strategies for responding to the existing housing crisis.

In 1987 we marked a half-century of federal involvement in meeting the nation's housing needs. Beginning with the Housing Act of 1937, the federal government, seeking solutions to the problem of ''one-third of a nation ill-housed,'' initiated two major strategies that defined national housing policy for decades. First, through a program for national mortgage insurance, the federal government created the private long-term mortgage credit market and the opportunity for widespread homeownership. Second, through the public housing program, it assumed responsibility for the capital costs of public housing and thereby reduced the cost of such housing to residents. The first strategy was premised on a belief in the mixed economy and demonstrated the creative interplay between the government and the market. By minimizing risks to lenders, and thus widening the market for mortgages, the government allowed the market to provide housing for a majority of households. The second direction, direct funding of housing production, reflected a recognition of the limits of the market. One hundred and fifty years of experience made it clear that the market could not produce enough inexpensive decent housing for everyone. If every household was to be housed, the government would have to use a mix of strategies and resources. For the next quarter-century, the major strategies employed were credit enhancement through federal mortgage insurance and, in effect, capital grants to local public agencies to build, own and rent housing at a reduced cost to people who could not afford to obtain decent housing through the private market.

Achtenberg focuses on a strategy developed subsequently by the federal government to complement the policies adopted in 1937. She considers the decision to involve private industry in the ownership, development, and management of housing for lower-income Americans. On June 30, 1961, John F. Kennedy, citing the 25 million Americans who lived in substandard housing and the large number of households who could neither afford decent housing in the private market nor qualify for public housing, signed a new housing bill. The legislation made available direct loans, at the federal borrowing rate, to private developers, both profit and nonprofit, to build housing for people of moderate income, that is, those earning up to 95 percent of the area median income.

The idea was simple and not very revolutionary; it was designed to widen the constituency served by the private market. By reducing the cost of financing, housing costs would be reduced and more households would gain access to housing through the private market. The issue of the relative roles of the public sector and the private sector had, in fact, been debated since 1937. The 1961 legislation, which engaged the private sector in the development and ownership of federally subsidized low-income housing, institutionalized a preference for using the market to provide decent housing for all citizens. In the 25 years since embarking on that course, through starts and stops and the various permutations of combined subsidies, the federally assisted housing stock of about four million units is now roughly divided one-third public ownership (through the public housing programs) and two-thirds private ownership (both profit and nonprofit). Federally assisted units represent about 25 percent of the housing affordable to people who earn less than $10,000 a year, or one out of every five American households.

Achtenberg expresses concern that federally assisted, privately owned housing will not continue to be available as affordable housing for low- and moderate-income households. She warns that, as low-income use-restrictions and other subsidies lapse, hundreds of thousands of currently available affordable units will likely be lost to the nation's low-income housing inventory. She is not alone in her concern on this issue. Henry Schechter, director of Housing and Monetary Policy for the AFL-CIO, has stated, "The idea of depending on private enterprise to develop low-income housing turns out to be a fool's paradise in the end. As I look back on forty years in the housing field, it was a mistake."[1]

Achtenberg's proposal is to transfer all assisted housing to social ownership, to end the failed experiment of private sector, for-profit ownership of low- and moderate-income housing. I question the capacity of nonprofits and tenant co-operatives to assume ownership responsibility for this resource, and argue for a more diversified approach that will continue private sector participation with appropriate restraints.

The belief that involving the private sector in the ownership of low-income housing was a mistake is based on the well-founded expectation that private owners will take advantage of current economic conditions to maximize profits at the expense of low-income tenants. Economic circumstances have changed dramatically since the housing programs involving private ownership were conceived and first implemented in the 1960s. Since that time, the value of housing in many cases has soared, not through labor or the risk of capital, but as a result of housing shortages and inflation, while the incomes of eligible households have remained steady or declined. General market conditions have made the type of housing developed under these programs a scarce resource. The goal of the Great Society's Section 236 program was to produce 600,000 units of assisted housing a year. Instead, that number was barely achieved over the program's life. Private owners now see the prospect of realizing current market value for this housing by selling or refinancing the projects for a higher-income constituency.

This was not the economic incentive that attracted the private sector to the program in the first place. The original incentives were highly leveraged investment; risk reduction as a result of mortgage insurance and subsidies; developer, builder, and management fees; and tax benefits that produced equity and profits. These incentives were successful in attracting private enterprise and capital to the assisted housing market. It simply was not anticipated at the inception of the program that a dramatic rise in market values would lead to a windfall to owners and displacement of tenants.

Federal housing programs created opportunities for investors and owners, but today the market allows those opportunities to be maximized at the expense of the groups the programs were meant to assist. This was not the intended result, and it is reasonable to attempt to develop means to protect our valuable low-income housing stock from the effects of the open market.

It is very likely that much of the existing federally assisted stock can be preserved as affordable housing, as the author suggests, by extending favorable tax treatment for low-income use. A tax code provision that would forgive the tax due on sale of a low-income housing project if no cash were received by the seller would open a new door to transferring projects to new owners who would continue low-income use. Tax forgiveness would be available only for a disposition approved by the appropriate regulatory agency, either HUD or the Farmers Home Administration, to a nonprofit, a tenant cooperative, or a private owner who undertakes to maintain the affordability of the housing under the original programs.

While it is impossible to estimate the number of owners who actually would take advantage of such a program, this incentive would satisfy the needs of many investors. In fact, most syndicators of low-income housing anticipated selling their projects for $1 over the mortgage at the end of the tax benefit period. Investor return was calculated on the value of the stream of tax benefits received during the ownership period and did not depend on appreciation in the value of the property itself. In addition, the expected payment of a tax at capital gains rates on the difference between the projected sale price (mortgage amount plus $1) and the investors' negative basis was considered in calculating the return offered by the investment. If investors were relieved of this tax, their overall return on investment would be increased significantly. Such an increase would likely serve as a compelling incentive to transfer the housing for low-income use.

Incentives for maintaining low-income use can be complemented by disincentives to selling out low-income housing to the highest bidder. The current market value of housing is largely a creation of fortuitous circumstances, due in part to the federal government's actions. The government could recognize this fact by imposing a "conversion" tax that would reflect the value of the contribution of the subsidy stream to the unit's market value. Such a tax would lessen the profits available through sales and tend to preserve units for low-income use.

Outright charitable contributions of assisted housing projects to nonprofit ownership might be encouraged by relaxation of the charitable contribution provisions enacted in the Tax Reform Act of 1986. Eliminating charitable donations of low-income housing as a preference item under the Alternative Minimum Tax would encourage high-income investors to divest themselves of ownership. In the past few years, several 501(c)(3) organizations have been formed for the express purpose of acquiring assisted housing through donation or bargain sale, to preserve low-income use.

The full impact of the prepayment problem referred to by Achtenberg will be felt less than two years from now. Congress has time to correct the design flaw in the structure of the programs and retain this stock. The additional cost required to find an equitable solution is insignificant in relation to the $130 billion replacement cost for the inventory. Taking steps to preserve the nation's privately held low-income housing inventory does not resolve the question of whether or not depending so heavily on private enterprise to meet our nation's low-income housing needs was unwise, but if the prepayment issue is not resolved, the answer certainly will be that it was a costly way to go about it.

If all Americans earned or received enough money to pay the full cost of decent housing while being able to afford the other necessities of life, the private market would be able to meet the nation's housing needs. This reasoning underlies the Reagan administration's housing voucher program. Vouchers, like food stamps, supplement income and give people the means to bid for housing in the private market. The merit of this approach is that it maximizes choice. The problem, of course, is that there is an inadequate supply of housing affordable within the limits of the voucher program. Between 1974 and 1983 the number of units renting for $250 or less decreased from 10.8 million to 8.8 million, while the number of households earning less than $10,000 annually increased, during the same period, from 8.9 million to 11.9 million. The National Low Income Housing Coalition's "Rental Housing Index" shows that by 1985, not a single state in theory had a supply of low-rent housing (units renting at or below 30 percent of half the area's median income level) greater than the number of households in the state at or below that income level. Whereas in 1980 ten states had a theoretical surplus of affordable units to the number of low-income households, by 1985 no state had a surplus, and over 17 states had a gap of better than two to one, as compared to only two states with so wide a disparity in 1980. Clearly there is an increasing shortage in the supply of housing affordable to potential voucher recipients.

If we are serious about providing housing for low-income households, we must support housing programs that increase supply both through preservation of the existing stock and the construction of new housing. Over the past 50 years almost all conceivable forms of ownership and combinations of subsidies have been used. Following the original subsidies of mortgage insurance to private lenders and direct capital grants to local public agencies, came mortgage interest subsidies under the Section 236 and 221(d)(3) programs and later tax-exempt bond financing through state agencies. Operating subsidies were added to the public housing program in 1969, and in 1974 these subsidies were provided to privately financed housing in the form of guaranteed rental contracts under the Section 8 program. Section 8 combined the idea of mortgage interest reduction subsidies with the idea of project-based tenant income subsidies that had been tried in 1965 as the Rent Supplement program. Capital grants for almost any housing purpose were made available under the Housing Development Grant (HODAG) program. Favorable tax treatment for investment in low-income housing has been a source of equity capital. With the withdrawal of the federal government, state and local governments with the imagination and will to replace federal funding (at least partially) have channeled funds to housing through similar programs.

These programs have provided ample opportunities to test alternative means to produce adequate housing. It seems clear that several strategies are needed. Efforts to develop housing for a target income population must include subsidies adequate to ensure that all housing costs can be met, if tenant rents are to be restricted to an affordable level of income. In the Section 236 and 221(d)(3) interest reduction programs, these subsidies were simply not deep enough for households with incomes below $7,000. This was the most significant threat to the survival of the housing stock discussed by Achtenberg. Regardless of the form of ownership, without the addition of subsidies for over 300,000 units through the Section 8 Loan Management program, the housing would not have survived long enough to face the prepayment problem on the horizon.

However, Achtenberg's major point is that unrestricted private ownership of low-income housing will ultimately result in the selling out of the interests of low-income tenants in pursuit of the highest profits. Without retroactive changes in the 221(d)(3), 236 and Section 8 programs and creation of new incentives to maintain low-income use, she will be right. This does not necessarily mean, however, that ownership of low-income housing should be left to nonprofits, tenant cooperatives, and public agencies.

Any assessment of the potential of ownership by cooperatives, nonprofits, and public agencies must begin with an evaluation of their activities thus far. With rare exceptions, low-income cooperatives function at disappointing levels. The critical constraints lie in management difficulties rather than legal limits. In order to be successful, cooperatives need management and business skills that often far exceed their current capacity.

While there are increasing numbers of able nonprofits, they are not yet numerous enough to be significant housing providers. Nonprofits first began to play an important role in federally assisted housing programs under the Section 202 program for the elderly introduced in 1959. Their effectiveness and political strength is demonstrated by the fact that Congress continues to fund the 202 program, albeit at a much reduced level. Less impressive testimony about the effectiveness of nonprofits was their performance as sponsors and developers in the 221(d)(3) and 236 programs. Achtenberg fails to acknowledge the many inexperienced and undercapitalized nonprofit-sponsored projects that failed under these programs. Without a dramatic increase in the number of capable nonprofits, there simply would not be enough sponsors to support social ownership of housing at any significant scale.

The nonprofit community certainly can play a major role as a housing provider. Those community corporations that have stayed in the trenches since the 1960s and have inspired other organizations are important players, especially when housing is viewed as part of a larger economic development effort. The absence of major federal housing programs over the last few years has caused many, if not most, private developers to leave the low-income housing field. This has created a tremendous opportunity for growth of the community-based housing sector. In order to take advantage of this opportunity, community-based interests must become better organized and work together more compatibly and efficiently. National organizations such as the Local Initiatives Support Corporation and the Enterprise Foundation must be strengthened in order to better coordinate use of the considerable contributions of charitable organizations and more forcefully advocate the interest of client groups.

Local public agencies that provide low-cost housing can also play a role in reducing the economic tension between the goals of increasing private ownership and long-term access to low-income housing. The fact is, however, that of the approximately 3,000 local public housing authorities, fewer than 350 own and operate more than 500 units. Obviously, the overall capacity of these organizations to affect the future of the nation's housing delivery system is currently limited. Since their recent exile from federally supported housing programs, however, some local housing agencies have developed new roles. They have become local financiers, as well as managers, of housing. Building on their considerable experience as housing providers, these agencies are in a position to play a positive role in addressing the nation's low-income housing needs.

To some extent, there is a chicken-or-egg effect of public policy on the housing delivery system. On the one hand, supportive public policies encourage and bolster the use and development of public agencies, nonprofit organizations, and tenant cooperatives as housing owners, allowing these institutions to respond more effectively to housing need. On the other hand, these public-purpose housing providers play a critical role in encouraging development of policies that give nonprofits and cooperatives a role in providing housing. The set-aside to nonprofits of 10 percent of the funding under the new low-income housing tax credit program is certainly the result of advocacy on the part of public-purpose providers.

Should housing advocates pursue only this direction for future development and preservation of low-income housing? Should they seek to exclude profit-motivated private owners from a future housing delivery system?

As a practical matter, given the present capacity of public purpose housing providers, it is unrealistic to expect them to develop an adequate supply of low-income housing. An alternative is to encourage the private sector to address the needs of low-income groups. As demonstrated above, profit motivation in low-income housing can be structured around the rewards for enterprise in successfully building, developing, and managing housing. It does not need to depend on long-term speculative ownership. The key is to figure out how to capture private investment capital and entrepreneurial talent, while at the same time keeping the housing out of the speculative real estate market.

One means to accomplish this is to separate actual ownership of low-income housing from eligibility to receive tax benefits for investing in the production and maintenance of low-income housing. We have learned that private investment capital drawn to low-income housing by tax benefits does not require the incentive of gain on sale, just as it does not depend on project cash flow for a return. This indicates the potential for separating investment in low-income housing from a traditional ownership interest in that housing. Nonprofits, tenant cooperatives, even public agencies should be given the right to sell tax credits to corporations or individuals.

As a method for raising private capital for housing, the tax credit program is a major improvement over past tax incentives because of its rent restrictions and willingness to target benefits to low-income households. It does not, however, face the issue of what happens to the housing in private ownership at the end of the 15-year restricted period for low-income use. On the other hand, the existence of the tax credit program provides another source of capital by inducing owners of existing assisted housing to transfer their projects to new owners willing to continue low-income use-restrictions in return for tax credits. This $9 billion tax credit program is more likely to produce the capital needed to preserve low-income housing stock than are direct appropriations for conversion of that stock to social ownership, as advocated by Achtenberg. Direct appropriations could be, however, a useful tool, and to the extent possible, within the current political climate, should be brought to bear on the problem.

Better programs and more money for affordable housing will be found in a mixed economy of private entrepreneurs, investors, nonprofits, tenant cooperatives, public agencies, and families who cannot afford the full cost of housing in the private market.

While leadership in establishing commitments and providing funding is needed from the federal level, the appropriate mix and match of programs and subsidies can best be determined at the state and local level, where need and housing resources vary greatly. In any case there is a need to involve both the public and private sectors in the effort. Government at all levels, builders, developers, managers, for-profit and nonprofit owners, renters, investors, and lenders all need to play a part in the housing economy that meets a need so important to the quality of the lives we lead.

NOTES

1. Comment made in an article by W. John Moore, ''Expiring Subsidies,'' *The National Journal* 18 (1986): 1888.

11

COMMUNITY-BASED HOUSING IN MASSACHUSETTS: LESSONS AND LIMITS OF THE STATE'S SUPPORT SYSTEM

Rachel G. Bratt

This chapter is a piece of a larger study that has two major goals: to determine what has been learned from past subsidized production programs, and to develop a proposal for rebuilding a low-income housing policy (Bratt, 1989). The arguments presented here are premised on conclusions drawn from earlier phases of the work—much of which reviewed and consolidated findings of previous studies (Bratt 1985; Bratt 1986a; Bratt 1986b; Bratt 1987a; Bratt 1987b). Those conclusions can be summarized as follows:

- There is still a need for more low-cost housing, and the unassisted private sector will not or cannot meet this need. Significant government subsidies will be required to help low-income people attain decent shelter.
- Housing allowances or cash vouchers will not stimulate low-rent housing production. Therefore, there is a need for a new or revised subsidized production program.
- Subsidized multifamily housing can be good housing, and levels of satisfaction among tenants of subsidized housing are generally high.
- Producing subsidized housing through the for-profit private sector has some serious drawbacks, since the needs of these developers almost inevitably conflict with the broad public objective of long-term maintenance of a supply of decent, low-cost housing.
- Public housing is, overall, much better than most people believe, and a revised program should be an important component of federal housing policy.

Partial support for this work was provided through a grant from the Monroe Trotter Institute (formerly the Institute for the Study of Black Culture), University of Massachusetts, Boston.

- The experiences with tenant management and other initiatives involving community sponsorship of both new and rehabilitated housing indicate that there is enormous potential in using community groups to develop and manage their own housing.

This last assertion is the starting point for the current paper. Over the past 15 years, a set of state agencies in Massachusetts have evolved into an impressive support system for community-based housing. The Massachusetts experience is instructive because it serves as an example of how the public sector can provide top-down support to bottom-up housing activities. The first section of the paper examines the roots of community-based housing and presents a brief overview of some of the major strengths and weaknesses of the approach. The remainder of the paper focuses on the Massachusetts experience with community-based housing and addresses the following questions: How and why did the Massachusetts system of support for community-based housing groups evolve, and how does it currently operate? What insights can be drawn from the Massachusetts experience about the potential for creating additional state-level systems for supporting community-based housing?

ROOTS OF COMMUNITY-BASED HOUSING

The current generation of community-based housing groups has several types of ancestors—the early housing philanthropists; the nonprofits of the 1960s; and the community-based sponsors in the 1970s who formed limited partnerships. Although some groups in the latter two categories overlapped (for example, nonprofits also operated in the 1970s), various types of community-based housing groups were dominant at different times over the last two decades.

The Early Philanthropists

Long before the formal entry of nonprofits onto the housing scene in 1959, some nineteenth century reformers saw the need to limit the amount of profit in housing low-income people. By the turn of the century, a small-scale movement had formed to provide model tenement houses, "philanthropy plus 5 percent."[1] The goals of the movement were straightforward: to provide decent housing for the poor while yielding a modest profit for investors.

The legacy of the model tenement movement was mixed. On the one hand, such efforts pioneered in providing light and air to interior rooms, an "advance that was in sharp contrast to the tenements being built by speculators" (Meyerson, Terrett, and Wheaton 1962, 293). On the other hand, some model tenements turned into slums that were as bad as any produced by the private market. Further, according to Lawrence Veiller, a prominent housing reformer of the period, speculative builders had produced vastly more buildings, most of which were highly objectionable: "For every 13 people who have been provided with model tenements, 1,000 others have been condemned to live in unsanitary ones" (Friedman 1968, 86). Catherine Bauer, another key reformer, pointed out that the economics of the model tenement plan were ultimately unworkable. The model builders wanted "to provide good dwellings, on an 'economic' basis, at a price which everyone could pay, and without disturbing or even questioning any part of the current social-economic system"; it was an "impossible job" (Friedman 1968, 87). Thus, even at the turn of the century, it was acknowledged that decent low-cost housing was a goal that ran counter to the economic realities of housing production. Housing has always been expensive to build and, by definition, low-income households often have inadequate resources with which to pay the real cost of shelter.

The First Generation of Nonprofit Housing Developers: 1960s

From the federal government's entry into subsidized housing in 1937 until 1959, housing for low-income households was produced and managed through local public housing authorities. In 1959, however, the first in a series of housing programs which permitted private sponsorship of subsidized housing was enacted. The Housing Act of that year authorized direct below-market interest rate (BMIR) loans to private nonprofit groups to sponsor subsidized housing for the elderly, through the Section 202 program. Section 221(d)(3), enacted in 1961, authorized the federal government, through the Federal National Mortgage Association, to purchase mortgages at a 3 percent interest rate. For-profit or nonprofit developers were eligible to receive these low interest loans. Section 236, enacted in 1968, also authorized interest rate subsidies. Instead of the public financing arrangement of the Section 221(d)(3) program, the Section 236 subsidy went toward lowering the interest rate on mortgages, which were provided by private financial institutions, to as low as 1 percent.

Nonprofits in the Section 202 program enjoyed a good reputation. Although they were only partly responsible for the program's success they earned well-deserved praise and credibility as competent housing providers (Bratt 1989). Unfortunately, the experiences of nonprofits in the subsequent programs were not nearly as positive, and nonprofit sponsorship of multifamily subsidized housing acquired a generally negative reputation. Many well-meaning church, civic, or union groups with little prior experience in housing often found themselves unable to maintain the developments once they were built. In addition, many nonprofit groups were lured into the projects by for-profit builders, contractors, or consultants, who often bailed out after they pocketed their fees (Keyes 1971; HUD 1972). In view of these circumstances, it is not surprising that nonprofit projects failed at two to four times the rate of for-profit developments (GAO 1978; Friedland and MacRae 1979).

In addition to the unique problems confronting nonprofits, some structural defects in the Section 221(d)(3) and 236 programs also proved troublesome. Among the most significant flaws were the lack of any requirement for funds to be set aside to deal with unforeseen expenses and a subsidy formula that could not increase if additional resources were needed (BRA and BUO 1973; HUD 1978; GAO 1978). When utility costs skyrocketed in the early 1970s due to the oil crisis, owners of subsidized housing were faced with several difficult options for trying to meet increased operating expenses: raise rents; decrease maintenance and management services; cut into profits; or default on mortgage payments. Different strategies were chosen to try to keep the projects afloat but, overall, the results were grim. By 1978 less than one-third of the subsidized developments were financially sound (HUD 1978).

While all owners of subsidized housing found themselves between a rock and a hard place, the nonprofit sponsors had fewer options than did other owners. With limited assets, nonprofits did not have the option of using some of their own resources to make ends meet. Further, choosing either to reduce maintenance or increase rents was antithetical to the goals of the nonprofit groups. As one community sponsor of subsidized housing—who was 15 months behind in mortgage payments—put it: ''We had to make a decision: do you let people stay cold or do you pay the mortgage? Who are we to serve, the government or the tenants?'' (Urban Planning Aid 1973, 41). When faced with the decision of whether to provide housing services to tenants or pay debt service to financial institutions, some nonprofits chose to put their limited resources into the developments and to allow the projects to default. This suggests that an important reason behind the higher financial failure rate for the nonprofits was their desire to operate the buildings as well as they could given a shortage of funds.

Although it appears that the social commitment of the nonprofits may have created a situation that left them vulnerable to default and criticism, this commitment also produced a record that had many unequivocal benefits:

- By June 1970 nonprofits had sponsored about 28 percent of all units built under the Section 221(d)(3) BMIR and 236 programs.[2]
- Nonprofit sponsors used the rent supplement and the leased housing programs proportionally more frequently than did for-profit developers, thereby making units more affordable and available to lower-income people than those in the latter (Disario 1969; Keyes 1971).[3]
- A comparison of nonprofit and for-profit developments in Boston revealed that tenants in the former paid lower average rentals than those in the latter (Disario 1969).
- The same study also found that nonprofit developments had more three-, four-, and five-bedroom apartments than did other developments.
- Research conducted by HUD (1975) disclosed that projects built by nonprofit sponsors served a greater number of needy families than those built by limited-dividend sponsors.[4]
- A 24-city evaluation revealed that nonprofit sponsors of 221(d)(3) housing were more likely to undertake projects in urban renewal areas than for-profit developers (Keyes 1971).
- Many community-based sponsors openly confronted the toughest housing issues: central city rehabilitation, utilization of minority contractors and developers, and involvement of tenants in management decisions (Keyes 1971).
- The Urban Institute found that cooperatively-owned and nonprofit housing was, in general, more effectively managed than for-profit developments (cited in GAO 1978).

The early nonprofit housing groups operated in an institutional setting that makes these successes even more impressive. Although the Housing and Urban Development Act of 1968 included two sections explicitly intended to assist nonprofit groups, HUD did not aggressively administer the programs, and neither was fully utilized. These sections addressed two needs of nonprofit agencies: Section 106(a) authorized funding to provide information, advice, and technical assistance for nonprofit groups involved with housing construction or rehabilitation for low- or moderate-income families; Section 106(b) provided "seed money" loans to nonprofit housing sponsors. It was not until 1972, however, that HUD set aside $1 million to fund the Section 106(a) program. This money came from $6.7 million of so-called "excess" funds in the Section 106(b) revolving loan fund (HUD 1975). HUD's unsupportive attitude toward these programs is also revealed by the Department's questioning whether Section 106(b) seed money was necessary "in addition to . . . private sources of funds . . . [and whether the reasons for Section 106(b) were] sufficient to justify a $150,000 a year program" (HUD 1975, 21).

Although HUD's unwillingness to actively support Section 106 only adds another page in the long history of the agency's non-consumer orientation, it is noteworthy that lawmakers foresaw the need for funding and technical assistance for nonprofit housing sponsors. If Section 106 had been funded and used extensively, two key ingredients of a community-based housing system would have been put in place. As it turned out, however, technical assistance and funding to cover start-up costs had to be aggressively pursued by nonprofits, rather than easily obtained through federal appropriations. The lack of funding for these programs contributed to the overall impression of a fragmented non-system in which nonprofit community-based housing activities were forced to operate. With skimpy financial resources and few outside supports, many nonprofit groups got burned out after finishing one development. The knowledge that the group acquired was rarely used again, and new groups wanting to produce housing had to start at the beginning.

A few community groups that did not have a housing focus departed from this general pattern. Community Development Corporations (CDCs) that were well-funded through Title I-D of the Economic Opportunity Act of 1966, and later through Title VII of the Community Services Act of 1974, have had more resources available to them and have been considerably more durable (Abt Associates 1973; National Center for Economic Alternatives 1981).

Another group of community-based organizations that were supported by both the old Office of Economic Opportunity, and the Model Cities program, were the Housing Development Corporations (HDCs). As forerunners to many of the community-based housing groups that exist today, the early HDCs represented significant initial efforts to institutionalize the technical and financial resources needed to make nonprofit housing development possible (Keyes 1971). Nevertheless, they probably revealed as much about the problems associated with the way in which community-based housing development was operating as what was right. A major evaluation of HDCs summed up the situation: "They are saddled with goals and objectives that are far beyond their resources to achieve'' (Keyes 1971, 169).

Writing from the perspective of this period, Michael Stegman (1972, 246) questioned whether nonprofits would ''ever contribute significantly to improved living conditions in the inner cities via the housing production route.'' More optimistically, however, he suggested that community-based nonprofit organizations ''still may become significant producers of new housing for low-income and moderate-income families'' (1972, 256). According to Stegman, the key to this potential success was to be found in nonprofits forming joint ventures with for-profit partners.

Nonprofits Form Limited Partnerships: 1970s

Starting in the early 1970s, community-based housing sponsors, which, up to that time, had been nonprofit groups, did indeed begin to form limited partnerships with for-profit developers. The push for this new form of ownership grew out of the two key problems faced by the early nonprofits: inadequate financial reserves and a lack of technical expertise.

The limited partnership was uniquely suited to address these issues. First, by entering into such an arrangement, the community sponsor could attract the participation of a for-profit developer as a general partner. The for-profit developer's experience, financial backing, and political clout were enormously helpful in negotiating the complexities of the development process. Second, the partnership could take advantage of substantial financial benefits through the federal tax system, thereby creating reserves for construction overruns or future maintenance expenses.[5]

Before passage of the Tax Reform Act of 1986, these financial benefits resulted from a process known as syndication. This allowed owners of a housing development to sell shares to investors (limited partners), who, in turn, enjoyed significant tax savings. All rental property depreciates for tax purposes, and these paper losses could shelter portions of an owner's other income. Since nonprofits have no taxable income that needs sheltering, the depreciation losses that flowed from a project were wasted so long as the housing was owned solely by a nonprofit group. If, however, the nonprofit formed a limited partnership, the limited partners could buy into the project and then, as partial owners, were entitled to a percentage of the depreciation generated by the project. The buy-in funds were paid to the general partners—the nonprofit group and the for-profit partner if there was one. The latter saw the money as a key source of profit and motivation for participating in the project, while the nonprofit used it as a cushion against increased costs, as a way to provide the project with more amenities, or as seed money with which to launch new projects.[6]

One of the most successful community-based housing groups that has used the limited partnership approach for developing and rehabilitating housing is Boston's IBA, *Inquilinos Borricuas en Accion* (Puerto Rican Tenants in Action).[7]

IBA has its roots in a protest organization that came together in the late 1960s demanding a community-oriented use for a parcel of urban renewal land. Eventually, IBA won the right to develop the land and constructed almost 400 units of subsidized housing and rehabilitated another 200 units.

A few community organizations such as Jubilee Housing in Washington, DC, have been able to purchase and renovate multifamily buildings without using the syndication approach. Relying primarily on donated labor and money from private individuals and foundations, Jubilee owns and operates six buildings with a total of 213 units.[8]

Most modern community-based housing groups such as IBA are very different from the earlier nonprofit housing sponsors. For one thing, the former are more financially sound, in large part because many groups have been able to take advantage of Section 8 New Construction and Substantial Rehabilitation subsidies. Section 8 was a significant improvement over the Section 221(d)(3) and 236 programs, since it takes into account increases in operating expenses. HUD's commitment to paying the difference between a fair-market rent and 30 percent of a tenant's income provides protection against financial difficulties and operating shortfalls as long as the fair-market rental price set by HUD accurately reflects market conditions. As part of the Reagan administration's cutbacks in domestic spending, however, the Section 8 New Construction and Substantial Rehabilitation programs are not receiving new funding. This phase-out of federal subsidies for housing production will result in a loss of both needed units and fledgling community-based housing groups.

In comparison with their predecessors, the current generation of community-based housing groups also is less likely to quit after one development, often launching additional housing and social service projects. Many contemporary groups have highly professional staffs that are competent in housing finance, development, and management. These groups also have been the beneficiaries of resources provided by a handful of organizations operating at the national, state, and local levels. At the national level, private nonprofit groups such as the Enterprise Foundation, the Local Initiatives Support Corporation, the Center for Community Change, and the National Housing Law Project have been providing significant technical and financial resources to community-based housing initiatives. Several cities—notably Boston, New York, Chicago, and Minneapolis—also have at least one public or nonprofit agency that assists community-based housing groups. And, at the state level, Massachusetts has pioneered a series of programs that has begun to emerge as a support system for community-based housing activities.

Figures on the accomplishments of the present generation of community groups involved with housing rehabilitation and construction are not available. Based on the few available surveys of this type of housing development (Marshall 1981; Cohen and Kohler 1983), and this author's general familiarity with the field, however, it is likely that total production has amounted to (at most) 50,000 housing units by 200–300 community groups.

WEAKNESSES AND STRENGTHS OF THE COMMUNITY-BASED HOUSING STRATEGY

Although good data on the level of community-based housing is not available, it is safe to conclude that these efforts contribute in only a very small way toward addressing overall low-income housing needs.[9] Thus, the first criticism of the community-based housing strategy is that it has achieved only a limited volume. Second, it may divert community organization and action away from confronting fundamental causes of housing problems (that is, that housing is built and managed on the private market only when it is profitable to do so, and the cost of shelter is a function of the need for investors to make substantial profits). Third, it forces community groups to think and act like for-profit developers. In acting as both the general partner in a limited partnership and as a landlord, the community-based sponsor is required to accept the basic operations of the housing finance and real estate system. It is ironic that to provide community-based housing, the nonprofit group usually enters into a for-profit limited partnership (Schuman 1986). Fourth, if localities were dependent upon community-based groups to produce most, if not all, of the needed low-income housing, there is a real possibility that many neighborhoods that have dire housing problems, but which lack a strong organizational capacity, would be unable to address these needs. This would, in effect, operate as a de facto "triage policy" and could present serious problems for low-income households and neighborhoods. Fifth, the self-help overtones of community-based housing can make it easy for public officials to ignore the federal responsibility for achieving the nation's housing goals. By initiating projects themselves, community-based groups can, unwittingly, let the government off the hook for providing housing resources. Finally, community-based housing has been criticized for being inefficient and slow. Groups with no experience and little expertise are pushed into a highly technical and intricate arena. Housing, it can be argued, is simply too complex for novices.

Although the weaknesses of community-based housing programs are sobering, several responses can be made. First, concerning the low levels of production and rehabilitation, it must be remembered that community-based housing groups have functioned without significant financial and technical resources. Not until a full-blown support system is in place would the criticism, "they can't produce enough housing," be valid.

Second, while community-based housing initiatives may divert attention from more fundamental problems, they do directly alleviate housing problems, although on a small scale. Encouraging people with inadequate or no shelter to shun a community-based housing strategy and, instead, to organize to protest the system may never lead to a roof over one's head. The issue is short-term versus long-term goals, and the lack of decent, affordable housing forces many groups, quite understandably, to pursue an expedient path. Although community-based housing itself may be unable to change the system, it can heighten political awareness of how that system operates. Launching any type of housing initiative requires participants to learn a great deal about banking, finance, federal programs, and local codes and regulations. This type of education is certainly related to building a political consciousness that would be needed for a more fundamental agenda for change. More optimistically, it is possible that community-based housing initiatives may actually serve to hasten community demands for more sweeping changes. A successful community-based housing program can be a very real symbol that socially oriented solutions are feasible.

Third, despite the willingness of community-based groups to become players in the market economy, they still are much more likely to undertake non-market types of projects. Neighborhoods that a for-profit developer would avoid and housing that has been abandoned by the private market often are the targets of community-based developers. Furthermore, community-based sponsors have demonstrated their willingness to break the rules of the real estate system, by refusing to make mortgage payments rather than reduce services.

The fourth criticism—that many neighborhoods with serious housing problems, but without a strong organizational capacity would be excluded if community-based housing were the only vehicle for housing production and rehabilitation—is a potentially serious one. Rather than advocating a single solution, however, (that is, community-based housing), what is needed is a multifaceted housing policy that would rejuvenate the public housing program. The community-based housing strategy cannot and should not be expected to meet the entire low-income housing demand (Bratt 1985; Bratt 1986a).

Fifth, although community-based housing can be confused with self-help, and could encourage federal complacency, this need not be the case. What is needed is for the community-based housing movement to be supported by a public system of financial and technical assistance. In this way, public responsibility for providing decent, affordable housing for all would be explicit. This type of system would also address the sixth criticism that community groups are too slow and must rediscover what others already know. By creating a comprehensive technical assistance network, community groups could obtain the needed information quickly and professionally. Although housing is complex, community groups have shown that they can master the intricacies of development, finance, and management.

More positively, community-based housing also can provide a host of benefits for individuals, as well as for the local neighborhood. Community-based housing groups have demonstrated their capacity to view housing as only one aspect of the overall needs of low-income residents. Once a community-based housing development has been built, the group often launches needed social services, such as elderly, daycare, and employment programs. A community-based housing development also is likely to be a stabilizing force against gentrification. Furthermore, a community group that has gained credibility by building housing may have an increased chance of being consulted when any major public initiative for that area is being contemplated. Finally, there can be many important psychological benefits for the individuals involved in community-based housing initiatives. Empowerment, control, and security are some of the personal benefits that developers and residents in a community-based housing development are likely to achieve.

In summary, the weaknesses of the community-based housing strategy appear to be less persuasive than its actual and potential strengths. This overall positive evaluation, particularly when combined with the enormous need for decent low-cost housing, makes it important to understand and develop public policies to support community-based housing programs.

EVOLUTION OF THE MASSACHUSETTS SUPPORT SYSTEM FOR COMMUNITY-BASED HOUSING

A key assertion of this paper is that, given sufficient financial and technical supports, community-based groups could be central to a new strategy for producing, rehabilitating, and managing housing. Massachusetts has created a set of programs that are quickly evolving into a model support system for community-based housing. Although other states and cities have one or more of the components of such a system, the Massachusetts model is by far the most fully developed (Sidor 1982). Ironically, the major pieces of this system did not start with a focus on housing—the original emphasis was on community economic development.

During the late 1960s the needs of inner-city low-income neighborhoods began to receive increased attention. First, although the federal community development programs left a mixed legacy for urban neighborhoods and their residents, they did serve to focus attention on problems of the cities. Urban renewal was an easy target for criticism, as thousands of low-income units were lost, and whole "urban villages" demolished. In their place, luxury apartments, offices, and civic centers became the concrete symbols of the inequities of the "urban/Negro removal" program.

The federal community development programs that followed—the War on Poverty and Model Cities—although more focused on trying to assist low-income neighborhoods, often were viewed as only token improvements, and program goals rarely lived up to expectations. In addition, although "community control" and "maximum feasible participation" became the buzzwords of the mid–1960s, lawmakers gave ambiguous messages about whether neighborhood residents or the local chief executive would actually hold the reins of power. As inevitable controversies arose, the neighborhood emerged as a significant locus of activity, if not necessarily control. Whether community groups coalesced through protesting urban renewal plans or by vying for power with city hall, a new generation of leaders and activists emerged, and there was a fresh awareness of the problems facing the inner city.

Consciousness about poor urban dwellers in general, and blacks in particular, also was raised by the Civil Rights movement. Although there were no geographical boundaries to inequality or the movement, the plight of blacks became synonymous with inner-city problems. This link became fixed when, in the summers of 1966 and 1967, frustrations in black communities gave way to full-scale urban riots.

At about the same time, a third set of events was unfolding that also contributed to an increased awareness of the problems facing urban neighborhoods, particularly those neighborhoods in older industrialized states such as Massachusetts. Traditional manufacturing firms began to close down, or relocate to sunbelt locations, in large part as a way to employ cheaper nonunion labor, reduce taxes, and utilize more modern manufacturing facilities. The result for the cities was often disastrous, as tax bases declined and fiscal crises became a major topic of concern.

By the early 1970s community activists, some political leaders, and a handful of academics began to see potential in a completely new urban agenda. Two positive approaches emerged: black capitalism and community economic development. The former emphasized assisting black entrepreneurs to enter the economic mainstream, while the latter focused on a collective response to poverty which viewed community control as the critical ingredient.

The Massachusetts Community Economic Development Program: 1978–83

In Massachusetts, the community economic development movement received significant support from a group of local politicians, activists, and academics. This coalition was crucial to the creation of the state program.

Community Development Finance Corporation (CDFC). Following more than a year of negotiation and debate, a bill was signed in 1975 which created the Community Development Finance Corporation (CDFC). In exchange for giving CDFC the proceeds from the sale of $10 million in state general obligation bonds, the state received all the agency's common stock, thereby becoming its sole owner. CDFC's mandate was to function as a development bank that would make equity investments, which are relatively risky and difficult to obtain, as well as loans that would be paid back over a period of time. CDFC's funds were to be targeted to Community Development Corporations (CDCs) operating in blighted areas.

Very briefly, a CDC is a nonprofit organization that is controlled by local residents to help guide the improvement of an economically distressed area. Membership in a CDC is open to all adults living in the specific geographic area, and the majority of the CDC's board must be elected by its membership. Other board members may be appointed, but they must be public officials or represent other nonprofit groups operating in the area. Although all CDCs share the broad objective of enabling residents to exercise greater control over the local economy and improve the quality of goods and services in their communities, the specific goals and activities launched by a CDC can vary considerably.

As mentioned above, some of the first CDCs received substantial federal funding during the late 1960s and 1970s.

The requirement that CDFC channel its funds through CDCs gave clear support to the view that projects should be controlled by and operated for the benefit of community residents. CDFC's operation was unique because of its willingness to take equity positions in risky ventures, its explicit focus on economically distressed areas, and its restriction to working with only one type of client, the CDC.

Due to a legal delay in the sale of CDFC's bonds, the first investments were not made until 1978. During the next three years, CDFC found it enormously difficult to locate and package attractive deals. By the end of 1981 only 21 investments with a value of $3.6 million had been made. Despite the original assumption that lack of capital was a major deterrent to development in depressed areas, there was relatively little demand for funds. This was due in part to the fact that at the start of CDFC's operation, there were only a handful of CDCs in the state. Further, the CDCs that were functioning had a great deal of difficulty attracting experienced staff and locating skilled entrepreneurs who could put together sound business ventures.

Another key problem in CDFC's early years was that many of the original investments ended in failure. Of the first 25 ventures financed, 14 were closed and liquidated and two had to be reorganized. As of early 1984 the remaining nine loans had either been repaid or were current 1984. According to Nancy Nye, then vice president of CDFC, "This compares reasonably well to the SBA [Small Business Administration] documented 55 percent failure rate of small businesses, particularly considering that all the CDFC ventures are located in distressed areas and by the very nature of the investment are higher risk than a general sample" (Nye 1984).

Along with the slowness in making investments and the high rate of failure of the early loans, CDFC also had a disappointing record in stimulating job creation. As of the end of 1983 the agency could claim that only 474 jobs had been created or retained through CDFC investments (CDFC 1984).

Community Economic Development Assistance Corporation (CEDAC). The need for a new agency that would provide technical assistance to CDCs was acknowledged by Massachusetts lawmakers even before CDFC realized that demand for its capital was weak and that only a relatively small number of CDCs were eligible to receive investments. The Community Economic Development Assistance Corporation (CEDAC) was created in 1978 to provide technical assistance to CDCs. CEDAC's main functions were to assist groups in becoming CDCs and then to assist them in the initial stages of economic development planning and in the preparation of business plans for CDFC financing.

In its early days CEDAC had always been much less financially secure than the well-capitalized CDFC. Technical assistance is a much "softer" type of activity than financing, and it is difficult to measure direct outcomes of such efforts. Although technical assistance may be an essential ingredient in a given project, its contribution to producing new jobs or housing often is overlooked partly because the bulk of technical assistance usually comes early in the process. Also, technical assistance providers sometimes choose not to take credit themselves, playing intentional 'behind-the-scenes' roles, thereby enabling the CDCs to receive full praise for their accomplishments.

CEDAC also faced major hurdles due to a shift in the state's political administration. Although supported by the liberal Governor Dukakis, CEDAC did not start its operation until early in the King administration's term, in 1979. Governor King's view of CEDAC went from direct opposition to tolerance, but without the active support of the state's chief executive, CEDAC was forced to seek funding from the legislature on its own. Governor King further compromised a sound working relationship between CDFC and CEDAC by requiring the former to contract for services from CEDAC, in lieu of direct state funding. According to CEDAC personnel, this damaged their credibility and compromised their effectiveness (CEDAC 1983).

All of these factors contributed to CEDAC's shaky funding history. Whereas CDFC was capitalized with $10 million of state-secured funds, during CEDAC's first four years of operation (1978–82) it received only $250,000 from state appropriations. During that period, it received another $700,000 through two federal sources, the Comprehensive Employment Training Act and the Economic Development Administration, neither of which provided guarantees for future funding.

Despite these impediments, CEDAC managed to hold on during the lean King years, providing technical assistance to community organizations and, perhaps even more importantly, learning from their experiences and mistakes. By the end of its first four years, CEDAC concluded that:

- For CDCs to be in a position to undertake development, they must have a clear organizational agenda, an indigenous reason for existing, and strong leadership. CEDAC's technical assistance could not replace or create these attributes.
- The agency needed to be more aggressive in assisting CDCs to initiate developments, by identifying viable projects that could be undertaken by eligible organizations.
- Nationally, CDCs that were involved with real estate development had been more successful than those involved with business ventures (CEDAC 1983).

Community Enterprise Economic Development Program (CEED). The third major component of the state's economic development system is the Community Enterprise Economic Development Program (CEED). A forerunner of this program became operational in 1976 (two years before CDFC's first loan was made). In response to a request for proposals issued by the Massachusetts Executive Office of Communities and Development (EOCD) for "production-oriented as opposed to social service- or advocacy-oriented" community development projects, 44 applications totalling almost $1 million were filed by nonprofit groups. With $69,000 available, however, only four grants could be made (EOCD 1984).

Three of these awards went to community groups involved with business ventures, while the fourth was for a land-use study—none related to housing.

Despite the small size of the pilot program (or perhaps, because of it), there was a great deal of enthusiasm for the state to create an ongoing capital fund to help nonprofit groups finance planning and start-up activities. In 1978 the Massachusetts legislature created the CEED program, with an appropriation for fiscal year 1979 of $142,450. Between 1978 and 1983, 39 organizations received over $1.5 million in CEED grants. During the early years of the CEED program, staff assisted numerous groups with the initial stages of organizational development, including incorporation, formulation of community development plans, and board training. Yet it was not until 1982–83 that the "organizational efforts [began to] bear fruit, as the material outputs of CDCs began to blossom" (EOCD 1984).

Unlike CDFC and CEDAC, during CEED's early years there was significant involvement in housing. In 1982, CEED-funded CDCs rehabilitated or created over 350 units of housing, and in 1983 the number increased by more than 50 percent to 530 units.

Overall, by 1983 the state-funded economic development program could boast several important achievements. First, the number of CDCs in the state increased from eight in 1976 to over 50 in 1983. Second, the total state investment in CDCs leveraged $127.9 million in other public and private investments for industrial, commercial, and housing development. And third, across the state, CDC projects created or retained 4,000 jobs (EOCD 1984).

Conceptually, the state's economic development program included many of the key pieces of a support system for CDCs. First, the CEED program helped in the earliest stages of a group's development and provided a unique source of funding to hire staff and pay overhead costs. Next, CEDAC provided the young organization with technical assistance, such as marketing analyses, economic feasibility studies, and financial packaging, as it moved toward project development. Finally, CDFC provided financing to help launch sound business ventures. Although there was sometimes overlap in providing technical assistance, particularly between CEDAC and CEED, the functions of the three agencies were, for the most part, distinct and complementary.

From Economic Development to Housing Development—1984

As discussed in the previous section, Massachusetts' economic development system was primarily oriented toward providing technical assistance and financing to CDCs involved with business and job creation activities. Only CEED programs included an explicit housing and real estate development focus. A 1983 CEDAC progress report noted the three main reasons behind its early focus:

> [B]ased on the earlier successes of established CDCs, it appeared that community-based groups could successfully develop housing without assistance from a support institution

like CEDAC. Furthermore, CDFC, which was the primary financing target for CEDAC-assisted projects, would not finance real estate. Lastly, there was a sense among board members that job creation was a primary objective for CEDAC and an overriding and inadequately addressed problem in locales that qualify as CEDAC target areas (CEDAC 1983).

Several factors contributed to CDFC's and CEDAC's decision to move into housing, some of which had to do with their experience with economic development, while others related to the positive attributes of housing as a vehicle for community development.

First, there was enormous frustration about the difficulty of finding the right kinds of business deals to finance. An analysis of the early community economic development program in Massachusetts observed that:

> [T]echnical assistance, useful in turning good venture concepts into sound business plans, could not generate good venture concepts. . . . In order to stimulate demand at CDFC, CEDAC's effort turned to finding local entrepreneurs who wanted to start businesses. Yet, it soon became apparent that it is primarily the quality of the entrepreneur, not the business plan, that makes for a good investment. CEDAC staff discovered the lessons bankers learned years ago: management experience and expertise is indispensable and very hard to find. Community zeal can achieve great things but the delicate navigation of and single-minded attention to a business' health, like the expertise acquired by surgeons or highly trained workers, cannot be found or developed easily in most communities (Bratt and Geiser 1982).

Second, the record of CDFC's investments was, overall, disappointing. Although this record may not have been significantly worse than the failure rate for all small businesses, given the level of support being provided through the state system one would have hoped that a much higher percentage of investments would have been successful. In order to justify state funding, CDFC's investments, while high risk, would have to be put together better than the average small business deals. Housing, it was hoped, would provide more opportunities for successful investments.

A third reason for abandoning the economic development approach was the constraints imposed by low-income neighborhoods. Firms that leave an area usually do so because of an inability to make a profit in the first place and, by definition, residents in low-income areas have little money with which to purchase goods and services. Thus, CDCs often sponsored ventures with inexperienced entrepreneurs in areas already abandoned by more savvy businesspeople.

Fourth, the low-income nature of the neighborhood notwithstanding, almost any business venture is faced with an uncertain market once it is operational. In contrast, a decent unit of affordable housing is virtually guaranteed to find an eager tenant.

In addition to the desire to pursue something different in view of the experiences with economic development, there were some positive pressures for the state agencies to move into housing. First, the rehabilitation and construction of housing by community-based groups was already a familiar and successful activity in Massachusetts. Largely because of the work of Greater Boston Community Development, Inc. (GBCD), the notion that good, affordable housing could be produced and managed by nonprofits was relatively well-accepted throughout the state. Incorporated as a nonprofit organization, GBCD provides technical assistance to community-based sponsors of housing for low- and moderate-income residents. Its primary goal is to "enable community organizations to control the development and management of housing which will best serve the needs of lower income families, elderly and handicapped people" (GBCD 1980, 5). Although in many respects it operates similarly to a private developer, GBCD's first priority is to help community-based groups achieve their own housing and community development goals. Since 1964 GBCD has assisted over 30 nonprofit housing sponsors to develop over 4,000 units of housing.[10] In addition, GBCD manages over 1,500 units of housing, some of which it also played a role in developing.

One of GBCD's most important contributions has been the way in which it has used the limited partnership, and more recently, the low-income housing tax credit, to benefit community-based housing sponsors. GBCD claims that it has "structured limited partnerships so as to maximize the financial benefits to the sponsor and the development while protecting the sponsor's tax-exempt status and control over the development." With a staff of almost 60 (including about 38 people involved in property management and maintenance), the agency continues to vigorously advocate for, initiate, and provide technical assistance to community-based housing activities.

Staffs of the state's economic development agencies began to feel the push to get into housing. According to Nancy Nye, "Housing was what the CDCs were doing or wanted to do and, to be responsive, CDFC needed to move in the direction."[11] Similarly, Carl Sussman, executive director of CEDAC, stated that they "finally became convinced that the resources to do housing development were not really available to most of the CDCs in the state."[12] The interest in housing on the part of community groups was also stimulated by the dramatic need felt in many low-income communities. Private market forces, combined with the withdrawal of the federal government from subsidized housing production, severely affected an already limited supply of affordable units.

Second, as a community development initiative, housing is more satisfying than the more ambiguous pursuit of economic development. A CDC-supported venture that creates a handful of jobs does not have the same visual impact as watching a formerly vacant lot become the site of newly constructed housing or an abandoned building being renovated. Housing is always a concrete and visible neighborhood-oriented activity.

Third, during the early 1980s HUD began to pursue a policy of allowing foreclosed multifamily Section 221(d)(3) and 236 developments to be sold to the highest bidder to be used for market rate housing. The threat of this happening in Boston mobilized an effective campaign that persuaded the local HUD area office to give priority to new buyers who would be committed to maintaining the low- and moderate-income nature of the developments. Faced with this situation and committed to preventing the possible loss of thousands of low-income units, state officials responded to the need to salvage the HUD-foreclosed housing.

The shift into housing was rapid. Within a few years, virtually all of CEDAC's activity and about half of CDFC's loans were going toward housing initiatives. CEDAC has been directly responsible for helping CDCs rehabilitate some 2,000 units of housing. With this sense of accomplishment, most observers agree that the shift from economic development to housing development was the right decision.

Filling in Some Missing Pieces

Although the key pieces of the Massachusetts support system for community-based housing were rooted in the community economic development movement, several additional agencies and programs also play important roles.

Massachusetts Housing Finance Agency (MHFA). Created in 1966 through an act of the Massachusetts legislature, the Massachusetts Housing Finance Agency (MHFA) was one of the country's first state housing finance agencies. Since 1970, when construction on the first MHFA-financed housing began, the agency has made loans totaling more than $3 billion to finance the construction and rehabilitation of about 62,000 apartments (MHFA 1987). MHFA (as well as other state housing finance agencies) operates by issuing tax-exempt securities. The proceeds are used to make loans at below-market interest rates to private nonprofit or for-profit developers who agree to set aside 25 percent of the units for low-income tenants (defined according to public housing limits). Although CDFC provides a much-needed source of capital that often has made the difference between a project being launched or not, MHFA is set up to provide construction or permanent financing for large-scale housing developments. This source of financing, with its clear public purpose, is a critical component of the state's overall support system for housing, including community-based initiatives. Unfortunately, caps on permitted levels of tax-exempt financing instituted in the Tax Reform Act of 1986 have threatened the functioning of all state housing finance agencies.

Massachusetts Government Land Bank. The Massachusetts Government Land Bank was created in 1975 in response to a Defense Department announcement that it would be closing five military installations in the state. The Land Bank's mandate was to "aid private enterprise or public agencies in the speedy and orderly conversion and redevelopment of certain lands formerly used for military activities to non-military uses" (Massachusetts Government Land Bank 1985). Capital was provided through $40 million in general obligation bonds, thereby giving the Land Bank a financing capacity to cover any expenses incurred in the course of its redevelopment work. With the agency's authorization due to expire on June 30, 1980, and with several of the conversions nearing completion, a handful of state legislators sponsored legislation that extended the Land Bank's life and broadened its powers. According to the chairman of the House Commerce and Labor Committee, a clear rationale for the Land Bank's continuance was that in the process of fulfilling its original goals, "it had acquired the skills that could be applied to other areas of development" (Massachusetts Government Land Bank 1985, 7).

With the new state legislation, the Land Bank was empowered to acquire, develop, and sell surplus state property as well as surplus federal property located in Massachusetts and blighted open or substandard properties. Since its mandate was broadened, the Land Bank has financed the production or rehabilitation of over 1,200 units of housing. Several projects were developed by nonprofit community-based groups.

In addition to the CEED program, EOCD administers an array of programs that are targeted to or can be used by community-based housing groups.

Special Project Fund of the Community Services Block Grant. Under terms of this fund, a portion of the Massachusetts Community Services Block Grant for fiscal year 1989 (about $370,000) was targeted to community-based nonprofit groups. One of its main focuses was to provide funding for "projects which demonstrate innovative ways to expand availability and affordability of existing housing for low-income families and individuals" (EOCD 1985, 1).

Small Cities Community Development Block Grants. A portion of the federally funded Small Cities Community Development Block Grant is targeted for organizational support of community-based nonprofit development organizations operating at a regional or multi-community level in rural sections of the state.

Commonwealth Service Corps. Through this program, individuals are paid from a fund of over one-half million dollars to serve in community-based neighborhood development and service delivery projects. Not only do these individuals gain valuable work experience, but they also provide much-needed human resources to nonprofit groups, many of which operate on skeleton budgets.

Neighborhood Development Front Money Loan Fund. Using $300,000 in federal Community Services Block Grant monies, a revolving loan fund was established to provide seed financing for real estate development projects sponsored by nonprofit community-based organizations. Aimed at filling a "critical financing gap," the specific purpose of this fund is to provide the "front end capital required to bring residential and commercial real estate projects, designed to benefit lower-income residents and to support local neighborhood revitalization objectives, to the point where development financing is committed by other public and private sources; at which time the seed loans will revolve for reuse in other neighborhood real estate projects" (Tierney 1984).

Neighborhood Housing Services. EOCD has created a special program to support the ten Neighborhood Housing Services corporations in Massachusetts. For fiscal year 1989, $835,000 was appropriated to supplement other public and private funds that assist individual homeowners in rehabilitating their properties, and to support other neighborhood rehabilitation projects.

Housing Abandonment Program. Initiated by EOCD in fiscal year 1985, the Housing Abandonment Program reimburses community-based and tenant organizations for expenses associated with financing the rehabilitation of tax-delinquent, abandoned, or deteriorated residential properties. Funded at a level of $832,000 in fiscal year 1989, the program is aimed at helping economically depressed neighborhoods recapture a stock of much-needed housing.

Organizational Development Fund. Another new EOCD program, the Organizational Development Fund, was created to supply a source of money (up to $2,500 per grant) to help young CDCs cover some of the out-of-pocket costs (such as lawyers' fees) associated with forming a new organization.

EVALUATION AND OBSERVATIONS

An Outline for an Evaluation of the System

A thorough assessment of the Massachusetts system that supports community-based housing activities is not possible at this time. Little data presently exists for most of the relevant measures, such as housing impacts, neighborhood/market impacts, social impacts, or organizational impacts. For each of these measures, a substantial amount of information would have to be collected. Relevant data to assess housing impacts would include the number, physical quality, and cost of units produced and rehabilitated, as well as an assessment of the quality of maintenance over time. Impacts on the neighborhood or local market often are more difficult to determine. Researchers would want to collect information on the extent of public and/or private investments in housing, retail, or commercial areas, and public facilities. In addition, changes in socioeconomic groups, evidence of forced displacement or gentrification, and indicators of neighborhood stability (for example, homeownership rates and community perceptions) would be studied. The social impacts of community-based housing activities could be assessed by determining whether they were supplemented by social service programs; how the perceptions of residents in the buildings have changed (particularly with regard to feelings of well-being, security, and control); and whether there was evidence of an increased sense of empowerment among leaders or participants in the housing development process. Finally, the impacts on the community-based housing organization itself could be evaluated in terms of the organization's ability to manage its properties, the extent to which it succeeded in launching additional production and rehabilitation projects, and its ability to act as a voice for residents in public or private controversies or development schemes.

In order to broaden our understanding of the capabilities and limitations of community-based housing, the state or an academic or research institution should launch a longitudinal research project that will systematically gather this type of information. But since the above list of measures is, at the present, still a wish list, we are faced with the immediate problem of assessing how well the Massachusetts system of supports for community-based housing is working. In the absence of hard facts, the following is presented, less as an evaluation than as a way of understanding what the Massachusetts experience already reveals about how government can support community-based housing. Pointing out some of the areas that are likely to present future problems also is important, both for those involved in the state system as well as for others with hopes of building similar programs.

Observations from the Massachusetts Experience

The state appears to be a good level of government through which to channel community-based housing programs. There has been very little work on the idea of institutionalizing a system of support for community-based housing initiatives. Altogether, six distinct proposals can be identified. The first, which includes the broader economic development agenda, was proposed by the Twentieth Century Fund Task Force. They called for "the building of a nationwide system of support for community-based economic development programs" whose objectives would be "to enhance the effectiveness of community development corporations and to enlarge their capacity for self-help" (1971, 12). Included in the proposal were seven key elements, although how they were to be administered was not discussed. The second proposal, suggested by Keyes (1971), outlined the development of metropolitan or state-level Community Housing Corporations that would act as conduits for Section 106 funds and provide technical assistance and financial packaging services to local housing groups, similar to GBCD's present operation. The third proposal, presented by Egan et al. (1981), did not call for any single programmatic initiative; rather, they suggested that policymakers and government officials change their attitudes to be more supportive toward what they call mediating structures—neighborhood, church, family, and voluntary associations. The fourth proposal, outlined by Mott (1984) and sponsored by the National Low Income Housing Coalition, and introduced as legislation by Rep. Joseph Kennedy (D-MA) as the "Community Partnership Act, called for the creation of a new Community Housing Supply Program that would target federal funds for housing production and rehabilitation projects controlled by neighborhood residents and/or tenants. Federal, state, and local governments would share in disbursing the subsidy money but, unlike Keyes' proposal (1971), no new agency would be created. A fifth suggestion, to create a community-based housing supply program, was outlined in earlier papers by this author (Bratt 1985; Bratt 1986b). Similar to Keyes, in this proposal GBCD is also seen as an important model for new local technical assistance organizations. A federally supported Community-Based Housing Support Corporation would help in the creation of new GBCD-like agencies and would help channel public and private financial resources and technical assistance to community-based groups. The sixth proposal was developed by Erdmann (1987), who advocated a key role for states in assisting community economic development initiatives. His study recommends that states examine their own unique needs and tailor their programs accordingly, rather than trying to replicate any one state's system. Thus, no single model of support for community-based organizations is advocated. Finally, the Rouse Commission report (National Housing Task Force 1988) recommended that 10 percent of a proposed first-year $3 billion additional allocation for housing be set aside for nonprofit community-based housing organizations. The new funds, part of a "Housing Opportunity Program," would go to state and local governments, with a minimum of federal regulation. HUD would be directed to administer the new program with a maximum of flexibility to enable localities to design programs to meet their own needs.

Not surprisingly, none of the above proposals suggested a system of supports for community-based housing nearly as complex as the one created in Massachusetts. In part, the complexity of the Massachusetts system may be due to its piecemeal evolution and its original emphasis on community economic development, rather than housing. Although it is possible that the other models would offer clear advantages, it does not appear that the state is a good conduit through which to channel community-based housing programs:

- The state can pass legislation, create new programs, and put significant resources into those programs.
- The power and prestige of the governor and executive departments can facilitate program development and coordination.
- The state is in a good position to assess local needs.
- State housing finance agencies have proven to be effective entities for channeling housing resources and providing housing services (Betnun 1976).
- The state is a manageable size for operating community-based housing systems.

In contrasting a state system with a federal support system, however, the former does reveal some weaknesses:

- Some states would never adopt a community-based housing system, thereby leaving many people and localities without the needed resources. Only a federal support system would have the ability to reach the entire country.
- The amount of money needed to launch and sustain a community-based housing system is substantial, and it is unlikely that any state would have the resources necessary to do the job thoroughly.

A progressive liberal Democratic administration is more likely than a conservative Republican administration to support a community-based housing system. Although this point is fairly obvious, it is a reminder that there are some important distinctions between this country's two major political parties.

At the federal level, we have had ample evidence that liberal Democrats are much more likely to support housing subsidy programs than are conservative Republicans, such as President Reagan (who virtually dismantled the nation's housing programs). Further, over the past 25 years, it has been the Democrats who have created programs that were, at least at the level of rhetoric, oriented toward empowering poor people. The War on Poverty and Model Cities, despite significant weaknesses, did encompass some of the values that underlie a community-based approach to housing. More recently, President Carter's Neighborhood Self-Help Development Program (which provided a modest supply of funds directly to community groups, and which was quickly removed from the federal agenda by President Reagan) is another demonstration that liberal Democrats have more aggressively explored neighborhood-based solutions to housing and community development problems.

The Massachusetts experience has shown that a liberal Democrat, Governor Dukakis, has done much more to support the community-based housing agenda than the conservative Governor King. Under Governor King (1979–82), CEDAC was almost eliminated; there was very little program development and there were few efforts toward coordination.[13] In contrast, it was during Governor Dukakis' first term (1975–78) that the three major community economic development initiatives—CDFC, CEDAC, and CEED—were launched. Further, during Governor Dukakis' second and third terms (1983) the EOCD has been staffed by individuals with extensive prior experience in community-based housing who have a genuine commitment to the approach. Together, they have begun to develop "A State Strategy for Neighborhood Development" (Tierney 1984) and have developed a host of new programs in which important gaps were identified. For example, since 1983 EOCD has launched the Housing Abandonment Program and the Organizational Development Fund. In addition, EOCD has been directing several of the other programs its administers, such as the Small Cities Community Development Block Grants, the Community Services Block Grant, and the state Section 705 public housing program explicitly to CDCs involved in housing development.

Another important aspect of the emerging state system is the willingness to allocate increased funds into the various programs. Most striking is that CEED now is operating on a $2.2 million yearly budget—50 percent more than the total CEED expenditures between 1978 and 1983 of $1.5 million.

Finally, Governor Dukakis' EOCD is aware that coordination is a critical component of a community-based housing system. Alert to potential overlaps in the system, particularly between EOCD and CEDAC, EOCD staff spent much of the first six months of 1983 working out the institutional links between CDFC, CEDAC, and EOCD. A key result was that CEDAC's board was reconstituted to make the agency less independent and to define its operation more explicitly as an arm of EOCD—EOCD's deputy assistant secretary for Neighborhoods and Economic Opportunity now chairs the CEDAC board.

But although the Democrats look good when compared with their Republican counterparts, no federal administration has been willing or able to articulate or carry out a comprehensive system of supports for community-based housing.

Potential for replication may be questionable. It probably would be difficult to replicate the Massachusetts system because of private sector opposition. Even in Massachusetts, it is unclear whether the system ever could have been launched from scratch, particularly if the original focus of the state system had been housing instead of community economic development. Although the state's economic development program was not going to compete with private entrepreneurs (since it was to provide employment and business opportunities in areas that had been abandoned by the private market), the creation of CDFC and its capitalization were, nevertheless, the subjects of intense legislative debates. While the community economic development program ultimately prevailed, it did so only by a slim margin.

The question is: Could a support system for community-based housing, that to many may appear to be taking business away from private, for-profit developers, get the needed support? Even though the unassisted private sector is not interested in producing low-income housing, for-profit developers are certain to be against any program of subsidies to build low-income housing that does not include them. The homebuilders and real estate trade associations always have been vehemently opposed to the conventional public housing program, which does not rely on private developers and owners. Conversely, these groups historically have been strong advocates of subsidized housing programs in which they had a role.

Massachusetts' support system for community-based housing may have some qualities of a lucky accident. Community economic development was proving difficult to carry out and there was strong support for the state to become more involved with low-income housing, notwithstanding opposition by the private sector. Although it may only be coincidence, at about the same time that the state began to support community-based housing, Governor Dukakis spearheaded an initiative designed specifically to assist private developers in undertaking rental developments. The SHARP program (described below) provides a significant financial incentive for all private developers—both for-profit and nonprofit community groups—of predominantly market-rate rental housing. While it is easy, and possibly erroneous, to ascribe causality, SHARP may have helped deflect opposition to the emerging community-based housing agenda. Thus, in considering how a state-supported community-based housing program could be replicated, it is important to consider who the likely opponents would be and how their objections can be handled. Aside from these political considerations, the Massachusetts state program could, conceptually at least, be replicated.

Targeting of resources is important. The young and growing Massachusetts support system has pursued a strategy of deciding what programs are important and then has sought funding to implement them. This approach speaks to the debate about whether it is better to fund broad goals through block grants or to specify more explicit program guidelines and fund them through categorical grants. Massachusetts has enjoyed the flexibility provided through several federal block grant programs, but as for developing its own strategy, it has chosen to initiate new categorical programs when it felt a particular need. The new Neighborhood Development Front Money Loan Fund is a good example of the way in which the state has defined a problem and then created a program in response.

A public support system for community-based housing initiatives cannot guarantee that the programs will be truly community-based. Experience with the state's early community economic development program revealed the difficulty inherent in a level of government trying to stimulate local responses to problems. If an effort is to be community-based, what role, if any, is appropriate for a public body? According to Annette Rubin-Casas, former director of EOCD's Office of Community Economic Development for Community Non-Profits, before CDFC became involved with housing, some CDCs were created that were not truly community-based. Local entrepreneurs needing assistance to launch a business could help develop a CDC that would then serve as a conduit for state funds.[14] In pursuing a housing agenda, however, CDCs may be developing as more obviously community-based organizations. Michael Tierney, EOCD's assistant secretary for Municipal Development, has stated: "In venture development the CDC is dependent on entrepreneurial skills; in housing development the CDC is the entrepreneur."[15] The CDC that coalesces around housing goals and develops a project is almost certain to be responding to the needs of the community. It is unlikely that there could be ulterior motives. Nevertheless, it remains to be seen whether the state's community-based housing system will be successful in providing "top-down" supports to truly "bottom-up" activities.

Individual commitment and expertise is essential. The Massachusetts community economic development program emerged from the social commitment and vision of a handful of community activists, academics, and legislators. Two factors were essential to the successful adoption of a housing agenda: the conviction of many committed professionals that community-based housing was "the way to go," and their willingness to work extremely hard. As one astute observer recently put it: "Hernandez, Edgerly, Whittlesey, and Clancy are the best in the country at making community development happen" (Robb 1985, 65).[16] Yet a system such as the one operating in Massachusetts is not the work of just one or even a few people. Although there have been some impressive leaders, the system could not work without the scores of committed and competent staff people at the public and quasi-public agencies and at the CDCs themselves.

Quasi-public agencies are important components. Quasi-public agencies such as CEDAC, CDFC, and MHFA play critical roles in the state system. Although it is theoretically possible that many, if not all, of the functions performed by CEDAC could be carried out by EOCD, state line agencies in Massachusetts are not permitted to perform the banking functions of CDFC and MHFA. Also, the ability of these agencies to pay more than the state's maximum salaries has allowed them to be more competitive with the private sector and to attract high-quality personnel and hire costly consultants when necessary. Finally, quasi-public agencies are more able to move quickly and avoid some of the red tape that is an unavoidable part of a state bureaucracy.

The system needs to be flexible. Even in the short period during which the Massachusetts system has been operating, the need for flexibility has become apparent. The shift from community economic development to housing development was a radical one, and it is a credit to the people involved that there was a willingness to change. The ability to acknowledge problems in the system and make necessary adjustments was also apparent when CEDAC became more closely controlled by EOCD.

New pressures for change are inevitable, and the system still has some important challenges facing it. For example, there still is some overlap in the system, particularly in the area of technical assistance. Second, with the cost of land and buildings skyrocketing in Massachusetts, many community-based housing developments that were financially feasible only a few years ago or that benefited from opportunities to acquire land cheaply through the urban renewal program would now be impossible because site control would be too expensive. Third, a handful of older CDCs in the state are being confronted with new responsibilities, such as how to manage their services and investments. The state will have to begin to develop assistance programs to address the needs of the more seasoned CDCs. Finally, the state system is going to have to be clever and adaptable to get through the years of minimal federal support. The last two observations point to what could become the Achilles heel of the Massachusetts system for community-based housing: as good as the overall program may be, the system is dependent on federal policies, as discussed below. The inability of the state to function completely on its own suggests that a comprehensive community-based housing system would have to be supported, if not necessarily implemented, by the federal government.

The system does not include "deep" subsidies. The kind of subsidies available through the federal Section 8 New Construction/Substantial Rehabilitation program, which guaranteed tenants low rents while providing owners with adequate operating funds, are not provided by the state. Although Massachusetts has several subsidy programs, none provides deep subsidies to community-based housing sponsors (or, for that matter, any private developer). Massachusetts' Section 705 is the state's public housing program and usually operates through local housing authorities.[17] Section 707 provides rental assistance similar to the Section 8 existing program, and the SHARP program provides loans (which effectively lower the interest on the mortgage to as low as 5 percent) to private for-profit or nonprofit developers who agree to set aside no less than 25 percent of the units for low-income tenants. Without a public supply of money that can be used to substantially lower rents, the Massachusetts system, however, comprehensive and exemplary, may face serious problems. The economics of housing production/substantial rehabilitation for low-income people simply do not work without substantial public subsidies.

The system depends on existing Internal Revenue Code regulations, which are subject to change. Although one could visualize a subsidy system that would include generous front-end or rental subsidies to make development financially feasible, in political terms this is very unlikely in the near future. The federal tax system has provided the major incentives for producing privately owned, publicly subsidized housing. Recent changes in the IRS code dramatically reduced the attractiveness of real estate investment in general, and subsidized housing in particular. With pre-1986 syndication schemes no longer available, community-based groups must now rely on the Low-Income Housing Tax Credit, which is due to expire after 1989. Without the tax credit, and without other deep subsidies, community-based housing, as it presently is produced in Massachusetts and elsewhere, almost certainly would be infeasible.

The Massachusetts system encompasses many of the key components of a community-based housing system. In particular, it includes many types of technical assistance, specially targeted programs, and several of the necessary funding and subsidy mechanisms. Deep subsidies are not provided, however, and the system is dependent on existing IRS provisions. There are other weaknesses or omissions in the Massachusetts system: while several agencies provide technical assistance, the system does not offer technical assistance for groups other than the community organizations, such as banks and public agencies that are needed to support the community-based housing program. In addition, since it does not include a land acquisition and land banking program, community-based groups must compete for land and buildings with private speculative developers. Another drawback of the Massachusetts system is that it does not yet include a comprehensive evaluation system. A thorough assessment of the impacts of the Massachusetts system should be undertaken, as outlined above.

FINAL NOTE

This study of community-based housing and the evolving Massachusetts support system has argued the following:

- The current generation of community-based housing sponsors operate differently from the earlier nonprofits in that they are unlikely to disband after one development, are more professional, and have been the beneficiaries of resources provided through several nonprofit organizations.
- There are many positive attributes of community-based housing, including an ability to provide decent-quality housing, a willingness to tackle tough projects, an interest in launching social services programs, an effort at providing safeguards against displacement, and an attempt at increasing opportunities for resident control and empowerment.
- The provision of housing may be the most suitable vehicle for launching community-based development projects as it is both more observable than economic development initiatives, and less risky.
- The Massachusetts system of supports for community-based housing presents an exciting model that, theoretically, could be emulated by other states. Refinements in the system

should be based on a thorough evaluation of its impacts and costs.• Despite the many strengths of a state-based system, the federal government must play a role by providing deep housing subsidies and/or tax incentives. In addition, the possibility of the federal government playing a role in implementing a nationally-based support system for community-based housing should also be considered.

In conclusion, the Massachusetts system of support for community-based housing—or any systems designed to replicate it—may continue to operate only at the margin of our present housing system. If that is the case, such systems will constantly be facing an uphill fight to sustain their programs. More optimistically, the Massachusetts model could become a centerpiece of a revised federal housing policy, and a tangible symbol of a new commitment to the universal right to decent shelter.

NOTES

1. Model tenements that were produced for no profit rather than for limited profits were extremely rare. Edith Wood, writing in 1919, knew of only two (Friedman 1968, 76).

2. Author's calculation from data supplied in Keyes 1971.

3. Clancy et al. (1973, 49) points out that "a high level of rent supplement or leased housing units in a Section 236 project create a more difficult management situation requiring much greater input of management staff time."

4. However, the same report (p. 7) also noted that "limited dividend sponsored units serve minorities more than nonprofit sponsored units do," adding, "no plausible explanation can be suggested for this situation."

5. Although there were many good reasons to involve for-profit investors in low-income housing deals, until the so-called "use restriction" period terminates it will be unclear whether nonprofits will be successful in guaranteeing the long-term affordability of their low-income units. (See also Chapter 10 by Emily Achtenberg.)

6. Among the many changes in real estate investing which, overall, had the effect of making such investments far less attractive, the Tax Reform Act of 1986 also created a new three-year Low-Income Housing Tax Credit. Similar to the sale of depreciation benefits to wealthy investors, these tax credits are sold by owners of low-income to limited partners in exchange for equity contributions.

7. During IBA's early years it joined with a for-profit co-general partner. However, as IBA has gained expertise, it has been the sole general partner for its developments.

8. Whether a present-day community-based housing group would choose to develop housing as a nonprofit or through a limited partnership would depend on the goals and particular situation facing the group. For a thorough evaluation of the various forms of ownership available to a community-based housing sponsor, see National Housing Law Project 1982.

9. This section is based on a fuller assessment of community-based housing that appears in Bratt 1986b.

10. These data include the accomplishments of GBCD's predecessor, South End Community Development. GBCD was formed in 1970.

11. Author's interview, April 17, 1985.

12. Author's interview, May 2, 1985.

13. There may also be other reasons for Governor King's antipathy toward these programs, such as a desire to destroy anything associated with his predecessor, Governor Dukakis.

14. Author's interview, April 17, 1985.

15. Author's interview, April 14, 1984.

16. Jorge Hernandez was, until his death in early 1986, the long-time executive director of IBA, a CDC; William Edgerly is the chairman of the board of the State Street Bank and Trust Company, and was pivotal in the creation of the Boston Housing Partnership, a public-private venture with a major emphasis on the role of community-based sponsors; Bob Whittlesey was the founder of GBCD and currently is executive director of the Boston Housing Partnership; Pat Clancy is the executive director of GBCD. The statement was made by Mitchell Sviridoff, former president of the Local Initiatives Support Corporation, a Ford Foundation-funded organization that channels private foundation and corporate funds to community-based programs.

17. In fiscal year 1984, for the first time, EOCD provided Section 705 funds to community-based nonprofit housing sponsors located in areas where local housing authorities were unable to initiate family housing development (Tierney 1984).

REFERENCES

Abt Associates. 1973. "An Evaluation of the Special Impact Program Final Report," vol. 1, Summary. Prepared for the Office of Economic Opportunity, contract no. B00-5181. Cambridge, MA.

Betnun, Nathan S. 1976. *Housing Finance Agencies: A Comparison Between States and HUD*. New York: Praeger.

Boston Redevelopment Authority and Boston Urban Observatory. 1973. "Subsidized Multi-Family Rental Housing in the Boston Metropolitan Area." Boston, MA.

BRA. See Boston Redevelopment Authority.

Bratt, Rachel. 1989. *Rebuilding a Low-Income Housing Policy*. Philadelphia: Temple University Press.

———. 1986a. "Public Housing: The Controversy and Contribution." In *Critical Perspectives on Housing*, edited by R. Bratt, C. Hartman, and A. Meyerson. Philadelphia, PA: Temple University Press.

———.1986b. "Community-Based Housing Programs: Overview, Assessment and Agenda for the Future." *Journal of Planning Education and Research*. 5 (Spring): 164–77.

———.1987a. "The Role of Citizen-Initiated Programs in the Formulation of National Housing Policies." In *Citizen Participation in Decision Making*, edited by S. Langton and J. DeSario. Westport, CT: Greenwood Press.

———.1987b. "Private Owners of Subsidized Housing vs. Public Goals: Conflicting Interests in Resyndication." *Journal of the American Planning Association* 53 (Summer): 328–36.

———. 1985. "Housing for Low Income People: A Preliminary Comparison of Existing and Potential Supply Strategies." *Journal of Urban Affairs* 7 (Summer): 1–18.

Bratt, Rachel G., and Kenneth Geiser. 1982. "Community-Based Economic Development: The Massachusetts Experience." Tufts University. mimeo.

CDFC. See Community Development Finance Corporation.

CEDAC. See Community Economic Development Assistance Corporation.

Clancy, Patrick E., Langley C. Keyes, Jr., Edward H. Marchant, and Robert B. Whittlesey. 1973. "The Role of Nonprofit Organizations in the Housing Process." Report to HUD. mimeo.

Cohen, Rick, and Miriam Kohler. 1983. "Neighborhood Development Organizations After the Federal Funding Cutbacks: Current Conditions and Future Directions." Prepared for U.S. Department of Housing and Urban Development, Division of Policy Development and Research, Contract order no. HUD 7177-82. Jersey City, NJ.

Community Development Finance Corporation. 1984. "Annual Report." Boston, MA.

Community Economic Development Assistance Corporation. 1983. "A CEDAC Progress Report: Its Past Experience and Its New Directions." Boston, MA.

Disario, Rita Michele. 1969. "Nonprofit Housing Sponsors: An Evaluative Study." M.C.P. thesis, Massachusetts Institute of Technology, Cambridge, MA.

Egan, John J., John Carr, Andrew Mott, and John Roos. 1981. *Housing and Public Policy: A Role for Mediating Structures*. Cambridge, MA: Ballinger.

Erdmann, Robin J. (ed). 1987. "States and Communities: The Challenge for Economic Action." Vol. 2. Washington, DC: National Congress for Community Economic Development.

EOCD. See Executive Office of Communities and Development.

Executive Office of Communities and Development. 1985. "Community Services Block Grant Special Project Fund, Request for Proposals, FY 1985." mimeo.

———. 1984. "The Community Enterprise Economic Development Program: A Survey of CEED-Funded CDC Activities, 1979–1983." Boston, MA.

Friedland, J. Eric and Duncan C. MacRae. 1979. "FHA Multifamily Financial Failure: A Review of Empirical Studies." *Journal of American Real Estate and Urban Economics Association* 7 (Spring): 95–122.

Friedman, Lawrence. 1968. *Government and Slum Housing*. Chicago: Rand McNally and Company.

GAO. See U.S. General Accounting Office.

GBCD. See Greater Boston Community Development.

Greater Boston Community Development, Inc. 1984. "Building Communities." Boston, MA.

———. 1980. "A Decade of Housing Services: 1970–1980." Boston, MA.

HUD. See U.S. Department of Housing and Urban Development.

Keyes, Langley. 1971. "The Role of Nonprofit Sponsors in the Production of Housing." In *Papers Submitted to Subcommittee on Housing Panels on Housing Production, Housing Demand, and Developing a Suitable Living Environment*, part 1. Committee on Banking and Currency, U.S. House of Representatives, 92nd Cong., 1st sess., pp. 159–181.

Marshall, Sue. 1981. "A Profile of Revitalization Projects Being Implemented by Neighborhood Development Organizations." Washington, DC: The Urban Institute Working Paper 1457-01. Prepared with the assistance of Jennifer Blake.

Massachusetts Government Land Bank. 1985. "Tenth Anniversary Report." Boston, MA.

Massachusetts Housing Finance Agency. 1987. "Annual Report." Boston, MA.

Meyerson, Martin, Barbara Terrett, and William L.C. Wheaton. 1962. *Housing, People and Cities*. New York: McGraw Hill.

MHFA. See Massachusetts Housing Finance Agency.

Mott, Andrew H. 1984. "Making Affordable Housing a Reality." Testimony presented at a hearing before the Subcommittee on Housing and Community Development of the Committee on Banking, Finance and Urban Affairs, U.S. House of Representatives, 98th Cong., 2nd sess., June 28, pp. 211–27.

National Center for Economic Alternatives. 1981. "Federal Assistance to Community Development Corporations: An Evaluation of Title VII of the Community Services Act of 1974." Prepared for the U.S. Community Services Administration. Washington, DC.

National Housing Law Project. 1982. *The Subsidized Housing Handbook*. Berkeley, CA: National Housing Law Project.

National Housing Task Force. 1988. *A Decent Place to Live*. Washington, DC: National Housing Task Force.

Nye, Nancy. 1984. "Six Years Later: The Experience of the Massachusetts CDFC." *The Entrepreneurial Economy* 2 (March): 11–12.

Robb, Christain, 1985. "Rehabbing the American Dream." *The Boston Globe Magazine*, March 31.

Schuman, Tony. 1986. "The Agony and the Equity: A Critique of Self-Help Housing." In *Critical Perspectives on Housing*, edited by R. Bratt, C. Hartman, and A. Meyerson. Philadelphia, PA: Temple University Press.

Sidor, John. 1982. "State Assistance for Community Economic Development." Council of the State Community Affairs Agencies.

Stegman, Michael A. 1972. *Housing Investment in the Inner City*. Cambridge, MA: MIT Press.

Tierney, Michael. 1984. "A State Strategy for Neighborhood Development." Massachusetts Executive Office of Communities and Development. mimeo.

Twentieth Century Fund. 1977. *CDC's: New Hope for the Inner City*. New York: Twentieth Century Fund.

U.S. Department of Housing and Urban Development. 1978. "Final Report of the HUD Multifamily Property Utilization Task Force." Washington, DC: U.S. Government Printing Office.

———.1975. "Housing Production with Nonprofit Sponsors." A staff study. Washington, DC: U.S. Government Printing Office.

———.1973. "Housing in the Seventies." Washington, DC: U.S. Government Printing Office.

———.1972. "Report on Audit of Section 236 Multifamily Housing Program." Office of Audit, report no. 05-02-2001-5000. Washington, DC: U.S. Government Printing Office.

U.S. General Accounting Office. 1978. "Section 236 Rental Housing: An Evaluation with Lessons for the Future." Report to the Congress of the United States by the Comptroller General PAD 78-13.

Urban Planning Aid. 1973. "Community Development Corporations: The Empty Promise." Cambridge, MA: Urban Planning Aid.

COMMUNITY-BASED HOUSING IN MASSACHUSETTS: COMMENT

Howard J. Sumka

No discussion of housing delivery systems would be complete without considering the role of the community-based, nonprofit sector. Non-profit sponsors became a cog in the federal housing machinery in the 1960s and, despite some considerable problems, they have grown in importance and sophistication over the past two decades. Professor Bratt begins her chapter with the assertion that "there is enormous potential in using community groups to develop and manage their own housing." She then goes on to review the emergence and maturation of the community housing sector, the potential for nonprofit sponsors and the problems that can dilute their effectiveness. Finally, she describes a number of programs of Massachusetts state government agencies that, she believes, constitute at least the basic structure of a comprehensive state support network for community-based housing.

In this brief comment, I will try to draw out some of the issues to which the chapter alludes and which I think bear more consideration. I will consider how we define community-based housing, how local support mechanisms assist community-based efforts, and how research might shed additional light on the needs of community-based housing providers and the role of states.

Before getting to these issues, however, it may be worthwhile to lay out some assertions of my own. I have no disagreement with the basic premise of this chapter regarding the potential importance of the community housing sector. It

The views and conclusions in this chapter are solely those of the author and should not be construed to be those of any agency of the U.S. government.

seems to me, however, that a few additional assertions are required to help frame the discussion. First, the production, management, and maintenance of housing—including that for lower-income families—is fundamentally a responsibility of the private, for-profit sector in this country. A corollary assertion is that housing is, among other things, an economic commodity produced under a system of market incentives that economize on the use of the scarce resources needed to produce it.

If one accepts these parameters, it is not necessary to apologize, as does Professor Bratt, for the past performance, the production potential, or the current behavior of community-based housing sponsors. These sponsors serve a particular portion of the housing supply. Their performance should be measured not in terms of total volume (although volume is important to examine) but in terms of how well they serve the segments of the market to which they are especially well-suited—or, alternatively, to which the private sector is poorly suited. One must also recognize that community-based housing producers must secure investment capital for their housing and manage it well with the resources they have. This requires them to behave similarly to for-profit developers, which Professor Bratt equates to consorting with the devil. I think it is constructive to look at community-based housing as neither an exclusively private commodity nor an exclusively public good. It is a mixture that demands a combination of market discipline to conserve resources and community ownership and management to fully protect the long-term interests of the residents.

With this mixed-good concept in mind, we can turn to the issue of defining community-based housing. Professor Bratt's paper implies that ''community-based'' and ''nonprofit'' are synonymous, although a caution is presented in the final observations. This is misleading. It seems to me that the fundamental requirement of community-based housing is that residents have a continuing and meaningful responsibility for the management of the building or an ownership interest in it. This criterion excludes a substantial portion of nonprofit housing which has been developed over the years by various types of organizations, usually operating under one of the federal subsidy or insurance programs. Where the residents have no formal role in the management of the building or in basic decisions about its future, nonprofit sponsorship differs only marginally from that provided by for-profit organizations. The same cost and management problems affect both types of sponsors equally and—their presumed community interest notwithstanding—nonprofit sponsors find themselves having to make the same hard choices as those made by for-profits. Moreover, their lack of experience often gets them into deeper trouble faster.

Resident management or ownership creates a unity of interest that can produce the fiscal and social discipline necessary to ensure a building's stability. Tenant management demonstrations in public housing as well as experiences with lower-income cooperatives have consistently produced fewer maintenance and vandalism problems and higher rent collection rates than typical for lower-income rental housing.

The record of lower-income cooperatives is not, however, unblemished. Numerous cooperatives never get off the ground; others succumb to financial and management problems. To succeed, cooperatives must meet their financial requirements, ensure that the tenants are trained in ownership skills and responsibilities, and operate as an efficient decisionmaking body. Support provided thus far by the federal government has been primarily in the financial area, in the form of grants and below-market interest rate loans to support development, rental assistance payments to compensate for the inability of residents to pay full market rent, or special subsidies for replacement needs and deferred maintenance items. We know generally what it takes to keep multifamily housing on sound financial footing, and we should by now know the advantages and drawbacks of the various subsidies and incentive structures.

What we do less well, and often not at all, is provide the kind of technical support that is essential for community-based housing to survive over the long term. Professor Bratt sees Massachusetts—where an array of financial and technical services is provided by different state agencies—as an exemplary case of a comprehensive support system at the state level. This, she argues, is a model for other states to follow, and she may very well be right. The system seems to have grown like Topsy, however, and to have evolved from economic development into housing activities per se almost by default. Its experience to date is insufficient to allow any considered judgment to be made about its effectiveness or, more generally, the potential for supporting community-based housing at the state level. I would suggest that before subscribing completely to the support model provided by Massachusetts, we take a careful look at other support systems or delivery models that community-based housing sponsors can call on. We might then examine the resource needs that remain unmet and consider explicitly whether the state is the best level of government at which they can be provided. This is a larger task than can be accomplished here, but it might be useful to consider two examples of community-based housing delivery systems.

One model gaining attention, although still a relative rarity, is the Mutual Housing Association (MHA). Although MHAs take many forms, one version uses vertical integration of development and management tasks, and horizontal integration of multiple projects to provide a form of resident control that avoids the pitfalls of cooperative ownership. Residents do not own an equity share but are members of the association by virtue of having paid a modest initiation fee. They are normally entitled to lifetime residency as long as they abide by the rules of the association, and they are expected to participate in the management of the building. The MHA commonly serves as an umbrella organization, developing new projects which it manages and supports. Other variations of MHAs take the form of federations of independent cooperatives. Whatever their specific form, the MHA is a model for providing some of the benefits of ownership to households that do not have the means or the desire to be share-owning cooperators. At the same time, the MHA coordinates the provision of technical and management services, allowing it to realize scale economies and combine technical resources into an efficient local support system.

Another model is the city-wide, or national, technical assistance provider whose services are available to community-based housing developers and sponsors on a contract basis. These organizations provide essential services to community-based groups through either individualized training in housing maintenance and management or by conducting regular courses for community-based housing groups. This model has been used in multifamily homesteading programs, and has been widely employed in New York City in the management of the *in rem* housing stock. It has the advantage of drawing on the expertise of people who have considerable experience in community-based housing, or in specific aspects of for-profit housing development and management. Generally, the technical assistance providers are viewed as peers by those who are receiving the services. The use of private organizations allows the recipient to elect specific services and to select from among a number of organizations.

Lower-income cooperatives, MHAs, and technical assistance providers have drawn on support from a variety of sources. Local governments have generally used CDBG funds to provide rehabilitation grants, write down mortgage interest rates, or support technical assistance. They have also provided abandoned buildings that have been used in homesteading or other reuse projects. Private foundations have also supported technical assistance and often provided up-front capital for development projects. The primary federal role has been related to financing and mortgage insurance, although some support for technical assistance has been made available with federal government resources.

The states traditionally have not been significantly involved in the provision of housing, although the role of state housing finance agencies has grown. As the federal government withdraws as a major supporter of housing and neighborhood programs, there is a greater need for state and local government involvement. As a rule, responsibility for financial support, in the form of capital grants or long-term mortgage subsidies, should lie with higher rather than lower levels of government. Thus, the state, rather than the municipality, can best fill the gap left by the reduction of federal assistance. It is less clear who should provide technical assistance, however. Arguments can be made for state systems, but there are also arguments for using local authorities. Perhaps the most promising strategy would be for states to use their ability to raise revenue or grant tax relief to direct resources into a housing technical support system available either through local governments or exclusively from qualified nonprofit providers.

It is not clear how a comprehensive support system for community-based housing should be structured, or from what level of government it should be delivered. There is, however, a wealth of experience that can be tapped to assist in the development of the structure of such a system. The needs of community-based housing sponsors can be ascertained from the experiences of cooperatives, MHAs, technical assistance providers, and others operating at the grassroots level. An analysis of the extent to which MHAs or other forms of collaboration among cooperatives and nonprofits have helped overcome the most serious difficulties of community-based housing would be instructive. So, too, would be a review and assessment of the programs undertaken by a number of state and local governments. A recent HUD survey of state activities that support housing and neighborhood programs uncovered 40 programs operating in 20 states. In addition to Massachusetts, New York and California each have an array of programs available. An analysis of the experiences and effectiveness of the individual state programs and their relationship to both local and federal activities would shed considerable light on the potential for a state support system.

With the federal government becoming less generous in its housing subsidies and local governments facing increasing demands on their limited resources, it is logical to look to the states for help. Professor Bratt has opened this avenue of inquiry, but considerable work needs to be done to develop truly effective support systems for community-based housing.

12

A PROGRESSIVE HOUSING PROGRAM FOR AMERICA

Institute for Policy Studies Working Group on Housing (Richard P. Appelbaum)

Until quite recently, for most middle-class Americans the security of homeownership appeared to be a realistic expectation—part of middle-class America's birthright. The explosive development of suburban detached dwellings, the availability of federally-insured long-term mortgage financing, and the postwar rise in average real income all contributed to that expectation. For over half a century the proportion of renters steadily declined, so that by 1980 two out of every three American households had attained homeownership.

The poor never shared in the American dream. For minority households, elderly renters living on fixed incomes, female-headed households, and a significant number of working-class white families, ownership was at best a distant promise, a vague hope for one's children. Yet so long as most middle-class Americans felt secure in the dream, national policy was effectively able to ignore the needs of those who were denied it.

During the past ten years significant numbers of middle-income Americans have seen the dream recede, replaced by a reality of rising housing costs, de-

This chapter is based on a program drafted by the Institute for Policy Studies Working Group on Housing, a component of IPS's Alternative Program for America project. Richard P. Appelbaum had primary responsibility for putting the Program into written form, and presented this chapter at the May 1985 VPI-IPS conference. Emily Achtenberg, Chester Hartman, Peter Marcuse, and Michael Stone drafted, organized, and edited major portions of the Program. Peter Dreier, Jacqueline Leavitt, Christine Minnehan, and Carole Norris also provided or edited drafts of specific sections. Other Working Group members include John D. Atlas, Arthur Collings, Bob Goodman, Daniel Lindheim, Michael Rawson, Florence Roisman, and Joel Rubenzahl.

clining affordability, reduced choice, and insecurity of tenure. It is no longer possible to provide decent, secure, and affordable housing to the majority of Americans. Partly this is due to the economic conditions of the post-Vietnam War period: chronic inflation, long-term increases in unemployment, stagnation in growth, and recurrent deep cycles of decline and recovery. These conditions have resulted in a steady erosion in living standards for many middle-class Americans, while at the same time reducing the number of available housing units.

Although the President's Commission on Housing (U.S. President's Commission on Housing 1982, xvii) assures us that "Americans today are the best-housed people in history," this is not the case. (See Chapter 1 by John Weicher, for a contrary assessment.) A brief comparison with Sweden is instructive. In 1965 Sweden embarked on a ten-year program to bring affordable housing within reach of its entire population. The United States made a similar public commitment three years later. The rates of anticipated new construction were unprecedented in both countries, approaching 10–13 units per thousand people, foretelling a one-third increase in the respective housing stocks over a ten-year period. The United States, lacking any real means to implement its goals, fell short 4.5 million of the projected 26 million units, or almost one-fifth. Of the 6 million targeted subsidized units, only 2.7 million were built—a shortfall of 55 percent (Stone 1980). Sweden, by way of contrast, overreached its ten-year target, achieving construction rates 20–25 percent higher than previous levels (Nesslein 1982, 241). With housing regarded as a right rather than as a commodity, Sweden by the mid-1970s had achieved its goal of providing adequate and affordable shelter for its entire population (Headey 1978; Appelbaum 1986a).

THE DIMENSIONS OF THE HOUSING PROBLEM

It is not simply in comparison with other countries that the United States has suffered a decline in its housing standards; those standards have dropped with respect to its own recent past as well.[1] Over the past decade the supply of available housing has decreased relative to need. For homeowners the vacancy rate has remained consistently low at between 1 and 2 percent, while for renters it declined from 7.1 percent in 1980 to 5.9 percent in 1983 (U.S. Bureau of the Census 1984a, 371). No significant number of apartments were being built at the end of the 1970s, leading the U.S. Comptroller General (1979) to characterize rental housing at that time as an "endangered species." It is estimated that approximately 2.4 million housing units must be constructed each year to keep pace with demand (COIN 1979, 56). We have not come close to realizing that figure since 1974, and in the highly cyclical building industry annual production has frequently been half that amount (U.S. Bureau of the Census 1983, Table 1). Unemployment in the construction industry has paralleled declining construction, reaching a high of 22 percent by the end of 1982 (U.S. Department of Labor 1982). Although construction has recovered somewhat in the past couple of years, most observers believe that recovery was a short-term response to anticipated changes in the tax laws, which will remove many existing tax shelters from real estate. During 1984 and the first quarter of 1985, apartment starts fluctuated widely, ranging from a seasonally adjusted eleven-year annual high of 650,000 units to a low of under 400,000 (*Business Week* 1985, 124–25). The 1986 Tax Reform Act has had an extremely adverse short-term impact on apartment construction. Market simulations predict an annual reduction of some 160,000 apartment units over the next five years (Apgar et al., 1985,1).

This decline in supply is reflected in a parallel decline in affordability. For renters, housing costs are increasing almost twice as fast as incomes: between 1970 and 1983, median rent rose 192 percent while median renter income rose only 100 percent (U.S. Bureau of the Census 1984a). In 1970, 40 percent of all renter households paid at least 25 percent of their income for housing, and 25 percent paid at least 35 percent (U.S. Bureau of the Census 1972, Part C). But in 1983, the latest year for which data are available, the proportion paying 25 percent or more had increased to 59 percent, and 40 percent paid more than 35 percent. An astonishing 6.5 million renter households in 1983 devoted at least one-half of their income to housing (U.S. Bureau of the Census 1984a, Part C). Growing costs are reflected in utility bills as well as sales prices and rents. The Consumer Price Index (CPI) for fuel, oil, coal, and bottled gas rose from 110.1 in 1970 to 675.9 in 1981, and has since dropped slightly, to 646.0 by mid-1984. In that same 14-year period, electricity prices rose by 252 points, compared with a 194 point rise in the CPI for all items (U.S. Bureau of the Census 1984b, 482). This increase was especially felt in the economically depressed frostbelt communities of the Northeast and Midwest.

Needless to say, problems of affordability are felt unequally by different groups, with female-headed, elderly, minority, and farmworker households impacted the most. For example, 81 percent of all households earning less than $10,000 pay 25 percent or more of their incomes for housing, while only 2 percent of those with incomes of $50,000 or more pay this much (U.S. Bureau of the Census 1984a). The median rent-to-income ratio for renter households earning less than $3,000 was a stratospheric 60 percent and above (the *Annual Housing Survey* does not provide more specific figures at this level); for renter households in the $3,000–6,999 income class, the median ratio was 55 percent; and for renter households in the $7,000–9,999 class, the median ratio was 39 percent (U.S. Bureau of the Census 1984a, Table A–1). It is estimated that fewer than half of these poorest households are able to find rental units that cost 25 percent or less of their income; in fact, using the 25 percent standard, it is estimated that nationally there is a shortage of 4.1 million units for those earning under $7,000 (Dolbeare 1983).

Ten percent of female-headed households live in housing that is officially rated as inadequate, as compared with 7.5 percent of all households (U.S. President's Commission on Housing 1982, 9). Low-income, minority, and female-headed households are more likely to be displaced, even though their housing options are more limited (U.S. Department of Housing and Urban Development 1981, 38).

While there is significant and growing disparity between renters' and homeowners' incomes, the latter have also experienced serious housing affordability problems. Between 1970 and 1983, the median sales price of existing homes more than tripled, from $23,400 to $70,300 (U.S. Bureau of the Census 1984a). During the same time, mortgage interest rates on conventionally financed single-family homes rose by over half--from 8.4 percent to 13.4 percent. Based on a conventional 30-year loan for 80 percent of the sales price, monthly mortgage payments increased *four and one-half* times over the thirteen year period—from $143 to $640. It is worth noting that while 60 percent of this increase can be attributed to the increase in sales price, the remaining 40 percent is due to the rise in mortgage interests rates. In the peak year of high mortgage interest rates—1981—first-time homebuyers represented only 13.5 percent of the sales market, as compared with 36 percent in 1977 (U.S. League of Savings Associations 1982). Among homeowners with mortgages, 32 percent pay more than one-quarter of their income on housing-related expenses, while 15 percent pay more than 35 percent (U.S. Bureau of the Census 1984a, Table A–1).

Although housing quality improved somewhat during the first three postwar decades, substantial quality problems remain, particularly with regard to neighborhood conditions. In 1983 over 17 million households indicated that neighborhood crime was a problem, and over 8 million households felt that bothersome neighborhood conditions (noise; lack of street repairs; intrusive non-residential activities; odors, smoke and gas; trash, litter and junk; or boarded-up or abandoned buildings) were so severe that they would like to move (U.S. Bureau of the Census 1985, Table A–3).

But even individual units—despite improvements in the standard measures of crowding, plumbing facilities, and dilapidation—continue to experience persistent problems in maintenance and services. In 1983 over 2 million households reported exposed electrical wiring; 10 million households reported signs of mice or rats; and over 6 million households reported signs of water leakage from their roofs (U.S. Bureau of the Census 1985, Tables A–1 and A–2). The problem of neglected maintenance, followed by housing abandonment, is a growing one in many large cities; New York City alone has lost 30,000 units a year for this reason (Marcuse 1979; Stegman 1982).

Lack of residential security is also a growing problem. According to government estimates, 600,000–850,000 households—some 1.7–2.4 million persons—are forced to move each year because of private market activity. Over 40 percent of such moves are attributable to increased housing costs, with the sale of the apartment accounting for another 23 percent (U.S. Department of Housing and Urban Development 1981, 25–26). While tenants are most vulnerable to being forced out of their homes, homeowners are increasingly threatened by mortgage foreclosures and eviction. Nearly one in 16 home loans are more than 30 days in arrears (Jones 1985). In many areas, high foreclosure rates are a function of rising monthly payments under graduated payment mortgage arrangements, while housing values are not rising and in some cases are falling below the amount still owed to the lender (King 1985). Regional economic hardship can of course produce widespread mortgage foreclosures: whereas in early 1985 the national foreclosure rate was 2.5 per 1,000 mortgages (up from 1.8 in 1981), in Oregon, with its declining timber industry, the rate was 8.7 (King 1985).

Homelessness is the extreme outcome of displacement and affordable housing shortages. Recent estimates for the New York City area indicate as many as 50,000 homeless, while the figures for Los Angeles suggest almost 40,000 (U.S. Department of Housing and Urban Development 1984, 14). While HUD estimates a national homeless population of 250,000–350,000 (U.S. Department of Housing and Urban Development 1984, 19), this figure almost certainly is a considerable underestimation (Appelbaum 1986b). Other estimates have placed the figure at 2–3 million (U.S. Department of Housing and Urban Development 1984, 9).[2]

Finally, it is important to realize that housing problems often have broad social consequences. Housing, after all, is much more than shelter. It provides social status, access to jobs, education, and other services; and the structure for economic, social and political relationships. Racial segregation in housing, which remains severe, limits educational and employment opportunities for minorities even as it forces them to pay more of their income for declining services. Housing design and locational patterns reinforce the traditional division of labor within the male-dominant family, foster unpaid work in the home, and restrict opportunities for female labor-force participation (Saegert 1981; Rothblatt et al. 1979). In this way, housing both reinforces and perpetuates economic and social divisions that exist within the larger society.

SOURCES OF THE PROBLEM

There is a principal underlying cause to these problems, which in our view explains the inability of our society to provide adequate, affordable housing for all segments of the population: housing—a necessity of life—is treated not as a social good but as a commodity.[3] Housing in our society is produced, owned, operated, and sold in ways designed to maximize profits, rather than to provide needed shelter. The consequence is waste and inefficiency in production and allocation; a highly volatile housing economy; chronic shortages, particularly among lower-income households; and a growing gap between incomes and housing costs.

Profits at all levels add considerably to the cost of housing, since they are cumulated throughout the production, sales, and consumption process as each participant seeks to maximize the return. Profits typically accrue to the owner of the land on which the unit is built, who may realize a speculative gain; the financial institutions that make the construction and mortgage loans, whose profits are included in the interest and fees charged; the general contractor and subcontractors during the construction phase; the building material providers, which are frequently large corporations with few incentives for cost control (Schlesinger and Erlich 1986); and finally, each successive owner, who hopes to realize a profit every time the property is sold.

Speculation, the buying and selling of property for short-term profit resulting from inflation, can result in significant short-term price increases. In housing, speculation is encouraged by a mortgage financing system that permits a small down payment to leverage control over a substantial investment. Speculation was in part responsible for the major price increases that occurred in California during the late 1970s, as speculative investment capital flowed into local housing markets in search of quick, relatively safe profits. Speculation is wasteful and inefficient, and can be extremely damaging to low-income neighborhoods, whose residents can quickly be priced out of the housing market.

Since virtually all housing construction and purchase is financed through private credit, residential mortgages are a significant portion of total private debt in the United States, averaging around one-third over the past 15 years. In 1980 residential mortgages amounted to nearly $1.1 trillion—an amount that far exceeded corporate debt and was even greater than the debt of the United States government (Stone 1986). Furthermore, residential mortgage debt has placed an increasing burden on the overall economy. As of 1984 it was equal to 41.4 percent of the gross national product, compared with 36.4 percent in 1970, and just 13.5 percent in 1946 (Stone 1986, Table 3.2)

This heavy dependence on private debt financing renders housing costs and starts highly susceptible to fluctuations in the credit markets. The use of credit for speculative purposes also siphons off credit from industry and other productive uses, rechannelling it into inflated housing markets, and thereby depriving the national economy of needed investment capital (Downs 1980). Finally, debt financing threatens overall economic stability, since during a deep recession significant numbers of mortgage failures threaten banks, reverberating throughout the entire financial structure.

Rising interest rates drive up the cost of financing mortgage payments. While higher monthly payments may have a somewhat dampening effect on demand, any resulting decline in sales prices is more than offset by the higher monthly payments. Interest rates also add significantly to the cost of construction, since most construction is financed with temporary private loans. Construction loan interest is one of the most rapidly rising components of housing production costs (the other is land; see U.S. President's Commission on Housing 1982, 181).

From the perspective of the local housing economy, interest rates are externally determined: they do not reflect local supply and demand conditions, but rather national and international credit markets and federal monetary policy. Since the Federal Reserve System uses high interest rates and credit control as its chief means of fighting inflation, housing consumers suffer greatly during times of anti-inflationary monetary policy, confronting high interest payments and a general scarcity of credit.

The highly cyclical nature of housing production is the direct result of such reliance on private credit. One consequence has been a significant impairment of the long-run productive capacity of the housing industry (U.S. President's Commission on Housing 1982, xxi, 182; Solomon 1981, 200). The cost of idle plant and construction equipment during slack times is recaptured in higher prices for those housing units which are built. Construction workers require higher wages to offset those periods when they will be unemployed. Builders face a high degree of risk, which they cover through higher profit margins, a cost that is passed on to consumers. Estimates of increased production costs resulting from cyclical instability run as high as 15–20 percent (COIN 1979, 57).

Tax policies contribute both to artificially high housing demand and speculation. For homeowners, federal income tax deductions for interest and property taxes encourage the purchase of more expensive housing than would be affordable in the absence of such deductions (U.S. Congressional Budget Office 1981). Prior to the 1986 Tax Reform Act, the ability to depreciate the purchase value of income property over relatively short periods encouraged its resale as soon as the bulk of depreciation benefits were exhausted—usually five or six years. This, in turn, contributed to the treatment of rental property as a speculative investment, in which returns were calculated in terms of short-term yield rather than long-term income potential. While the 1986 Tax Reform Act weakened such depreciation benefits, it did not do away with them entirely.

Finally, the other sources of high housing costs include property taxes, which are highly regressive, and local government restrictions on development, which can also add to housing costs although in recent years their impact has been substantially less than is generally believed (Gilderbloom and Appelbaum 1988, Chapter 6).

THE FAILURE OF CURRENT APPROACHES

Federal housing programs date back to the Depression, and over the years have included low-interest loans, mortgage-interest subsidies, rent supplements, publicly owned low-income housing, and—in the case of military housing—direct public financing as well as ownership. Many programs have been targeted to specific groups, such as the elderly, rural households, or very low-income households. Federal programs have never reached more than a small fraction of those in need, however, because in the United States housing has never been regarded as an entitlement. The largest federal outlays for housing, in fact, have gone to upper middle-class homeowners in the form of deductions for mortgage interest and property taxes, which cost the Treasury $49.4 billion in 1984—more than has been spent under all HUD-assisted housing programs since the inception of public housing in 1937. Sixty percent of these deductions go to taxpayers in the top 10 percent of the income range (Dolbeare 1983, Figure 2.1, 67–68).

Public housing and rent supplements are the two principal programs that have been directed at low-income populations. The former originated in the National Housing Act of 1937 as a pump-priming public works program and has served the needs of returning veterans after 1945. It wasn't until the massive urban renewal and slum clearance programs of the 1950s that public housing became largely identified with low-income populations. As large public housing projects became "last resort" housing for the economy's cast-offs, they frequently suffered form official neglect in the form of chronic underfunding, poor maintenance, and bureaucratic management. While public housing is owned by public agencies (local housing authorities), it is built by private contractors and financed with bonds, and its costs thus reflect both private profit maximization and the instabilities of the private credit markets.

The other major low-income housing program consists of rent supplements to poor tenants under Section 8 of the National Housing Act. Under this program, participating landlords agree to charge qualifying tenants fair-market rents, which are based on prevailing rent levels as determined by HUD. The government then makes up the difference between this market rent and the tenant's rent payments, set at 30 percent (formerly 25 percent) of monthly income. During times of rapidly rising rents, this program is highly inflationary, with the average direct subsidy cost for a new unit of Section 8 housing estimated in 1982 at $4,000–$5,500 per year (U.S. Department of Housing and Urban Development 1982), and nearly twice that amount in high-cost New York City—figures that doubtless are much higher today.

When all low-income housing programs are considered together, there are some 4.5 million housing units that currently receive some form of direct subsidy, of which 3.4 million are administered by HUD, with the remainder in rural areas administered by the Department of Agriculture's Farmers Home Administration. The HUD-administered units include 1.2 million units of public housing and about 1.3 million households receiving Section 8 payments (Dolbeare 1983, Table 2.6).

Notwithstanding the fact that these programs reach fewer than one out of every four households living in poverty, the Reagan administration has subjected them to deep budget cuts. New budget authority for HUD's subsidized housing programs in recent years has fallen from $30.1 billion in fiscal year 1981, to $8.7 billion in fiscal year 1983, $9.9 billion in 1984, and $10.8 billion in 1985 (LIHIS 1985). The Reagan administration's proposed budget for fiscal year 1987 originally called for *no* additional budget authority. Between 1981 and 1989, budget authority for subsidized housing will have dropped by four-fifths. When President Reagan came to office, seven dollars were spent on the military for every dollar on housing; when he leaves, the ratio will be forty-six to one (LIHIS 1988). For existing subsidized units, the administration has proposed reducing the stock through demolition, conversion, and sale. HUD at one time planned to sell or demolish 100,000 public housing units over a five-year period (Bureau of National Affairs 1983).

As housing difficulties extend further into the middle class, the federal government's present approach is to trust to the marketplace, all but eliminating its own already minimal role. We believe that this is a prescription for disaster during the coming decade.

OBJECTIVES OF A JUST HOUSING PROGRAM

The program begins with the assumption that every person is entitled to adequate housing in a decent neighborhood at an affordable price, with secure tenure, and that the special housing needs must be met of women, minorities, and other traditionally disadvantaged in the housing market. There are seven central objectives of such a housing program.[4] They are:

1. *Expand the amount of housing under social ownership*. By "social ownership" we refer to housing that is operated solely for resident and community benefit, is subject to resident control, and cannot be resold for a profit. Social ownership may take many forms, including direct public ownership by government or nonprofit entities, collective ownership by resident-controlled corporations or neighborhood councils, non-equity or limited-equity cooperatives,[5] and limited-equity ownership of single-family homes. Residents of socially owned housing will pay rent according to true ability to pay, and will have the right to permanent occupancy as long as they comply with reasonable tenure obligations.

2. *Expand social production and increase social control over the housing production process*. Although in the immediate future most aspects of housing production will continue to be performed by the private sector, in the long run all housing that is produced under our program will be subject to social ownership and control. By this we refer to an increasingly strong public and/or community development sector, with a growing role for worker-controlled nonprofit and public construction companies. Social ownership will be encouraged through technical assistance and funding to nonprofit suppliers and developers. Within this framework, we envision a substantial amount of new housing construction to meet the needs of newly formed households, to replace lost or unrepairable units, to reduce overcrowding, and to facilitate mobility and choice. National multifamily housing production targets will be set in conjunction with local housing development plans. Additionally, the existing housing stock will be converted to social ownership where feasible and upgraded to appropriate standards of safety, livability, space, and energy-efficiency.

3. *Expand direct public financing of housing production and ownership, thereby reducing the dependence of housing on privately controlled debt and equity capital*. The dependence of housing production, ownership, and improvement on private mortgage credit must be greatly reduced. Accordingly, the proposed housing programs will be financed with direct grants wherever feasible, in much the way that we have funded substantial portions of the military's family

housing inventory. This housing would therefore be permanently debt-free, with no mortgages or bonds to repay. At the same time, a growing portion of the existing stock will be converted to social ownership, and the mortgage debt on such properties will be paid off over time and eventually eliminated.

4. *Control speculative private use and disposition of land.* Land is a scarce resource, acquiring much of its value by public action. Land has a pervasive influence over community life. Its control is an indispensable element in planning for society's needs. Its rising cost is a significant deterrent to housing development and sound community planning. The amount of land under social control and ownership is to be significantly expanded, and existing public lands preserved, through government and community land-banking. Public control over private land will also be achieved through a variety of regulatory, tax, and planning measures.

5. *Increase resident control over housing and neighborhood decisions.* To ensure that local housing programs are responsive to the needs of low- and moderate-income and minority neighborhoods, the residents of such neighborhoods should be increasingly involved in development and service decisions. Such control must operate within a basic nonexclusionary framework. Residents should exercise control over private development decisions that affect the well-being of their neighborhood. At a minimum, this means that any private development activities must involve neighborhood input, and, where determined to be detrimental, should be strongly regulated so as to minimize adverse impacts.

6. *Eliminate the discriminatory, exclusionary, and oppressive uses of housing, and affirmatively address the housing needs of special groups.* Racial minorities, women, children, and the low-income elderly are among the principal groups that continue to suffer pervasive discrimination and exclusion in most housing markets. These forms of oppression must be ended. Beyond that, an affirmative effort must be made to provide housing in forms and locations that address the special situation of such groups, as well as safeguard the right to remain in place or move to other neighborhoods of choice. Housing resources must also be targeted for the revitalization of existing minority communities, while at the same time expanding the right of mobility for minority residents by providing increased housing options in other neighborhoods of choice. Efforts are also needed to develop housing of appropriate size, type, and design to free women from oppressive domestic conditions.

7. *Allocate housing resources on an equitable basis, and provide adequate resources to meet housing needs.* Funds should increasingly be targeted for purposes that benefit low- and moderate-income and minority households. In the long run, in order to provide decent, affordable housing and viable neighborhoods, the level of resources allocated to housing must be substantially increased. A major shift in spending priorities—most notably, away from military spending—is necessary to provide sufficient funding to meet the housing objectives of this program. Revenues must be generated in a progressive way, by eliminating inequitable tax loopholes and adopting progressive tax measures.

PROGRAM COMPONENTS[6]

The Progressive Housing Program for America takes as its point of departure the goal originally established by the National Housing Act of 1949: "a decent home and a suitable living environment for every American family." Building on this commitment, it declares that housing that is decent, safe, sanitary, affordable, compatible with resident needs and under democratic resident control is a universal national entitlement. It establishes that attainment of the national housing goal is a priority of the highest order, to which substantial public resources must be devoted. It assumes that local, state, and federal governments have a responsibility to use their powers to meet the housing needs of all segments of the community and offers four legislative acts that are designed to meet the above objectives:

1. The National Tenant Protection and Private Rental Housing Conversion Act is intended to protect private-sector tenants from arbitrary eviction, excessive rent increases, and undermaintenance, while facilitating the phased conversion of a significant portion of the private rental housing stock to various forms of social ownership.

The first objective—the protection of private-sector tenants—is to be achieved by the following measures:

- national just-cause eviction protections, setting forth minimal national standards governing evictions
- model ordinances that can be used by localities to demonstrate compliance with federal housing requirements, including ordinances governing rent increases, condominium conversions, demolitions, eviction protections, warranties of habitability, and resale price controls
- standards governing private rental housing management, including leasing and occupancy terms, residential services, collective bargaining, rent dispute adjudication, and grievance procedures

The second objective—phased conversion of private rental housing to social ownership—will be achieved by the allocation of federal funds and technical assistance to localities, which will establish the necessary legal mechanisms to facilitate conversions.

Purchase of privately owned rental units will be at market rates, with locally established ceilings to discourage speculation. Substandard housing that the owner cannot or will not bring up to code can provide one source of units for conversion at market value. There will be a standing purchase offer for low- and moderate-income rental housing at a reasonable price. Localities will be required to establish procedures facilitating the acquisition of rental property that is in mortgage foreclosure. Capital grants will be available to rehabilitate substandard units, if the owner agrees to deed the unit to the social sector under specified terms.

Each year 160,000 rental units are to be converted under this program, at an annual cost of $5.6 billion.

2. The National Homeowner Protection Act is directed at existing homeowners who, for economic or other reasons, are willing to deed their house to the social housing sector in order to obtain security of tenure and reduced housing outlays. By encouraging voluntary transfer of private homes to the social sector in exchange for enhanced affordability and improved maintenance, a new form of *protected occupancy* will be created for existing homeowners that also will bank a portion of the owner-occupied housing stock for permanent nonspeculative use. Where tenants wish to own their units, localities will also be encouraged to facilitate the conversion of rental housing acquired from private landlords to forms of individual and collective nonspeculative resident ownership.

Purchase of private homes will be achieved through several programs. A standing purchase offer will be made in exchange for lifetime security of tenure at affordable rent levels. An equity-participation program will provide an exchange of equity for a lifetime annuity and security of tenure. Direct rehabilitation grants for major capital repairs will be offered in exchange for an agreement to deed the property to a social owner at a future date or upon termination of occupancy. Finally, a foreclosure program will enable the homeowner to deed the property to a social owner in exchange for lifetime security of tenure at an affordable rent (a short grace period for buy-back is provided).

Each year 160,000 owner-occupied units will be converted under this program, at an annual cost of $8.0 billion.

3. The Subsidized Housing Preservation Act is intended to protect the existing stock of federally subsidized housing, including public housing as well as nonprofit housing constructed with federal subsidies. This inventory of some 3.4 million units, which represents a multi-billion dollar capital investment backed by the federal government, is a national resource which, once lost, would be far more costly to replace. Currently, many subsidized housing tenants are forced to pay considerably more than they can afford for substandard units, are subject to arbitrary management practices, and have limited security of tenure. Further, an increasing number of units are in danger of being lost from the subsidized inventory through demolition, private resale, and conversion to market-rate housing (especially as their bonds or subsidy contracts expire or their mortgages become ripe for prepayment). (See Chapter 10 by Emily Achtenberg).

To address these problems, the Act seeks to improve the affordability and livability of the subsidized housing stock, ensure security of tenure, and increase resident control for existing and future low- and moderate-income tenants. At the same time, the Act provides mechanisms to assure the permanent retention of existing subsidized units, enhance existing public and nonprofit ownerships, and facilitate conversion of privately owned subsidized units to forms of nonspeculative social ownership.

These objectives are achieved by providing for protections against arbitrary eviction, the loss of assisted units through conversion or demolition, and undermaintenance and neglect. The quality and affordability of the existing assisted housing stock is secured by reserving such units exclusively for low- and moderate-income households, by providing adequate operating subsidies where necessary, and by providing capital grants for necessary upgrading. Rents in public housing will be determined on the basis of an "ability-to-pay" formula that takes into account non-housing expenditures, rather than the simple percent of income formula that is presently used (See Chapter 13 by Michael Stone.) Conversion of the privately owned assisted housing stock will be facilitated through a combination of subsidy incentives and regulatory enforcement. Finally, responsible management is ensured through adequate funding, technical assistance, and maximal opportunities for residential participation.

Some 81,000 HUD-held units will be converted annually to the social housing stock under this program, at a yearly cost of $1.3 billion. Additionally, 500,000 existing social units will be modernized annually, at a cost of $5 billion.

4. The Social Housing Production and Financing Act provides for the production, rehabilitation, and financing of social-sector housing. It calls for redirecting all federal housing-related financial aid to production and substantial rehabilitation in the social sector, or for the conversion of privately owned units to social ownership. All social-sector production and rehabilitation will be restricted to low- and moderate-income housing. Production under this Act will initially be by any developer willing to comply with its requirements, but in the long run technical assistance and funding will be targeted toward nonprofit developers.

Financing will be by means of direct grants, funded through the federal budgetary process, much as large parts of the military family housing stock is funded.[7] Funding will be available for land-banking, and for universal operating subsidies where necessary to bring costs down to affordable levels. As with public housing, affordability will be determined on the basis of an "ability-to-pay" formula that takes into account nonhousing expenditures.

The program calls for 200,000 units annually of new construction, at an annual cost of $12.0 billion, and 400,000 units of substantial rehabilitation, at an annual cost of $8.0 billion. The operating subsidy program, projected to reach some 6.5 million units annually, is estimated to cost $13.0 billion.

PROGRAM IMPLEMENTATION THROUGH MANDATED LOCAL HOUSING PLANS

The federal government will establish guidelines, set forth requirements, and provide funding. State governments will have primary responsibility for oversight. Localities will be required to design and implement complying programs, with demonstrated local compliance a threshold requirement for receiving federal funding for any programs that impact housing.

The federal government will fund the programs, with HUD serving as a secondary enforcement body. HUD will be empowered to withhold funds from non-complying states and localities. State governments will designate a lead state agency as the primary enforcement body, and will empower that agency (or another agency, if appropriate) to administer programs in localities that are unable or unwilling to do so. Regional entities will be empowered to determine regional fair share housing needs.

Localities will implement the various provisions of the Acts as follows:

- needs assessments will be conducted to determine fair share housing requirements, the quality of the existing stock, all land and units suitable for inclusion in the social sector, relevant existing government programs and constraints, and the needs of special groups (disabled, single parents, farmworkers, minority groups, elderly, low-income)
- goals and objectives will be explicitly established, with measurable performance indicators
- four-year ''rolling action plans'' will promote all the objectives of the Acts, including the provision of adequate sites, balancing governmental regulation with housing needs, mitigating the negative impacts of private- and public-sector commercial and industrial development activities, and providing for public input into the planning process
- annual program revision will be required, with a thorough reevaluation every four years
- individuals and groups will be granted standing before HUD to assure compliance

REFORM MEASURES

A number of measures are provided to improve the housing situation of low- and moderate-income households in the short run. These are compatible with the assumptions of the overall program, yet do not require a fundamental restructuring of the existing housing delivery system. Some of these are local measures that can be adopted to satisfy the federally mandated local housing plans, and are therefore not appropriate for federal legislation.

Tax reform measures will modify the existing tax structure, which, as we have seen, is inequitable, inefficient, and contributes to speculation and waste in the housing sector. The following reforms will be included:

- As the long-run effects of our program are realized, the homeowners' deduction would be ended. This could only occur, however, as part of a genuine tax reform that eliminated inequities and thereby significantly reduced the tax burden of low- and middle-income households.
- In the long run, depreciation will be eliminated altogether, substituting a realistic schedule for writing off capital improvements.
- A national deed-transfer tax would be enacted in the short run, with the tax inversely graduated to length of holding. In the long run, a virtually confiscatory windfall profits tax on all sales of rental housing would be enacted to end speculation.
- Tax-exempt bonds will be used exclusively for social housing programs in the short run, and eliminated altogether in the long run as a wasteful and inefficient means of raising revenues.
- Local tax reform could include progressive real property taxes, which charge higher rates for more highly valued property, while providing circuit-breaker relief for low-

income property owners. Luxury housing taxes could also be enacted locally, with funds going to social housing.

Financing measures would be adopted to steer private credit toward social housing objectives. Any housing that benefits from such measures must be offered for sale to the social sector at a previously agreed price after a designated period. These measures must apply to all credit institutions with equal force. They include:

- differential taxes on credit institutions, rewarding preferred lending, using revenues for social housing
- loan set-aside requirements for social housing objectives
- differential reserve requirements, with lowered reserves for institutions that meet social housing goals (the reserves could be used for social housing objectives)
- below-market interest requirements for a designated percentage of loans, which could then be used to meet social housing objectives

LONG-RANGE GOALS

Our hope is to provide housing that meets the needs of those low- and moderate-income households not served by the present system. We believe that society has an obligation to provide affordable housing to all segments of its population. To achieve this end, we offer long-term measures that can serve as a guide for future action. We firmly believe that as the housing situation worsens, these measures will come to have broad appeal.

The rights of use ordinarily associated with private ownership are secured and enhanced by our program: security of tenure, privacy, the right to modify one's living environment. Only the right to profit in housing is unavailable to those households who choose this alternative. Because such housing is nonprofit with respect to production, financing, and ownership, its cost will include only operating and maintenance expenses, representing a significating reduction in expenses to residents. (For single-family homeowners with mortgages, principal and interest payments represent, on average, 65 percent of total monthly housing expenses (Hartman and Stone 1986). Eliminating financing costs would thus reduce monthly housing costs for such households by nearly two-thirds.) Nonetheless, subsidies will be provided where necessary to ensure that rent payments reflect true ability to pay. Social housing is operated only for resident and community benefit.

The social housing stock will increase both as a result of our production programs and from conversion of market housing to social ownership. At the same time, existing housing which is subject to some form of social ownership or control—such as public housing, limited-equity cooperatives, and some assisted housing—constitutes a national resource threatened with demolition or sale to private ownership. Our program will arrest these processes, maintaining and enhancing the existing stock.

Speculation in housing cannot disappear overnight. Many adjustments are necessary as we move from a housing system characterized by inadequate and overpriced accommodations in segregated and insecure neighborhoods to the kinds of residential environments that are our goal.

We now have an opportunity to implement a program that can benefit low-, moderate, and middle-income tenants and homeowners. The growing elusiveness of homeownership for the vast majority of tenants and the decreasing ability of low- and moderate-income homeowners to benefit from their housing as an investment make tenure distinctions less important. At the same time, increasing neighborhood problems create a basis for common action. Moreover, the traditional housing solutions of subsidies and tax incentives for the rich, combined with federal credit manipulations, seem less and less workable, even to those who view them as desirable. Needed is a program that can alter the terms of existing public debate on housing, that challenges the commodity nature of housing and its role in our economic and social system, and that demonstrates how people's legitimate housing needs can be met through an alternative approach.

NOTES

1. This section is partially adapted from Achtenberg and Marcuse 1983.
2. The HUD study suffers from significant methodological flaws which render its conclusions doubtful. For a collection of critical analysis and testimony, see U.S. House of Representatives (1984).
3. For detailed analysis, see Stone 1980, 1983; Rybeck 1982; the collection of readings in Hartman 1983; Bratt et al. 1986; Sternlieb and Hughes 1981; U.S. Comptroller General 1979; and U.S. President's Commission on Housing 1982.
4. This section is partially adapted from Achtenberg and Marcuse 1983.
5. Under limited-equity form of ownership, tenant-owners acquire a share in the cooperative, which holds a blanket mortgage for all the units. Typically, the share is equivalent to the down payment for the unit—perhaps 10–20 percent of its value. When the owner wishes to leave the cooperative, the share is resold (to the cooperative) at the original value, plus an annual appreciation set by common agreement or state law at a low level (in California, state law presently limits annual appreciation to 10 percent). Cooperative members thus cannot sell their units at market value; they can only sell their share at a controlled rate of appreciation. This feature serves to maintain the affordability of housing, a goal regarded as paramount to individual owners' ability to maximize their profits.
6. The program was introduced as legislation on June 1, 1988, by Rep. Ron Dellums (D-CA), as HR4727.
7. See Chester Hartman, "Military Family Housing: The Other Public Housing Program," Washington, D.C.: Inst. for Policy Studies, unpublished.

REFERENCES

Achtenberg, Emily Paradise, and Peter Marcuse. 1983. "Towards the Decommodification of Housing: A Political Analysis and Progressive Program." In *America's Housing Crisis: What Is To Be Done?* edited by Chester Hartman. Boston: Routledge and Kegan Paul.

Apgar, William C., H. James Brown, Arthur A. Doud, and George A. Schink. 1985. "Assessment of the Likely Impacts of the President's Tax Proposals on the Rental Housing Market." Cambridge, MA: Joint Center for Housing Studies of M.I.T. and Harvard University.

Appelbaum, Richard. 1986a. "Swedish Housing in the Postwar Period: Some Lessons for American Housing Policy." In *Critical Perspectives on Housing*, edited by Rachel G. Bratt, Chester Hartman, and Ann Meyerson. Philadelphia: Temple University Press.

———. 1986b. "Testimony on *A Report to the Secretary on the Homeless and Emergency Shelters*." In *Housing the Homeless*, edited by Jon Erickson and Charles Wilhelm. New Brunswick, NJ: Rutgers University Press

Bratt, Rachel G., Chester Hartman, Ann Meyerson (eds). 1986. *Critical Perspectives on Housing*. Philadelphia: Temple University Press.

Bureau of National Affairs. 1983. *Housing and Development Reporter* 10:42 (March 14).

Business Week. 1985. "How Tax Laws Pushed Apartment Owners Into Overdrive" May 13: 124–125.

COIN (Consumers Opposed to Inflation in the Necessities). 1979. *There Are Alternatives: A Program for Controlling Inflation in the Necessities of Life*. Washington, DC: COIN.

Dolbeare, Cushing. 1983. "The Low-Income Housing Crisis." In *America's Housing Crisis: What Is To Be Done?* edited by Chester Hartman. Boston: Routledge and Kegan Paul.

Downs, Anthony. 1983. *Rental Housing in the 1980's*. Washington, DC: The Brookings Institution.

———. 1980. "Too Much Capital For Housing?" *The Brookings Bulletin* 17:1 (summer).

Gilderbloom, John I., and Richard P. Appelbaum. 1988. *Rethinking Rental Housing*. Philadelphia: Temple University Press.

Hartman, Chester (ed). 1983. *America's Housing Crisis: What Is To Be Done?* Boston: Routledge and Kegan Paul.

Hartman, Chester, and Michael E. Stone. 1986. "A Socialist Housing Alternative for the United States." In *Critical Perspectives on Housing*, edited by Rachel G. Bratt, Chester Hartman, and Ann Meyerson. Philadelphia: Temple University Press.

Headey, Bruce B. 1978. *Housing Policy in the Developed Economy*. London: Croom Helm.

Jones, John A. 1985. "Record Delinquency Rate a Sign of Home Affordability Crisis." *Investor's Daily*, May.

King, Wayne. 1985. "A Rising Tide of Foreclosures." *New York Times*, October 20.

LIHIS (Low Income Housing Information Service). 1988. "The 1988 Low-Income Housing Budget." Washington, DC.

LIHIS. 1985. "The 1986 Low-Income Housing Budget." Special memorandum no. 21, February. Washington, DC.

Marcuse, Peter. 1979. *Rental Housing in the City of New York: Supply and Conditions, 1975–1978*. New York: Department of Housing Preservation and Development.

Nesslein, Thomas S. 1982. "The Swedish Housing Model: An Assessment." *Urban Studies* 19: 235–46.

Rothblatt, Donald, Daniel J. Garr, and Jo Sprague. 1979. *The Suburban Environment and Women*. New York: Praeger.

Rybeck, Rick. 1982. *Meeting America's Housing Needs: A Progressive Agenda*. Washington, DC: The Conference on Alternative State and Local Public Policies.

Saegert, Susan. 1981. "Masculine Cities and Feminine Suburbs: Polarized Ideas, Contradictory Realities." In *Women and the American City*, edited by Catherine Stimson et al. Chicago: University of Chicago Press.

Schlesinger, Tom and Mark Erlich. 1986. "Housing: The Industry Capitalism Didn't Forget." In *Critical Perspectives on Housing*, edited by Rachel G. Bratt, Chester Hartman, and Ann Meyerson. Philadelphia: Temple University Press.

Solomon, Arthur P. 1981. "Flawed Analysis of Market Trends Fuels Assaults on Housing Expenditures." *Journal of Housing*, April: 194–200.

Stegman, Michael. 1982. *The Dynamics of Rental Housing in New York City*. New York: Department of Housing Preservation and Development.

Sternlieb, George, and James W. Hughes. 1981. *The Future of Rental Housing*. New Brunswick, NJ: Center for Urban Policy Research.

Stone, Michael. 1986. "Housing and the Dynamics of U.S. Capitalism." In *Critical Perspectives on Housing*, edited by R. Bratt, C. Hartman, and A. Meyerson. Philadelphia, PA: Temple University Press.

Stone, Michael. 1983 "Housing and the Economic Crisis: An Analysis and Emergency Program." in *America's Housing Crisis: What Is To Be Done?* edited by Chester Hartman. Boston: Routledge and Kegan Paul.

Stone, Michael. 1980. "The Housing Problem in the United States: Origins and Prospects." *Socialist Review* 52 (July-August): 65–119.

U.S. Bureau of the Census. 1985. *American Housing Survey: 1983*, Part B, "Indicators of Housing and Neighborhood Quality by Financial Characteristics, U.S. and Regions." Series H–150–83. Washington, DC: U.S. Government Printing Office.

U.S. Bureau of the Census. 1984a. *American Housing Survey: 1983*, Part C. Washington, DC: U.S. Government Printing Office.

U.S. Bureau of the Census. 1984b. *Statistical Abstract of the United States*. Washington, DC: U.S. Government Printing Office.

U.S. Bureau of the Census. 1983. *Housing Starts*. Construction reports, series C20–83–2 (February). Washington, DC: U.S. Government Printing Office.

U.S. Bureau of the Census. 1972. *Census of Housing: 1970. Metropolitan Housing Characteristics, U.S. and Regions*. Report HC(2)–1. Washington, DC: U.S. Government Printing Office.

U.S. Comptroller General. 1979. *Rental Housing: A National Problem That Needs Immediate Attention*. General Accounting Office report to the Congress, CED 80–11. Washington, DC: U.S. Government Printing Office.

U.S. Congressional Budget Office. 1981. *The Tax Treatment of Homeownership: Issues and Options*. Washington, DC: U.S. Government Printing Office.

U.S. Department of Housing and Urban Development. 1984. ''A Report to the Secretary on the Homeless and Emergency Shelters.'' In *Joint Hearing Before the Subcommittee on Housing and Community Development and the Subcommittee on Manpower and Housing*, U.S. House of Representatives, May 24. Banking Committee Serial no. 98–91. Washington, DC: U.S. Government Printing Office.

———. 1982. *Recent Evidence on the Cost of Housing Subsidy Programs*. Office of Policy Development and Research report to the U.S. Congress. Washington DC: U. S. Government Printing Office.

———. 1981. *Residential Displacement: An Update*. Office of Policy Development and Research report to the U.S. Congress. Washington, DC: U.S. Government Printing Office.

U.S. Department of Labor. 1982. ''The Employment Situation: November 1982.'' Bureau of Labor Statistics, Release no. 82–454, December 3.

U.S. House of Representatives. 1984. ''HUD Report on Homelessness.'' In *Joint Hearing Before the Subcommittee on Housing and Community Development and the Subcommittee on Manpower and Housing*, May 24. Banking Committee Serial no. 98–91. Washington, DC: U.S. Government Printing Office.

U.S. League of Savings Associations. 1982. *Homeownership: The American Dream Adrift*. Chicago: U.S. League of Savings Associations.

U.S. President's Commission on Housing. 1982. *Report of the President's Commission on Housing*. Washington, DC: U.S. Government Printing Office.

A PROGRESSIVE HOUSING PROGRAM FOR AMERICA: COMMENT

Morton J. Schussheim

The chapter by Professor Appelbaum raises large and disturbing questions about how we provide, use, and misuse housing in America, about the wisdom of our relying on the market and private, profit-motivated initiatives to meet the nation's housing needs, and about the efficacy of past government programs in addressing the nation's housing problems.

Over the past decade we have seen a shift away from direct government involvement in the production and management of housing toward less regulation and more reliance on private enterprise. This shift is apparent not only in the United States and Britain but also in some socialist countries, most notably Hungary. In each case it seems to reflect dissatisfaction with past public sector efforts to address national needs and to be premised on the assumption that the market can and will do at least as well as the state in providing housing to different groups.

The proposals offered by Appelbaum and his associates would halt the shift toward increased privatization of housing. They are based on an analysis of the circumstances and unmet needs of those who have been largely neglected by the traditional market—minority families, the elderly, the handicapped, female-headed households, farm laborers, and the poor. As they point out, renters were paying more of their incomes for gross rent in 1983 than in 1970, and home-ownership is less affordable today than a decade ago, due to higher relative interest rates, house prices, and operating expenses.

Whether or not one accepts Appelbaum's general assertion that this country's overall housing standards have declined over the past decade (at least relative to need), it is clear that there is a significant housing problem in this country and that it most acutely affects low-income households, minorities, the elderly, and female-headed households. While for most in these groups the main problem is cost burden, many also must face insecurity of tenure or endure substandard physical conditions. Almost five million households report living on a street with boarded-up buildings. Given the evidence we have on the degree to which these groups' housing needs have not been met by either the market or public sector programs, it is difficult to argue against some shift in national policies.

The Appelbaum group agrees with those who argue that it is time for a shift away from existing policies. Unlike the proponents of increased privatization of housing, however, they argue for an increased, though transformed, public sector role. They propose the creation of an entire new sector, called "social housing," to supplement and largely replace existing public efforts.

According to the Appelbaum group, establishment of a social housing sector, if organized according to the outline provided, would have several advantages over continuation of existing public efforts. First, if the production of social housing were financed by capital grants rather than depending on borrowing in private capital markets, the actual cost of housing would be reduced and low-income households would have improved access to housing. Second, if the social housing sector were organized to give tenants a major voice in management of the environment, it would serve as a means to empower those who, until this point, have largely been left out of the political process. Social housing would address the housing needs of currently excluded groups even as it would give them increased control of their lives.

Largely ignoring the obvious question of how, in an environment of extreme competition for scarce resources, it will be possible to convince Congress to provide resources adequate to fund their proposal, and making very optimistic assumptions about the potential for large-scale and long-term successes in the area of tenant-managed housing, the Appelbaum group calls for four specific pieces of legislation to create a social housing sector.

The first is called the National Tenant Protection and Private Rental Housing Conversion Act. It is intended to protect private-sector tenants from arbitrary evictions, excessive rent increases and undermaintenance while facilitating the phased conversion of a significant share of private rental units to social housing. It is clear that rent control or "ordinances governing rent increases" is a central feature of this act. The fact that rent controls are likely to discourage the production of new rental units or the maintenance of existing apartments is evidently of little concern. It is somehow assumed that the social housing sector, financed with plenty of federal dollars, will be able to absorb any private rental properties that cannot survive under rent control. The costs of this act are put at $5.6 billion annually.

The second piece of legislation is the National Homeowner Protection Act. Applicable to socially owned or subsidized housing, this law would restrict sale, conversion, or demolition of such housing, prevent economic displacement of low-income residents, and prohibit eviction of tenants except for egregious behavior. Tenants would be granted lifetime tenure. Evidently, the authors place little credence in the findings of some observers that lifetime tenure in public sector housing in Britain has dampened the willingness of workers to move to areas of improved job opportunities. The potentially adverse effect of lifetime tenure on the mobility of workers goes unrecognized. In any case, the annual cost for this program would be $8 billion.

A third element of the proposal is the Subsidized Housing Preservation Act, designed to protect existing federally subsidized housing, including public housing, from conversion, demolition, undermaintenance, and neglect. The cost of such a program, which includes provisions for tenant management and technical support, is estimated at $5 billion a year.

The Social Housing Production and Financing Act, which would limit the federal housing-related finance effort to production and rehabilitation within the social sector, is the fourth and most expensive of the Acts. Federal grants adequate to finance the level of production required to meet the housing needs of the target groups would be at the level of $20 billion annually, with another $13 billion needed annually for operating subsidies.

In order to get some perspective on the scale of commitment required to carry out the policies proposed in these Acts, it is useful to note that under the FMHA Section 514/516 farmworker housing program which supplies a precedent for federal grants for the production of low-income housing, the amount obligated for Section 516 grants since 1974 has averaged $12 million a year. When that figure is compared to the annual $50 billion price tag for the proposed programs, the precedent seems somewhat less than compelling.

It is very doubtful that the proposed package can serve as the basis for any administration's housing program. Such a prospect reminds one of Theodore Sorensen's reflections on what a President can and cannot do. After two years as Special Counsel to President Kennedy, Sorensen wrote:

> [A President] is free to choose only: 1) within the limits of permissibility; 2) within the limits of available resources; 3) within the limits of available time; 4) within the limits of previous commitments; and 5) within the limits of available information (Sorensen 1963, 23).

The Appelbaum group seems unprepared to accept resource or political limitations. They ignore the fact that allocating $50 billion to one sector has consequences—that increased support for housing would be just as likely to be at the expense of Social Security or health benefits or a program to deal with acid rain as with defense commitments. Nor do they recognize the limitations of information or understanding or market dynamics—that, for example, an unanticipated withdrawal of builders, lenders, or investors from private rental housing might produce severe short-term housing shortages and market disruptions.

But although the Appelbaum package as a whole lacks credibility for policy advisers, it is not without potentially usable ideas.

- Limited-equity cooperatives is one such idea. It is not a brand-new concept, but it fits well with the Appelbaum emphasis on tenant identification with and control of the buildings and neighborhoods they live in.
- The buy-out of rental buildings that might otherwise be lost to the housing inventory is, with appropriate safeguards, an approach worth trying.
- The proposal to shift from a homeowner tax deduction for mortgage interest to a capped tax credit would be a move toward equity—a notion endorsed by a number of mainstream economists.
- The idea of a progressive transfer tax on luxury apartments and homes, with the proceeds earmarked for subsidized low-income housing, has some appeal, especially in a period of budget stringency when funds for low-income housing will be scarce.

There are many intriguing and challenging ideas in this very ambitious package. One need not subscribe to the entire package to acknowledge that it is an imaginative and carefully elaborated schema for improving the housing conditions of low-income people in America.

As President Kennedy wrote, to govern is to choose. Many would choose a different kind of program—one that retains market discipline and incentives for producers and investors while at the same time addressing the needs of tenants and low-income people. While the market approach has fallen short in providing decent housing for low-income people, so have the efforts of countries that place less emphasis on the market and more on government. A friend who has studied housing policies in many countries recently said, "There is no one way to approach the problem of raising housing standards for low-income people."

We need a variety of practical tools, not a holistic theory of what might be. In housing policy, as elsewhere, the perfect is the enemy of the good.

REFERENCE

Sorensen, Theodore C. 1963. *Decision-Making in the White House*. New York: Columbia University Press.

13

SHELTER-POVERTY IN BOSTON: PROBLEM AND PROGRAM

Michael E. Stone

This chapter argues, first, that most housing problems in Boston and throughout the nation are ultimately the result of the squeeze between inadequate household incomes, on the one hand, and the cost of profitably providing housing, on the other. It also argues that housing costs and incomes together are the most decisive determinants of the overall quality of life for families and communities. Third, it contends that the long history of inadequate attempts to cope with the affordability problem not only has failed to solve the problem, but indeed has contributed to the broader and serious problems of the overall economy, with resultant impact on Boston's budget, employment, and other vital areas, as well as its housing market.

Each of these three themes suggests, correspondingly, a major direction for public policy. First, housing policies—at the local as well as the state and national levels—must be coupled with and include policies for increasing and redistributing income. Second, housing policies must be formulated with explicit recognition of and attention to their capacity to affect the quality of life far beyond the provision of decent, affordable housing. Third, there can be no solution to the housing problem without a solution to the broader political and economic crisis, but at the same time there can be no solution to the broader problems that does not deal with the structural roots of the housing crisis.

The housing affordability problem in Boston is examined quantitatively through the lens of a concept called "shelter-poverty"—a sliding scale of affordability reflecting the interaction among incomes, shelter costs, and the cost of nonshelter necessities. The approach provides a model for housing needs assessment that can be utilized in any locality, as well as for the country as a whole. Applied to Boston, the concept reveals that a family of four would have needed an income of $28,000 to have been able to afford the median-priced, unsubsidized two-bedroom apartment available in the city in 1985, while an elderly couple would have needed an income of $14,000 to have been able to afford the median-priced one-bedroom apartment. Nearly 40 percent of the households in Boston were shelter-poor in 1985, compared with one-third in 1980. Most are renters, and most have incomes of under $10,000. The city's booming economy not only has failed to benefit a sizable portion of the people of Boston, it actually has exacerbated their housing problems, through rampant speculation, wholesale condominium conversions, property tax increases, arson for profit, and loss of support for public and subsidized housing, all of which have been part of the boom.

In view of the deep sources and pervasive consequences of the housing problem, a solution must be based upon the following principles:

- the establishment of housing as a right rather than a commodity
- the promotion of social, nonprofit production and ownership of housing
- the reduction and eventual elimination of credit in the production and transfer of housing

(An elaboration of these principles may be found in Chapter 12, by the Institute for Policy Studies Working Group on Housing.)

A set of policy proposals, consistent with the above principles, are presented for beginning to deal with the housing problem in the city. While addressed to the particular situation of Boston, nearly all of the proposals are appropriate and adaptable for most localities throughout the country, affirming the possibilities yet acknowledging the limitations of local action, especially with regard to the third principle.

Although the structural changes required to truly solve the housing problem must occur nationally, local policies aimed at both the housing cost and income sides of the problem can begin to make an impact locally while serving as models for large-scale reform. Because of fiscal constraints and continued skepticism about the efficacy of traditional spending programs, the proposed policies focus primarily on institutional change rather than major expenditures. Local leaders, local governments, and community groups have the potential to exert great leadership and initiative nationally for a new understanding of the nature and causes of the housing problem, and thus for new kinds of policy directions to effectively address this profound problem of Boston and our entire society.

THE NATURE OF THE HOUSING PROBLEM

Most housing problems can be traced logically or historically to the problem of affordability—the squeeze between incomes on the one hand and housing costs on the other.[1] Problems of physical condition and space, security of tenure, community viability, the amount, type, and location of new construction, and the allocation of public and private financial resources to housing—that is, not just the obvious cost problems of rents, utilities, taxes, interest rates, and sales prices—are ultimately traceable to the squeeze between incomes and housing costs.

Several aspects of the relationship between incomes and housing costs are important to understand. First of all, the interaction between incomes and housing costs is fundamentally different from the relationship between incomes and the cost of any other necessity of life. Why should this be so? Housing is physically quite different from other consumption items: it is large, durable, tied to location, and generally must be purchased as a complete dwelling unit, not as a shopping basket of separately selected items (like rooms, facilities, amenities, location) in the way that food and clothing are purchased. And because housing is not literally consumed the way that food is, and thus is not purchased anew on a regular and frequent basis, once a household begins to consume the services of a particular dwelling it is relatively hard to alter the amount and type of housing services consumed; that is, it is much harder to move than to, say, switch food stores or food items or defer buying new clothing. What this means is that the amount that we have to pay for housing tends to be rather rigid and inflexible. Housing costs thus tend to represent the first claim on the disposable income of a household. Everything else generally has to fit into what remains of the income after paying for housing. To be sure, in extreme emergencies people are going to buy food to stay alive even if it means not meeting their housing expenses, but in general people adjust their other expenditures to fit the constraints of their housing costs and incomes rather than adjusting their housing costs to fit their other expenses.

Furthermore, because of the bulkiness of housing, its immobility, and its attachment to land, when one purchases housing one is not just obtaining the services of the dwelling but the advantages and disadvantages of the location, in terms of social environment, physical environment, accessibility, municipal services, and so forth. The amount that a household can and does pay for housing thus determines the character of the entire environment in which they live—not just the quality of their dwelling unit—in a way that is unmatched by any other consumption expenditure.

A NEW AFFORDABILITY SCALE

The conventional view of the housing affordability problem is based upon a certain notion of how much people reasonably can be expected to pay—namely, the frequently invoked 25 percent of income rule-of-thumb. Even this rule-of-thumb is subject to various adjustments and interpretations, depending upon one's point of view, prevailing economic conditions, and one's political position. At different times and in different situations, anywhere from 20 to 30 percent has been considered appropriate.

What follows is a challenge to the assumption that any particular percentage, regardless of what it is, makes sense. This does not mean that it is impossible to arrive at a quantitative standard of affordability, but rather that one particular percentage should not be applied in all cases. As suggested in the above analysis of the distinctive nature of housing costs, a more logical and defensible approach is to use a sliding scale of affordability to establish reasonable housing costs for any household.

Imagine two very different households of comparable disposable (that is, after-tax) incomes, one a single person, the other a single parent with five children. What would be the difference in the cost of non-shelter necessities of life based upon some specified level of adequacy for these necessities? Obviously, the large household would need substantially more for its non-shelter necessities than would the small household to achieve comparable material quality of life. This implies that the larger household can afford to spend a smaller share of their comparable income for housing than can the small household, if they are to meet their nonshelter needs at the given level of adequacy.

Similarly, two households of the same size but different after-tax incomes would require about the same amount to purchase a comparable non-shelter standard of living.This would of course leave less to spend on shelter for the family with a lower income. The higher-income household thus could afford to spend more on housing, as a percentage of income as well as in dollars.

The above examples capture the principle that, due to the special character of housing costs, there is a maximum amount that a household reasonably can be expected to pay for shelter, and that the amount will vary based not just on household income but also on other household characteristics. There simply is no single percentage of income that can transcend differences among different types and sizes of households. In general, for a given level of income, smaller households can afford to spend more money and hence a higher percentage of income for housing than can larger households, if both households are to have comparable ability to pay for other necessities, such as food and medical care.

In the market today, most households do not pay what they actually can afford; many pay more, while some pay less. This variation does not reflect free choice among limitless opportunities. Opportunities do not match need and ability to pay. As a result, people pay what they must in order to obtain shelter, and then cannot adequately meet their non-shelter needs. I have labeled such a state "shelter-poverty," a situation that does not refer to inadequate housing, but rather to deprivation of nonshelter necessities resulting from having to pay a more-than-affordable amount for housing.

In order to operationalize the concept of a sliding scale of affordability, it is necessary to determine what constitutes a minimum level of adequacy for non-shelter items and what would be the cost of achieving this minimum level, recognizing that the cost will certainly be different for each size household and will change over time as prices change; it will also vary geographically with climate and price differences, although geographical averaging is possible.

The Bureau of Labor Statistics' (BLS) Lower Budgets are used to establish the cost of nonshelter necessities at a minimum level of adequacy.[2] Utilizing these figures, scaled for various size households, and taking into account income taxes and Social Security taxes, I have operationalized the sliding scale of affordability developed above. Figures 13.1 through 13.6 present the scale for Boston for 1985. They reveal, for example, that in 1985 on average a family of four with a gross income of under $23,500 could not have afforded as much as 25 percent for shelter; indeed, if their income was under $16,000 they could not have afforded anything for shelter and still met their non-shelter necessities at the minimum level specified by the BLS Lower Budget. One-person, elderly households, on the other hand, could have afforded 25 percent for shelter at an income of about $5,000 and a greater percentage at higher incomes (if they have full medical insurance), but six-person households needed an income of over $38,000 to have been able to afford 25 percent of income for housing in Boston in 1985.

SHELTER-POVERTY IN BOSTON

In order to determine the extent and distribution of shelter-poverty among Boston households, it is necessary to match the sliding scale of affordability against actual housing expenditures. Housing expenditures for renters in Boston for 1985—cross-tabulated by income and household size—have been obtained from the Boston Redevelopment Authority Household Survey and matched against the affordability scale in Figures 13.1 through 13.6 (Boston Redevelopment Authority and Neighborhood Development and Employment Agency 1985).

This analysis reveals that more than 61,000 renter families—nearly 42 percent of all renter households in Boston—were shelter-poor in 1985. In 1980, by way of comparison, a little over 58,000 renter households were shelter-poor, 37 percent of renter households.[3]

Yet while the number of shelter-poor renters was increasing, the available rental stock was shrinking. In 1980 there were over 131,000 private rental units in the city of Boston; by 1985 there were fewer than 122,000. More than 13,000 apartments in multi-family structures were converted to condominiums during this period, a loss not nearly offset by the net addition of about 2,400 private rental units in one-to-four-family buildings and the net addition of 2,700 subsidized private and public units (Goetze 1985).

Among those renters with incomes of under $10,000, 85 percent (46,500 families) were shelter-poor in 1985, compared with 59 percent in 1980. Shelter-poverty is especially concentrated among these lowest-income families, who accounted for 76 percent of the shelter-poverty among renters. Most of the balance had incomes of $10,000 to $15,000, with a rate of shelter-poverty of 51 percent, comprising another 9,000 families unable to afford their housing in 1985.

Shelter-poverty is thus a pervasive problem in this city. Yet the quantification

Figure 13.1
Maximum Affordable Shelter Cost in Dollars—2 Married Adults and Children (Boston, 1985)

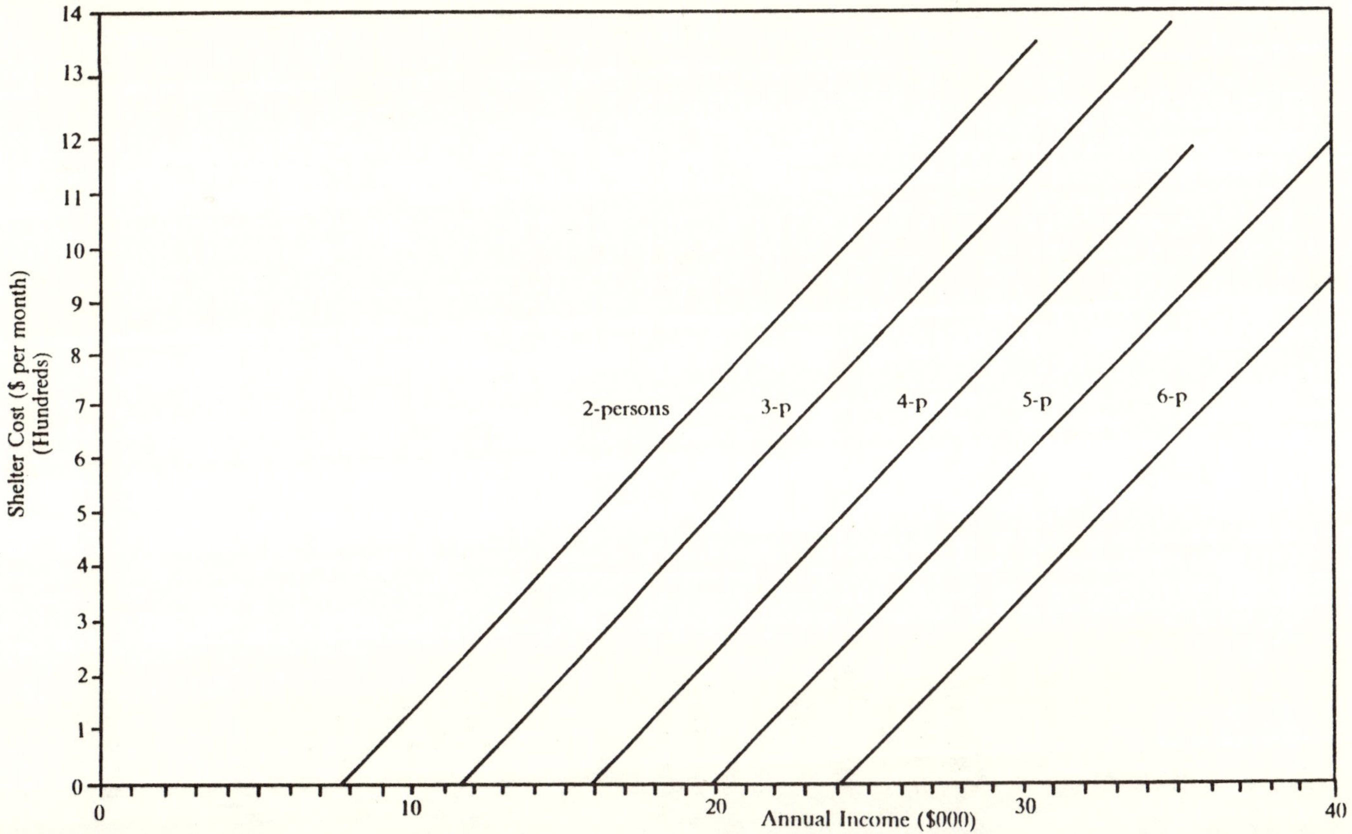

Figure 13.2
Maximum Affordable Shelter Cost as Percentage of Income—2 Married Adults and Children (Boston, 1985)

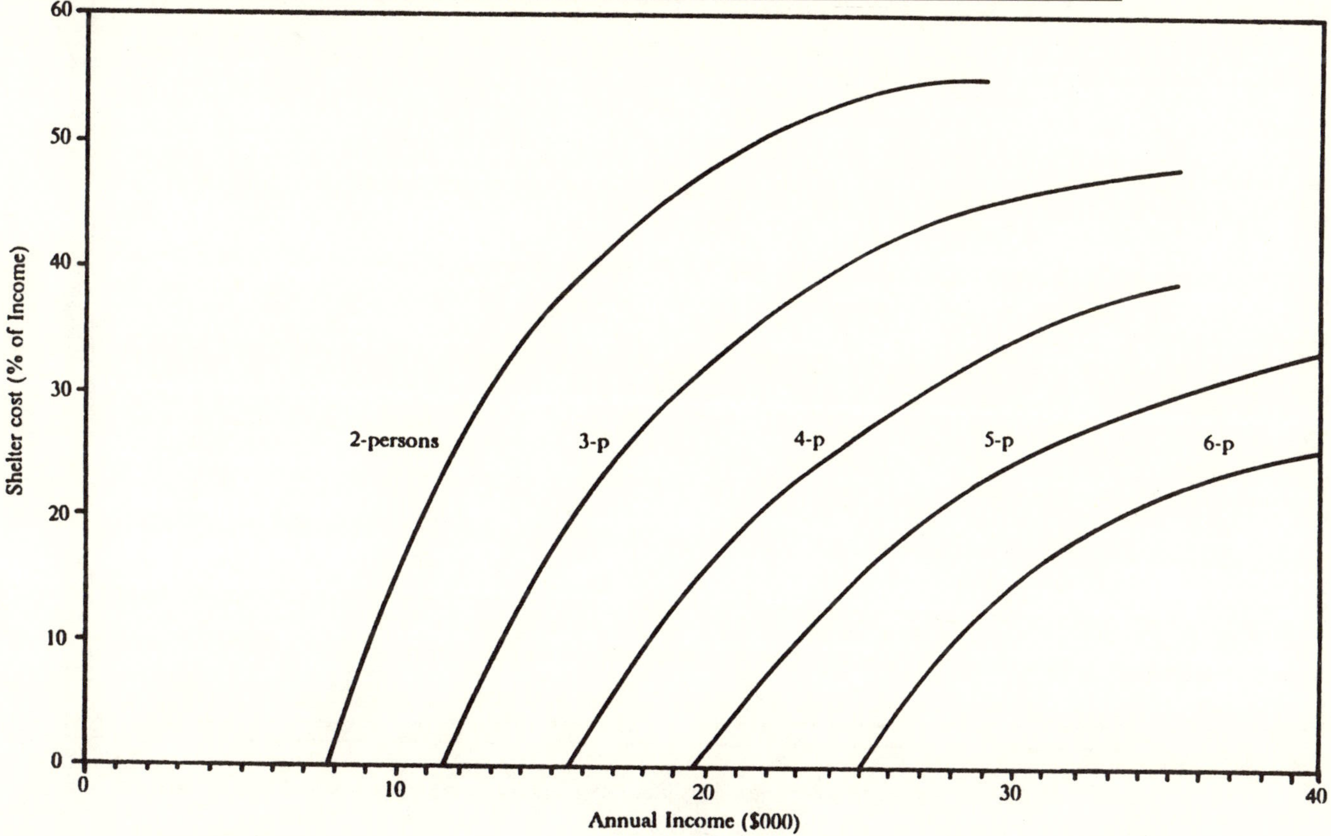

Figure 13.3
Maximum Affordable Shelter Cost in Dollars—Single Adult and Children (Boston, 1985)

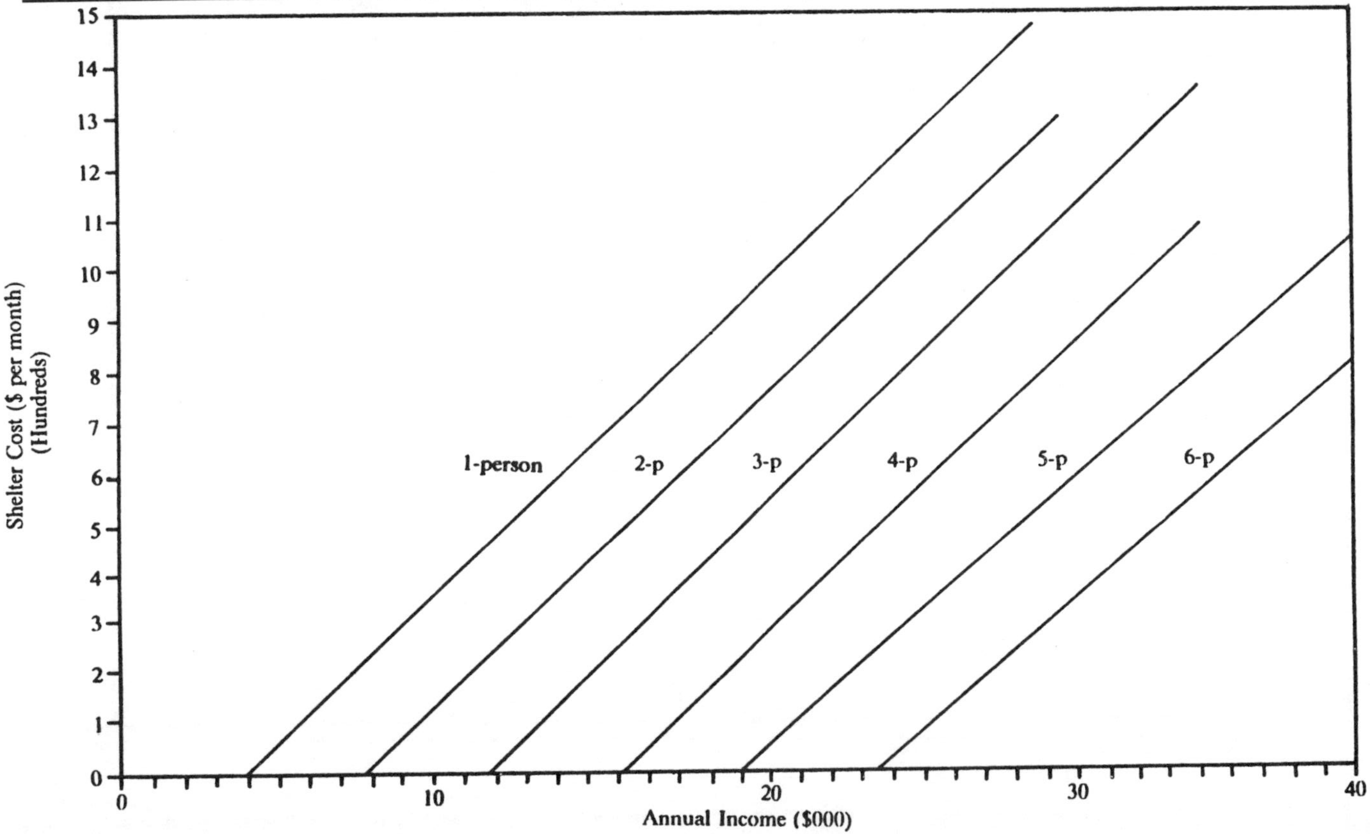

Figure 13.4
Maximum Affordable Shelter Cost as Percentage of Income—Single Adult and Children (Boston, 1985)

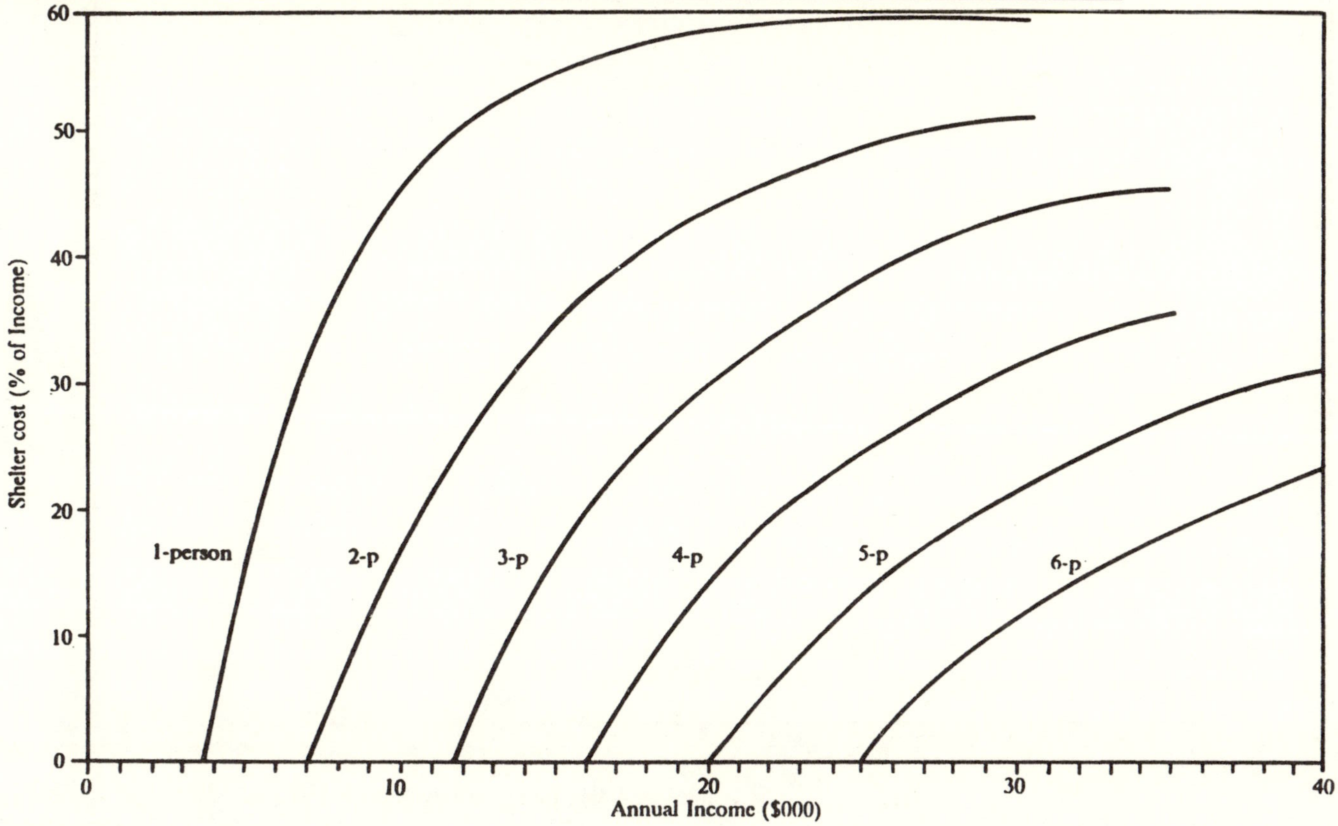

Figure 13.5
Maximum Affordable Shelter Cost in Dollars—The Elderly (Boston, 1985)

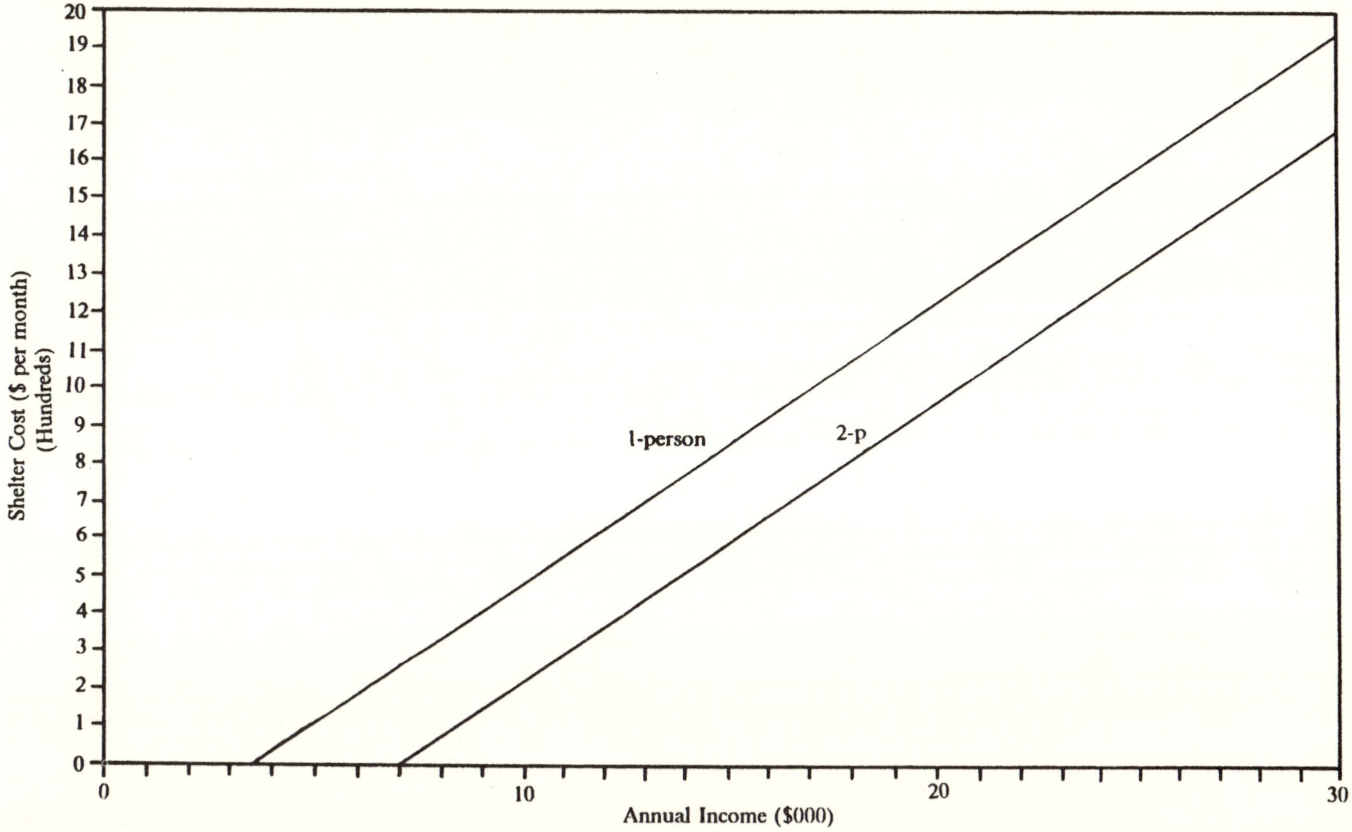

Figure 13.6
Maximum Affordable Shelter Cost as Percentage of Income—The Elderly (Boston, 1985)

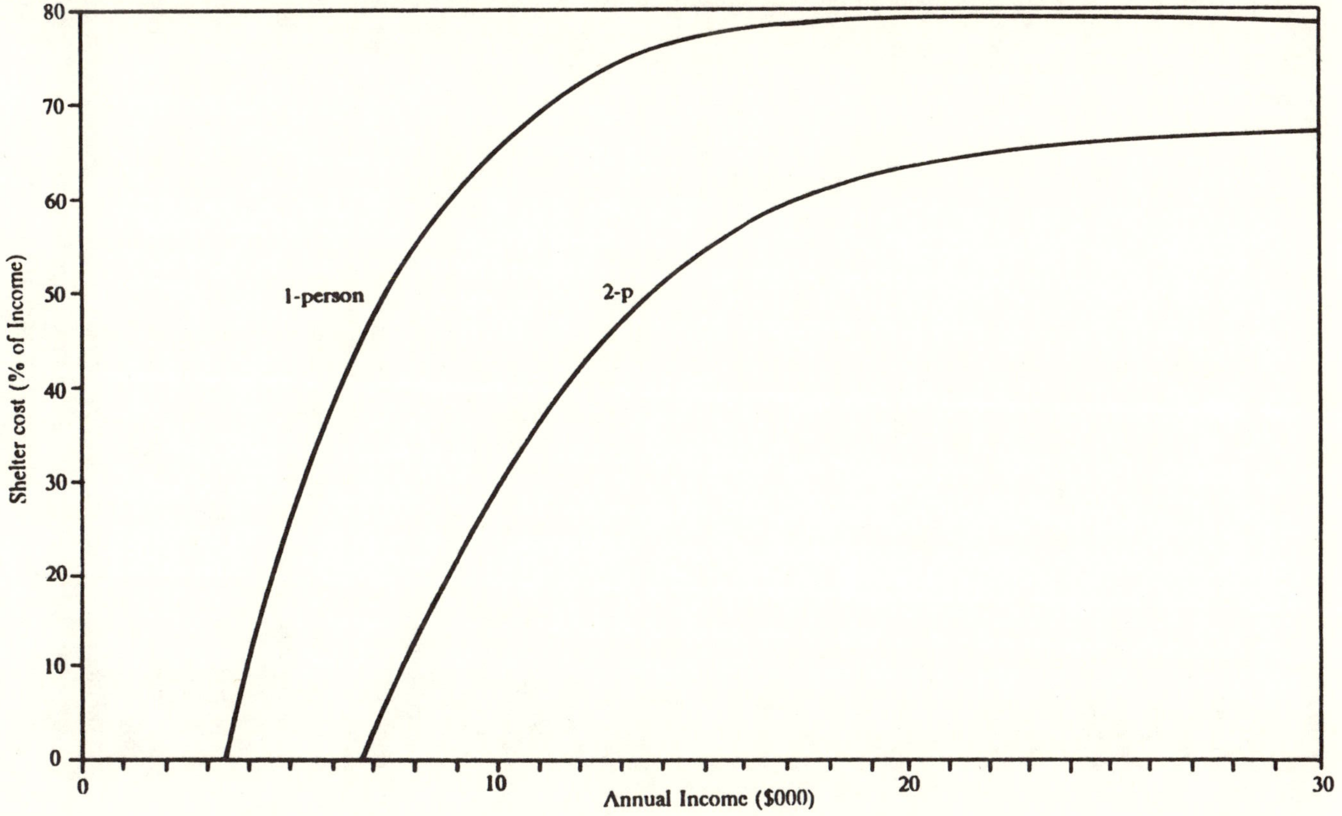

of housing affordability in this way cannot be said to exaggerate the problem, for, comparing the incidence of shelter-poverty with the extent of households paying more than 25 percent of income for shelter, we find that 54 percent of all renter households—and 86 percent of renters under $10,000—were paying over 25 percent in 1985.

The shelter-poverty approach may in fact be a relatively conservative measure of the affordability problem. It is, however, more sensitive to the effect of household size on ability to pay than is the traditional 25 percent measure. Thus, while 42 percent of all renter families in Boston were shelter-poor in 1985, just 35 percent of one- and two-person households were shelter-poor; by contrast, 51 percent of three- and four-person renter families and 76 percent of five-or-more-person families were shelter-poor.

Unfortunately, the 1985 survey did not obtain housing cost data for homeowners, and even Census and American Housing Survey data are for owners of single-family houses only, so it is not possible to determine precisely the extent of shelter-poverty among homeowners in Boston, a city with an unusually high number of owner-occupied two-, three-, and four-unit buildings. It is possible to make a rough estimate, though, utilizing the 1985 BRA survey's breakdown of income relative to household size among homeowners. If a homeowner family of a given size and income is as likely to be shelter-poor as a renter family of the same size and income, then about 33 percent of Boston homeowner households were shelter-poor in 1985, including 90 percent of homeowner households with incomes under $10,000. In numerical terms, since there were about 65,000 owner-occupied units in the city in 1985, excluding condominiums (Goetze 1985), this would suggest that over 18,000 homeowners were shelter-poor in 1985, compared with nearly 16,000 in 1980. Of course, long-term owners of a given size and income are probably somewhat less likely to be shelter-poor than equivalent renters (due to fixed-payment mortgages secured at historically lower interest rates), but more recent buyers are more likely to be shelter-poor than renters of the same income and household size, so this estimate has some uncertainty in both directions. Since these figures exclude condominium owners, some of whom are probably shelter-poor, it can be said with considerable confidence that at least 18,000 homeowner families in Boston were shelter-poor in 1985.

With 61,000 shelter-poor renter families and 18,000 shelter-poor homeowners in Boston, there are nearly 80,000 families—almost three-eighths of the city—faced with a squeeze between their incomes and housing costs that leaves insufficient resources to meet their other basic needs adequately.

Another view of the affordability problem of people seeking housing in Boston may be obtained by analyzing ads for private rental units. While advertised rents tend to be somewhat higher than rents paid in occupied units, the data are still quite useful for understanding the housing affordability problem.

The results of a survey of over 3,400 apartment ads that appeared in the *Boston Sunday Globe* in the winter and spring of 1985 are summarized in Figure 13.7.

Figure 13.7
Rents of Private Unsubsidized Units Available for Rent (Boston, 1980–87)

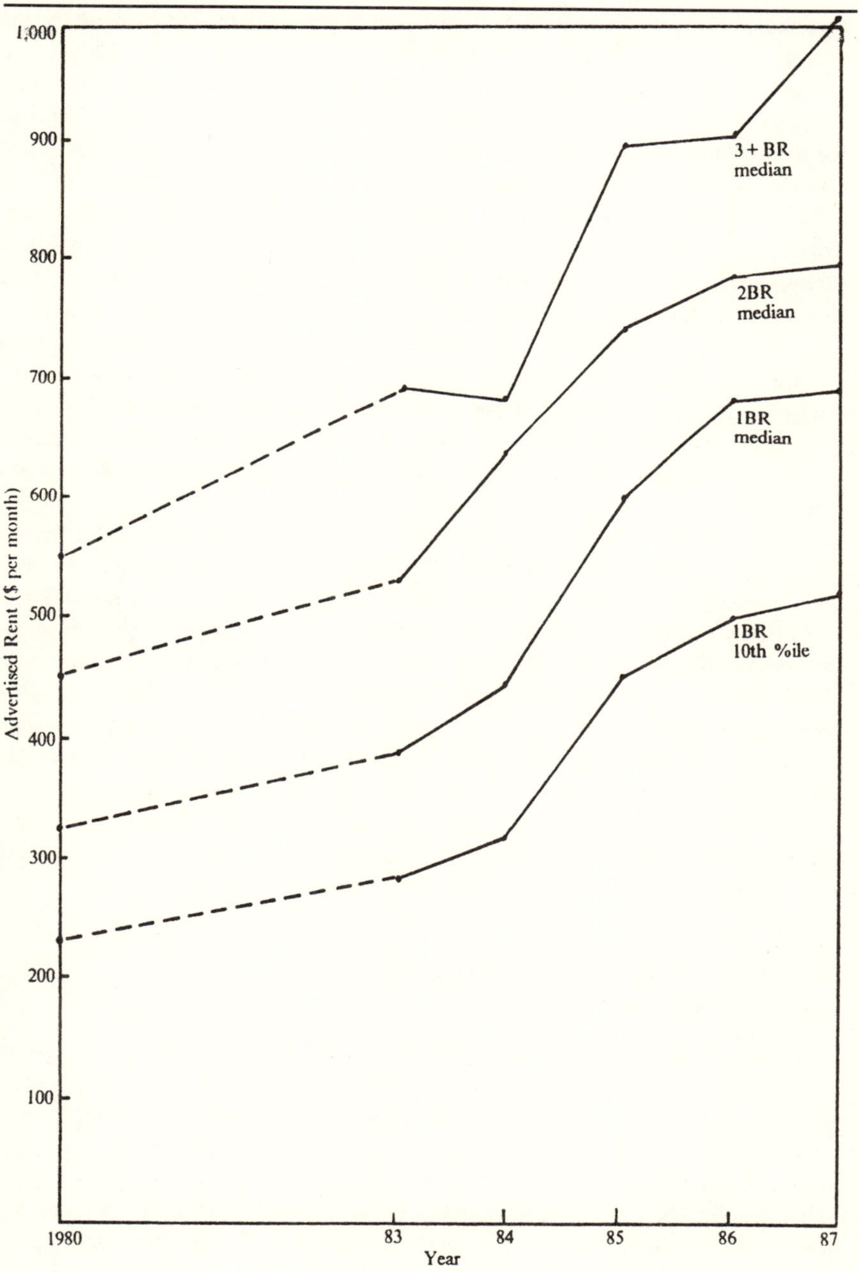

Source: Boston Sunday Globe (apartment ads, 3-week intervals, first and second quarter of each year)

Of these, about one-eighth were studio apartments, about three-eighths were one-bedroom, about three-eighths were two-bedroom, and approximately one-eighth were three-or-more-bedroom units; that is, three-quarters of all the advertised apartments had one or two bedrooms. The median rent of these 3,400-plus available units were $670; the tenth percentile was $440. Virtually no apartments, other than studios, were available at rents of less than $400 a month. The median rent for one-bedroom units was $618, for two-bedrooms $737, and for three-plus bedrooms $888. An unpublished survey using the same methodology conducted during the same period of 1983 yielded median rents of about $400, $535, and $700 for one-, two-, and three-plus bedroom units, respectively. That is, in a period of just two years, from 1983 to 1985, rents of available private apartments in Boston increased typically by about $200 a month. Thus, if a family had moved in 1983 and again in 1985, they would have needed an increase of $2,400 in their annual income over this period to be able to obtain a comparable apartment—even if none of their other expenses had increased. And a similar survey of over 4,500 ads for the first four months of 1987 found that the median had increased to $736 and the tenth percentile to $510 a month; virtually no units, other than studios, were available for under $500 a month (see Figure 13.7).

The distribution of private market rents by unit size can be matched against the housing affordability scale in Figure 13.6 to get a more complete picture of the income/housing cost gap (see Figures 13.8 through 13.10). Households of one or two persons needed an income of at least $15,500 to be able to afford the median-priced one-bedroom unit for rent in Boston in 1985; if they were below $10,000, nothing was affordable in the private market.Three- and four-person households needed nearly $28,000 for the median-priced two-bedroom units; if their income was below $20,000, nothing was affordable. Most dramatically, five-or-more-person households needed an income of at least $38,000 a year to be able to afford the median-priced three-bedroom apartment, and below $29,000 could afford none of the few available units.

SOME CAUSES AND CONSEQUENCES OF THE HOUSING PROBLEM

Housing affordability problems in Boston occur within a context of long-term national economic instability, as well as local forces of uneven development, in which the private ownership and development of land and housing has been a crucial ingredient. Over the past three decades, the Boston economy has undergone a dramatic transformation, writing off much of its declining commercial and manufacturing base, and, building upon its traditional strength in finance and higher education, becoming a regional, national, and international center of high technology, medical, and other services as well as finance and education, with an employment structure of high-paying technical and managerial jobs on

Figure 13.8
Percent of Available 1-BR Apartments Affordable by 1 and 2 Pers. Hhlds. (Boston, 1985)

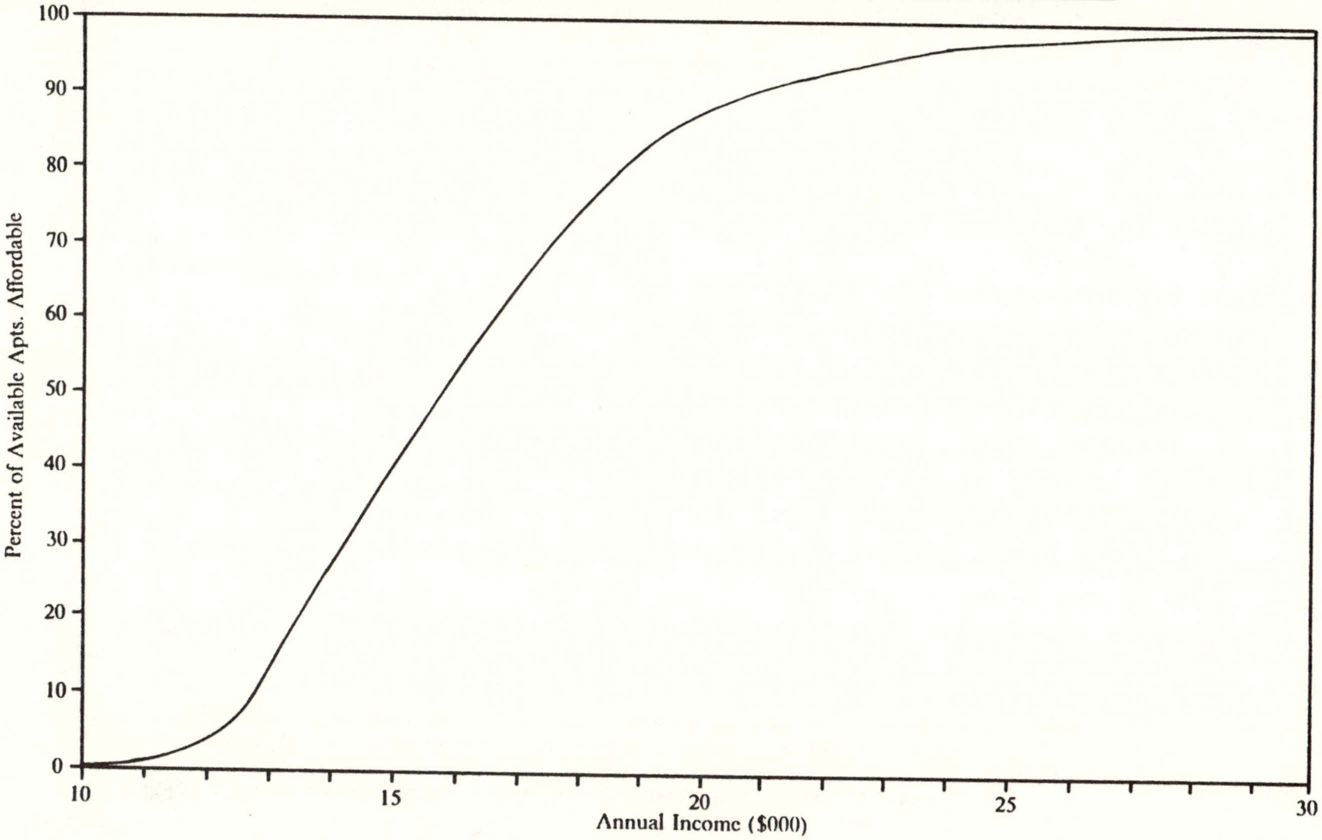

Figure 13.9
Percent of Available 2-BR Apartments Affordable by 3 and 4 Pers. Hhlds. (Boston, 1985)

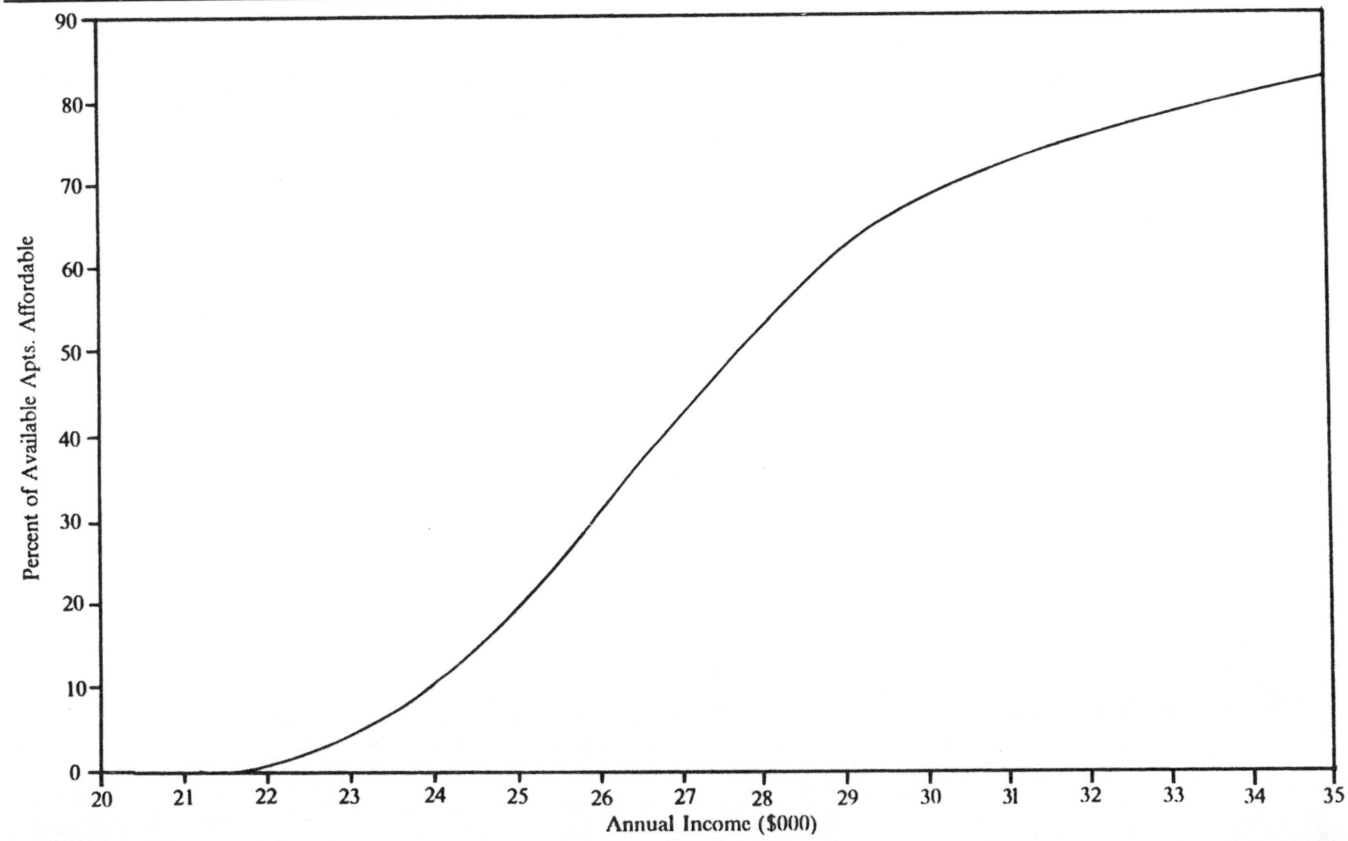

Figure 13.10
Percent of Available 3-BR Apartments Affordable by 5 and 6 Pers. Hhlds. (Boston, 1985)

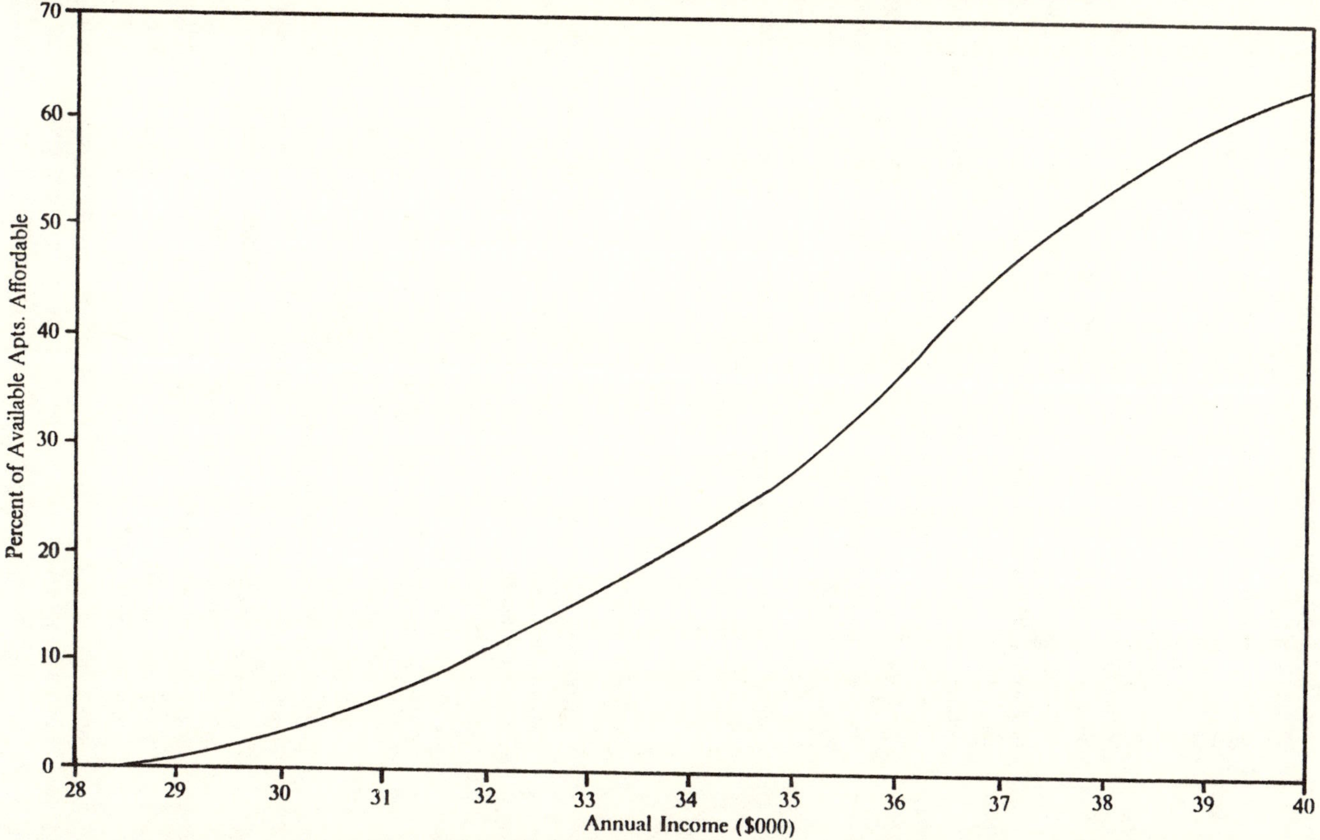

one side, and low-wage service and clerical jobs on the other (Gaston and Kennedy 1985a, 1985b, 1987; Stone 1978a; 1978b).

The result for the residential communities of Boston itself and many older inner suburbs has been waves of disinvestment and speculative reinvestment—at various rates and in various forms. While soaring rents and sales prices, condominium and luxury rental conversions, "upscale" arson (to clear out tenants and generate cash for luxury rehab), and publicly supported urban renewal have swept across even more neighborhoods, lower-income people have been and continue to be displaced, and in communities of color especially this process has followed earlier rounds of abandonment and "downscale" arson (Gaston and Kennedy 1987; Brady 1983; Frisby 1986a, 1986b, 1986c, 1986d; for a detailed analysis of the situation of Boston's black community in relation to the "New Boston," see Clay 1985).

Meanwhile, the city government's dependence on property taxes and borrowing has caused continuing fiscal problems: earlier revenue inadequacy has not been relieved by the booming real estate market because a state-wide property tax revolt has restricted this revenue source, even though lower-income homeowners now face substantial tax increases as their assessed valuations rise (Achtenberg and Stone 1977; Stein 1986; Quill 1986a, 1986b).

A WAY OUT?

Strategies consistent with traditional conservative and liberal perspectives cannot adequately resolve the problems generated in the process outlined above. The conservative solution can be called a "managed depression." Conservatives have argued correctly that there can be no solution to the housing crisis without controlling inflation and that federal bail-out of the housing industry will not really solve the problem but will add to the federal deficit and to inflation. Their approach therefore has consisted of tight money and high interest rates on the monetary side; on the fiscal side they have provided tax cuts for large corporations and wealthy individuals to shield them from austerity, while severely cutting housing and community development, income maintenance, and social services spending in order to try to offset the tax cuts and increased military spending.

The conservative approach appears to some people as no more than a cynical attempt to protect big business and the wealthy from austerity while weakening the security of the working class (Piven and Cloward 1982); to others—including some who may dislike or disagree with these policies—it may seem like a realistic attempt to avoid cataclysm. Regardless of this perspective, however, the conservative approach will fail because the high social costs it imposes and the obvious inequity in the distribution of these costs will lead to political rejection. True conservatives have often had a fairly accurate understanding of the limits of liberal capitalism and have understood what is required economically to keep the system afloat. However, their policies involve a degree of social and economic injustice which has never been tolerable for very long by the majority of Americans. Thus, in the long run the conservative approach will not ever be fully played out, except under a far more authoritarian regime than we now have.

On the other hand, liberal policies, which in the past have always had and undoubtedly will again have greater political appeal, will lead unwittingly but inevitably to an unmanaged depression—to a genuine financial collapse—with uncertain but potentially terrifying social and political consequences. With the understandable goals of relieving austerity, assuring a little greater equity, and bailing out the housing and lending industries, the liberal approach would involve increased federal spending to maintain most housing and other social programs and to provide bailouts to distressed thrift institutions, builders and homeowners while only marginally increasing taxes and slowing the rates of growth of military spending. Thus, despite their declarations of a commitment to cut the federal deficit in order to reduce inflation and credit competition, the fiscal policies offered by liberals would almost certainly increase the federal deficit.

Liberal monetary policy involves, of course, an easing of tight money in order to accommodate the federal government's credit demands without crowding out housing, consumer borrowing, state and local governments, and other businesses. In the very short run, the effect would be a further boost to the economy and a reduction in defaults and bankruptcies by individuals and businesses, but soon inflation and speculation would again stretch the credit bubble beyond real growth in the economy, making a crash a very real possibility.

The only sensible and workable alternative, then, to managed versus unmanaged depression is one that goes beyond the conservative and liberal approaches and instead begins to deal with underlying causes: maldistribution of income, overdependence on credit, and ownership and investment arrangements that encourage speculation (in housing and industry) rather than production, employment, and social well-being.

A substantial amount of work has already been done and is continuing on the development of policies and programs for dealing with these causes and their consequences, both on an immediate emergency basis and in a long-term, more structural way (Achtenberg and Stone 1974; Stone and Achtenberg 1977; Hartman and Stone 1978). A national housing program to restructure the American housing system may be found in Chapter 12 of this volume (see also Hartman 1983; Hartman and Stone 1986).

A HOUSING PROGRAM FOR BOSTON

The following housing policy proposals constitute an elaboration of previous local efforts (the 1980 platform of the All-City Housing Organization and the City Life Housing Platform), incorporating some new ideas as well as some already being tried in Boston and elsewhere. The theme and commitment that unifies these proposals into a coherent program is "Housing as a Human Right" (Episcopal City Mission n.d.)[4]

While the emphasis is on the housing market side of the housing problem, some attention is also given to local options for addressing the income side of the affordability problem. In addition, even though in this era of federal austerity the focus is on local initiatives, the larger context must simultaneously be confronted, as the analysis has shown. There is thus included some discussion of possible roles for local leaders in addressing the housing problem and its causes at the state and national levels.

The set of policies proposed for the housing market side of the problem are presented under the following six major goals:

- preserving affordable rental housing
- facilitating homeownership without speculation
- preserving and upgrading government-assisted housing
- producing housing for nonspeculative ownership
- generating and channelling funds for social production and ownership
- establishing and enforcing a local Housing Bill of Rights

I. Preserving Affordable Rental Housing

Although more than 20 percent of the housing units in Boston are subsidized, most low- and moderate-income renters do not receive subsidies and, as the analysis has revealed, are shelter-poor. They are thus in need of measures which can at least limit—if not reduce—the cost of their housing. Some such measures can deal directly with the cost of housing. Others can have the effect of reducing displacement of low- and moderate-income people, as displacement usually results in both the loss of relatively lower-cost units and in displacees paying more for whatever housing they eventually obtain. Still others can permanently remove existing private rental housing from the speculative market. The following policies are proposed in this area under two subgoals.

A. Protect tenants and enhance the viability and affordability of the private rental housing stock.

1. Strengthen rent, eviction, and condominium-conversion controls. In the mid–1970s, when Boston had fairly strong rent control, which covered nearly all units except apartments in owner-occupied two- and three-family homes, about 85,000 units were under rent control. Since 1976 about 65,000 apartments have been removed from the rent control system—about 50,000 through vacancy decontrol and 15,000 through condominium conversions and substantial rehabilitation.

As one of his legislative priorities following his election in November 1983, Mayor Raymond Flynn urged the City Council to enact a slightly revised version of the Boston Home Protection Act which he had first introduced while still a member of the City Council. Under the revised Act, vacancy decontrol would be repealed, with the rents of recontrolled units set on the basis of average citywide increases in operating and maintenance expenses and property taxes since decontrol; thus, the rents of many units would be reduced below current levels. The Act would allow rent increases only for documented increases in operating expenses and property taxes; there would be an automatic reduction for code violations, a tenant consent requirement for capital improvements other than to correct code violations, and capitalization of the cost of repairs over their useful lives. Exemptions from coverage would be limited, and evictions for condominium conversion as well as other conversions likely to result in substantial displacement would not be permitted. To date the Council has only enacted several weaker bills, which continue vacancy decontrol but do strengthen eviction protections and provide tenant-initiated rent grievance procedures for decontrolled units.

It is time to recognize rent and eviction controls as an integral and permanent feature of local policy and regulation, analogous to zoning and housing codes. There is no reason why a competent city administration cannot administer such regulations efficiently and fairly. The principal difficulties of rent and eviction controls stem not from their existence, but from uncertainty about their duration and inadequacies in their administration. Recognizing that rent and eviction controls are neither stopgap measures nor the be-all of local policy for rental housing, the city of Boston should establish a stronger system (equivalent to that of Cambridge and Brookline) and then direct its energies more to other necessary housing policies.

2. Strictly enforce the State Sanitary Code, with community and resident participation, using condemnation where appropriate, and encourage the Housing Court to use the Boston Citywide Land Trust (see section B1 below) and nonprofit community development corporations (CDCs) as receivers.

3. Require owners of rental housing to use fire insurance proceeds to restore fire-damaged buildings for existing residents. Arson-for-profit has proven to be a terrifyingly effective way for some landlords to deal with the income/housing cost squeeze. To stop this crime will require active municipal and neighborhood monitoring of property transactions and landlord behavior. But it will also require elimination of the financial incentives. The city administration should at least seek home rule authority—and indeed lead statewide efforts—for fire insurance reform. There should be limitations on the disbursement of fire insurance proceeds in the event of incendiary or suspicious causes; the city should be named loss payee, as mortgage holders now are, with the power to ensure and require that rental property be restored to habitable condition substantially equivalent to prefire conditions, and that a fire not be an excuse for removal of the housing from rent-controlled stock. In addition, landlords should be required to have sufficient coverage to pay relocation expenses and housing costs in excess of prefire levels for displaced tenants for a period of one year. These measures, along with much greater commitment to criminal investigation, can help save both affordable housing and human lives.

4. Establish statutory life tenure rights for tenants who continue to pay their

legally established rent and do not interfere with the rights of other tenants. The just-cause eviction protections now provided to tenants in rent-controlled and vacancy-decontrolled apartments in Boston provide considerable security of tenure, although condominium eviction protection is not absolute. Also, tenants in buildings that never were under rent control do not have such just-cause eviction protection. In addition, although Massachusetts has fairly strong protections against retaliatory evictions, as well as eviction defenses for substandard conditions, active organizing and education are also essential. The Eviction-Free Zone in Roxbury and Jamaica Plain, which was announced in the fall of 1985 by a coalition of community groups, can provide a model for legal defense and political action,[5] in conjunction with statutory life tenure. The city's rent control enabling law may permit establishment of such tenure for all tenants, but a more legally secure approach would be the enactment of the proposed state just-cause-for-eviction bill.

5. Legislatively recognize the rights of tenants to form unions and bargain collectively.

6. Strengthen the enforcement powers of the Boston Fair Housing Commission to protect the rights of renters. The Boston Fair Housing Commission was established by the city in 1982 in response to documented patterns of racial discrimination and segregation in housing, which led to threats from HUD to withhold Community Development Block Grant (CDBG) funds if the city continued to fail to promote fair housing. The Commission has, however, only had the power to investigate and not to penalize violators, thus leading to minimal improvement in housing opportunities.

7. Support financial assistance to enhance affordability and protect tenants against homelessness. While the city government is not in a financial position to provide direct rental assistance, and federal cutbacks in Section 8 rental assistance will no doubt be felt for some time, efforts should be made to get the state government to expand its rental assistance. Although expansion of the state Chapter 707 rental assistance program is an obvious measure, a less apparent but equally important possibility in assisting affordability for many low-income families is Aid to Families with Dependent Children (AFDC). About 70–80 percent of AFDC recipients live in private rental housing, and the Welfare Department admits its grants are too low to afford decent housing. (See also Chapter 6 by Sandra Newman and Ann Schnare.) Statewide political and legal efforts are underway to substantially increase AFDC grants, focusing particularly on the problem of increasing homelessness among AFDC families and the inadequacy of the grants to cover the cost of private market rents (Bennett 1985; Massachusetts Coalition for the Homeless 1986; Stone 1986a).[6] Local officials and housing activists should join in such political and legal efforts.

B. Reduce speculation and facilitate conversion of the private rental stock to nonspeculative forms of ownership.

Private rental housing is increasingly being recognized as an anachronism, at least by those landlords who are converting to condos, abandoning their buildings, or burning them for the insurance money. To the extent that city policies make conversion and arson no longer available or profitable, and to the extent that tenant militancy has resulted in greater legal protection and municipal enforcement, landlords who wish to bail out should be able to do so in ways that are not harmful to tenants. Therefore, mechanisms must be established—or existing mechanisms more fully utilized—to facilitate conversion of private rental housing to forms of social or nonspeculative ownership, such as non-equity or limited-equity co-ops, mutual housing associations, life estate condominiums (that is, establishing the possibility of eventual speculative resale but ensured life tenure for existing occupants), ownership by community trusts or public ownership.

In order to achieve such transfer of ownership without increasing rents but with compensation to the former owner, it would be necessary first for the new ownership entity to assume any existing mortgages, perhaps with a renegotiated interest rate plus restrictions on refinancing prior to sale or mortgaging at inflated amounts in order to pull out equity. Second, the departing owner might receive not cash but a mortgage for the agreed equity, with the monthly payment on this mortgage not exceeding the cash flow the former owner realized (unless the old mortgage could be renegotiated at a lower rate, in which case the former owner could get more, thus providing an incentive not to inflate mortgages just before sale).

Patterns of private ownership, financing, and disinvestment in rental housing often are quite elaborate and bizarre, so there is great need for an improved legal framework, technical assistance, and strong tenant organizations to engage successfully in negotiations for such property transfers. This approach will not, of course, provide the resources necessary for physically upgrading the multi-family buildings taken over—that again will require public resources—but it will mean a reduced rate of rent increases, retirement of much outstanding mortgage debt, and greatly increased resident and community control over, responsibility for, and security in multi-family housing, at very little cost.

1. Establish a right of first refusal for tenants in private rental housing (assignable to nonprofit CDCs, the Boston Citywide Land Trust (BCLT), or other appropriate entities) to purchase their properties at a discounted price, with forgiveness of back taxes, for conversion to nonspeculative ownership.

2. Encourage lenders in the process of mortgage foreclosure on non-owner-occupied buildings to offer a nonprofit CDC or the BCLT right of first refusal to acquire the building for the mortgage balance plus foreclosure costs (that is, a non-auction sale). The nonprofit would then offer resale-restricted, below-market individual or co-op ownership to low- and moderate-income buyers (with first right of refusal to any tenants in the building). Such a process (without interim CDC ownership) has already occurred in at least one HUD-foreclosed multi-family development in Boston, which has been sold to a limited-equity resident co-op, and similar sales are under negotiation for several others. By utilizing CDCs or the BCLT as interim owners (possibly even financing such

transfers), private lending institutions could facilitate conversion of foreclosed buildings to nonspeculative resident ownership while avoiding the responsibilities of interim ownership associated with HUD-foreclosed buildings.

3. Facilitate conversion to limited-equity co-ops of multi-family buildings, occupied by low- and moderate-income tenants, that have responsible owners with limited financial resources. Technical assistance and rehab grants should be provided for such conversions. (Indeed, public rehab money might be tied to such conversion at present or at some agreed future point.) Internal financing should be used as much as possible, that is, purchase-money mortgages between tenant-buyers and owner-sellers as a way of both minimizing closing costs and providing a below-market interest rate to buyers, with a satisfactory return to sellers.

4. Accelerate conversion of multi-family buildings with irresponsible owners. Aggressive use of code enforcement and receivership with irresponsible landlords, as discussed above, should be coupled with the requirement that such landlords negotiate sale to a nonspeculative owner within one year, following which condemnation proceedings would be used to acquire and convert to nonspeculative ownership.

5. Provide local resources and support increased state and federal resources for technical assistance, seed-money loans, equity grants, rehab financing, and operating assistance to resident, community-based, and citywide entities that acquire existing private rental housing for nonspeculative ownership and manage it for resident and community benefit.

6. Transfer city-owned rental property (tax title, condemned or surplus) at a nominal price to tenants, nonprofit CDCs, or the BCLT for conversion to nonspeculative ownership.

7. Enact a tax on the speculative turnover of housing. The most affordable housing without direct subsidies is that which has been held, without refinancing, by the current owners for 10, 15, 20 years or more, so that the residents are not paying for speculative increases in values and financing at high current rates of interest. A useful tool for discouraging short-term ownership, dampening speculative pressures, and also raising some revenue is a local tax on speculation.

Although in Massachusetts state enabling legislation is required for such a local tax, Boston and other municipalities should be able to craft an appropriate framework. The two basic ingredients are the definition of speculative gain and the rate of taxation. Since the state constitution requires a flat rate of taxation, in order to discourage short-term holding and rapid turnover the definition may involve a sliding scale: for example, in the first year, the entire gain could be defined as speculative; in the second year, 95 percent; in the third year, 90 percent; and so forth, so that property held more than 20 years would be subject to no tax. Alternatively, any gain over and above the Consumer Price Index increase during the ownership period could be defined as speculative. The tax rate on the speculative gain should then be as high as is constitutionally possible, with at least 70 percent probably being the minimum for the tax to be effective.

8. Support acquisition by the Boston Housing Authority of some existing one-

to-four-family homes on a scattered site basis to house large low-income families, with emphasis on community assistance and resident self-help to further reduce housing costs as well as promote other social objectives.

II. Facilitating Homeownership Without Speculation[7]

The attractions of homeownership are undeniable: most of us desire the security of tenure and control over our living space that homeownership offers, along with the possibility of relatively stable housing costs, some equity accumulation, income tax benefits, and a sense of full community membership and social status that homeownership may provide.

Yet conventional homeownership is not without problems: high acquisition costs and interest rates have made it difficult for all but the wealthiest to buy their first home; the risks of mortgage foreclosure and tax foreclosure undermine the security this tenure seems to offer; the popular homeowner tax benefits are highly regressive, flowing almost entirely to homeowners with incomes of over $30,000; and, sadly, homeowners may place the enhancement of property values above the preservation and enhancement of community, developing resentment toward neighbors who are tenants or who are regarded as being of lower social or economic status. Finally, they often ride the wave of speculative increases in property values that can deprive other members of the community of the possibility of homeownership.

The challenge, then, is to find ways of facilitating the positive aspects of homeownership while overcoming the negative ones. To be sure, full realization of this goal will ultimately require changes nationally in our concepts of housing and our distribution of income. Nonetheless, there are a number of feasible local and immediate strategies that can achieve the objectives of:

- increasing opportunities for low- and moderate-income community residents to achieve individual or cooperative homeownership through below-market prices and/or financing
- maintaining continued affordability for future owners and ensuring community stability by establishing resale restrictions
- increasing security of tenure and housing affordability for existing low- and moderate-income homeowners through foreclosure protection, equity conversion, tax relief, and rehabilitation grants

Policies for achieving these objectives are presented below under two sub-goals.

A. *Enhance security of tenure and affordability for existing lower-income homeowners and improve the viability of the resident-owned housing stock.*

1. Reduce property taxes for low-income homeowners through the use of existing legal mechanisms (Tilly 1985). The city already possesses the legal authority for the tax assessor to exempt a portion of the assessed valuation of a home from taxation for reasons of financial hardship. Indeed, the law allows up to 90 percent exemption. The city thus could readily implement a program that

would reduce the housing costs of low-income homeowners by as much as $100–200 a month.The city administration would only be required to establish criteria for eligibility and a formula establishing the amount of assessed valuation to be exempted.

One readily available framework for determining eligibility is the income limits for federal Section 8 rental assistance. Since these limits constitute an established and generally accepted standard of eligibility for housing assistance, their use should pose no legal problems in defining financial hardship.

The formula for the amount of assessed valuation to be exempted could reflect the shelter-poverty approach to affordability, providing the greatest exemption for households with the lowest incomes and most people; a simple mathematical formula or tables could readily be devised for this purpose. If, on the other hand, political considerations dictated an even simpler formula based just on a few income categories, one reasonable formula might be 90 percent exemption for eligible households under $5,000 income, 70 percent for those between $5,000 and $9,999, 50 percent for those between $10,000 and $14,999, and so forth.

Depending upon the formula used, implementation of such an affordable property tax program in Boston would result in tax increases of about 1-2 percent for other property owners (Tilly 1985). It thus would be possible to provide quite substantial affordability relief to low-income homeowners at very modest cost to the rest of the community.

2. Establish equity conversion options for low-income elderly homeowners, providing income for life, as well as lifetime security of tenure and maintenance services, in return for deeding the house to a nonprofit entity. Reverse annuity mortgages are a mechanism that lending institutions have begun to offer to older homeowners who have paid off their mortgages and happen to live in areas with rising and relatively high property values: the homeowner gets an annuity for life or a term, secured by the equity in the home and repaid upon death or at the end of the term out of the owner's estate by selling or refinancing the home. Boston should investigate the creation of such a program for lower-income homeowners, using municipal borrowing or CDBG funds to make the annuity payments. The mortgage lien could provide for the BCLT to have right of first refusal to buy from the owner's estate, with the share of annuity payments provided by CDBG funds being used to write down the cost.

Another version of this model would be for the Boston Citywide Land Trust, or other nonprofit entity, to purchase the home of an elderly low-income homeowner, offering in return a life estate and an annuity equal either to full housing costs or the difference between full housing costs and what the seller could afford to pay under the shelter-poverty standard. In this way, the resident would be assured of life tenure at a truly affordable cost. In Buffalo, New York, a program of this sort using CDBG funds has been in operation for several years (Edmonds 1984, 13, 28; Brown 1986).

3. Support and provide foreclosure relief for low- and moderate-income home-

owners. The city should use its persuasive powers to encourage private lending institutions to exercise forbearance in foreclosing on unpaid mortgages on the homes of low- and moderate-income homeowners, and should endorse state legislation to ensure maximum forebearance and relief by lenders.

In addition, Boston should explore establishing a foreclosure relief program analogous to the program for elderly homeowners described above. For qualifying low-income homeowners who have not been able to resume mortgage payments even after lender forbearance, the city should use CDBG or other funds to provide financial assistance for one year, or perhaps at most two years. The assistance should bring the homeowner's outlays down to the shelter-poverty affordability level, in return for which, whenever the owner wishes to sell, the Boston Citywide Land Trust will have the right to buy at a price yielding no more than a limited-equity return to the seller. As an alternative, if the owner is unable to resume full mortgage payments within a specified time, the terms of assistance could require that the owner deed the property to the BCLT, subject to the mortgage but with no cash payment, in return for a life estate and housing payments permanently based on the shelter-poverty affordability scale. For low-income homeowners facing the loss of both their shelter and their investment to foreclosure proceedings, this program provides security of tenure and affordability. As a voluntary program, people would always have the option of going through foreclosure proceedings and taking their chances at the foreclosure auction.

4. Provide grants and low-interest loans for low- and moderate-income homeowners to pay for repairs and weatherization. Under its Housing Improvement Program, Boston has been using CDBG funds for over a decade to assist homeowners with rebates of 20-50 percent. The program has had great impact, but several modifications may help with the affordability situations of low-income owners and maintain long-term affordability of some of the existing owner-occupied stock. Some owners cannot afford necessary repairs and energy improvements at all; they should be able to receive outright grants for these costs, with imposition of a lien that requires repayment of the grant if and when the owner or owner's heirs sell and with the right of first refusal by the Boston Citywide Land Trust to buy at such time. Indeed, many municipalities use CDBG funds for partial homeowner grants or rebates, with liens to permit recovery and recycling of the funds when the property is sold. This proposal just goes a step further in order to address the more serious barrier to homeowner repairs while serving long-term objectives of future removal of housing from the speculative market.

B. Reduce speculation in the owner-occupied housing stock and increase individual and collective opportunities for nonspeculative resident ownership.

1. Enact a tax on the speculative transfer of housing. The speculation tax discussed under rental housing should apply to owner-occupied housing transfers as well, except where such transfers are necessitated by personal hardship (loss

of job, divorce, and so on). It would not penalize long-term homeowners, but would diminish speculative fever and enhance long-term affordability, while returning to Boston some of the windfall gains that are realized.

2. Link homeowner relief programs, such as equity conversion, foreclosure assistance, and rehab grants, to transfer of title to a nonprofit entity so that future transfer can be at below-market prices to lower-income buyers, with permanent resale restrictions to maintain nonspeculative ownership.

3. Transfer city-owned property (tax title, condemned or surplus) that is suitable for homeownership either directly to lower-income buyers or to interim owners such as nonprofit CDCs or the BCLT at a nominal price, with deed restrictions to ensure permanent nonspeculative resident ownership. Whenever city-owned property is disposed of for homeownership, two deed restrictions should be incorporated to ensure and maintain affordable nonspeculative ownership: (a) when the property is sold, the sales price would be set so as to yield to the seller return of the original down payment plus the (depreciated) cost of capital improvements, increased by the Consumer Price Index (net of any cash obtained through refinancing); (b) when the owner wants to sell, a nonprofit CDC or the BCLT would have the right of first refusal to buy at the limited-equity price; the nonprofit in turn would sell the house to another eligible low- or moderate-income household at the below-market price, possibly with below-market financing, including the same resale stipulations for the new owner.

4. Utilize the right of first refusal policy for rental properties to facilitate creation of limited-equity resident cooperatives.

5. Allocate funds for technical assistance, seed-money loans, equity grants, rehab financing, and operating assistance to the BCLT, nonprofit CDCs, the Boston Housing Partnership, and other appropriate entities that facilitate acquisition of housing for conversion to forms of nonspeculative homeownership.

Many of these strategies rely upon deed restrictions to prevent speculative windfalls. Of course, in a runaway speculative market there is always the risk that some people might try to get the speculative increase in value through the private market despite the deed restrictions. Several possible mechanisms can avoid this problem. One would be to give the residents (as individuals or co-ops) title to the building while vesting land title in the BCLT. Another would be to place a municipal lien on the property at the time the nonspeculative title is established; the lien would be for the (as yet undetermined) amount of any increase in value over and above the limited-equity increase stipulated in the deed. In this way, there would be no incentive for the owner to sell to a speculator or high-income person, since the seller could not keep the windfall and there would be a disincentive for a speculator or high-income person to buy because there would be a continuing lien (and hence a cloud on the title) for further increases in value.

A fundamental principle underlying these strategies is that the community and the government at all levels have an obligation to facilitate more affordable homeownership for community residents in the present while simultaneously contributing to community stability and housing affordability over the long term. It is thus entirely reasonable, appropriate, and indeed cost-effective for public policy to declare that anyone acquiring, improving, or retaining a home with public and community assistance must accept a measure of public and community obligation in the form of explicit resale stipulations. Anyone not willing to accept such stipulations would always be free to enter and operate in the unregulated housing market, but without public and community assistance. Community development policies should provide opportunities to individuals in ways that clearly and simultaneously benefit the community.

III. Preserving and Upgrading Government-Assisted Housing

Over 20 percent of housing in Boston is subsidized, either through the Boston Housing Authority (BHA) or forms of government assistance to private owners. The extent of shelter-poverty reveals the need both for more subsidized units and for subsidies more appropriate to need. Yet at the same time, there are factors working to reduce the amount of assisted housing, factors that the city administration will need to oppose if the housing affordabilty problem is not to worsen. The city itself has limited power over most subsidized housing, but the following represent some elements that comprise a policy of support for the preservation and improvement of this vital resource. The specific policy elements are organized under three sub-goals.

A. *Preserve the existing supply of publicly owned and state- and federally-subsidized housing for lower-income people.*

1. Prevent private resale of public housing and conversion of subsidized housing to market-rate rentals or condominiums. Under court receivership the Boston Housing Authority began substantial efforts to improve existing public housing. However, in some cases the housing may be turned over to private ownership, with the risk that it will not always be for low-income residents. Also, the process of redevelopment has involved a substantial reduction in the total number of units in many of the developments. The city should therefore make every effort to ensure that there is no sale or transfer of public housing, except perhaps to nonprofit or nonspeculative resident ownership with permanent restriction to low-income use.

The city may have some direct leverage over the disposition of privately owned subsidized developments in former urban renewal areas and should exercise this legal authority to ensure that these developments remain both subsidized and out of the speculative market. In instances where the city has no direct legal power, political leadership plus technical assistance to nonprofit and resident groups interested in taking over the housing should be provided. (See also Chapter 10 by Emily Achtenberg.)

2. Require prior one-for-one equivalent replacement of assisted units that must be removed from the housing stock for socially necessary reasons.

B. Protect tenants in government-assisted housing and enhance its affordability and viability.

1. Support the upgrading of existing public housing. Although federal dollars to modernize existing federal public housing and to convert and upgrade state-aided public housing have been reduced substantially, Boston should commit a proportion of its diminishing CDBG funds to public housing, not in proportion to the fraction of all housing units in the city, but rather to the fraction of all low- and moderate-income households. In addition, state modernization funds should be aggressively pursued and efforts made to increase such funding to improve the public housing stock that has not yet been upgraded.

2. Advocate and support changes in the rent formulas for public and subsidized housing, along with adequate operating subsidies. The shelter-poverty scale reveals that larger and lower-income families in public and subsidized housing especially are paying more than they can afford despite the subsidies, while some of the smaller households with incomes approaching the income limits could indeed afford to pay somewhat more. The most immediate way of making the housing more affordable and allocating subsidy funds more appropriately, on the basis of true need, would be to change the definition of income used in determining tenant rents. Efforts have been made at the congressional and state levels (with limited success so far) to change the definition of income so as to provide for per-person deductions (rather than the traditional deductions for minor children only) and make these deductions at least $600 per person. With tenants paying 30 percent of their income net of these deductions, larger and lower-income families in subsidized housing would actually pay up to $30 a month less than they did under the pre-Reagan 25-percent-of-income formula. Smaller and higher-income households would pay more than under the old 25 percent formula but less than under the new federal formulas.

Again, while local government does not have a direct role in establishing these rent formulas, it can participate actively with others in seeking such changes, along with increased appropriations for operating subsidies so that enhanced affordability does not occur at the expense of even greater reductions in necessary maintenance of the housing.

3. Reduce property taxes and seek reduction of mortgage debt in privately owned assisted housing.

4. Strictly enforce local codes and require repairs in subsidized housing.

5. Increase security of tenure, collective bargaining rights, warranties of habitability, tenant services, and affirmative protection of the rights of minority residents in public and assisted housing.

C. Increase nonspeculative ownership of government-assisted housing.

1. Use local code enforcement, tax title, redevelopment, and political powers to compel HUD and the Massachusetts Housing Finance Agency to foreclose on assisted properties whose owners do not responsibly manage them. Such foreclosures should then lead to transfer of the properties to nonspeculative resident or community owners on favorable terms.

2. Limit local discretionary assistance, such as property tax reductions, rental assistance, and rehab grants, to subsidized projects currently owned by or optioned to limited-equity resident co-ops, nonprofit CDCs, and other nonspeculative entities.

3. Use political leverage to create a right of first refusal for tenants in subsidized developments to purchase their housing at a discounted price for conversion to limited-equity co-ops. Such a right should be assignable by the residents, if they choose not to own, only to nonprofit organizations or the Boston Housing Authority.

4. Allocate resources for technical assistance, seed-money loans, equity grants, and operating assistance to entities engaged in conversion of subsidized housing to nonspeculative ownership.

IV. Producing Housing for Nonspeculative Ownership

It is easy to say that there ought to be more federal and state funds for the production of subsidized housing. The reality, of course, is that drastic federal cutbacks continue, while state aid for subsidized housing production, even in Massachusetts, will not come close to offsetting the federal cuts. Boston obviously should actively work to restore and increase funding, especially for state- and federally-aided public housing, while aggressively seeking and utilizing whatever funds are available. There are some types of local initiative, though, which are possible and which also should be pursued aggressively, rather than placing all hope and blame on the state and federal coffers. Policy proposals are presented under three sub-goals.

A. *Increase public and community control over land for housing use.*

1. Utilize the BCLT for permanent nonspeculative ownership and land-banking potential sites for future community-based development. Community land trusts are being proposed and established in many parts of the country as vehicles for property ownership and controlling land for social purposes (Institute for Community Economics 1982; Institute for Community Economics). The idea of a housing and land trust for Boston has been suggested for a number of years, and in the fall of 1985 the BCLT was incorporated as a nonprofit, charitable foundation, with a board made up of community organizations.

The BCLT should be able to receive land and vacant buildings, holding them for community-based development when resources become available; the land would remain in trust, with development rights assigned to a CDC. It should also be able to receive occupied buildings, as discussed above, in some cases for permanent ownership and management or, where feasible, for eventual transfer to other nonprofit or nonspeculative forms of resident ownership. Single-family as well as multifamily housing can enter into this process, as there is no reason why limited-equity and community repurchase stipulations cannot be attached to single-family dwellings, just as they are being applied to co-ops and condominiums.

2. Maintain existing public ownership of land suitable for housing, using the ground lease mechanism to facilitate and regulate development.

3. Discourage land speculation through taxation and tax incentives to transfer land to the BCLT for land-banking for eventual community-based development.

B. Increase public and community control over housing development.

1. Use public site control, design review, permit approval, taxation, and other mechanisms to ensure compatibility of housing development, design, occupancy, and management programs with public and community objectives.

2. Require developers building on public land or receiving any form of public subsidy to joint-venture with community-based or other nonprofit developers. Such community and nonprofit sponsors should be assured of having substantial control over development and operations and an option upon completion to convert the housing to nonspeculative ownership.

3. Establish neighborhood councils, with a majority of representatives selected or designated by community-based nonprofit organizations, to approve and monitor housing development projects within the framework established by public and community objectives.

C. Support social development for nonspeculative ownership.

1. Promote development of new public housing. While the Boston Housing Authority was in receivership, the court quite properly required it to focus on revitalizing existing public housing developments and restricted development of additional units. While redevelopment of existing public housing projects has brought hundreds of units back into habitable condition, it also has permanently eliminated hundreds of others. The extent of shelter-poverty in the city reveals the need not only to replace the lost units, but to increase the stock of public housing beyond mere replacement. With a new administration in City Hall and new leadership at the BHA, receivership ended in 1984. Working now with a long-absent degree of cooperation, the city and BHA should be aggressively seeking to expand and obtain state public housing development dollars, especially for scattered-site family housing, while exercising leadership nationally to restore federal public housing funds.

2. Provide resources for seed-money, technical assistance, equity grants, rehab/construction financing, and operating assistance to nonprofit CDCs, the Boston Housing Partnership, and other social developers (see Chapter 11 by Rachel Bratt). While the claims on local and limited federal and state community development funds are great, the challenge is to focus this money in ways that will have the greatest benefit for those most in need. Such dollars certainly will not go very far if used for capital grants, even though such grants can have the greatest impact on what residents end up having to pay for newly built or substantially rehabilitated housing. More broadly distributed funds may seem like a more equitable approach in the short run, but may also have little long-term impact unless used to facilitate institutional change rather than just provide

financial assistance. Thus, whatever limited funds are provided to assist housing production should contribute to increasing the amount of housing under permanent community, public, or nonspeculative resident ownership.

3. Ensure that community-based development for homeownership has the same types of deed restrictions as the disposition of publicly owned buildings. While CDCs traditionally have concentrated mainly on the development of rental housing because of the availability of federal rental subsidies plus private funds from equity syndication, some have been devoting more of their efforts to developing below-market homeownership opportunities, especially as rental subsidies have dried up. Although CDCs are emphasizing making such housing affordable to existing residents, they are also in excellent position to ensure continuing availability and affordability for community residents by including resale requirements when they sell the completed housing.

4. Use condemnation and receivership provisions, homeowner relief programs, and tenant right-of-first-refusal legislation to make occupied housing in need of rehabilitation available for social development and nonspeculative ownership.

5. Provide technical assistance, resources and support to cooperatively owned or community-based nonprofit materials suppliers and construction companies, including preferential purchasing and contracting by public agencies and publicly assisted developers.

V. Generating and Channelling Funds for Social Production and Ownership

Although the possibilities for generating substantial amounts of social capital at the local level for housing acquisition, rehabilitation, and construction are, of course, severely limited, there are a number of intriguing possibilities for raising funds and many opportunities to better target the funds that are available. The policies in this area are presented under three sub-goals.

A. Expand existing resources and develop new funding sources for the production and preservation of affordable housing for nonspeculative ownership.

1. Strengthen the linkage formula and target the funds for development of nonspeculative housing. Linkage between downtown development and neighborhood housing has become a widely recognized and supported concept in Boston, as it has in many other cities experiencing a commercial development boom (see Chapter 9 by Dennis Keating). The mayor and many members of the City Council participated in the promotion of the concept, which now is being implemented administratively through the zoning code. The formula originally adopted for developer payments—on office developments of over 100,000 square feet, $5 per gross square foot (with the first 100,000 square feet exempted), paid in over 12 years beginning with completion of the project—represented a fairly weak compromise.

With tremendous development pressures continuing, Boston is in a very good position to require a higher rate of payments, paid in over a shorter time period, and for major developments beyond those of the downtown commercial area. Thus in the summer of 1985 a Linkage Action Coalition was formed by some of the most broadly-based groups representing homeowners, private housing tenants, and public housing tenants. The Coalition has demanded that the formula be increased to $10 per square foot, to be paid in its entirety at the start of construction, and with no exemption for the first 100,000 square feet (although projects of under 100,000 square feet would still not be covered). The Coalition also demanded that there be a policy of "inclusionary zoning" for new luxury housing, under which at least 10 percent of the units would have to be for low- and moderate-income people (a higher percentage if public dollars or land are involved). In November 1985 the mayor responded by increasing the formula to $6 per square foot, with the extra dollar designated for job training rather than housing; payment of the housing portion now will be over seven years and the job portion over two years, and payments will begin up front (Advisory Group 1983; Frisby 1985a, 1985b; Quill 1985; Scharfenberg 1985; Snyder 1986).

The other significant and particularly relevant issue is the allocation of linkage funds paid by developers. Although the funds began to flow in during 1986, with as much as $37-$52 million expected over the next decade under the old formula (and possibly 50-100 percent more than this under the new formula and new estimates of development demand), the Housing Trust, which is to allocate the money, is also a source of some contention regarding types of eligible developers and amount of affordable housing, and has had difficulty establishing clear guidelines for operation. Clearly, the greatest long-term impact on affordability will be achieved by utilizing the resources as direct capital grants, or very low–interest loans for use in rehabilitation or new construction for nonprofit or nonspeculative ownership, through community-based developers and the BCLT. If the amount of funds estimated under the old formula were to be allocated as direct capital grants, as many as 500-800 new units could be produced, or at least twice that many rehabilitated, at rents of about $300-$400 a month; as partial grants or nominal-interest loans, the funds expected under the old formula could produce twice as many units, but at rents of $700-$800 a month. Greater funds under the new formula could produce some combination of more units and lower rents. The Linkage Action Coalition has focused on income guidelines to ensure that the housing will be for the most needy, and has also raised demands for nonprofit development and nonspeculative ownership.

2. Explore the use of a portion of municipal pension funds for financing new construction and substantial rehabilitation. Pension funds are discussed with increasing frequency as a potential financing pool not yet significantly tapped for housing. They certainly do not offer the potential for providing funds much more cheaply than other sources, but at the municipal level (as well as the state level and by unionized workers) they do offer the possibility of using a portion of locally generated resources for the direct benefit of the community. Since the

funds would be used in the form of loans and at competitive interest rates, the only way in which such money could help to alleviate the affordability problem is on a long-term basis, by having funds targetted, as with other sources mentioned above, for housing that remains independent of inflating property values and costly refinancing.

3. Create new state or local trust fund revenues for affordable nonspeculative housing from a tax on speculative real estate transfers, unearned interest on property tax and insurance escrows held by lenders, excess interest on security deposits, and other appropriate sources.

4. Strengthen Urban Development Action Grant (UDAG) payback terms and urban renewal transfer/termination penalties on developers and require luxury housing developers to contribute to or build lower-income housing ("inclusionary zoning").

5. Tap new state trust funds, such as the Massachusetts Housing Partnership revolving fund ($35 million) and the Massachusetts Government Land Bank Thrift Fund ($100 million) for developing and acquiring affordable housing for nonspeculative ownership.

6. Press for increased state funding for public housing, rental assistance payments, and targetted SHARP (State Housing Assistance for Rental Production) funds for nonprofit developers.

7. Promote the expansion and targetting of private social financing sources. The Episcopal City Mission (ECM) Housing Seed Money Loan Fund and the Boston Community Loan Fund tap socially concerned donors and investors for funds to assist community groups developing affordable housing. While modest in size (the ECM Fund has loaned about $1 million), such sources have provided essential funds without the complexities of public or bank procedures.

B. Better utilize available public funds to increase the production and preservation of affordable housing.

1. Direct capital grant and loan programs, discretionary local funds, and available subsidies to projects that are maximally affordable. Whatever public funds are available, such as federal UDAG, State Community Development Action Grants, HODAG (federal Housing Development Action Grants), CDBG, SHARP, MHFA, linkage fees, UDAG paybacks, federal Section 8 and state Chapter 707 rental assistance, should be committed solely to projects that:

- maximize the number of units available to and occupied by lower-income households
- maximize the affordability of such units, especially to very low-income families (using the shelter-poverty standard)
- maximize the duration of lower-income use

C. Maximize the availability of resources for the preservation and production of affordable housing on a nonspeculative basis.

1. Target all capital grant, loan, and rental assistance funds on a priority basis

to housing owned by or optioned to residents, nonprofit CDCs, and other appropriate entities on a nonspeculative basis.

2. Support increased state bonding authority and appropriations for public housing development, modernization, and operating subsidies.

3. Support increased state funding for programs such as the Massachusetts Community Economic Development Assistance Corporation (CEDAC), Community Enterprise and Economic Development (CEED), and Community Development Finance Corporation (CDFC) which now provide money loans, technical assistance, operating funds, interim financing, and other forms of support for community-based, nonprofit housing sponsors, and earmark additional locally controlled discretionary funds for such purposes.

VI. Establishing and Enforcing a Local Housing Bill of Rights

A number of these proposals presented here would increase the rights of residents in various ways and indeed begin to move toward the notion of affordable housing as an entitlement. It is therefore worth considering bringing these various measures together into a package that legally affirms and codifies elements scattered in various laws and regulations. But even if this were not possible statutorily, the city government could certainly prepare materials and provide services in a way that interconnects the various rights residents have. Expressed in this way, the major tenets of such a program would be as follows:

- statutory life tenure (eviction protection) for all tenants who continue to pay their rent and do not interfere with the rights of other tenants
- life estate security for homeowners under the equity conversion and foreclosure relief programs
- strict enforcement of the State Sanitary Code, with community and resident participation, and use of receivership and condemnation where appropriate
- legislative recognition of the right of tenants to form unions and bargain collectively
- strengthened anti-discrimination enforcement by the Fair Housing Commission
- public education, outreach, publicity, and technical assistance to housing residents and groups on their housing rights and how to exercise them individually and collectively

INCOME POLICIES

Apart from these measures aimed specifically at the housing market, local officials can undertake a number of methods to enhance housing affordability from the income side. Local officials are always working to bring in and create new jobs for residents, and this will of course continue. It is possible to have at least as great a positive impact, though, on the income of Boston residents through efforts directed at job access and the structure of existing jobs.

Job access policies certainly include efforts to improve the quality and availability of education and training. They also should involve the reaffirmation and strengthening of a policy of "Boston jobs for Boston residents" and support for affirmative action (and not only for jobs where the city government has direct leverage). The local administration can also undertake efforts to increase access to suburban job opportunities, by supporting improvements to existing transportation systems and developing special job-oriented transportation links.

Job creation and job access endeavors, as important as they are, will do little to solve the housing affordability problems of Bostonians if the jobs pay low wages and offer little or no prospect for improvement. Local government therefore needs to look at its own internal job structures and provide models and exercise political influence to alter private-sector employment patterns. Unionization is an essential institution for workers themselves to participate in establishing not only their wage levels but also career development and training opportunities; local government leaders can help create a climate that supports workers' rights to unionize and utilize their unions in these ways. Comparable worth is a concept whose time is long overdue; the mayor's commitment to the concept should not only improve the incomes of women workers, especially in city government, but can provide an example for the private sector in Boston. Finally, city government can directly develop and assist other employers in developing career ladders and job-upgrading programs, both to help individual workers improve their situations and also to restructure jobs, so that there is enhancement of prevailing levels of skill and productivity as well as of income.

MUNICIPAL LEADERSHIP

Imaginative and aggressive municipal leaders can begin to have an impact on the housing problem and its causes at the state and national levels in a number of forums, such as by testifying and lobbying; participating in national organizations of mayors and municipalities; contributing to party platforms; and speaking before and providing educational materials to housing and community development advocacy and professional groups.

While all of these areas of activity are fairly obvious, the potentially original element is the content. Rather than arguing primarily for increased dollars and local control—as important as these are—what our municipal leaders can offer that is most significant is, first, local models for housing action and institutional change; and second, persuasive arguments on the seriousness of the crisis and passionate support of the following measures for dealing with it:

1. Cut the federal deficit and begin to distribute income downward by:

- cutting military spending
- closing tax loopholes, including housing-related tax benefits
- eliminating the federal income tax for all lower-income households

- explicitly targetting housing and economic development subsidies and incentives to entities that engage in productive, nonspeculative investment

2. Impose credit controls and credit allocation in order to:

- deflate the credit bubble
- decrease use of credit for speculation
- ensure an adequate supply of low-cost credit for productive investment in housing construction and rehabilitation, rebuilding decaying infrastructure and creating job-producing industry

3. Control prices through a combination of:

- explicit controls
- use of federal and state tax codes to penalize speculation
- incentives to transfer housing, land, and enterprises to forms of nonspeculative (resident, community, worker, consumer, public) ownership

Boston's leaders are uniquely equipped to guide and inform our community and also to advocate broader policies such as these, to begin dealing with the roots of the housing problem while avoiding economic disaster.

Acknowledgments

I especially wish to thank William Magee, Jr., for the use of his skills, his energy, and his computer to carry out the 1985–87 rent survey and derive the 1985 shelter poverty affordability scale. The organization of the Housing Program for Boston in this version was developed in collaboration with Emily Achtenberg, but I am fully responsible for the discussion and the final phraseology. Specific pieces of the program have benefited from discussions with the following people: Janice Fine of Boston Fair Share, on Boston linkage; Michael Kane of the Boston Affordable Housing Coalition, on an affordable property tax for Boston; Bob Van Meter of the Massachusetts Tenants Organization, on Boston rent control; and my fellow members of the Technical Support Group for the Eviction Free Zone (Steve Fahrer, Pat Feeley, Mauricio Gaston, Rick Guidel, Marie Kennedy, Regina Placid, Boyce Slayman, Aura Suarez, and Ken Wade), on nonspeculative homeownership. I also want to thank Deborah Oriola of the Boston Redevelopment Authority Research Department for providing special cross-tabulations from the 1985 Neighborhood Survey. Finally, I wish to thank Leslie Jay Corn for having put an earlier version of this chapter onto disk to facilitate editing and revision.

This paper is a substantially revised and updated version of a paper with the same title prepared in 1983 for the John W. McCormack Institute for Public Affairs of the University of Massachusetts at Boston.

Notes

1. To be sure, not all housing problems are simply reducible to the affordability squeeze. In particular, housing discrimination has a dynamic of its own; restricted housing opportunity for oppressed people and groups is in part an affordability problem resulting

from lower incomes caused by discrimination in education and employment, but clearly there is housing discrimination that is not solely a function of income differences. In addition, some problems associated with or growing out of the design of housing are the result of certain assumptions and conventions about household structure and composition; the role of household members—most particularly the role of women—cannot be fully understood in terms of cost or affordability constraints.

2. The most controversial aspect of using the BLS Lower Budget is whether it provides a reasonable definition of minimal level adequacy. The BLS itself has altered its official position on this matter since the budgets were first published in the late 1960s. At the time the Lower Budget was first being developed, the Bureau declared:

> The lower-standard budget will represent a minimum of adequacy. . . . The lower-standard budgets are expected to be more appropriate than the moderate budget for use in establishing goals for public assistance and income maintenance programs in the current decade (Bureau of Labor Statistics 1967, vii).

By contrast, since the early 1970s the cover statements accompanying the published sets of family and elderly budgets have included such statements as "The budgets are not intended to represent a minimum or subsistence level of living," or "The budgets are not intended to represent a minimum level of adequate income or a subsistence level of income."

The change in the official BLS interpretation of the Lower Budgets undoubtedly reflects the retreat by the federal government from a commitment to substantial income redistribution necessary for an income maintenance program with a reasonably adequate minimum support level. Since this retreat was associated with the growing economic difficulties of the U.S. starting in the late 1960s and with the change of administration in 1969, the published disclaimers must be discounted somewhat on political and ideological grounds. At the same time, there are some conceptual and methodological problems associated with the BLS budgets, but no operational alternative has yet been put into place. In 1978 the Bureau began a project to revise the Family Budget Program; an Expert Committee on Family Budget Revisions was established, but its final draft report—"New American Budget Standards," completed in May 1980—was never published or acted upon. The analysis summarized here had thus been carried out using the BLS Lower Budgets, recognizing certain limitations but hoping that it will contribute to rekindling debate on income distribution and the definition of a minimum adequate standard of living.

The Reagan administration decided to eliminate the BLS Family Budget Program beginning in fiscal year 1983; this means that the last published budgets were for autumn 1981. Unless and until the Program is revived or a new one established, it will be necessary to update the the budgets by applying the Consumer Price Index (CPI) for specific items to the various budget components, in the same way the BLS itself updated the budgets.

The 1985 affordability scale for Boston has thus been derived from the BLS Lower Budget for 1981, updating each budget component by using the increase in the Boston CPI for the corresponding component from September 1981, to September 1985.

3. The figures on the incidence of shelter-poverty in Boston in 1980 are from Flynn 1981, based upon application of the 1980 shelter-poverty affordability scale to housing cost cross-tabulations from the 1980 Boston Household Survey conducted for the Boston Redevelopment Authority by the University of Massachusetts at Boston Center for Survey Research.

4. On February 22, 1986, the Episcopal City Mission held a one-day "Housing Con-

sultation'' on the theme of ''Housing as a Basic Human Right,'' bringing together community activists, nonprofit housing agency staff people, and progressive housing bureaucrats from the city and state; in addition, in the fall of 1985 the Massachusetts Coalition for the Homeless began planning for a state-wide ''Right to Housing'' campaign to amend the state constitiution to declare housing a basic human right.

In the fall of 1986 and again in 1987 signature campaigns to launch the amendment process fell slightly short of obtaining enough signatures due to organizational difficulties, but provided experience for a legislative campaign to achieve the same end.

Substantial support for the campaign was generated in the spring of 1987 by a hearing on the Right to Housing Amendment before the state legislature's Joint Committee on Housing and Urban Development. A large number of community, labor, and religious groups endorsed the proposed amendment, and in response the Committee unanimously voted a favorable report.

The Right to Housing project has, in addition, produced a comprehensive and extensively researched position paper establishing the legal and moral bases for the Amendment and explaining the legal and policy implications of its potential enactment (Massachusetts Right to Housing Project 1987).

5. In the fall of 1985 a broad-based coalition of community groups, with back-up from the Legal Services Center and progressive planners, declared the Roxbury and Jamaica Plain sections of Boston to be an ''Eviction-Free Zone'' (Technical Support Group 1986).

In order to realize this declaration, the Legal Services Center pledged to make its considerable skills and expertise available to all residents of the Zone to prevent or at least delay indefinitely any attempted evictions. In addition, the Technical Support Group was prepared to assist resident groups in efforts to convert buildings to various forms of nonspeculative, resident-controlled ownership, and to obtain financial and non-financial resources for ownership and physical upgrading. The weakest element in implementing the concept has been the difficulty in organizing active resident involvement, particularly in the Roxbury portions of the Zone.

6. In the fall of 1985 a group of homeless AFDC recipients and two support organizations brought suit against the state, claiming that, given the high and rising costs of housing, AFDC levels are too low for parents to be able to raise their children in their own homes. In June of 1986 Superior Court Justice Charles Grabau found for the plaintiffs, ruling that the AFDC grants failed to meet statutory standards of adequacy, and ordering the state to act affirmatively to remedy the situation. The state acknowledged the inadequacy, but appealed the judge's order, declaring executive and legislative discretion in setting payment levels. In August 1987 the State Supreme Court upheld Justice Grabau's ruling, but the governor and legislature have refused to appropriate the necessary funds.

7. This section draws extensively on Stone 1985 and 1986c.

REFERENCES

Achtenberg, Emily Paradise, and Michael Stone. 1977. ''How Bankers Engineer Economic Policy.'' *The Real Paper,* September 10.

———. 1974. *Tenants First! A Research and Organizing Guide to FHA Housing*. Cambridge, MA. Urban Planning Aid, Chapter 9.

Advisory Group on Linkage Between Downtown Development and Neighborhood Housing. 1983. Report to the Mayor. Boston, October.

Bennett, Philip. 1985. "Homeless Welfare Recipients Sue State Officials." *Boston Globe,* December 11.

Boston Redevelopment Authority and Neighborhood Development and Employment Agency. 1985. *Household Survey.* Conducted by the Center for Survey Research of the University of Massachusetts at Boston.

Brady, James P. 1983. "Behind the Burning of Boston." *The Boston Globe Magazine,* October 23.

Brown, David W. 1986. "Reverse Mortgages: Proceed with Care." *Boston Globe,* March 22.

Bureau of Labor Statistics. 1967. "City Worker's Family Budget for a Moderate Standard of Living." Bulletin 1570-1, Autumn 1966. Washington, DC: U.S. Government Printing Office.

Clay, Phillip L. (ed). 1985. *The Emerging Black Community in Boston.* Boston: Institute for the Study of Black Culture, University of Massachusetts at Boston.

Edmonds, Sherry. 1984. "House Rich but Cash Poor: An Informational Packet on Home Equity Conversion." Boston: Massachusetts Department of Elder Affairs, October.

Episcopal City Mission. No date. "Housing: A Basic Human Right." ECM Policy Statement, Boston.

Flynn, James F. 1981. "The Need for Public Housing in Boston." Boston: Community Service Program, College of Public and Community Service, University of Massachusetts at Boston.

Frisby, Michael K. 1986a. "Arson Report Cites Two Hub Areas." *Boston Globe,* March 12.

———. 1986b. "City Hall Declares Arson Study Flawed." *Boston Globe,* March 13.

———. 1986c. "Flynn Aides Had Advance Word on City Arson Study." *Boston Globe,* March 14.

———. 1986d. "Crusader on Arson in Spotlight." *Boston Globe,* March 17.

———. 1986e. "Flynn Offers MCAD Housing, Jobs Plan." *Boston Globe,* March 22.

———. 1985a. "Developers Await Linkage Changes." *Boston Globe,* November 11.

———. 1985b. "Flynn Would Tie Linkage Fee to Jobs Plan." *Boston Globe,* November 12.

Gaston, Mauricio, and Marie Kennedy. 1987. "Capital Investment or Community Development? The Struggle for Land Control in Boston's Black and Latino Community." *Antipode* 19.

———. 1985a. "Roxbury: From Disinvestment to Displacement." *The North Star* 2 (Fall).

———. 1985b. "From Disinvestment to Displacement: The Redevelopment of Boston's Roxbury as a Case Study of Inner City Communities of Color." Boston: Roxbury Technical Assistance Project, College of Public and Community Service, University of Massachusetts at Boston.

Goetze, Rolf. 1985. "Boston's 1985 Housing Stock and Comparisons with 1980, by BRA Planning District." Boston Redevelopment Authority Research Department, November.

Hartman, Chester. 1983. *America's Housing Crisis: What Is To Be Done?* Boston: Routledge and Kegan Paul.

Hartman, Chester, and Michael E. Stone. 1986. "A Socialist Housing Program for the

United States.'' In *Critical Perspectives on Housing,* edited by Rachel Bratt, Chester Hartman and Ann Meyerson. Philadelphia: Temple University Press.

———. 1978. ''Housing: A Socialist Alternative.'' In *The Federal Budget and Social Reconstruction,* edited by Marcus G. Raskin. New Brunswick, NJ: Transaction Books.

Institute for Community Economics. 1982. *The Community Land Trust Handbook*. Emmaus, PA: Rodale Press.

Institute for Community Economics. *Community Economics,* various issues.

Massachusetts Coalition for the Homeless et al. v. Michael S. Dukakis, Governor, Philip W. Johnston, Secretary of Executive Office of Human Services, and Charles M. Atkins, Commissioner, Department of Public Welfare. 1986. Suffolk Superior Court, Civil no. 80109.

Massachusetts Right to Housing Project. 1987. ''Right to Housing Amendment: Position Paper.'' Draft, March 17.

Piven, Frances and Richard A. Cloward. 1982. *The New Class War: Reagan's Attack on the Welfare State and its Consequences*. New York: Pantheon Books.

Quill, Ed. 1986a. ''Property Valuations Soar in Hub.'' *Boston Globe,* March 13.

———. 1986b. ''Rise in Property Values Shows Hub Gaining in Popularity, Observers Say.'' *Boston Globe,* March 15.

———. 1985. ''Flynn's Proposal to Expand Linkage Under Attack From Three Groups.'' *Boston Globe,* November 13.

Scharfenberg, Kirk. 1985. ''Boston's No. 1 Challenge: Affordable Housing.'' *Boston Sunday Globe,* December 22.

Snyder, Sarah. 1986. ''Midprice Condos Offered for City's OK of Project.'' *Boston Globe,* March 14.

Stein, Charles. 1986. ''Housing Prices in Boston Area Up 38%.'' *Boston Globe,* February 21.

Stone, Michael E. 1986a. ''AFDC, Housing Costs, and Homelessness.'' Testimony prepared for the Committee on Human Services, Massachusetts General Court. March.

———. 1986b. ''Housing and the Dynamics of U.S. Capitalism.'' In *Critical Perspectives on Housing,* edited by Rachel Bratt, Chester Hartman, and Ann Meyerson. Philadelphia: Temple University Press.

———. 1986c. ''Homeownership Without Speculation.'' *Shelterforce,* November/December.

———. 1985. *Homeownership without Speculation*. Boston: Roxbury Technical Assistance Project, College of Public and Community Service, University of Massachusetts at Boston, November.

———. 1978a. ''Boston's Political Economy: Some Thoughts on How to Approach the Analysis.'' Unpublished.

———. 1978b. ''Overview of Changes in Boston's Political Economy and Geography.'' Unpublished.

Stone, Michael, and Emily Achtenberg. 1977. *Hostage! Housing and the Massachusetts Fiscal Crisis*. Boston: The Boston Community School, Chapter 5.

Technical Support Group. 1986. ''Eviction-Free Zone.'' Boston: Legal Services Center. February 22.

Tilly, Chris. 1985. ''The Affordable Tax Plan: Tax Relief without Loss of Revenue.'' Paper prepared for the Boston Affordable Housing Coalition, August, and submitted by the Coalition to Mayor Raymond Flynn on October 18.

SHELTER-POVERTY IN BOSTON: COMMENT

Peter D. Salins

It is only possible to describe the task of discussing Michael Stone's sweeping paper as a daunting prospect. First, the paper covers so much ground that one would need a paper of almost equal length to deal with the various analyses and proposals it contains. Second, the paper is premised on a large number of assumptions and produces propositions that certainly would be challenged by most mainstream housing analysts. Given the impossibility of debating all of Stone's assumptions and propositions, it is necessary to limit comments on his paper to a discussion of several critical arguments and the general thrust of his recommendations.

The first critical argument is, of course, his analysis of the problem of housing affordability. According to Stone, housing affordability is a function of something defined as "shelter-poverty," which he estimates afflicts 42 percent of all of Boston's renter families and 85 percent of all *poor* renter households. These estimates are the result of applying measures produced by: taking a household's gross income, subtracting what the Bureau of Labor Statistics (BLS) once defined as the sum necessary for all non-shelter expenditures in its "lower-standard" budget (for 1981 with a CPI escalator) and comparing the shelter residual with what the household actually pays for rent. If the actual rent exceeds the residual, the household suffers from shelter-poverty.

While this measure represents an interesting conceptual wrinkle in the longstanding (and simplistic) percentage-of-income criterion (such as 25 percent or 30 percent) for determining housing affordability, it is methodologically flawed. Its use as such a measure is premised, of course, on the validity of the now discontinued BLS lower-standard budget, and the accuracy of data on Boston household income and housing expenditures drawn from a single 1980 Boston Household Survey. Whether or not this is an appropriate premise, the concept itself is curious, regardless of the data used. There is no question that poor people are indeed poor, and the very essence of poverty is the inability to afford the range or quality of goods that more affluent people can. But why isolate only shelter as the dependent variable? One could just as soon use Stone's methodology and treat food (even more a necessity than housing, although Stone claims people always pay their rent first) as the residual and identify a construct called "nutrition-poverty." (Note: if housing is indeed the first item to be covered, the other parts of budget are the real residual.)

Frankly, it seems preferable to use the more traditional approach to determine whether people need assistance in one or another functional category by identifying the number of families who are actually ill-housed, ill-fed or lacking in some other essential and to what degree. Maybe on this basis we would still find 42 percent of all tenant households affected, but it would provide a more useful operational tool for housing policy than Stone's novel, but artificial, shelter-poverty construct.

If there are likely to be questions about Stone's measure of housing affordability, there will certainly be serious reservations about his policies to relieve shelter-poverty. Those reservations will begin with the items in his long catalogue of proposals:

- permanent rent and condo-conversion controls
- fire insurance controls
- housing turnover tax
- city-funded grants and loans for repair
- reverse annuity mortgage
- foreclosure relief
- property tax abatement
- transfer of private housing to a nonprofit (he calls it nonspeculative) community land trust
- upgrade existing public housing
- change rent and subsidy formulas for public housing
- a housing trust fund to finance nonprofit housing
- develop new public housing
- use CDBG funds to underwrite the construction of new nonprofit housing
- use pension funds for nonprofit housing
- legislate statutory life tenure for all tenants
- effective "life security" for all homeowners (with reverse annuity and foreclosure relief programs)

- condemn and turn over to the nonprofit housing trust all buildings with code violations
- allow tenants to form unions to bargain with landlords

And if these housing measures are not enough (because they do not deal with the inadequate income which is the denominator of shelter-poverty and do not necessarily guarantee sufficient income distribution), we have the following national macro-policies:

- cut military spending
- repeal the 1981 (ERTA) tax cut
- close tax loopholes—especially the housing market ones
- eliminate the income tax for low-income households
- impose credit allocation and controls
- impose national price controls

This is indeed a breathtaking array of proposals, leaving, as it were, no stone unturned (pun intended). Let us disregard altogether the federal level recommendations, and let us disregard redundancy among the housing proposals and isolate the key ideas. It is actually breathtakingly simple: ''Property is theft.'' In almost every instance the idea is to eliminate private ownership of not just rental but all housing. First, these proposals are aimed to make private ownership unattractive, or unprofitable, what with rent control, conversion restrictions, turnover taxes, foreclosure restrictions, punitive code enforcement, lifetime tenure, tenant bargaining and so on. Second, they mean to transfer—through a variety of devices, and to the maximum extent possible—privately owned housing to the nonprofit sector in order to eliminate that all-purpose scourge of the present housing system: speculation. Finally, they depend on a variety of devices—either tax levy resources (preferably from Washington) or taxes on nonresidential development (which presumably remains private and therefore speculative)—to subsidize the operations of a community land trust inventory which is correctly expected to be not only nonprofitable but *un*profitable, running at a loss.

Since there is no place in this country, or elsewhere, where quite this type of nonprofit housing Elysium can be found and examined, there is no empirical basis for testing whether or not it can work. (We do, of course, have considerable experience with outright public ownership of housing, which can range a great deal in quality, but happens to be quite dismal in Stone's native city.) Before we commit scarce resources to such an experiment, however, it would be useful to see a great deal more conjecture as to the details and operational mechanics of a housing market where these recommendations might be implemented. Skeptics would certainly raise a number of objections.

With no profit motive to drive housing production, such an experiment would depend on bureaucratic initiatives by public officials or those responsible for managing the trust set up for the purpose of ensuring an adequate supply of new and rehabilitated housing. Given that the range of prices/rents would necessarily be very narrow under a system in which price reflects "ability-to-pay" considerations rather than the cost or market value of the unit, there may well be problems creating incentives for the production of new stock. This, when linked to the fact that a vested tenant could not be dislodged, would be expected to create extreme shortage of housing. No longer being able to ration housing by price, I suspect we would see hair-raising levels of scarcity, competition, and inevitably, of course, a vigorous black market as our life-tenured tenants illegally sublet and move to the suburbs. The reason we do not dare—even in the most interventionist of times—to consider the collectivization of food production is that we know we would soon go hungry. The collectivization of housing, as Michael Stone proposes, would doubtless force those within the reach of his kind of housing market to go unhoused. In conclusion, however attractive such utopian housing proposals as Stone's might appear on first glance, neither political nor economic analysis commends them to us for serious consideration.

INDEX

ABOUT THE CONTRIBUTORS

EMILY PARADISE ACHTENBERG is a housing consultant and urban planner working primarily with community-based nonprofit organizations in the Boston area. Her research and practice currently focuses on the preservation of federally subsidized housing. She has been a visiting lecturer in the urban planning programs at Tufts University and the Massachusetts Institute of Technology.

WILLIAM C. APGAR, JR. is associate professor at the John F. Kennedy School of Government, Harvard University, and associate director of the Joint Center for Housing of Harvard University. His research focuses on issues relating to housing and community development as well as urban and regional economic development.

RICHARD P. APPELBAUM is professor and chair of sociology at the University of California, Santa Barbara. His research and publications are in the area of social theory, urban sociology, urban public policy, and housing market analysis.

EUGENIE LADNER BIRCH is on the faculty of Hunter College/CUNY, where she teaches housing and planning history. She has taught a ''Women and Housing'' seminar with Donna E. Shalala and has edited the proceedings of the seminar's first year's activities, as *The Unsheltered Woman: Housing Issues in the Eighties*, published by the Center for Urban Policy Research. She is currently co-editor of the *Journal of the American Planning Association*.

ELIZABETH ELLEN BOWYER is on the staff of the Richmond Field Office of HUD. She is also a master's student in the Urban Affairs Program at Virginia

Polytechnic Institute and State University, where she is completing her thesis on the sensitivity of state housing policies to the housing needs of rural residents.

RACHEL G. BRATT is associate professor in the Department of Urban and Environmental Policy, Center for Public Service, at Tufts University, specializing in housing and community development. She has served as member of the Consumer Advisory Council of the Federal Reserve System and the Multi-family Advisory Committee of the Massachusetts Housing Finance Agency.

ANDREW S. CARRON is a vice president of The First Boston Corporation and manager of mortgage research. He directs research on the mortgage-backed securities market, advises thrift institutions on asset-liability management, assists in new product development, and consults with the trading and sales departments on emerging investment opportunities.

PHILLIP L. CLAY is associate professor of Urban Studies at the Massachusetts Institute of Technology where he teaches courses in social and demographic aspects of planning, housing, and community development. He is former assistant director of the MIT-Harvard Joint Center for Urban Studies.

CUSHING N. DOLBEARE has been a consultant on housing and public policy since 1971, specializing in the problems of low-income people and the impact of federal legislation and programs. She is founder of the National Low Income Housing Coalition and of the Low Income Housing Information Service.

PETER DREIER is director of housing for the Boston Redevelopment Authority and housing advisor to Mayor Raymond Flynn of Boston. Prior to his government positions, he taught sociology and urban studies at Tufts University.

ANTHONY S. FREEDMAN is a partner in the Washington firm of Powell, Goldstein, Frazer and Murphy, where he specializes in housing finance and development. He was formerly deputy assistant secretary of housing policy and budget for HUD.

CHESTER HARTMAN is fellow at the Institute for Policy Studies in Washington, DC and has taught at Harvard, Yale, Cornell, the University of California at Berkeley, and the University of North Carolina. He is founder and chair of the Planners Network, a national organization of progressive urban and rural planners.

W. DENNIS KEATING, associate professor, Department of Urban Studies, Cleveland State University, is a lawyer and planner whose work focuses on housing and community development policy issues. He has been a consultant to federal, state, and local housing and community development agencies and community housing groups.

PETER MARCUSE is a lawyer and urban planner. He has been chair of the Los Angeles City Planning Commission and the Housing Committee of Community Board 9 of New York City, and is a member of the Planners Network and the American Institute of Certified Planners. He is professor of Urban Planning at Columbia University.

MARILYN MELKONIAN is president of Telesis Corporation, which develops and raises equity capital for affordable low-income housing. She was formerly deputy assistant secretary for multifamily housing of HUD and has practiced private and public law.

ANN MEYERSON was formerly assistant professor and program director at the Metropolitan Studies Program at New York University. She is co-editor of *Critical Perspectives on Housing* with Chester Hartman and Rachel Bratt (Temple University Press, 1986).

MARY K. NENNO, associate director for Policy Development, National Association of Housing and Redevelopment Officials, has been engaged in the housing and community development field for 30 years. Her most recent publication is *New Money and New Methods: A Catalog of State and Local Initiatives in Housing and Community Development.*

SANDRA J. NEWMAN is associate director for research at the Institute for Policy Studies at Johns Hopkins University. Her research has focused mainly on the housing problems of disadvantaged households—both the nature of those problems and the effectiveness of interventions to correct them.

DOUGLAS R. PORTER heads the Urban Land Institute's research program in development policies and regulations. He and his staff are responsible for monitoring and reporting on trends in federal, state, and local regulations and court actions affecting the development process. Before joining ULI in 1979, Porter was employed for nearly 20 years as a development and planning consultant.

SARA ROSENBERRY is associate professor and assistant program head of Urban Affairs and Planning, Virginia Polytechnic Institute and State University, where she teaches courses on public policy, planning theory, and comparative social welfare. Her research activities focus on issues relating to welfare policy development in the advanced capitalist democracies.

PETER D. SALINS is professor and chair of the Department of Urban Affairs and Planning at Hunter College. He is the author of *The Ecology of Housing Destruction* and editor of *Housing America's Poor*. He is currently review co-editor of the *Journal of the American Planning Association*.

ANN B. SCHNARE is vice president of ICF Inc. in Fairfax, Virginia. She is an economist with extensive experience designing, conducting, and managing research on housing costs, urban housing markets, government housing programs, and urban demography.

MORTON J. SCHUSSHEIM has worked on urban problems and housing in city hall, state government, and federal agencies. He has been on the faculty of Case Western Reserve University and the University of Pennsylvania and has served as assistant administrator for Program Policy in the Housing and Home Finance Agency. He is currently Senior Specialist in Housing with the Library of Congress in Washington, DC.

MICHAEL A. STEGMAN is professor and chairman of the Department of City and Regional Planning at the University of North Carolina at Chapel Hill, where he teaches graduate courses in housing markets and real estate investment analysis. In addition to his teaching and research, he has served as Deputy Assistant Secretary for Research at HUD and as a member of various state and local commissions and task forces.

GEORGE STERNLIEB is professor of Urban and Regional Planning as well as founder and former director of the Center for Urban Policy Research at Rutgers University. He has served on the President's Task Force on Urban Affairs (1980–81), U.S. Census Advisory Committee on Population Statistics, the National Research Council, Advisory Board on the Built Environment, and the Board of Trustees of the Urban Foundation Institute.

MICHAEL E. STONE is professor of Community Planning and Social Policy at the College of Public and Community Service, University of Massachusetts, Boston. He began his professional career in planning with the Model Cities Program in Trenton, New Jersey, later working for a private social science research and consulting firm in Boston and for Urban Planning Aid, an OEO-funded community organizing and advocacy planning organization.

HOWARD J. SUMKA is with the Office of Housing and Urban Programs of the Agency for International Development, where he is responsible for research and development related to various aspects of urbanization and urban development in the developing countries. From 1977–85 he was director of the Division of Community Planning and Neighborhood Studies, Office of Policy Development and Research, at HUD.

JOHN C. WEICHER is associate director for economic policy at the U.S. Office of Management and Budget, on leave from the American Enterprise Institute, where he holds the F.K. Weyerhaeuser Chair in Public Policy Research. He specializes in the areas of housing, urban economic problems, and state and local government finance. He has served as Deputy Assistant Secretary for Economic Affairs at HUD, as well as director of the Housing and Financial Markets Research Program at the Urban Institute. Weicher has taught economics at Ohio State University and the University of California at Irvine.

ANTHONY M. J. YEZER is professor of economics at George Washington University. He has served on the editorial board of the *American Real Estate and Urban Economics Journal* and the *International Review of Regional Science*. Yezer's research and previous publications and are concentrated in urban housing and land markets, housing finance and consumer credit markets, and interregional migration.